A
Boy Genius
Grows Old

It's a Fascinating Life So Far

Doc Rivett

authorHOUSE™

1663 LIBERTY DRIVE, SUITE 200
BLOOMINGTON, INDIANA 47403
(800) 839-8640
WWW.AUTHORHOUSE.COM

This book is a work of non-fiction. Unless otherwise noted, the author and the publisher make no explicit guarantees as to the accuracy of

First published by AuthorHouse 2/1/2006

ISBN: 1-4208-7157-9 (sc)

Library of Congress Control Number: 2005906340
Printed in the United States of America
Bloomington, Indiana

This book is printed on acid-free paper.

To

<u>Aunt Flora Frances</u>
Who Made Me Possible

And

Shorty
<u>Elena Margareta Elisabeta Puccio</u>
Who Made Me (Somewhat) Civilized

A
Boy Genius
Grows Old

Francis S.
Doc Rivett

Recalling Some Memories

As far back as I can remember, I had a good memory. Good recall, too. People used to marvel at my ability to call up various obscure or arcane information out of my memory. Sometimes, my recall is too good for my own good. I am forever dredging up from my memory those embarrassing little incidents that most people are able to erase, or even replace, in the sober light of day.

Always, I have remembered (or recalled) things that other people might look up. I had to. I couldn't look up most of that stuff in a hurry: lousy files. Of course, I never tried to remember things I could look up easily, like Willie Mays's batting average in 1954, though I still recall every detail of The Catch off Vic Wertz in the World Series that year.

One of the things I recall that I probably should have forgotten goes back to the late 1930's. In one of my underemployed eras, I went to Albany one evening to visit friends at the *Times-Union* sports desk and dun the sports editor for some money due me for covering sports events in the Troy Area. As I was about to leave, I realized I was broke. Not twenty cents for bus fare, nor even a dime to show good faith to the driver. When I mentioned my plight, a sportswriter named Henry Matteo, a slight, husky voiced man about ten years older than I, offered to lend me the necessary. I accepted with thanks, and I still remember his kindness and trust. What I can't recall is paying him back -- if I did. Henry is still around. At age eighty-nine, he had earned a Ph.D. in political science, and he'd remember. So why don't I dispel my doubt by just asking him? What, I should reveal a flaw in my recall, if I had repaid him? Or, perhaps worse, face a polite request for repayment with all that compound interest over all those years?.

1

I've been mentioning recall as well as memory, though I suppose many people regard them as the same thing. Ah, there's a difference, as I once told a colleague who complained that his memory wasn't very good. "I think your memory is OK," I told him. "You're putting all kinds of stuff into your memory all the time and whatever you put into your memory is still there. The real trouble is that you can put stuff in, but your recall doesn't bring it out." He felt reassured, I could tell, because he stopped complaining about his memory. He probably can't recall what his proper complaint is.

Memory like a photograph came to me early. I remembered clearly, as clearly as a Brownie box camera snapshot, riding up George Street atop a pile of our belongings in a handcart Pa was pushing. That was when we were moving from 37 George Street where I was born to 57 George Street to live with my grandmother. The reason, perhaps, that it all seemed so photographically clear was that it really was a photograph, and it was so impressive when I first saw it at age five or six that I truly believed that I remembered it right from the start. That would have been a great memory feat: recalling how I looked on top of a pile of furniture when I was already up there. Memorable!

I began developing my memory, and recall too, in earnest when I was a kid of eleven. I used to go to the movies in Troy on a Saturday: the whole works--two features, at least one a cowboy movie starring Tom Mix or Ken Maynard or Hoot Gibson or Harry Carey (we used to have a big joke about a cowboy double feature: Tom Mix in Cement and Harry Carey in Water), a serial, a couple of Selected Short Subjects, and a slightly aged newsreel--all for a dime. I had the required ten cents for admission, of course, but I had something else in mind. So I'd stand outside the American Theater and hold out a right hand showing a nickel and four pennies and, with a sad look, ask a passerby for that final cent: "Please, mister, I need another penny to get in the movie."

It was the early days of the depression, even before most folks called it a Depression, and a cent was within reason, a nickel was not. I was really trying to put together an extra nickel to buy a Tar- Baby--that was a hard molasses type candy on a stick and it lasted an entire show; in fact, some of the Catholic kids said they could make one last through first Mass on Sunday too. I mostly went to the American Theater because it was on River Street, where a lot of people might walk past. The movies there had no color, no sound, not even a piano, but it had TarBaby and other selected sweet things.

Be patient, I'm still talking about memory and recall. The way I learned memory and recall so quickly, and never forgot, is that I had to if I wanted to avoid being embarrassed or worse. If you pulled that "Mister, I need a penny more to get into the movies" on the same guy who just a couple of minutes ago had given you the very penny you needed, the poor recall was apt to result in a thwack across the ear, or a boot in the behind. So I remembered. And recalled. Fast.

A Profitable Recall

My recall -brought me greater profit a few years later when I was in Troy High School. I was taking Latin II and not doing too well in my marks because I was not doing too well in attendance. The teacher Frances McTammany thought I should be in class more often and doing more homework and she was holding my report card down to barely passing grades despite my high marks on tests. She also told me and told me and told me to come to class more and work more or I might fail, or, at least, I'd have to get a seventy-five on the Regents instead of the sixty-five that usually was a passing grade. As the Regents exam neared, she made me a one-sided bet: if I got an eighty-five or better on the exam, she'd give me a half-dollar. Came examination day, and I raced through the multiple choice questions, all easy stuff, to see what I could do with the major point-getter, the translation. I started to read the Latin and wow! it was a passage that Miss McTammany had covered in her grand preview review of the Regents a few weeks earlier. My recall turned on and scrolled up the memory line by line, word by word--just like a computer screen, only thirty or forty years ahead of its time. I thought it was wordperfect. When we went for our final marks, Miss McTammany greeted me with a big smile, the good news that I had a ninety-five on the exam, and a shiny solid silver half-dollar.

Plagiarism, of a Sort

Many years later, my excellent memory and recall caused me to commit plagiarism of a sort. That "of a sort" is no excuse for what I did, just an explanation. I had covered the graduation ceremony for an adult evening class and on the way back to the office, I visualized a punchy lead and story to match. So I quickly typed it, just as it had appeared to me. Next morning when I read my story, I had misgivings: it looked like something I had seen before. But where? And by whom? When I went to work, the reporter who had covered the graduation for the *Knickerbocker News* called. "That was a nice story you wrote last night," he told me, "but it was the same story you wrote last year." Nobody else noticed it, so I kept quiet about it too.

The people who praised my memory often asked how I did it. I couldn't remember any special way I recalled things. But I knew I didn't rely on mnemonics: the process of linking what you want to remember with something else, like initial letters. The only thing I recall along that line is from high school physics class: Roy G Biv, for the visible spectrum--red, orange, yellow, green, blue, indigo, violet. Otherwise, I thought mnemonics just clogged up the memory and complicated the recall.

An incident that occurred early in my Albany sportswriting career convinced me that mnemonics wasn't to be relied on. Too great a chance you'd press the wrong recall button. In those days it was not unusual for a sports writer to pick up a few extra bucks in what would now be deemed a conflict of interest, but then was an enhancement of interest, the interest in obtaining a living wage. Like many of my colleagues, I had qualified in the football officials' examination for just that purpose. And, in 1943, the football coach at Albany High asked me to referee a squad scrimmage, offered me five dollars. At the end of the game, he said he'd send me a check and "Oh, what are your initials?" I told him "F S." And he said: "That's easy to remember: F S for Fulla Shit." So a few days later, the check arrived, addressed to "B S." An error of some degree.

A Matter of Context

Mnemonics aside, much of memory and recall is contextual, especially memories of people. For years after my sportswriting career ended, people--well, they were always men--would say, rather challengingly, "Remember me?" Well, sometimes I did. But mostly, I had to say something like: "No. Sorry. Suppose I should." I just couldn't get a fix on why I should remember whomever. They had changed so much--as they soon admitted--getting older, heavier, grayer, or balder. And, most of all, they had molted the youthful plumage I was familiar with: the football helmet and pads, the baseball uniform, and sweaty basketball suit. But once I learned the name, I could tell him, usually, what high school he had gone to, what team he was on and, on good days, what position he played. It's all in context.

That is the introduction to my fascinating life. What follows is my memory, my recall, my context.

A Living Memorial

My birth occurred at the highest point in Green Island: the third floor over Fred Fletcher's grocery store at 37 George Street. It was not, however, a high point for either of us most closely involved. Ma was having a terrible time of it, and I emerged--with the help of a doctor named Armstrong--with a wry neck, a swayback, and a coating of the dark detritus of my delivery.

It was a perilous time to be born. The older people were being killed off in a World War; we newborns were threatened by the pandemic of influenza. Our life expectancy, I read much later, was reckoned at only forty years; that is, not more than half of us were deemed likely to attain a fortieth birthday.

But I was a dedicated baby, a living memorial to my aunt Flora Frances Rivett. The dates speak. Aunt Flora died of a heart attack on September 17, 1917; I was born on June 18, 1918, proof enough that Ma and Pa, who married in 1916, had gotten together in mourning. (Further evidence of Ma and Pa's early dedication to family planning is the arrival of my brother Douglas, on August 10, 1919, just nine months after the Armistice, on November 11, 1918, had ended the Great War.)

❑

Aunt Flora's death was a shock to everyone, though she had been ailing for some time. A weak heart, as I heard it, but not so weak that she was unable to gad about. On the Sunday she died, she had risen early for an excursion by train to Lake George. As the *Troy Times* reported next day, "She had gone upstairs to complete dressing when her mother heard a moan and a thud" as she fell dead. She was forty years old and still single, and, like many "girls" of the era, still living at home.

The old family home still held mementos of Aunt Flora--besides me. A watercolor, a still life, by Mister Hansen, with whom she had gone steady, and a small oval portrait of Aunt Flora, a handsome woman, a bit pale, and, in a niche in the parlor, an upright piano she used to play. (The piano vanished when I was six; the pictures were still there when I moved out and my sister inherited them.)

Tough in a Pinch

It hadn't taken long for the other kids to recognize my wry neck and sway back as a ground for disparagement. By the time I was in the first grade, age five, some kids were taunting me with cries of "crooked neck". Sometimes repeated so much that I would slink away crying. Until one day when a kid from across the street called me "crooked neck" in a really nasty way and I flung a small stone at him. I missed. He threw a stone at me. He missed. After a few more throws and misses, I bravely strode forward and grabbed him by the neck, thinking I might choke him. I wasn't sure how to do it, so I pinched the skin on his throat. Hard. He slunk away crying. As word of my fierceness in a pinch got around, the kids didn't taunt me so much.

A year or two later, Ma and Pa began to worry that the conditions I regarded as a nuisance might become a handicap. They enlisted the help of Professor Stephen Burke, who lived up on the next block on Hudson Avenue, who wasn't really a professor, but a physical culturist and they all used that honorific. He examined me--really, he just looked closely at the taut tendon on the left side of my neck--and offered a suggestion: massage that tendon with cocoa butter and that might loosen it. So Ma rubbed my neck every day, twice a day, with cocoa butter, and I tried to preserve its effect by not washing it off. Soon it was clear that the only effect was to impart a rancid odor toward weekly bath time. The tendon hadn't eased up at all.

❑

When I was, I think, eight years old, I learned I had another condition; one that didn't bother me, but caused older people to mutter their discomfort. We were on vacation at John Patterson's farm at Montcalm Landing on Lake Champlain, right near Fort Ticonderoga. (The Pattersons, who were old friends of Ma and Pa, took in summer boarders at their small farm.) The weather was drizzly, so we were in the farmhouse parlor one afternoon and I overheard a man telling Pa, "Your son acts like he has Saint Vitus dance."

Dancing with St. Vitus

Saint Vitus Dance is dressed up in more scientific language now: hyperkinesis, or attention-deficit disorder. Then, people said, "Oh, he'll grow out of it." Now, people prescribe some fancy drugs or a diet without sugar and other good stuff. I look back with pleasure on the lack of medical knowledge that spared me a life--at least a boyhood--of abstinence. Imagine being unable to go visit Pop McDermott's store, across Hudson Avenue from school, every morning and hem and haw for minutes over whether to spend that penny on *these here* chocolates with sprinkles that did not last long, but were six for a cent, or *those there* Mary Janes, several minutes of chewiness, but only two for a cent. Or, in fifth grade, imagine being refused permission to go over to Grady's drug store on George Street every day and charge a nickel candy bar to Pa's account. No hemming or hawing there; always a Hershey with almonds. (Both Pop McDermott and Mr. Grady were connected with the school, as janitor and head of the school board, in that order.)

❑

Growing up time was also the time of Couéism and Fletcherizing, and, without anybody telling me to, I practiced both till my attention span gave out. Couéism was named for the French savant Emile Coué, who preached a philosophy of self-improvement. It sounded so easy: just say *Ev-e-ry day in ev-e-ry way I am get-ting bet-ter and bet-ter* and you will. You had to say it a certain number of times and repeat it at specified intervals to make it work. Somehow I came up short. Fletcherizing was something you could get your teeth into. It was invented by a man named Horace Fletcher who said a long life was assured by complete mastication of food: chew every mouthful two hundred times, or something like that. He lived to seventy, so it seemed like a good idea. The trouble was that Ma cooked things so that there was not much chew left. Anyway, I giggled at the thought of Fletcherizing Graham crackers: Fletcher on the first floor, Graham on the second, at 37 George Street.

Well, It Was Home

We had moved from 37 to 57 George, in the middle of the next block, when I was about two years old, to live with Pa's mother, who was left alone by the death of my grandfather the doctor in January 1920. Fifty-seven George was a two-story wooden house that looked no better or no worse than its neighbors. Doctors did not live ritzily in those days; lacking the ability to perform medical miracles, they earned only marginally more than the people they cared for. But the house had central heating (the pipeless furnace warmed the center of the first floor) and a bathroom that included a tub, which set it apart from many of its contemporaries. The house was narrow and the rooms small (a nine by twelve rug was nearly wall-to-wall in the biggest), except for the office grandfather had added on the first floor and the fourth bedroom on the second. Dougie and I occupied that fourth bedroom and we had to mog through Pa and Ma's room to go downstairs or to the bathroom; we invaded their privacy only a couple of times that I recall. Later on, Pa had someone turn the office into a spacious kitchen, and the old tiny kitchen became a laundry etc room. He also had the second bedroom, Grandmother's room, turned into a large bathroom.

❏

I never knew much about Grandmother. She seldom came downstairs when I was beginning to notice such things. She was in her sixties, but on the few occasions I talked to her she said she was fifty-seven, which I later figured was the result of some confusion about the year she was born, 1857, or her address. Whenever she came down she was dressed all in black and looked sickly. The last time she came down to dinner which we called supper, she asked "Please pass the fried pickles" and pointed toward a serving dish. I followed the point, not the words, to a dish of fried sausages. Ever after, when we had fried sausages, we called them fried pickles.

After that evening, Grandmother stayed in her room, with Ma as her nurse, till the day she died in August 1928, probably with a little assistance. One day toward the end, while I was on the stairs--quiet for a change--I could hear Ma and our doctor talking, something about a little more morphine. Grandmother's funeral took place at home. She was laid out, in lavender, in a casket in the parlor. In the custom of the day, my brother and I were shunted off to spend the funeral day with Aunt Netty, Ma's sister, in Watervliet.

❏

Green Island was a good place to grow up--so good that I stuck around for thirty-two years, right up to two days before I was married. It was a small town, about forty-five hundred people, in a space, twelve blocks from top to bottom and seven (at the widest) from side to side. Center Street marked the division between Uptown and Downtown, a division that most people seem to have ignored. But not Ma and Pa.

Ma, in particular, regarded Uptown as an evil place, one to be avoided for safety of body and soul. The Irish live there, she proclaimed, and you better not let me catch you going up there. In her lexicon, Irish meant Catholic, as if the Pope lived in Dublin rather than Rome. How she came to feel so strongly anti-Catholic I never understood. Perhaps it was a case of needing someone to feel superior to. In expressing loathing, Ma used all the bad names for the Irish and the I-talians, usually combined with adjectives about their parentage and their hygiene. Pa shared her views, but, since he was seldom home or awake in the daytime, he had limited opportunity to express them.

Ma and Pa were flexible in their biases. They overlooked the I-talianness of those who lived on George Street. John Valletta, who lived across the street and worked in Manning Paper Company, was always Mister Valletta and I was allowed to play with the Valletta kids. (His brother-in-law Tony Carlucci, who lived Uptown and worked on the village garbage truck, was, on the other hand, always Tony.) A partial exception was Margaret Piccarillo, who ran a little store and ice cream parlor down in the next block. She was always treated cordially, but was spoken to and of as Maggie Pick. She didn't mind. Behind her back, she was the subject of some snickering for her prolonged "going together" with Frank Forcey, the nightshift policeman.

Such Hospitality

Ma and Pa took it in stride when the Knights of Columbus--every one of them Catholic if not Irish--established their headquarters just one house and a double driveway from ours. We kids found the Knights hospitable, though perhaps unknowingly so. We played a kind of baseball in the driveway, either four to a side or "numbers" in which everyone took turns doing everything. We also found a way to sneak into the building and, found the pool table on the second floor and spent many an afternoon there. We were finally caught by the young caretaker Arthur Wallingford, who was just finishing college at Holy Cross and heading for medical school. We felt deflated when he simply told us to behave ourselves; we had expected that he would bawl us out. (Decades later, as a reporter, I encountered Arthur Wallingford again. He was a locally famous doctor and head of the Albany school board. We talked about Green Island, but never about the Knights' hospitality.)

Ma and Pa also disliked Jews, as a group, and used a whole lexicon of nasty names for them. They were limited in the exercise of their hostility, because only one Jewish family lived on Green Island. They were the Morses, Joe and Lena and their daughters, and they ran a drygoods store that Ma was dependent on, so they were ordained "good Jews". The only other "good Jews" Ma spoke of were Mrs. Toppall, whose husband was a tailor in Troy, and her son Lester; Ma met them at the baby doctor she took me to. Even the specialty shop owners in Troy who often afforded her credit did not escape Ma's contumely. Negroes also came abstractly under Ma and Pa's scorn; no Negro ever lived on Green Island and few even passed through.

❑

All that prejudice and Pa's odd working hours limited their opportunities for social life. They probably had more, though, than I was aware of. One night, Larry Connors and his wife Sophie (Uptown Irish) came to dinner. Once, Ma and Pa (and I) went to a party at Bill Hayes's house in Watervliet; Bill was a plumber who worked for our neighbor Mr. Jermain. Most memorable was the night we visited the Daltons, who lived across the street from my birthplace, to listen in on the Dempsey-Tunney fight--the famous long-count fight--on their big loudspeaker radio. Larry Connors, Bill Hayes, and Mr. Dalton were, to be sure, Irish and Catholic. Who's to explain?

Most times we went out, it was to visit the Grahams, who still lived in the second floor at 37 George. Mr. Graham was from the North of Ireland, an Orangeman, and he had a great marching sash, to note his rank, that he kept on display; his wife Lizzie was all English. Mr. Graham, a tall, well built man, worked at the Ford plant. Mrs. Graham was a very short woman, who would have been several inches taller but for her very bowed legs, the result of rickets. There were two Graham boys, Alec and Bobby. Alec was a little older than me, Bobby a little younger. In our younger years, we had great fun playing train with dining room chairs. I drifted away when I was twelve and heading for high school. A few years later the Grahams moved Uptown and Ma and Pa stopped visiting them. The visits were all one-sided; they never visited our house at all. But then, I hardly ever had any of my friends at our house.

When I started school, Ma sent my brother Dougie with me, even though he was only four. She figured she'd get some time for herself. I never learned what she did with that time. Ma was not alone in dispatching a younger kid to school; other four-year-old kids, went to first grade with their older siblings.

When I was in second or third grade Pa extended my geography to the Delaware and Hudson railroad yard office, across the tracks at the far end of Clinton Street. That day, he was checking what run with higher pay, or longer hours, was up for bid; he had been a trainman twenty-five years, since he was fifteen, and could choose from a lot of jobs. Later, he took me there whenever he went to bid for a different run or to send in a Form 280 report when he got hurt on the job, which was more frequent: usually a broken big toe or cracked ribs. The men at the yard office made a big fuss over me, and I was mightily impressed by my view of the work they did. Those visits also impressed me with something that Pa already knew: away was a lot more fun than home.

A Railroad Town Changes

Green Island had been a railroad town since the eighteen-thirties when some entrepreneurs discovered that it offered a nearly level route between Troy and the north. The railroad (that became the Delaware and Hudson) occupied a wide right-of-way from bottom, where it built a freight house, to top, the site of car and engine shops and a roundhouse, and, all the way, a five-track switchyard

But the times were changing. The D&H had moved much of its shop work to a new center in Colonie, three or four miles to the south. The Gilbert Car Works, which built railroad parlor cars, went bust, and John A. Manning moved his papermaking plant from Troy to that site, up in the next block. Not long after that, Henry Ford built a large parts plant at the Federal Dam, to capitalize on cheap electric power, and hired more men than ever had worked for the D&H.. In a few years, a man named Marshall from Troy opened a plant uptown that made auto brake linings of rubber and asbestos. The aromas of the curing rubber at Marshall's and the bleach at Manning's made breathing an adventure in the hot humid days of summer.

❑

Railroaders still held a lofty view of their importance, with train crewmen viewing themselves most important of all. As a trainman's son, I shared Pa's high regard for his colleagues (and himself). Pa was choosing runs that kept him away as many hours as possible. To make more money, he said, since wages were computed on a complex formula of miles and hours. In the midst of the Depression, however, he was deprived of much awayness, not to mention pay, when the D&H president concocted a scheme that eliminated daily overtime and reduced the Montreal run to ten round trips a month.

The Fun of Awayness

Pa introduced me to some of his far awayness. When he was on the Fast Freight, he took me along one night in the caboose. A near-disaster. Ma had made a lunch for me: a fried egg sandwich. A cold fried egg and a bumpy ride did not get along well. Later, Pa took me on Train 5 that left Albany about 5 p.m., northbound to Rouses Point. He was the baggageman, and I rode with him a while, then in a coach, and, for several miles, in the cab of Engine 604, on the fireman's seat (he was too busy to sit much). Coming south next day, as a milk train, we hit a loaded gasoline truck at a crossing a few miles north of Plattsburgh, and knocked it far enough that nothing could catch fire. Pa's awayness was very impressive.

❑

While Ma and Pa found vivid language to express their biases toward other people, they were less than adequate communicators in other ways. I grew to think that Pa adopted awayness to avoid trying to communicate with Ma. "Love" was not spoken at home. Little fond emotion was even displayed: no hugs, no kisses. Yet Pa could express his love quite eloquently in writing. At an early age, I discovered a letter he had written, hidden behind a framed picture, and intended to be read after he died. I refolded the paper and returned it as carefully as I could. (By the time Pa died, even the picture had vanished.)

Pa and Ma were sometimes, about a dozen times in all, able to communicate with us kids with body language. As applied to our bodies. Pa used his razor strop, a leather belt about three inches wide that distributed the pain fully across the behind. Ma used the wooden back of a hairbrush, which concentrated the pain over the hip bones. Otherwise, Ma was a lousy communicator. For example, Dougie was still taking a bottle to bed when he was six years old, and Ma asked if he didn't think it was time to quit. He said: "Yes, but I thought you wanted me to keep on taking it." Right then he swore off the bottle--the milk kind.

Saved by a Cap Gun

One afternoon when Pa was overcome by a hangover or, worse, perhaps a fit of depression, he attempted a terminal method of communication. He took his straight razor in hand and said he was going down cellar to kill himself. I don't know where Ma was, just that she was not where the action was. It was left to me to stop him. But how? Talking? I tried, and got nowhere. Crying? Likewise. He was a big man; I

was a little kid. I had a little cap gun in hand, on my way
out to play. As he walked through the old kitchen toward the
cellar door, I went up behind him, reached up as high as I
could, and, in desperation, whacked him with the cap gun on
the back of the head. Harder than I planned. Pa went down.
Out. I grabbed the razor, folded it and scrammed. I hid the
razor and myself. By the time I came back for supper, Pa
had recovered his senses and his good sense. He never said
a word about the afternoon's activities.

❏

I could not get as far away as Pa did, but, for a little
kid, I did pretty well. I started next door at Bennett's sheet
metal shop, watching with awe as the men turned a sheet of
galvanized steel into a giant stovepipe or bent and folded a
larger sheet into a cornice. Then on to Jermain's plumbing
shop another door away. Not much to watch there. Not much
fun for me, either, as Mister Jermain turned out to be a
tickler. By the time I was eight I had extended my awayness
to the stores in the next block down on George Street, the
block where I was born, to Larry Connors's gas station and
Mister MacAffer's newsroom and Harrison's market, which
used to be Fletcher's.

Going to Connors's or to MacAffer's was hanging
around, fun. At the gas station, I listened to Mr. Connors and
the other men tell each other stories I couldn't understand,
and I watched Mr. Connors pump gas (by hand) and hook up
batteries to the charger and fix punctured tubes (remember?)
and tires. The radio behind the counter was always on. That's
where I heard all about Lindbergh landing in Paris in May
1927. What a day! I ran outside yelling "Lindy has landed . .
. Lindy's in Paris" and on and on. There was no one out there
to hear me, but I was too excited to care. Everyone else was
still inside listening to their radios.

At MacAffer's, I talked with the older kids who
delivered the papers, and learned some swearwords and how
to play handball against the wall outside. Inside, I listened
to the older men, Mister MacAffer's friends, tell each other

more stories I couldn't understand. Once in a while one of them would say something about *yewgeenicks*, and give me a sidelong look; I didn't understand that either.

❑

My visits to Harrison's were all business. Ma sent me to shop for groceries and, sometimes, meat. Shopping was pretty easy: no choices. Milk was milk, eggs were eggs, cheese was cheese, butter was butter, dug out of a tub. Cold cuts were boiled ham and baloney and cottage loaf and headcheese. Meat was beef or pork, cut to order. Chicken was available, but some of it was called fowl; turkey was for Thanksgiving and Christmas. Cereals and canned stuff came in one size, one brand. All of which made it easy for a kid to get what his mother wanted. You were supposed to ask one of the Harrisons--Clarence, who owned the place, or his wife the cashier, or his brother Chester, who handled the produce--to get the stuff off the shelves behind the counter. Except me. I learned where everything was and helped myself. No money needed: Ma had a book at Harrison's, which she paid up on payday.

A few years later, I learned it hadn't worked that way. Whenever we could not buy something I wanted, Ma explained that we were broke. Not poor, just broke. On my last shopping trip to Harrison's I learned how broke we were. Helping myself as usual, I grabbed a jar of Rogers Pickled Lamb Tongues. Mr. Harrison said, "Wait! You can't have those; you can't have any luxuries, your mother owes too much." I was upset and I told him, "They ain't a luxury, we eat them all the time." Mr. Harrison insisted, "You can't have them; your mother owes seventy-nine dollars. No luxuries until she pays some of that." I left everything there and ran home. I told Ma. "That sonofabitch," she said, using her universal swearword. "I'll never buy anything there again. I'll pay him a dollar a week. That's the law." I didn't know Ma knew law, but she did what she said she would do. She found a new book at the tiny and not so tidy store of the DeMento brothers on Paine Street. They ceased being

I-talians right then and became those nice DeMento boys. She paid off the DeMentos' book every payday, at the same time she sent two dollars to the Harrisons.

We Stay Broke, not Poor

Our broke-ness continued. It's a good thing Ma kept telling me that we were broke, not poor. I knew a lot of kids that were poor, some really poor, and it didn't seem different from broke. Since all of us were in the same condition, I was not embarrassed to have holes in my stockings, or even in my shoes. We fixed up the holes in the soles with pieces of cardboard and sometimes the hole got so big that the cardboard fell out. When that happened I just kept on walking.

As soon as Ma knew I could cross the street without getting hit by a trolley car, she started sending me to the Morses' Eljay drygoods store across from MacAffer's to buy her necessities, like stockings and house dresses. Mrs. Morse knew that Ma wore service weight stockings and size something-and-a-half housedresses which came in pink or blue designs. Sometimes, Ma told me to pick up one of those packages--a square box wrapped in plain paper--from the shelf in front of the cash register. I didn't know for years what was in the box and when I learned it was Kotex, it made no impression anyway.

I had already done some shopping at Grady's, even though it was on the Uptown corner of Center and George Streets, and not just for candy at lunchtime. Mr. Grady filled prescriptions, mixed to order, not just pills counted out of a big container, and also sold patent medicines, a line of cosmetics (powder, rouge and one shade of lipstick), boxed candy, house paint, and window glass At holiday time, Pa would send me to fetch a box of chocolate covered cherries that he gave Ma. Once he sent me to get what I heard as *profillaticks*; when I told young Jack Grady what I wanted, he said "Oh, you mean rubbers" and he reached for a very small package and put it in a bag. I wondered about those rubbers; the only kind I knew were for the feet. Later, when Ma needed some special over-the-counter medicine, she sent me to Troy to buy it for her. I have forgotten everything about it except that one word on the label was *dysmenorrhea,* a word of wonderful sound, but, to me, no meaning

❏

Once I was allowed to cross George Street, I often went to the fire house on Clinton Street, the Gilbert Hose Company, to watch some of the men--too old or, like Mr. Gallenschutz who had two wooden legs, too disabled to fight fires--play pinochle at a big round table. I managed, by watching, to learn how the game was played and cheated at. Another attraction at the firehouse was the newspapers: the *Knickerbocker Press* from Albany and the *New York American.* They both had lots of stuff you couldn't find in the Troy papers.

For a time, young Chester Harrison, we called him Junior, was a special friend. Junior was a little older than me, and he talked me into getting up early, like five o'clock, on Saturdays to go to market in Troy with his father to pick out produce for the store. I wore out my welcome one Saturday morning when I reached the Harrison home on Hudson Avenue a bit early and Saint Vitus called "Junior!" a bit too loudly. When Junior came out, he told me, "My father says you can't come any more, you woke up the whole neighborhood."

Junior made it up to me by introducing me to the milkman, Gus Krugler, who, with his horse, delivered Collar City Creamery milk door-to-door in the very early morning. Soon I was getting out before four in the morning--weekends in the school year, every day in summer--to help Gus and his horse. Each day, when we finished deliveries way uptown, we rode back to the railroad crossing on George Street, put the feedbag on the horse, and dropped in to Ray Smallwood's grimy greasyspoon lunchroom for a mug of coffee and a sugar bun. Gus always paid the dime for mine. I went home; Gus went back over the route to collect. That fall, Gus got a new job and I began to sleep later.

❏

I kept finding new places to hang around. When a couple of men from Troy opened a new kind of meat market at the corner of George and Market Streets where the Harrisons had kept store before they bought Fletcher's, I was there, In the new store, the Boston Market, the meat was cut (or ground) in advance and displayed in a glass cooler case, so people didn't have to wait while a butcher got the order ready. Jim Houlihan, who ran the store, let me help some times when he prepared the hamburger or the ground round for Saturday's big sale; we dumped the ground meat that looked quite dark into a wooden tub, shook on a lot of white powder, and then poured on some water, and mixed it all together good. The powder made the ground meat glisten real red all day and helped it absorb all the water too, so people paid as much for water as for meat. Saint Vitus got me into trouble there one day after Mr. Houlihan had stacked up toilet paper into a grand display. Someone offered me a quarter to knock it down. Saint Vitus told me I needed a quarter. Mr. Houlihan told me I needed a new place to hang out.

That summer of 1929 I took my first airplane ride. The Ford Company had brought in a bunch of its tractors, fitted out to move dirt, and put them to work smoothing out a runway on the Prairie, which was past Uptown. Some of us walked up once in a while to watch but it wasn't as exciting as watching the steam shovel and the concrete mixer and the steamroller that were paving Hudson Avenue. To celebrate the airport's completion, someone brought in a new Ford Trimotor transport plane and offered rides for a fee. The fare for a kid was two fifty, which Pa provided, but my ride cost three bucks, as two quarters in change fell out of my pocket and rolled out of reach in the back of the cabin. The ride was a great thrill--bumping along the runway at seventy miles an hour, clearing the Marshall Asbestos plant by just a few feet, and soaring, wobbling with the air currents, over Watervliet and Troy and Lansingburgh and Cohoes, back to a bumpy landing. But I never saw our house from the air; I sat on the wrong side of the plane.

A Railroader—J.G.

That summer, I began hanging out at the yard office. I just walked up the stairs and said hello to some of the men I had met while visiting with Pa. Men named McDermott, and Murray, and Molloy--Charley, Tommy, and Gerry, when we got acquainted--all Irish, all Catholics, all nice to a kid who should have been someplace else.

One visit had led to another and soon the men were asking me to sharpen some pencils, or clean the pencil sharpener, or clean the glass globes on the lanterns. Things that the clerks didn't like to do. I was there every day I could be. One of my first outside chores was to scrounge around the empty milk cars parked on a siding nearby and gather a bucket of ice for the water cooler. I had to compete with many neighbors who did not have the money to buy it.

The yard clerks took me along when they went through the yard and taught me some of the tricks of the trade: how to "bleed" the airbrakes with a chunk of coal stuck under the lever (there was always coal or coke around), how and where to chalk switching directions on a freight car. Even how to throw a switch. Not only taught. They let me do those things. A couple of times, when everyone else was busy, I even took a train order on the special phone, direct from the dispatcher. My voice had deepened to adult range most of the time and the dispatcher never asked who I was. (Someone else had to rewrite it though; my penmanship did not look grownup.) They also taught me how to stamp the cards that directed the return of empty cars to Green Island--spelled Troy on the card. I learned that task so well that I thought I could do it with my eyes closed. One day, I must have done it that way, for I went through a whole train full of coke cars, fifty or so, and stamped each of them one line too low, which meant the cars were returned empty to Wilkes-Barre, a couple of hundred miles off course. That was serious enough to bring someone from the main office to check, but not serious enough to get me barred from the office. I stuck around until the yardmaster retired later that year and the new guy let it be known that he could not stand having a kid around.

It was just as well. When school started again in September, I went to Troy High, and I had other places to go and other things to do.

The Official Word: Genius

I knew for sure what Miss Belle Ayres was going to say when she rose with some dignity and much arthritis from behind her desk on the little platform in the corner of our eighth grade room, right by the rope with which she rang the school bell. I mean exactly. That morning in June 1930, everyone knew that Miss Ayres was going to announce the names of the two highest honor students, the valedictorian and the salutatorian. I knew--so did my friends--that the valedictorian was me.

After all, I was a genius, as I had known since sixth grade

So I was only half listening as she began her little speech. Until she said: "The salutatorian is Francis Rivett." Even before I knew the words, let alone their meanings, I learned about hubris and nemesis, as Miss Ayres went on to say: "The valedictorian is Agnes Iozzo," which she and we pronounced *Yutz,* pretty close to the real I-talian sound. Second. And to a girl. A true embarrassment, and especially so for a kid who was a genius.

❏

Miss Cannon, whose first name I learned much later was Anna, had come to teach at James Heatly School after School 2 uptown was closed, and she broke the news of my genius to me when I stayed after school one day to help her with a special project. She had been working on another project, a graduate course, I think, and looked up the scores on intelligence tests over the years in Green Island. I heard her say, "You are a genius." Not near, not kind of. Real genius. I took it to heart. Being a genius, I knew, meant I wouldn't have to work hard any more. And that's why I became salutatorian.

But, even as a genius, I still had to explain to Ma and Pa (when he came in off his run on the railroad) why I had not been valedictorian. While any other kid named salutatorian would have skipped home, touching only every third flagstone, I dawdled most of the way. Of course, I hurried away from school, so I wouldn't have to explain why I told those other kids the wrong information. I knew what to expect from Ma. "How could you do this to me?" she'd say. "I've been telling everybody how bright you are and you're not even as smart as that little I-talian"--I substitute I-talian for Ma's phrase--"girl from Paine Street." It turned out that I was right about Ma. Word for word.

Pa Offers Some Words

And Pa: I figured he would blame someone else for my plight; with him, I could do no wrong, even when I did. What I wasn't sure about was whom he would blame and what words he'd use. When he came home, late and hungry--he had slaked his thirst--I thought I'd wait to tell him, but Ma couldn't wait. Pa got mad. He lit into Belly Ayres and Blinky DeMille, the superintendent of schools whose first name was George and who had an uncontrollable blink to his eyes, with his railroad language, which aspersed the parentage and hygiene of its objects in various compoundments. Pa also appealed to Christ in intimate terms: by first name, first and last name, and more fully Jesus Henry Christ, and, for emphasis, Jesus Henry Christ and All Hands Around, or Jesus Henry Christ and All Thirty-Seven Thousand Apostles. To his credit, though, Pa, in his chewing out, generally eschewed the sexual intercoarsenesses that mark so much discourse these days.

❑

Ma suffered her wounded pride in silence for a few days. As did I. Ma probably recovered first. I could still be the star of the show, outshine that little I-talian girl, and Ma could be mother of the star, which suited her fine. As salutatorian I was to give a kind of welcoming speech, only a couple of minutes long and hewing to a certain style. I was sure I could write it myself. But Ma could not forget or forgive my having led her astray. She turned for help to her best friend, Mary Dalton, who ran the office for Bennett's shop next door. Miss Dalton had the perfect answer: she would ask her sister the Sister, who also was a teacher, if she would write something nice for me. It took only a couple of days. When Ma read it, she thought it was very nice. So did I, even if I could have done better.

I Learn How to Speak

With speech in hand, Ma turned her attention to the other details. Of course, I had to look nice. That meant a new suit, with long pants, not knickers. Off we went to Troy, where Ma took over the shopping. She found what she wanted in one of the stores where her credit was still good, though she otherwise spoke disparagingly of its Jewish owner. I thought the suit was OK; it came with a baseball bat thrown in, the first I ever owned that wasn't put together with tacks and tape.

Then I had to sound nice. I figured that was easy: I knew how to recite things. I used to draw applause at Sunday school parties for my rendition of:

I went to the animal fair;
The birds and the beasts were there.
By the light of the moon
    I could see the baboon
Combing his long gray hair.
The monkey he got drunk
And sat on the elephant's trunk;
The elephant sneezed
    And fell on his knees
And that was the end of the monk.

I also used to recite another piece, a much longer one, that started like this:

In what way it happened we do not know, but Chinese voyagers . . . and rolled on and on out of memory.

All pretty good performances, I thought. Ma didn't think they were good enough. So we took the trolley again to Troy where I could take elocution lessons from a lady who once performed with a little theater group in Troy. We got together in her parlor, which was jammed with furniture that didn't leave much room for the gestures she insisted I learn. It took three or four visits to get everything down pat.

A New Suit; A New Me

In the midst of all these preparations, Mrs. Kenyon, who lived in the same house as Miss Ayres and was the Green Island "reporter" for the *Troy Record*, took me and Agnes to Troy to have our pictures taken. (Mrs. Kenyon was an old friend of the family and her husband Hank sometimes took us for a ride in his flivver. I never knew Mrs. Kenyon's real first name; our family always called her "Min," after the lady in *The Gumps* comic strip.) I wore my new suit and new necktie. That was the first time I had my picture taken by a real photographer, and I could see the difference it made. I looked handsome and dignified, two things I knew I wasn't. Agnes looked prettier than I thought she was, with her kind of Mona Lisa smile framed by dangling coils of dark hair. They were printed in the *Troy Record*, along with a story about our graduation and all the awards.

I was given two awards: one I expected, one I didn't. The one I expected was the Anna L. Cannon award in English, on merit. The award I didn't expect was the Board of Education gold medal for best student. Nobody ever said how the selection was made. But I'm sure Pa told Mr. Grady how disappointed he was that I hadn't been named valedictorian. Mr. Grady had been a friend of the family since the time he started his drugstore and grandfather, Pa's father, already was a well-established physician.

Whyever I was given the medal, I enjoyed it; it almost made up for not being valedictorian. A funny thing: Agnes Iozzo didn't even get the silver medal, and she was supposed to be the best. No, the Board gave the silver medal to June Fleming who came from Uptown. Looking back, I wonder if that was a case of discrimination against an I-talian or affirmative action toward a girl from Uptown. Agnes Iozzo did win a couple of other awards. On merit.

I was pleased to get the Cannon award. Miss Cannon was my favorite teacher right from the day I walked into her sixth grade room at the start of the second semester, about a half year past my ninth birthday, and a year or two younger than my classmates.

The Origin of Genius

It was the custom in the early nineteen twenties to give every kid entering school the Stanford-Binet intelligence test. The scores didn't matter, though, until Miss Cannon looked mine up. All the kids were put in the same classroom, with the same books, and the same everything. Some of the younger ones, including my brother, were kept back another year. One boy that I knew was kept even longer: a big boy (he must have been ten) named Billy Harrison, who acted like a three-year-old, which is what he was when he was hit by an auto and knocked into perpetual three-year-old-ness.

❑

As salutatorian, I stood on the stage in Saint Joseph's Hall and spoke Mary Dalton's sister's piece to my twenty-six classmates and all our parents and some friends. It was the biggest place I had been in, the only one on Green Island big enough to hold all of us. I cannot remember how I got through that evening. Not stage-fright, more like stage-amnesia. People told me afterwards that I was wonderful.

Miss Cannon came by and congratulated me for being salutatorian and for winning her award. She mentioned that if I had worked a little harder I could have been valedictorian and probably won the other prizes too. She was not criticizing me, just stating the facts. I don't remember any of the other teachers talking to me, but they probably did; they just were not in the same class with Miss Cannon.

I had entered Miss Cannon's class ahead of schedule because I was able to move through the fifth grade in half a year. An early touch of genius, no doubt. I nearly didn't make it, because, just before the end of the first semester, I took sick. Really sick. I used to get sick a lot in grade school. Sometimes really sick, but mostly no-homework sick or approaching-thunder sick. The teachers couldn't tell the difference because the main symptom was always the same: my customary pallor turned ghastly. So, when in mid-class I told the teacher I didn't feel well, she quickly let me out of class so I could dash the two and a half blocks home. It was better for me to be sick, meaning "throw up", at home than in school. Going home was not comforting.

The Lord's Accounting

If I was suffering the approaching-thunder sickness, Ma, who was just as scared of thunder as I was, would watch me shiver and blanch as the boom-booms reverberated and say: "That's the Lord punishing you." I had no idea what I had done to warrant such horrible punishment. After a while, I just concluded that the Lord was a lousy bookkeeper or had confused my record with someone else's. When I was really sick, the extent of Ma's solace was to say: "That's your meanness coming out." With her, I never ran out of meanness.

I took care of the Lord's bookkeeping, with the indirect help of St. Mark's Episcopal Church, when I was about eleven years old. It wasn't religious help--the church and I already had parted company--but geographic. One summer morning, about 5 a.m., Gus Krugler and his horse and I were caught in a tremendous lightning storm just as we reached the church. We parked under a giant elm tree to provide the horse some shelter and Gus and I climbed up on the milk cases as far as we could to avoid getting wet. As the lightning flashed and the thunder roared, I felt sick and sicker. Even in the dim light, Gus noticed how pale I looked. "Scared of the thunder?" he asked. Sensing another lecture about the Lord's bookkeeping, I nodded. "Nothing to be scared of," he said. "If you hear the thunder, that means the lightning missed you." I regained my natural paleness and never again have I let a thunderstorm confuse me about the Lord's bookkeeping. I never told Ma what Gus told me; I just let her think everything was now OK for me and the Lord.

(Why had the church and I parted company a year or so earlier? A matter of principle. The choir director had begun lecturing me about coming each Wednesday to practice so that my boyish alto voice could be trained. If I didn't, he said, he'd have to take back my red and white choir uniform. I didn't and he did. And I stopped going to church.)

Goodbye, Miss Knapp

That time in the fifth grade I had pneumonia. Getting over it, and some people didn't, took a long time. I missed maybe three weeks of school. But Miss Knapp had promised to promote me to the sixth grade in January. And she had sent my little brother home one day with a wonder drug of the day for me: a half-pint of vanilla ice cream. When I returned to school, Miss Knapp had bad news: I was going to stay in her room. For your own good, she said. When Pa came home that evening, I told him about Miss Knapp's perfidy. He also knew my own good. Pa went up the street and talked to somebody and soon I was in sixth grade.

Miss Knapp should have been glad to be rid of me. Earlier that term, she and I and old Saint Vitus had a little dustup that resulted in her hearing the wrath of Pa. Miss Knapp had just finished lecturing the class, no one in particular, about gnawing at their fingernails. It has to stop, was her message. Right now. If I ever see . . . That's just when Saint Vitus put my thumb tip to mouth. Whack! Miss Knapp wielded a swift ruler. I told Pa; he told someone his views. Miss Knapp never spoke about what she had heard.

❑

The fifth grade wasn't the first time that Pa had made his umbrage known in school. The first time was just a few days into first grade, when the teacher Mary Gilboy tried to cure my left-handedness. Not as forcefully as some teachers did to other kids, like tying their left hands to their sides. Miss Gilboy was more subtle. She was content to lecture me. "The inkwell is on the wrong side for you," she said. "And you'll get ink all over your fingers when you rub them across whatever you've written." And so on. I knew my own good, even in first grade, was staying the way I was. I told Pa. He told Miss Gilboy, or someone, and she let me alone.

She was right: the inkwell was a long reach and ink always dripped on the desk or the paper, and I did rub my knuckles across the stuff I had written. My penmanship was not up to Palmer method standards. It still isn't. (Poor Miss Gilboy killed herself by sticking her head in the gas oven when I was in third grade. It wasn't my fault.)

While I continued to write left-handed, I also continued to do almost everything else right-handed, except hold my fork. That ambiguity in handedness caused me some times to misinterpret someone else's left from right at a distance. As a Boy Scout at age twelve, I sometimes reversed the dots and dashes transmitted by wigwag signal from afar, resulting in some baffling messages. Whenever I sensed that I had dashed into a mistaken dot, I kept still about it. I didn't want to add to the confusion of our scoutmaster, who knew that I was much too smart to make that dumb kind of mistake.

Really Sick in First Grade

Oh, but I digress. First grade was the other time I was really really sick. I was five and a half years old when I went out one day near Christmas to play with some other kids. They were pulling me on a sled, because I felt terrible. My teeth were itching, which never happened before. After I went home, I didn't eat much--those itchy teeth. And then I had trouble breathing. Ma sent Pa up the street to get Doctor Silcocks. Right away, Doctor Silcocks knew I had diphtheria and he gave me a shot of something he called toxin antitoxin. Oh, that hurt; it's still a standard against which I measure pain. I soon recovered, but not quickly enough to keep the village health officer, also Doctor Silcocks, from placing a big red **QUARANTINE** sign on our front door. No one was supposed to go in or out of our house. No one did, through the front door. But Pa kept going to work, Ma kept going to the store. My brother Dougie had nowhere to go--he was too young to go to school without me--but he went some place where he caught chicken pox, which he generously passed on to me. As a result of all that, I missed a lot of school; I have no idea how much. No one ever mentioned that it might be better for me to stay in first grade another year.

The two principal mementos of my grade school career, the gold medal and the award from Miss Cannon, vanished long ago. The gold medal was, as I recall, about the size of a ten-dollar gold piece, pretty small. I am not certain where it went, but I'll bet that one of the itinerant gold buyers of the mid-thirties came to the house, found Ma in her usual fiscal state--not poor, but broke--and paid her a buck or two for it. I'm even less sure what happened to the award from Miss Cannon. The trouble is that I cannot even recall what it was: a medal, a certificate, or whatever. The only souvenir I have left from James Heatly School is a yellowed clipping from the *Troy Record* of June 24, 1930. And that long ago was folded so tightly that it has become two pieces.

An Ego Trip Into a Career

It was an ego trip, long before that phrase was coined. Not much of a trip, less than a mile. But it was a great trip for my ego and my ego needed all the trip it could get. I was a short, scrawny twelve-year-old, a high school freshman who still looked like an sixth-grader, if not younger. The trip was Pa's idea. Just before school started in September 1930, he told me he could get me a pass to ride Train 162 to school.

That first morning I walked the three and a half blocks to the depot with fervor. Train 162 chuffed in, steam spurting from the cylinders of the antiquated locomotive which had its cab perched atop its boiler. As it scuttered to a stop, I headed for the only car, a wooden day coach with a baggage compartment at one end. No one else was taking that train, a Toonerville Trolley with steam. The conductor Harry Court, an old friend of Pa's, greeted me by name. In the old coach, upholstered in red plush and dust, Harry never asked for my pass, which deprived me of the chance to show off to the eight or ten people already aboard, all commuters who had transferred to No. 162 at Cohoes, one station up the road, from an Albany-bound train from Saratoga Springs. They were all strangers. The only people I knew were the crew.

The ride was a fitting start to school. I wouldn't know many people there, either. I was going to Troy High School, because Green Island's school went only to eighth grade. I could have picked a couple of other high schools, but Troy was the big city, so its school had to be the best, I thought. A lot of my old classmates also were going to Troy High, but I wouldn't see much of them; most of the boys were taking shop courses, and the girls were in business classes. I was taking a college entrance course, mainly because my sixth grade teacher Miss Cannon told me to and partly because I was too smart, not to mention too clumsy, for shop and boys didn't take business.

After several days, Harry Court introduced me to an older man he called Doc Williams. He thought it great fun to introduce Young Doc, which was what the railroad men called me, to Doc. He explained that Doc Williams was a reporter for the *Troy Record*. He was the first reporter I ever met and I was impressed. He was a medium-sized man with glasses and a mustache who always wore a suit and tie and carried a genuwine leather briefcase. His first name, I learned, was Ralph, but I never learned where the Doc came from. I became more impressed as, morning after morning for the few minutes we were on the train, he told me, in a baritone mumble, how wonderful it was to be a reporter. Prosperous too, I figured, looking at his suit and that genuwine leather briefcase. Not like a railroader. By the end of the semester, I decided that's for me. (When I told Pa I was forsaking railroading for newspapering, he said I had chosen a poor role model. Of course, we didn't use that phrase then. Doc Williams's wife had killed herself, Pa said, and Doc did everything to help her but hand her the shotgun she used. Pa knew such things; I don't know how. A few years later I learned that Doc Williams was a poor role model for a better reason: he was a mediocre reporter who also couldn't write well.)

Alone and Overmatched

Troy High, at the beginning, was overwhelming. All of Heatly school would fit in one corner of the building; just the freshman class had more kids than all of Heatly, and even my homeroom had more kids than had graduated with me the previous June. I was not only lonesome but overmatched. From being the sole genius (and salutatorian), I was just one among a dozen or so of each, and as many valedictorians, and that was just the freshman class. There was more culture shock: instead of staying put in one room with one teacher all day, we had to move from room to room and teacher to teacher. And, from a town that had no Negroes and one

Jewish family, I met two classmates last-named Lewis: a husky Negro named Leon and a slight Jew named Sidney. Through it all, I kept one distinction: I was still the smallest kid in my class.

Instead of playing out in the schoolyard (there wasn't any), we had gym class every day and that introduced me to a new routine: a shower every day. Quite a contrast from the once a week tub bath at home. Quite a necessity too: the gym floor, made of some mysterious cork composition, had absorbed nearly two decades of dust and some of that dust stuck to each sweaty body that contacted it. The smallest kid contacted it most. And showering led to another discovery: I was the smallest kid in every way, a distinction I modestly tried to conceal.

A Very Stupid Remark

Amid all the strangers, I found one other Green Islander (or perhaps he found me), a senior named Sylvester Miccio who was one of the I-talians from lower Paine Street, the people Ma and Pa regarded so poorly. Sylvester tried to make me feel at home by introducing me to some of his friends. One asked me to repeat my name. With some annoyance I replied "Francis Rivett stupid." Calmly, he acknowledged: "Pleased to meet you, Francis Rivett Stupid." I learned one of the social graces. When Sylvester introduced me to other upperclassmen (no girls) I always responded politely. One of the boys I met this way was an upperclassman named Bill Atkinson, the tallest kid in school at six feet four or five. He wrote a piece in the school paper about how tired he was of walking on the curb in downtown Troy to avoid the awnings and of being asked *How's the weather up there.* (Bill went to Cornell to study architecture and wound up as a leading designer of women's clothes in the forties. From buildings to builds, you might say.)

Another shock was finding a cafeteria where you could eat right in school. In grade school we had an hour or so for lunch, which enabled us to stroll home, gulp down a sandwich or some leftovers, and hustle back to play in the Methodist church yard until the afternoon bell rang. With the cafeteria, you could buy a lunch already made or bring your lunch and eat at a table, then spend the rest of the time talking or reading. I began by buying my lunch every day--I convinced Ma that it was a vital part of going to high school--but quit after a few weeks when I ordered scrambled eggs and someone dumped a mass of tasteless yellow solidified glop on my plate. Good thing it was tasteless; I was afraid it would taste like it looked. After that I carried my lunch every day: a single sandwich of sliced white bread surrounding a smear of Miracle Whip Sandwich Spread, newly on the market. As I learned later, the spread was supposed to go with boiled ham or something, but just plain it was more satisfying than those scrambled eggs.

I Am a Newspaperman

My first real shot at newspapering came around the end of the first semester. (By that time, I had established a remote connection with newspapering. I was the scribe and it was my responsibility to tell the *Troy Record* once a week what was happening with Boy Scout Troop 17 at the Methodist Church. Nothing exciting.) One of the fellows Sylvester introduced me to told me the school paper, the *Purple Parrot*, was, as usual, in need of help, and he got me an invitation to work. No experience needed. No skills, either. So I became an advertising salesman, assigned to cadging a quarter per column inch from such firms as the Famous Lunch, the Alling Rubber Co. (a sporting goods dealer), and Lavender's book store. I was not able to cadge many quarters, so, to save the paper from bankruptcy, I was asked to write for it.

As it turned out, I didn't write much--only a couple of handwritten things. Instead, I edited. Oh, I know that's backward: you're really supposed to know how to write before you edit. But, working at the print shop, we had no choice; all the writing equipment was spoken for. The two guys who owned the shop, Dan Sullivan and Bart McGraw, used the two Linotypes, and their office girl kept us away from her typewriter. So the chief editor, Bill Malthaner, gave me a couple of lessons and we put together most of the *Purple Parrot* by clipping school news from the *Troy Record* and penciling in the changes that made it look like original material. Occasionally, one of the printers objected that he couldn't read the edited stuff, so I had to write it longhand, which may not have helped much.

For Me the Bell Tolls

Fairly early in my high school career, the Delaware and Hudson changed the schedule of Train 162 and then cancelled it, and I had to walk to school, with diversions not available to a train-rider. As a result, I was sometimes late. Not very late. I was in the building, chugging upstairs toward my homeroom, when the final bell rang. But you had to be in the room by then. Once I learned that two late entries were counted as one illegal (unexcused) absence, I decided that if I was going to be charged with an absence I ought to enjoy it.

I kept my pass just in case I would be going home when the Albany Belt Line local was leaving Troy. Most of the time, I walked home, nonchalantly ignoring the toll collector on the Green Island bridge, who would chant *toll bridge toll bridge* in an effort to collect two cents I didn't have. Many days, I met a couple of my friends and we hopped a ride on the back of a trolley or on the tailgate of a local horse-drawn delivery wagon. It was always easy to get off the Cohoes trolley; it had to stop at the George Street railroad crossing. The little four-wheel Watervliet trolley was something else: when the motorman saw us, he tried to speed down Albany Avenue so we couldn't get off. We stopped it by pulling the trolley off the wire and, when particularly annoyed, undoing the strap that held the cowcatcher up.

❑

I carried over from grade school my attitude toward homework: I thought it was boring and repetitious and I mostly didn't do any. In grade school, I could get away with it by announcing I felt sick and looking the part. The Troy High teachers wouldn't let me get away with that. As a result, I struck up an acquaintance with the principal Ernest J. Robinson and his secretary. Not social, all business. Whenever I came to a morning class without homework, the teacher sent me to the principal's office. After I had made a few visits, in which Mr. Robinson lectured me before ordering me to sit in the outer office and do the work, he cut short our relationship. He left it up to his secretary. She greeted me with a smile, without a lecture, and directed me to one of the writing chairs. I had company most days, but not often the same kids. With experience, I was able to use up the entire class period catching up on my homework. The secretary and I went steady for a long time.

Seminars at Lunch

Homework wasn't so great a problem for my afternoon classes, thanks partly to the cafeteria. Lunch period, the time we were not eating, offered a variety of social and academic opportunities. Some of the other geniuses, and just plain bright kids, gathered daily at one of the long tables to lunch and talk. Among them were the Wiberly brothers, whose father taught at RPI, and Ann Eldred, daughter of the superintendent of schools, and Beansy Cornell, whose old man was an alienist which is what shrinks were called then, and Margaret Reynolds, on whom I had a secret crush, and others whose names have faded. We discussed some important things, like the answers to questions likely to come up in the afternoon classes, which I found helpful in avoiding unnecessary study, and some unimportant things like books we had read and the philosophy of life. Since my reading habits and theirs differed, I mostly listened. And my years in Green Island had provided little background for me to discuss someone else's philosophy of life. Or mine. When that topic came up, my contribution was an occasional nod and "uh huh". The other kids didn't seem to notice or care.

❑

With the help of those lunchtime seminars, some studying, and a lot of luck, I passed all my classes in the first two years. Didn't even break a sweat. I was still busy on the *Purple Parrot* staff and learned that I was entitled to cut the last period study hall whenever I needed time to work on the paper. Or said I did. No one ever checked. Soon I learned that no one required a close accounting for absences of more than one period. So, when I tired of daydreaming of the great outdoors of Prospect Park, just up the hill and clearly visible from some of the fourth floor windows, I went out there. And when one of the movie houses had booked a great picture, I went. The movie houses weren't supposed to let school kids in on weekdays, but they never asked questions as long as you had enough dough: ten cents for most, fifteen at Proctor's which had vaudeville too. Once in a while someone tried to telephone home to verify where I was, or had been, but we had no phone, and by the time Ma had responded to a message left next door at Bennett's shop, she would say: "Oh, Francis wasn't feeling well." After we got a telephone, she gave the same response.

Some teachers in that span were memorable: Miss Etta McTammany, better known as Latin McTammany to distinguish from her sister Frances, known as Math; and John E. Howell in English II, who loudly identified himself as "Howell by name and howl by nature" and who had unerring aim with chalk or eraser to stir a nodding student; and Emily Cavanaugh, who taught French with a South Troy Irish accent, and Mary Alice Casey, so absent-minded that she ended every sentence in Geometry class with "what?" as if trying to catch us in absent-mindedness.

A Dream Goes Sour

By the start of my third year, my thoughts were turning to the goal of all student newspapermen: Troy High correspondent for the *Troy Record*. That was real ego stuff. I felt that I had a good chance at it. I already had an association with the *Record*: delivering a route in Green Island with about a hundred customers. The circulation supervisor, when I asked him, offered to say a good word for me.

My dream was soon shattered. I had encountered unsurmountable difficulty in one of my classes. I prospered as usual in French and Latin, did well enough in American History, taught by Irving Fancher, who precisely spat out his words over a Herbert Hoover type collar, and survived in Physics, under Thomas Treharne, despite my refusal to keep a lab notebook. The really important class was English III, in which I started poorly and went downhill. The real problem was that Miss Buckley (what was her first name?) insisted more strongly than the others that I turn in my homework and that I show up for every class. I quietly adhered to my strong views about homework and regular attendance. Miss Buckley prevailed. In one vital marking period, she inscribed a **48** in the proper square, which brought the year's average mark so low that I could not even take the Regents exam. I had flunked.

I applied anyway for the *Record* post, and I talked to the editor Dwight Marvin. He set great store by good marks in English, so I flunked out there too. He selected instead a classmate of mine named Thomas Tychonia. A few weeks later, my association with the *Record* ended: many of my customers were not able or willing to pay the twenty cents a week and the district manager wouldn't let me cut them off. I decided that I wouldn't pay the *Record* for papers I couldn't collect for.

Out of My Class

Besides losing a chance at being high school correspondent, I also lost my place in the Class of 1934. But I continued at Troy High. Even if I had to go a fifth year, I would still be only seventeen when I graduated. I smoothly progressed in my final years of French and Latin and whatever else. And, having taken English III to the bitter end the year before, I thought it would be a snap on second try. I was so sure that I would pass English III--hubris again--that I read my way through the college catalogues in the Troy Public Library, scores of them, seeking a college that I could afford and that would take me. The cheapest college I could find (really, one of several) was a state college in the Midwest that charged one hundred dollars a year for tuition. About ninety-nine more than I could scrape up. Many others offered free tuition but there was always a catch. High marks, for instance. Or some special qualification, like being the son of a graduate in the Class of '96, meaning 1896, or living in Swamp Hollow, Arkansas, or being the nephew of someone who fought in the Spanish-American War, or being able to play the violin left-handed. Not one free, or real cheap, place for a kid with pretty good marks, and world-class ability in skipping school and not doing homework.

That summer, I learned that Ma had an unsuspected attraction for men, or at least one man besides Pa. I had wandered into the darkened front parlor, with its green shades drawn against the setting sun, and sensed that someone was on the sofa in the corner where Grandmother had been laid out so many years before. I did not pause, but as I turned to leave, I noticed that Ma was there, with Nat Wood, a D&H trainman who used to come to our house to pay his union dues. But this time his mission was otherwise: he and Ma were necking. Without a word I kept on my way.

Without a word up to now. But I was pleased that Ma still had some life, and allure. In my mind, I wished her well.

❑

I should have, could have, breezed through English III that second time. All I had to do was to go to class every day and turn in my homework on time. But I couldn't, or wouldn't, change my ways, even for a different teacher. And the second time around was even more disastrous. In the crucial fourth marking period, she--the trauma, or something, has caused me to forget her name--anyway, she put down a well-rounded **O** for zero. No English III, and no prospect of graduating in a fifth year. In June, while nearly all my classmates received diplomas and left Troy High for good, I just left.

That summer of 1934, to show there were no hard feelings, I resumed my relationship with the *Record,* in a remote way. The *Record* conducted an advertising promotion, with first prize a trip for two to the Century of Progress World's Fair in Chicago. All you had to do was to collect coupons based on purchases from the participating merchants. It seemed pretty easy after a friend of Pa's gave me the coupons he received for buying a brand new Chrysler Airflow, a car whose design was decades ahead of its time. What a bunch of coupons! The man spent four hundred dollars--cash. I looked for my name near the top when the *Record* published its first standing. I was way down near the middle of the list: fourteenth. That turned out to be the highest I ever reached. But I persisted, nearly alone, though I heard the other kids were all getting help from clubs and church groups and the like.

I hung around the Public Service Market, on upper Paine Street, the first supermarket upstate, and picked up hundreds of coupons from people leaving the store. And I picked up hundreds more from Alice Mack, the cashier for the produce section at the market. She was an older woman, probably nineteen or twenty, and quite pretty, and

I had a crush on her. She requited that crush by asking her customers for some coupons and by collecting others that customers didn't ask for. Still, every time I looked at the standings I was down around eighteenth. The final standing was the most unkindest cut: twentieth place, just behind Thomas Tychonia. Again. My final tie to Troy High School.

My First Job; My First Firing

The people at Troy High had never told me in so many words to leave. I just knew I had worn out my welcome. I still had to pass English III and English IV and no one--let alone someone with my dismal record--had ever been allowed to do that at Troy High. So I had to find a school that would let me double up in English. As the new high school in Green Island still hadn't reached the senior year, there were only two left: Watervliet and Cohoes. Watervliet was smaller and closer, so I decided to try there first.

First I had to get Miss Norine B. Keating's permission to get into an English IV class, of which she was the only teacher in the school. Miss Keating was a formidable woman who, with her sister, occupied a large brick house with a double lot on the far side of Hudson Avenue, directly behind our house. The Keatings took in a couple of boarding students each year, boys who never were allowed to mix with our bunch. The Keatings took a dim view of our bunch because, in the summer, nearly every day, one of us dashed into their side yard to rescue a tennis ball or a spaldeen that one of the bigger kids had hit there from our makeshift ball field in a double driveway near our house. Usually the rescuer was the fastest of our bunch: me.

I approached Miss Keating with a mixture of fear that she would remember my forays into her yard and hope that she wouldn't. That subject never came up. Miss Keating was all business. No one ever had asked before to take English IV while still taking English III--for the third time yet. Whatever I did and said must have been right, for she agreed to let me into her class. I would take English III from Miss Fortanier. That left me needing one more class, not to graduate, but to get the school full state aid for my attendance. If I had given some thought to my career goal, I would have taken typing. But typing was only for business students. Since I needed something with no homework, I decided on shop.

While I was getting into Watervliet High, Pa asked an old drinking pal named Bill Skirving if he'd ask his son to help me out. Son Bill (his official name was William W.) was the Watervliet reporter for the Albany papers, *The Knickerbocker Press* and *Albany Evening News,* and also the adviser to the Watervliet Hi-Y club.

Watervliet High was a smaller, more hospitable place than Troy High. Not much bigger than the old Heatly School in Green Island. It was so crowded that it ran in two shifts: upper classes in the morning, lower classes in the afternoon. Part of the crowding was caused by the Great Depression, which influenced many kids, particularly boys, to stay on another year after graduation, or after they had given up hope of graduating. I joined those irregulars in a homeroom that occupied the right portion of the auditorium; the other side was a girls' homeroom.

❑

After getting acquainted at school, I sought out Bill Skirving. All I knew was what Pa told me: his office is in City Hall. So, after school, I went in the nearest door, into the police station, and asked the desk sergeant for Bill Skirving. "Hey, Skirv," he bellowed, "Somebody to see you." And a short, stubby fellow, in his early twenties, in shirtsleeves and with his tie loosened, emerged from a doorway, waved and called: "Hello, Doc, come in." I was impressed: I didn't think he'd know me.

It was the first newspaper office I had ever been in, not counting a class tour of the *Troy Times* several years earlier. Not much of an office, just enough space for its two desks, a filing cabinet, a coat rack and a spare chair. Skirving occupied the desk near the door, from which he could keep an eye and ear out for anyone passing by. As I learned that first day, Bill seldom let anyone pass unquestioned or ungossiped in his breathless, confidential way. The other desk, over by the wall, was occupied by the *Troy Times* reporter, a middle-

aged man named Whipple Rousseau who always kept his
tie tight and vest buttoned and his cigarette dangling from
his lips, spraying ashes over his ample front. He favored the
nickname Whip. It did not fit him. He still used an antique
Oliver typewriter, the kind with its type bars arrayed above
the platen; he and it fit well the image of the *Troy Times*, if
not the times.

Helping the Team

First off, Bill invited me to join the Hi-Y Club. It met
at the Troy YMCA, so I'd have to become a member there.
OK, I knew Pa would pay the fee. Within days a couple of
my club mates asked me to help the basketball team. But I
can't play basketball, I said. They wanted something else:
penmanship. Two of our best players are over the age limit,
I was told, and we can't win many games without them, so
we need to get their birth certificates changed. It proved
easy: a dab of ink eradicator, a touch of a pen, and the birth
years changed from 1915, or even 1914, to 1916. Apparently
none of our opponents cared enough to check the original
certificates, or perhaps they too lived in glass houses.

❑

The Hi-Y was fun, but a sideline. My main interests
were graduating from high school, and finding a way to get
into the newspaper business. To fulfill the former, I went
to school every day with homework complete and remained
alert in class (except possibly shop). And, for the latter, I
hung around Skirving's office. I had already read and
sometimes reread every book on journalism that the Troy
Public Library had in stock, a goodly number. Every book
explained, in pretty much the same order and sometimes the
same words, how to compose a news story: use an inverted
pyramid that put the main theme first and then pulled in
the details, and start with a resounding compilation of the
five Ws--who, what, where, when and why--and possibly an

H, for how. But none provided much guidance on how to get the story. Maybe hanging around would show me.

Skirving's career provided a lesson in the power of hanging around. He had begun hanging around the city room of the *Albany Evening News* when he was still wearing knickers and killing time before he picked up papers for the route he carried in the Port Schuyler section of Watervliet. His precocious hanging around paid off when one of the editors, accustomed to seeing him day in and day out, offered him a job as copy boy, even before he graduated from Watervliet High. It wasn't long, Bill told me, before he was promoted to reporter.

Skirving knew just about everyone who crossed the threshold of City Hall: all the city officials and workers, the police department, and even miscreants being escorted to the tiny lockup just past the press room. He offered a friendly greeting to strangers too: you could never tell who might have a story for you.

Running Out of the Times

In the meantime, Whip Rousseau sat at the keyboard of his Oliver typewriter, waiting for things to happen. In February 1935, something terminal happened: the *Troy Times* went out of business. That meant the end of a job for Whip. Just as abruptly, it meant the end of a hangout for me. My role model and mentor went to the Albany papers' Troy staff. The *Evening News* covered Troy with a four-page edition on pink paper that wrapped around the regular paper, perhaps a bit too gaudy for the good gray readers of the *Times*.

❑

I represented the Hi-Y Club at a state conference in Niagara Falls that winter. I wish I could say that it was a result of some distinguished achievement in Hi-Ydom. In truth, my strongest qualification was that I was able to go: Pa got me a roundtrip pass on the New York Central and anted up enough to cover my modest expenses. The other delegate Don Kershaw and I stayed with a young school teacher named Merrill May and his family. (Several years later, a different Merrill May became manager of the Albany Senators.) At the conference, we heard a lot of speeches urging pacifism as national policy, a popular theme in those days, but my dominant memory was of the ice-festooned Niagara Falls. The speeches sometimes were awful; that sight was awesome.

After a few days without a hangout, I went to Troy to look for Skirving. I found the Troy office on the second floor, over the Liggett Drug Store, in an oddly shaped building at Franklin Square, where Fourth Street and River Street and Grand Street met. The office door was open and I looked around. Inside the door a counter was supposed to inhibit visitors. Five desks were arrayed along the outer walls, each with its own Underwood typewriter. Skirving was in plain sight, so I walked in and said hello. He greeted me with his usual enthusiasm. He turned to the next desk and introduced me to his boss Julius Heller. And Julius said *Pleased to meet you* as if he meant it.

I eased my way into hanging around. Right from the start, though, Bill and Julius introduced me to everyone. Julius was about as tall as Skirving, not quite so wide. He was in (I guessed) his early thirties (or even younger and trying to look a bit older), with a skimpy mustache, glasses, cropped dark hair, and a booming baritone voice.

Meeting the Rest of the Staff

Julius and his staff of four reporters and a couple of stringers were competing with a couple of dozen reporters on the two editions of the *Record*. The most impressive of the group was Joe Horan, who moved with the dramatic air of Someone Very Important. And he was. Joe ranked second to

Julius. While Julius covered City Hall and politics and big crime stories and other major matters, Joe Horan covered the County Court House and whatever big stuff Julius didn't. Joe was impressively tall and slender, and the best dressed guy on the staff. He was an amateur actor and even offstage carried himself dramatically and seemed always to be looking down his nose, literally as well as figuratively, at the rest of us. Al Rockefeller, also tall and skinny but ruddy faced with chronic acne, was only a couple of years older than me. He was also the youngest guy I ever saw who wore a bowtie every day, and he covered Cohoes and Lansingburgh. Then I met Don Smith, the night reporter, who was short and rotund and good-natured. Unlike the others, who were all locals, Don had been in the newspaper big leagues, once touring the world as a feature writer for the *Public Ledger* in Philadelphia. A fondness for booze appeared to have been his downfall; he was reputed to be capable of downing a quart of whiskey a day and still functioning. The office manager was Mildred Best, who kept track of phone calls, time slips, and flashbulbs, and took what few classified ads trickled in. The display ad salesman, Joe Kennedy, a lanky late-thirtyish survivor from the *Times,* had his own little office adjoining the news office, except when it was taken over late each afternoon so Horan could broadcast the news over a local radio station.

Doing the Dirty Work

As I had learned, the key to successful hanging around is to do things other people don't want to do. Chores like emptying the pencil sharpener, going downstairs to the drug store, or across the street to the Morris Lunch (entirely to the Morris Lunch after Julius, eating at the drug store lunch counter, had tried to pick up a forkful of tuna salad and it walked away) for coffee or whatever, answering (when no one else could) the Troy phone but not, right away, the extension to the Albany switchboard, because Albany was not supposed to know I was there. My most essential chore was making sure that the day's copy got safely to Albany. Twice a night, at about six for the *Knick* and about eleven for the *News,* I had to walk down the block to the bus stop, hand the package to the driver and find out when he was due at the Albany terminal, then let the city desk know. Low tech, but reliable.

❑

As spring arrived, I heard that the high school baseball team had lost all the catcher's equipment and other stuff, and lacked the dough to replace it. I mentioned the incident at the office that afternoon. By then, the Albany office knew about me. "Call Floodie and tell him about it," Julius urged. Floodie was Warren Flood, who wrote a lively sports column for the *Knickerbocker Press.* He wrote his next column about it. As humor. The principal, E.J. Sanders didn't think it was funny. Floodie didn't mention my name, but E.J. detected my fingerprints, and upbraided me. He did not calm down even when I said: "But Mr. Sanders, it was true." I had not learned that people can put up with untruths, which they can deny, better than with truths, which they can't.

Dennis & Mr. Wilson

My marks remained high in English III and English IV. My record in shop was undistinguished, but perhaps that was a plus. The one kid who distinguished himself was Denny Nolan, a Green Island uptowner who had lost the sight of one eye when he was a kid. (I never learned just how that happened, but Ma was sure. "Be careful," she would admonish me as I tried to pry a knotted shoelace loose with the tine of a fork. "Be careful. That's how the Nolan boy lost his eye, doing just what you're doing." I was unable to visualize how anyone could poke out an eye while working on a knotted shoelace, so I ignored Ma and pried away.) Denny earned his distinction when, while turning a wooden tray on the lathe, he managed to have his work come loose, bounce off the floor, then the ceiling and splatter into several pieces. No one was hurt, but Mr. Wilson, the shop teacher, was scared as hell. (As I write this I suddenly notice the resemblance to a much later and still current comic strip that features Dennis and Mr. Wilson.)

Late in the school year, Miss Keating directed us to write a fairly long paper on a subject of our choice. I chose Social Credit, a political philosophy that had come to the fore as a way of getting out of the Depression. I spent hour upon hour at the library in Troy, looking up the basics of Social Credit, and the arguments for and against it. I wrote more than a dozen pages and turned in my essay on time. Miss Keating glanced at it, then asked (in an accusing way, I thought) "Francis, did you copy this?" Controlling my anger a little, I responded "No" with a great deal more vehemence than she had ever been vehemed before. No more talk. A few days later, I received an A+. Deservedly.

So it came to June and I was sure to graduate. Except for one thing. Someone discovered that I had never passed civics: one of the subjects the Regents required for a college entrance diploma. I had never taken it. Most kids passed civics in eighth grade, but our eighth grade teacher thought it was properly a high school subject and my high school teachers took it for granted that I had already passed. Mr. Sanders decided that I could take the Regents exam, but I would have to get at least seventy-five, ten points above the usual passing grade. I got a ninety-something.

A Photo Finish at 17

On June 25, 1935, seven days past my seventeenth birthday, I lined up with ninety-one classmates, sweltering in cap and gown on the hottest day of the season, to receive my diploma in Saint Brigid's Hall in Port Schuyler. Again, Ma and Pa had to endure sitting in a Catholic church hall. I was one of thirteen seniors who received a Regents college entrance diploma. When we all lined up for a group photo,

I found myself way down at the left end of the group, until E.J. slid in alongside me. He kept me in the picture.

Graduation freed me to hang around full time. Then a surprise: Skirving was going to the Albany office. But Julius took over my mentoring even more actively. As I was now hanging around in the evening too, Don Smith added to the mentoring. Skriving was succeeded (not replaced) by Mary Freeman, a strikingly unhandsome former *Troy Times* reporter.

The Value of Contacts

Julius emphasized the value of contacts. A contact, he explained, could open the door to information that a reporter otherwise would not be able to obtain, perhaps not even be aware of. Public documents were private, unless the reporter knew someone who might, for example, leave the document on a desk right side up and within the reporter's reading range. Or a cop who might whisper in passing (but don't say I told you) about some incident that never got recorded on the official blotter. In his years in Troy, Julius had developed contacts, some just by exercising his personality, others by doing favors the recipients had better not forget. I often heard him working his contacts on the phone, usually on a direct or even unlisted number, announcing in his big baritone voice: "This is JOOOL-ius; what do you know that I ought to know?" Sometimes JOOOL-ius would tell an official what he already knew, to the discomfort of the official. Julius also made friends of every cop in the area by treating them well in his stories.

Don Smith, working nights, had fewer opportunities to forge Julius's kind of friendships. But Don had one nonofficial contact worth nearly as much as all of Julius's: the night telephone operator in the Troy office of New York Telephone. She was Ena Ellithorp, a lonely woman working a lonely shift--not only were telephones scarce in the Depression, but nighttime calls were reserved for emergencies, and no one dared risk scaring a friend or neighbor by calling after dark. She was able to listen to nearly every call to the police, and she could call Don, at the office or at home, and let him to listen in.

Scattering Some Ashes

Not all of Julius's *contacts* were policemen and government officials. He had done favors for a lot of people who found ways to repay him. One was the owner of a small plane who often hired out for an odd job, like helping to strew the ashes of a dear departed over his favorite scenery. One sunny day, the pilot had such a commission and called Julius to offer him a chance to shoot some aerial photos. (Professionally made aerial photos were too expensive for newspapers.) Julius took me along. When we reached the Troy Airport, Julius handed me his Speed Graphic camera and box of photo supplies. "Get them out to that plane," he said, "so nobody can see them." And he went to meet the pilot and a grieving family. I walked to the far side of the plane, concealing my burden with my skinny frame. After the flight, Julius reported to the family that he had indeed dropped the remains on the community known as Alps. I smuggled the photo equipment back to Julius's car.

Later that summer, Julius took me to Lansingburgh, to the scene of a minor but spectacular fire. He took a couple of pictures of the general scene, then told me, "See if you can find someone who was in the building." I had no idea how to do it. But I wandered over toward a couple of young fellows standing in the doorway of a nearby store and asked if they knew anyone who had been in the building. They didn't say yes and they didn't say no, but the way they answered nudged my intuition. I beckoned to Julius. As soon as the young men saw the camera, they said yes they really lived in that house. Of course, Julius could have found those youngsters and just wanted to see if I could. I learned to trust my intuition.

One afternoon, a man in Watervliet called to report that he had seen someone walk into the Hudson River, just across from his house. We hurried to the scene. An old man had committed suicide. Afterwards, I called the tipster back. How did you happen to see the man? He told me that every day when he came home from work, he scanned the opposite shore. First time he had seen anything happen. Julius was pleased by my follow-up.

I Learn a Type of Typing

As the summer progressed, so did my usefulness. I knew that I'd never get a chance to be a reporter unless I could type. So I learned, after a fashion, and soon could produce fifteen words a minute. The fashion was that of Julius, a big bold two-handed attack on the typewriter. Julius used just his two index fingers; I snuck in a second finger on my right hand, which was odd considering that I am left-handed. My fashion was not very fast, but I could offer to rewrite some stories occasionally. The reporters were glad to avoid having to find a new angle to brighten the morning paper story for the afternoon, and vice versa. Two or three little items at a time led to bigger items for rewrite. I gradually built up speed, if not accuracy, in my typing, though I never learned to type right.

I was not the only hanger-around in the Troy office. There were several others: a varied lot that could easily have found roles in a play by William Saroyan or a folk opera by Marc Blitzstein. Foremost among them was Miles O'Brien--Miles Michael Johnston-Haight O'Brien, as he introduced himself--a short round man, round of head, round of dewlaps, round of belly. He was the oldest of the hangers, in age and tenure. Miles always wore tannish suits that matched his complexion, a sort of premature pancake makeup winter and summer. He smoked pre-tipped little cigars, and he wore a number of solid gold rings, and his smile showed a few gold crowns. Miles often brought his

training and experience as a process server (for the biggest
law firm in Troy) to bear by helping Julius obtain pictures or
documents from a bereaved, or otherwise unwilling, family.
Miles often regaled us on a slow evening with tales of his
activities in France during the World War (the only one at
that time). Some nights he wore the garb of a village priest;
some nights he posed as the village idiot. But every night's
tale had the same successful climax: he unearthed secrets
that help the U.S. Army win an important battle. They were
always good stories.

The other longtime hanger, and more, was Sidney
Grapp, a tall, skinny young man, with nose and chin too
large for his face. Sid was a senior at Rensselaer Polytechnic
Institute, a year or so older than his classmates, and he
covered doings at RPI on space rates. He was doing well
financially. RPI had recently fired an English instructor
named Granville Hicks for being too close to the Communist
party, a mortal sin at an institution that depended so heavily
on the success of the capitalist system. Since Mr. Hicks
was fighting back, Sid was sure of a story nearly every day.
Sid spent hours every day at the *Knick* office, and at the
Morris Lunch and at Ray Ryan's Unique Cafeteria (Unique
because a waiter delivered your order) downtown, and at
Hank McGrane's store and lunchery on the hill above the
campus. He was seen around the campus--except possibly
in class--so much that the president of RPI dubbed him "the
ubiquitous Mister Grapp." When the Hicks case lost its news
value, Grapp continued to find, or make, news on campus.
One of his biggest feats was the revelation that a beautiful
red-haired Russell Sage College student who sang on the
RPI radio station under the name of Cherry Winters was
Adelaide Moffatt, whose father was an oil millionaire even
during the Depression. (She went on to become a famed
night club chanteuse under her real name.) Another of Sid's
specials was a three-day wonder about another RPI student
who was the innocent offspring of the cuckolding of a major
financier two decades earlier.

Staying on a Good Side

More a visitor, a steady one, than a hanger was Jess Smith, a veteran of the World War who never told of his wartime exploits. Jess was a tall, lanky Oklahoman, who carried a large revolver; he had shown it to us. He often spoke, with scorn and loathing, about the county veterans' service officer, Dr. Joseph Judge. Jess had the notion, perhaps with reason, that Doctor Judge was depriving him of the full benefits he deserved for his undescribed disability. Sometimes Jess asked one of us to write a story about his complaints, and we did, making sure to discard it after he left. We suspected that his disability was shellshock and we wanted to keep on his good side in case his disability ever got the better of him. (Several years later, I saw a newspaper banner headline, something like **CRAZED VET KILLS 2, SELF,** and, even before I read the story, I knew that Jess Smith's disability had overcome him for the last time.)

Arthur Morton was a steady seasonal visitor. From September to May, he appeared about 10:30 one evening a week, with a press release, carefully and flowingly written in pencil on butcher paper, containing the coming week's schedule for "official visitations by District Deputy Grand Master Ralph Whoozis of the Independent Order of Odd Fellows . . ." Morton was an older man with a bushy mustache, who worked as a fry cook in a restaurant and his only suit and he were permeated by the smell of stale smoke. As he departed, someone usually shook the paper, in a futile effort to dislodge the kitchen odor. One night, he returned, he had forgotten one item, as the paper was being shaken while the shaker held his nose. We were more embarrassed than he was.

And there was Jim Hart, a gray-looking, gray-sounding fellow a few years older than me. He was a space rate reporter who covered his neighborhood, Beman Park, and Sycaway and Albia, as he had done for the *Times*. Jim did not spend much time in the office. When he came in,he often was accompanied by a couple of his pals. One was Bob Dean, a skinny lad who at age twenty had hitchhiked his way around much of the United States. The other was Arthur Wales, a handsome scion of the family that owned the Sunday *Observer-Budget*; he was headed for college in the fall. (Hart's grayness was misleading, as I learned a dozen years later, when I was a sportswriter at the *Times-Union*. One Friday night, I received an unexpected call: the police asking if I knew a guy named Jim Hart. Yep. He was in the Second Precinct, drunk and disorderly, and the cops wanted me to come and get him so he wouldn't have to go to court in the morning. I said I would but it would be late; there was a Joe Louis fight on that night. About midnight, a cop appeared at the sports desk with Hart and asked me to get him to Troy. Jim was even grayer than usual and contrite. He had been celebrating payday and got in an argument--he thought someone had stolen his topcoat--which the cops had resolved. It turned out that he hadn't been wearing a topcoat. I got him to Troy and on the proper bus for home.)

Rewriting for a New Cycle

Troy was a hot news town in the summer and fall of 1935. For a start, there was the Mike Kane murder trial, named for the victim, a cab driver in Hoosick Falls, at the far end of the county, who had been killed in a holdup months before. Joe Horan covered the trial, and he or Don Smith allowed me to rewrite the *Knick* story for the *Evening News*. My rewrite showed up only in the very early edition; Joe phoned in new leads as the trial progressed. Another time Horan covered a talk by Alexander Woollcott for the *Knick* and asked me to rewrite it for the *News*. That was fun. I used different words, but the same nasty slant. My first hatchet job! Everybody approved.

One afternoon in late summer I came to the office and found everyone busy and excited. A "world famed aviatrix," Ruth Elder, had been barnstorming from the Troy Airport in her Ford Trimotor plane, and it crashed on takeoff for her next stop. No paying passengers. Just her real pilot Captain Harry Hublitz and her crew of mechanics and ticket sellers. She and Hublitz were the only ones badly hurt. But Julius created a second story, of which he was a co-hero, when he found a judge who issued a waiver so that two of the crew could marry without the required waiting period. The main story became bigger about midnight when Captain Hublitz died in the hospital. Don Smith heard of it within minutes, courtesy of Ena Ellithorp. He called the city desk to say he was working on a new lead. Then he called the New York papers that he and Julius worked for on space rates and dictated new leads to their stories. After that, since our deadline was still several minutes away, Don again called the city desk and dictated a new lead for the *Knick*. I completed calling the rounds of local police agencies; no more news.

I'm Left Out of a Big Story

A few weeks later, another big story. On the way to the office in early afternoon, I found several people standing around at Franklin Square gossiping about a spectacular murder in the bank, across the street from our office. Once in the office, I was, to my chagrin, left out of the story. I saw some of the copy. John Healey, the principal of School 5, widely regarded as eccentric if not queer because he always carried a tiny dog wherever he went, had shot William F. Seber, president of the Manufacturers National Bank and head of the school board. (Several days passed before I learned the details which my colleagues apparently thought were too sordid for a seventeen-year-old to know. Mr. Healey had been suspended for a hearing on charges involving a young male pupil and he went to the bank to talk to Mr. Seber. In the course of the talk, Mr. Healey said "Will, are you calling me a cocksucker?" When Mr. Seber replied "Yes, John, I suppose I am," he learned, too late, that, in addition to his little dog, Mr. Healey also carried a little revolver.)

That summer I started my professional career; that is, I got paid as a reporter. There was a local tennis tournament in Prospect Park and the sports desk at the *Knick* wanted a story. No one was interested. So Julius asked me to cover it. I knew nothing about tennis, but I went. Someone kindly explained terms like "seed" and "forehand" and "backhand" and other arcana. I learned more than I needed; the sports desk wanted only a hundred words or so plus the summaries. At fifteen cents per column inch, a total of ninety cents. A week or so later, a swimming competition: I found another explainer, wrote another hundred words or so, with summaries, and earned a little over a dollar. The sports desk had other requests that summer: more tennis, a couple of swimming meets. Each time I found an explainer. Or should I say contact?

❑

Later that summer, I found a college I could afford: it was free. It was the Albany Collegiate Center, one of several such places the State had established to provide jobs for unemployed teachers, mostly of high school level. Classes were held after regular hours in the Albany High School annex, three bus rides from home.

A Lesson with Pay

I was in my second or third week there when my career took a new turn. A brand-new fire truck arrived in Green Island. Julius brought me along and told me to get the story. I found I had a contact or two, from having lived there since I was born, and I picked up all the information. Back at the office, I pounded out a several paragraph story and gave it to Julius. He read it quickly. "You've got all the facts all right," he told me, "and it would be all right for the *Record*. But we have to liven it up for Albany." He rewrote it, explaining each change he made. It seemed more his story than mine, but he allowed me to collect for it. A couple of bucks. I was convinced that I could learn more hanging around than I could in a collegiate center, so, at age seventeen, I became a college dropout.

❑

Julius gave me an early Christmas present. My little sister was seven years old on December 18, and Ma gave a little party for several little kids in the neighborhood. Julius came over and took a picture with old-fashioned flash powder; flashbulbs were too scarce for a kid's party. As Julius typed the caption, he read me the kicker line: "And a Good Time Was Had by All" and he said "When they see this in Albany, they're going to think you wrote it and put my name on it." I took it as a compliment.

Toward the end of winter, two little boys fell through the soft ice and drowned in Burden's Pond in the southeast corner of the city. Julius took me along, and gave me an assignment: go to the home of the six-year-old boy and get his picture. I didn't know how; I didn't ask how. Julius asked me to do something; I did it. The boy's mother came to the door. I said I was sorry about her little boy and asked if we could borrow his picture for the paper. If I looked the way I felt, she probably felt sorry for me. She brought out a nice framed picture of a nice looking kid, and said "He is a wonderful boy." I agreed. Present tense. It was the first time I ever had to do such a thing. And the last.

Covering the Home Town

After my success with the fire truck story, Julius let me cover other things in Green Island for pay, the usual fifteen cents per column inch. In a story about a Democratic nominating caucus for village offices, I wrote that each nominator had read the script from a paper that someone had handed him before the meeting. I named the someone. It was upsetting to the village fathers. At the next village board meeting, the Village President Jim Corr lectured me: "If you keep on writing things like that I'll have to keep you out of our meetings." I must have grinned, because he said, "That's no laughing matter." So I told him, "I was just thinking what a story **that** would be." Never another threat on Green Island. Not even when I persisted in trying to verify that a hit-run driver who killed a woman uptown was the assistant pastor at St. Joseph's Church. Everyone in the village except the police were outspoken about who the driver was and how he was: drunk. But his name never came out officially. I was shocked, shocked, to learn that my old mentor Bill Skirving (then in Albany) knew all about the case and didn't write it. He had, I suppose, a good reason: he was courting Jim Corr's older daughter Frances, whom he married.

❑

Don Smith told me that he had once discovered a good news story in the legal notices. Since I was working on space rates, I began perusing the finer print in the Albany papers and in the *Record*. Dull work. Nearly everything was a notice of a beer and booze license or a foreclosure sale. No news. Until one day, I came across a notice in the *Knickerbocker Press* that looked promising. It heralded the formation of the Biological Combustion Institute, Inc. by two local industrialists (yes, we used that term even during the Depression) and a physician from Brazil named Felix Octavio Pedroso; the industrialists' names have faded from memory. I showed the notice to Julius and hinted that maybe I should look into it. He decided that he should look into it. He found that the two local men had met Doctor Pedroso on a cruise, had learned of his theory of biological combustion and decided to support his discovery. Doctor Pedroso was in Troy and Julius talked to him.

The Saga of Dr. Pedroso

As soon as I read that first interview, I understood that it was too big a story for me. Doctor Pedroso had discovered a cure for practically everything: proper breathing. I was familiar with people who had discovered miraculous cures. My grandfather had formulated Dr. Rivett's Medical Discovery, a cure for at least a dozen ills. And fast talking, flashily dressed guys standing near their sign bedecked cars on the side streets off Franklin Square purveyed bottled goods that they said would cure even more ailments.

Doctor Pedroso was different. He was a tall, slim, fastidiously dressed man from Brazil, who offered no bottles but simply a method of breathing one's way to perfect health. Breathe in deeply, hold the breath for a specified time, breathe out slowly. It seemed too simple to work even on a hangover, but Doctor Pedroso said he could cure heart disease, even cancer. For proof of the latter, he pointed to himself. He had suffered throat cancer, he said, and cured it with his breathing regimen. At Julius's request, he let some local physicians inspect his throat; yes, they agreed, he had had a lesion there and only the scar persisted. They did not exactly endorse biological combustion, but they didn't condemn it either, which was good enough for Julius. In his first case, Doctor Pedroso brought a Cohoes woman back from the brink of heart failure. To Julius, that was more than a good news story, it was hope for a brother-in-law, who faced an early death from a heart condition. Julius asked Doctor Pedroso to work with the young man. All went well for weeks. Then the Cohoes woman died. Failure to follow the regimen properly, said the doctor. Other patients took turns for the worse. Doctor Pedroso's news value waned but Julius continued to write about him. Then the brother-in-law's condition worsened and he soon passed away. So, metaphorically, did Doctor Pedroso and the Biological Combustion Institute, Inc. I kept reading legal notices but all I got was eyestrain.

I Miss a Big Chance

About that time, I lost an opportunity to become a great radio performer, and, in the process, fell further in the esteem of Joe Horan, who already regarded me as a damn Chippewa. Joe had a daily, late afternoon, chore: reading the news for a local radio station. But merely reading the news was not enough for an accomplished thespian. Joe decided he could do one or two stories, the big stuff, in the manner of the March of Time, one of the biggest shows in radio, in which actors voiced the words of people in the news. For the program's debut, he assigned me to the role of the county judge, a man in his sixties with a high-pitched voice. I had a deeper voice, so I would have to really act. Luckily, we had time for a quick rehearsal. Luckily, because I fell victim to panic, and, ran, weeping, from the studio. Someone else became the judge. Joe never asked me again to march in his radio time.

❏

Late that fall one of the Albany reporters, George Laird, someone I knew only by voice, invited me to visit the home office. As soon as I could afford the bus fare, I took up the invitation. Perfect timing. That was Laird's last night at the *Knick*; he was becoming a public relations man for the power company, at its Buffalo office. Some of his colleagues were giving him a sendoff, and they invited me to come along. It was a modest do at the Plaza Grill, a half-block away, at the biggest table in the place, right under the big front window. The party began about 1 o'clock in the morning and only the start of the morning rush hour broke it up. (No closing time then, and no age limit, either.) We drank nickel beers--someone always seemed to buy me one--and talked and sang bawdy songs. A great party. I became one of the gang. (A quarter century later, I was a reporter for the *Times-Union* and George was back in Albany working for the power company. The first time I ran into him, he invited me to join him for a drink, which turned out to be several, as a guest of the power company. We held several reunions.)

As I revisited the Albany office, I was enthralled by the system of overhead belts and pulleys and gadgets that carried copy from the Associated Press and the United Press to the copy desk, and, on another line, to the composing room. But mainly I was there to broaden my acquaintance. Jerome

Walker, the city editor who was feared by the folk in Troy, turned out to be a pleasant and dignified man. I also met Dick Jackson, a sandy haired, mustached young reporter; Phil Mahar, a thin, intense police reporter; his brother Tom, likewise; Bill Taaffe, with a twangy voice that belied his local upbringing; Floodie and Al Maas, two large sports writers, and Frank Kelly, a copyboy who wanted to be a city fireman. And, on the ground floor near the entrance, the night cashier Dave Slick, a slight, sharp-featured fellow, who also was the night phone operator. First thing, he taught me how to operate the switchboard, through which every call into or out of the office flowed. When I filled in on the board he could take more time to gossip with the news carriers, and to eat his lunch or go to the bathroom.

Meeting Mr. Walker

Handling the switchboard was fun. Even on the night when I messed up a call for Mr. Walker. He told me the number and I dialed it. Almost at once he hung up. He called back: the same number, the same result. Again, he called back and gave me the number very slowly; I dialed it, he stayed with the call. Later I went to the city room, hoping that Mr. Walker wouldn't notice me; I recalled the stories in Troy about his impatience with bumblers. But he greeted me with a big smile. "That was you on the board, wasn't it?" he said, "I thought I recognized your voice. You know . . . I was trying to get a judge at his unlisted number and you got me another judge at his unlisted number; they're almost the same." It took me a while to figure out why he would be so cordial if I had messed up: I think he realized that he had given me the wrong number, or the right number wrong. They were close, he said.

❏

Some of the reporters in our Albany office, and those on the *Times-Union,* were trying to organize a union, part of the new American Newspaper Guild, but no one had

approached us in Troy directly. Judging from Julius's talk
about the Guild, they felt an approach would be futile. Then
came news that we had a new editorial director, assigned
from Gannett headquarters in Rochester. He visited the
Troy office, accompanied by Peg Steele, a chain-smoking,
almost good-looking, sobsister. His arrival in Albany had
been greeted by an anonymous article in the *Guild Reporter*
that was scurrilous though true, denouncing the editorial
efficiency expert, and a copy of it (bearing a scrawled note:
Take that, you skunk!) had been posted on a bulletin board.
So we met B. (for Byron, a name he never used) J. Lewis,
short, pudgy, and pasty faced. He lectured us at length about
the importance of zeal in pursuing stories and in writing
them. He took as his text the exploit of Phil Mahar, who
had worked forty-eight hours (or perhaps more), without a
break, to produce a brilliant scoop for the paper. Go thou
and do likewise, he was saying: ignore the blandishments of
the Guild and you'll wind up in newspaper heaven. I don't
recall that anyone but Julius got a chance to talk to him,
and not much at that.

Comes the Flood

In March of 1936, I made my first daytime visit to
the Albany office. Of all the people I met that day, only three
remain in my memory: Art Wood, the state editor; Harry
Fridman, the United Press editor, and Mike McArdle, the
ancient copyboy. Wood was editing the Troy copy that had
arrived by bus, and in particular a little story I wrote about
a dustup at the Heatly High School earlier in the week.
Just a short piece. I was dismayed when he drew two lines
through it, from top to bottom, about an inch in from each
side; it looked as if he was killing it. All he meant was to
indent the story and set it in boldface. He said it was a good
fun piece, being about my old teacher Miss Keating, who
had become principal of the Green Island school, and her
complaint that something un-American had happened. Art

headlined it like this: *And This Story/ Is Being Printed/ On Pink Paper.* I wandered up to the United Press office, in a kind of penthouse reached by a spiral staircase, and met Fridman, who impressed me as very young to be an editor for a wire service (as he was). I wanted to talk about newspapering; he talked about the trouble he was having with his powerboat. I was not sympathetic. Mike McArdle was small and frail looking, but usually carrying a pretty good load–of booze. But no one cared; he had been a copyboy since the *News* started business (and maybe before).

When I reached Albany that day, the Hudson River was rising, but no one took particular notice; it came up over its banks nearly every spring. On the way home, I stopped for a cup of coffee at a little lunchroom on State Street, called the Paddock, and met its owner-manager-counterman, a kewpie-looking fellow named Ed Murphy. We talked a bit; I was the only customer. He explained that he had named the place in memory of his old career: owning some slow racehorses. Off I went to the bus, after briefly watching the water rise in the railroad yard behind the Union Station. It still didn't seem important.

I dozed on the bus, until the driver stopped and asked, "Anyone know where we are?" Someone did. Inside the Watervliet Arsenal, because the river had flooded the main street, Broadway. He also knew how to get out and to Troy. I hustled to the office and reported my experience. By then, Julius had learned that we were in the midst of the worst flood in more than twenty years. He told me to write my story. Then he asked me to hang around for the duration. I covered a few stories about Green Island, including the washout of a culvert on the D&H railroad. I was able to get home for a few hours at a time. But mostly, I hung around, answered the phone, and did whatever anyone wanted done. A few days after the flood had subsided, I received a note signed by B.J. Lewis, thanking me with a check for five dollars.

A Light Show at a Fire

.That summer, Grapp covered another story with the office camera, Julius's trusty Speed Graphic, with a less felicitous result. Julius had taken the night off to take his wife to the movies, and a major fire broke out in a rambling one-story warehouse in Green Island. Grapp, as senior hanger around, grabbed the camera and headed for the fire. He was still out when Julius dropped in, heard about the fire, decided to go, too, and took me along. The fire was still burning brightly enough to take pictures by but above the red glare we saw the white light of a flashbulb. And another. We used them as a beacon to locate Grapp. "Got some great shots," he shouted, "Used six flashbulbs!" Julius reacted with shock. He roared, "Dammit Grapp, I could cover the Second Coming of Christ on less than six flashbulbs." I tried to stifle a laugh, but I didn't need to. Julius himself laughed at the thought of a Heller invoking Christ to a Grapp. But he never let Grapp use another flashbulb. Shortly after that, Sid changed his name to his mother's, Chertok, thereby changing puns on it from the excretal to the genital.

❑

Sid let me work with him on a couple of stories that year. When a well-heeled New York public relations firm took over the RPI Grand Marshal night as a grass-roots protest against hidden taxes (it imported thousand of bright new pennies to make the point), Sid covered it straight for the *Knick* with his new 35-millimeter camera. Then he and I worked all night at his room to print up more shots for an expose of the PR gimmick for one of the picture magazine, *Look*. I'm not sure it got published.

The other special was a longer-running affair: the birth and promotion of the Profiteers of Future Wars. A group at Princeton had organized the Veterans of Future Wars, a protest against wars future and past. Sid and a young red-haired red-bearded instructor at RPI (named Dugan) enlisted me in their satirical one-upping of the

VFW. I contributed a couple of one-liner slogans--one was Two Blondes on Every Lap—which indicated the breadth and depth of our protest. The Profiteers earned considerable mention in the local papers and received a favorable nod from a *New York Times* editorial.

A Lesson But No Lecture

More little stories, more lessons. One brought a lesson without a lecture. A young woman had given birth alone in a cellar apartment to a premature infant weighing less than two pounds. I had read a similar story a few days earlier in the New York *Daily News*. I recalled it so well that I wrote it again, almost word for word and for a lot of words. I didn't notice anyone editing it, but, next morning, I read a different and shorter version. I didn't ask. But I knew the message: we have to be a little brighter than the *Record* but not as hyped as the *Daily News*.

In midsummer, I lost another mentor, but gained in another way. Don Smith was transferred to the Albany office and I began to be paid a weekly salary. I was not on the payroll yet. Jim Hart became the night man on the payroll for sixteen dollars a week; I got the other nine dollars as we split Don's twenty-five dollar salary unevenly. Jim held seniority and that's the way the split was decided. I tried not to sulk, though I felt that seniority was a lousy way to decide something that important. But, what the hell!, nine dollars was a lot more than I ever had made in a week.

It turned out to be an artistic improvement too. While Jim stayed pretty much in the office, I was turned loose on real stories, like covering the city and county legislative bodies, with little preparation. Probably I would not have done so well without the help of another reporter, Joe Snyder of the *Record*. Joe was a tall, handsome fellow about ten years older than I, with a shock of golden hair that earned him the nickname Blondie, and was an excellent reporter. Joe introduced me to people and advised me what items could be left out. Without the malice that some veteran reporters might mix in.

As the outside man, I covered lectures by such as Walter B. Pitkin, the author of *Life Begins at Forty*, whose message I didn't get, and Senator Hugo L. Black, who came to Troy to boost the campaign of an old friend John Nyhoff for Congress, whose message I did get.

Asleep but Awake

On Election Night 1936--the year Franklin D. Roosevelt nearly shut out Alf Landon--I was kept busy, well into the next day. When we had completed the Rensselaer County tally, after midnight, Julius headed for the Albany office with all the tables, and took me along. Julius dashed off his main story there. We watched the compositors placing all the numbers in the page. Back to Troy. We both were pooped, but Julius was still boss, so he assigned me to stay awake and wait for a call from Albany about the Sunrise Edition coming up by bus, while he napped in the drug store's truss room, next to our office. I stayed awake, until just after six in the morning, when I realized I had not heard from Albany. I called the city desk. Someone said, "Kelly called somebody a few minutes ago." And, luckily for me, repeated the bus number and time. Just enough time to catch the bus. I never told Julius that I took the call once in my sleep and once awake.

❑

So life continued, at nine dollars a week, until the first of March 1937. Wondrous day! The Press Co., Inc., announced (and it was a big surprise to me) that it had reached agreement with Local 34 of the American Newspaper Guild on a new set of wages and working conditions. I would now receive reporters' starting pay of sixteen dollars a week.

I had demonstrated at last that it was possible for a kid fresh out of high school to hang around a newspaper office and wind up with a reporter's job. Even at the depth of the Great Depression. A kid can't do that now. He couldn't get past the security guard at the office door. And, if he could, he'd have to impress the human resources director with his degree and a polished résumé. There were no guards then. No human resources people. No questions, except *Doc, want to cover a tennis match?*

I felt grateful to the Guild for getting me such a substantial raise. And I quietly, or so I thought, sent an application for membership to one of the reporters I knew in Albany. I waited for my Guild card.

Names Make. . .Trouble

After three weeks of the new prosperity, Julius assigned me to type up a list of Russell Sage students and their male escorts to a prom. Editors always quoted the line attributed to Mark Twain but really said by someone else: *Names make news.* But what they practiced was: *Names replace news.* To me, it was a daunting chore. Any good typist could have breezed through it. I was not a good typist. I waited till close to midnight to start. I plodded through the list, read-a-name-type-a-name. At the start, I marked each page in top left corner to guide the editor in assembling the story. At first the slug-line (the technical name) was *Rivett/ Sage prom list/add 1*, and *add 2* and so on. Until, about one-thirty, I reached what would have been *add 5*; I was tired and ired. I took my anger out in the sluglines, changing them to *Rivett/Sage whores and pimps/add 5* then *add 6* and so on. Until nearly three in the morning. Still angry, I left the office, let the lock snap behind me, and went home.

The next day, really later the same day, I came to work and Julius called me in to the truss room. He didn't raise his voice. But he left no doubt about what he meant. I was a stupid kid. Imagine, leaving words like those on copy. Yeh, they were only sluglines, and were supposed to be blocked out at the desk, but suppose one of them got into the paper.

Think of it. Several minutes later, he concluded his talk and our relationship. I was fired. All I could say was Goodbye.

My illustrious career was at an end and I was only eighteen, if nearer nineteen. I went across the street to the Morris Lunch and had a cup of coffee. Then I went home. And I cried.

Hanging Around Again

Being fired is a saddening experience any time. At age eighteen, especially so. And compound the sadness when it's the first real job, gained after so much time and lost after so little. Even worse, to me: there wasn't any real reason for it. Oh, I had written some pretty stupid, even hurtful, slug lines, but nothing had *really* happened. They didn't get into the paper. They didn't even get beyond the first editor.

That, it seemed to me, was just unjust. I never had a chance to tell Julius Heller I thought he was being unjust. Not that it would have changed things. Julius sometimes didn't care about being just, only about being right. I never thought how he felt about my justness. He had been my mentor for nearly two years; he had given me a full-time job at part-time pay. He knew that I knew how he felt about the Guild. But he wasn't supposed to know that I had applied for membership. Ah, the arrogance of ignorance.

❏

For the first few days of joblessness--it seemed longer then--I moped around asking myself what to do next and getting no answer. Well, one answer. I wanted a job, any job, preferably the one I had held for two years going on three weeks. The trouble was that all I knew about getting a job was hanging around. Now I had no place to hang.

From force of habit, I kept on going to Troy. In denial, they would call it now. To the Morris Lunch. I soon learned from a former coworker over a cup of coffee that Julius had hired three people. What a boost to denial! One was the son of the local State Trooper captain (possibly in return for favors past); another was the only reporter for the *Cohoes American,* a daily of scornful repute, and the third--damned if I can recall. But it really was three.

I still held a far out hope that the Newspaper Guild might be able to set things right. I phoned Dick Jackson to ask if the Guild could help. He couldn't promise anything; the Guild never had filed a grievance before. The Guild did act: it claimed that the Press Co. Inc. had fired me unfairly for Guild activity. Preposterous, I thought then; applying for Guild membership wasn't much union activity. The company replied that it had fired me for economy. The company never mentioned the reason Heller gave me. The Guild, lacking experience in such matters, never brought up the subsequent three hirings to refute the claim of economy.

All Night for a Dime

My failure at vindication was accomplished within a few weeks, and by then I had gotten used to hanging around the Morris Lunch. I knew a lot of people there: the help and other customers. My customary fare was a mug of dark coffee, just a touch of milk, and a sugar bun, or maybe a hard roll; total bill in either case ten cents, financed usually by a handout from Pa. Even when I was gainlessly employed, I had often lingered for hours over a cup, chatting with one or another of the late night customers, and often with Earl Sharples, the night cashier, though I didn't learn his last name for a long time. One of the regulars was Marty Gordon, a slight, pinch faced waiter who came in every night after work. He signed me up, for a quarter, as a card-carrying member of the American Labor Party. That probably earned me a place in the dossiers of the FBI after Franklin Roosevelt, who had started the ALP as a second line on the 1936 presidential ballot in New York State, decided that it was just too far left, and replaced it with the Liberal Party. I hope that the FBI has since learned I was too young to vote back then and has therefore expunged my record.

After a few weeks. I decided to go ask for a newspaper job. Not knowing that the middle of May was much too late to get hired as a summer fill-in, I went to the Albany office of the papers I once worked for. Right up to the desk of B.J. Lewis, where I asked for a job, any job, even copyboy, for the summer. Mr. Lewis probably remembered me and why I was now looking for a job, but, I figured, if I really had been fired for economy, there ought to be no hard feelings. B.J. didn't even look up. "We won't be hiring anyone this summer," he told me in substance, "We'll be letting people go." Enough said. A brush-off, I thought. And so back to Troy.

Final Final Edition

I was still hanging around the Morris Lunch, when the bulldog edition of the *Knickerbocker Press* for June 30, 1937, came in. Big news. Bad news. It was the final edition, the very last. Gannett had agreed to give up the morning and Sunday *Knickerbocker Press*, and Hearst would move its *Times-Union* from evening to morning and continue its Sunday paper, unopposed. Gannett was left with the newly named *Knickerbocker News* alone in the afternoon. Nothing in the story about jobs, but clearly that hadn't been a brush-off from B.J. Lewis.

A few days later, Dick Jackson called me for help. Not for himself, as he had survived, but for others who hadn't. He told me several people I knew had lost their jobs after the management had shifted some of the Guild leaders to the *Knickerbocker Press*, setting them up to be fired. The Guild was going to the National Labor Relations Board. The next weekend I went to Albany to talk to the Guild lawyers and the NLRB field representative. They asked me about what Julius had said and done in opposition to the Guild. Julius never made a secret of any of it; given the normal volume of his voice, he couldn't have. Toward the end of the interview, I mentioned my visit to B.J. Lewis and his prophetic remark about letting people go this summer. Their first reaction: *hmmm, interesting, but . . .* On second thought, they decided it might be helpful; at least it wouldn't hurt.

Generally, the NLRB moved fast on union complaints, but it would be a few months until hearings would start. So I hung around some more, and hanging around worked a bit of magic. Not a newspaper job, but some work for money. Earl Sharples had decided he needed a night off, for some family event, so he had spoken to the manager Mr. Smith and it was all set: I'd work in his place next Saturday night. That was the busiest night of the week and I had never cashiered anywhere. So Earl coached me for an hour or so on Friday. That first night was a success, and soon Earl was taking other Saturday nights off, and Mr. Smith was asking me to fill in for his day cashiers, his wife and her sister. It was not my idea of a career, but it paid twenty-five cents an hour plus meals. No one ever asked which meal for which day. One afternoon, dinner was a small steak, dessert a pair of lamb chops. And, as a part-time employee I was entitled to an occasional cup of coffee and a sugar bun, or a hard roll, on the house, even when I was off duty.

An Added Hangout

There was a limit, I thought, on the hours I could hang around any one place. So, to fill the early evening, I became acquainted with the people at the Postal Telegraph office down the street: one blue uniformed messenger named Bill Keleher and one telegraph operator, about whom I recall only that he worked days for John Maloney, the local franchisee of the illicit Annenberg racing wire service. When Sharples learned of my early hangout, he suggested a practical joke on the busboy, a grown man of Italian heritage whom we called Mussolini for a fancied resemblance. The suggestion: a fake telegram ordering our Mussolini to report for service with the other Mussolini's army in Ethiopia. The message was delivered by the uniformed messenger. Damn, it was too realistic. Our Mussolini did not take it as a joke. He was not, we learned, a subject of the other Mussolini. There was hell to pay but all of us on the night shift at Postal Telegraph escaped with a bawling out and an admonition to never do nothing like that never again. We never did.

Mr. St. John, the manager at Postal, was quick to forgive. When the Buffalo *Times* (which vanished long ago) ordered Postal's package of coverage for a football game between Buffalo University and RPI, he gave me the paying assignment: two hundred and fifty words and a summary. Not enough to justify a Morse telegrapher at the game but he sent Keleher and his bike up the hill to the stadium to bring my copy to the office. I had no copy, just notes. So Keleher gave me a bone-shaking ride on the bar of his bike down the granite-block-paved Federal Street hill. Not very professional, but the *Buffalo Times* never knew. I wrote the story in the cozy Postal office and easily met the deadline. Mr. St. John said he'd keep me in mind for future assignments; none ever came.

Hanging around the Morris Lunch, even working there, seemed to offer no progress toward a newspaper job. Once more I went looking for work. I took the bus to Cohoes, a little over a mile and well over two journalistic generations away. to see what was available at the *Cohoes American*, a shabby little sheet published by Republicans in a thoroughly shabby city run by Democrats. Maybe there was an opening, for Heller had hired its reporter Jiggs Dillon. I peered through the window; there was Dillon. No opening. I caught the next bus home. All this time, I had not thought of applying for a job at the Troy papers. More denial. I was sure there must be a blacklist and I must be on it, else why would such a talented young man still be without a job

❑

One day when I wasn't cashiering, I got another phone call at home from Mary Freeman, who had survived the massacre in Albany. Could you meet me in Troy tonight, say about 9 o'clock? Sure, I said. I knew her purpose must be business because we were never really friendly, and I thought she was aggressively homely with the map of Ireland on her face and no topography on her body; she probably had an equally repulsed view of my attractions. She came to the point over the first beer she bought. If you would just forget all the things that happened in Troy, you know, the things Heller used to say about the Guild (was her message) and drop out of that case, you could be in line for a job in Albany.

She might have been a bit coy, but she was clear: if you're selling, we might be buying. No sale, Mary. I'm not that kind of guy. Anyway, I had already told the Guild and NLRB lawyers the whole story, a circumstance I did not mention to her. That first beer was the last. But, though still thirsty, I felt like a Hero of the Working Class, even if only a part-time member of it.

❑

It was early in 1938 before the NLRB hearings commenced in the cavernous echoing courtroom in the State Office Building in Albany. I was one of the last witnesses called by the NLRB. I was nervous, sweaty, but, as the board counsel posed easy questions, I calmed down. My answers traced the things Heller had said in despisal of the Guild to the Troy staff, and, on the phone, to people in the Albany office, including threats and warnings. Most times, I was interrupted by objections from Elisha Hanson, the national publishers' lawyer who represented the company. Mainly he objected that I could not have known whom Heller was talking to on the phone and that what I heard was only hearsay anyway. "Eavesdropper," Hanson thundered at me. I knew whom, and no one ever had to eavesdrop, but I was not allowed to say those things. Finally, the NLRB counsel brought up my conversation with B.J. Lewis, step by step, with nary a word from Hanson: no objection, no cross-examination. I left the room wondering if our lawyers had been right the first time: *hmm, interesting, but . . .*

A Job Offer at a Paper

At long last, in a phrase of the era, the hanging paid off. In the early summer of 1938 came an offer of work at--not yet for--the Sunday *Troy Observer-Budget*. The message of hope was brought by Art Wales, whom I had not seen in months. He had stopped at the Morris Lunch for a cup of coffee. He asked if I could work on a project for his uncle Gene Collins. Of course. The project was a grubby job of folding, collating and stapling together a printed program for the American Legion State convention, coming soon to Troy. It was real sweat work, but it paid the usual quarter an hour. My job was supposed to end when we had finished the programs. But Gene Collins felt bound to cover the convention copiously in the *Observer* and he hired me to do it. Temporary, he said. I do not recall what business the convention transacted, but conventions were not attracted to Troy for business, but for pleasure: the whorehouses were wide open. The one story I recall writing was a short about a bugler sounding taps over an empty whiskey bottle, a dead soldier, in the gutter on Broadway.

That was a foot in the door, the rest of me followed. The next week, something else had to be covered, for pay. I accepted the invitation. Likewise the following week and the week after. Soon I was employed part-time but steady. I can't recall how much (or, more likely, little) I was paid but I remember that the other employees sometimes discussed whether it was better to dash right to the bank on Friday to cash the paycheck or to wait until early next week, when the cash for ads and circulation would have come in. With me, Friday won.

Another Chance at a Job

About the time I had established my position at the *Observer*, I began hanging around the *Troy Record* too. Joe Snyder and I met on the street and he invited me to drop in at the Record "any time". So I did. He welcomed me. Soon I dropped in again. And again. And then fairly often, usually roosting near the desk of Jack Maloney, a reporter who was a graduate of Columbia School of Journalism, with a master's degree, and now was supplementing his pay check by running a small motor court in Mechanicville. So much for a master's degree.

Now I had two places to hang around. What a vast difference between them, though only a block and a half apart. The *Observer-Budget*, a mid-nineteenth century weekly in a nearly twentieth-century city, was housed in a, well, in a house on the uphill side of the railroad tracks. A house strengthened to hold the four Linotype machines on the second floor and job presses and a small metal melting pot on the third. It was cramped and quaint to the edge of woebegone. The *Record* was on a prominent corner within a block of the business section in a building that had been designed for a daily newspaper--two of them, morning and afternoon. The building had been recently expanded. It was bright and clean.

The *Observer* had changed little since Michael Collins founded it in the 1880s to advance his political career; the *Budget* part of its name came from another Sunday paper that Collins acquired in the early 1900s. The second generation of Collinses ran it more, it seemed, as a memorial to their progenitor than as a business enterprise. Around the office, the original was usually mentioned as The Senator, in the hushed, reverential tone due someone who had served long and with distinction in the United States Senate; he had actually served a few undistinguished terms in the State Senate.

❏

The Collinses, there were seven of them, struggled to make a living from the *Observer*. They might have prospered if they had to support only themselves. But they had a dozen or so other mouths to feed: four fulltime typesetters and a foreman, two part-time press operators, a bookkeeper (also part-time), and, fulltime, an ad salesman, a city editor and a reporter, and the latest addition, me. A remarkable roster for a paper that sold only five thousand copies (at a news stand price of ten cents), though the Collinses reported it as fifteen thousand, a figure they arrived at by adding together the three separate eight page press runs required to get out a twenty-four page paper. Their financial salvation was the profit from printing legal briefs and court papers.

The Collins family was as remarkable as the paper. Frank, the oldest brother, a dour looking but slyly humorous man, was the editor, which means that he wrote (or cribbed from the *Boston Post*) a couple of editorials, edited the telegraph news and put Page One together on Saturday night, and worried whether Gene Hayes would be able to get to Cohoes on Friday to prepare his customary page of what passed for news. (I wondered then why Frank was so worried about Cohoes; I think now it was because the *Observer* was paid to cover the city felicitously.) Gene, the youngest brother, a Colonel Blimpish figure, was the entrepreneur of the family, starting (and soon folding) a weekly for southern Rensselaer County, for which I worked a couple of weeks, and publishing a souvenir volume about the 1938 State Constitutional Convention. (He had an edge on some of his siblings: his wife had a steady job as a school teacher.) The other brother, Eddie, overweight and loud and perennially ruddy faced from rosacea, was the ad salesman-designate, though most of the selling was done by a hustling little guy named Steve McLaughlin.

A Working Sister

Only one of the sisters worked at the *Observer*: Helen, who was the society editor, filling a couple of pages each week with news of engagements, weddings and membership teas. She also dispatched several photographs to a photoengraver in Philadelphia and worried till the engravings arrived (always) just in time. Oldest sister Alice, who walked with a cane and was married to a man named Armstrong and who lived in New York, dispatched a weekly column of Gotham gossip in the form, and often the words, of O.O. McIntyre, and complained to Frank about the paucity of her income from the family paper. In 1939, she visited Troy and brought along Allen Markley, a tall, tweedy, pipe-smoking consultant, to search out more money for her. The other sisters, Rena who was Art Wales's mother, and Marie, married to a lawyer named Spain, rarely even visited the *Observer.* Art Wales didn't spend much time at the paper either, just enough to help pay his way through college. He worked at a couple of other local papers before he decided a better living lay at the other end of the typewriter. He died in 1993 at age seventy-three, after retiring as vice president of SCM, the typewriter manufacturer. Marie Spain, the last offspring of The Senator, died in the spring of 1994 at age ninety-two.

The two fulltime news employees were remarkable too. Al MacNaughton, a gnomish old man (he made sure nobody knew just how old) with a sly smile, a sneaky wit, and an eyeshade, was the city editor. His principal chore was to compile each week a three-column compendium of events covered by the *Observer* ten, twenty and thirty years before, a period most of the *Observer's* readers seemed still to be living in. He also updated local items from the Saturday *Record* and covered the police beat. Soberly. The only reporter was Hayes, who, at fortyish, still had the black Irish good looks of an altar boy, though his wavy hair was beginning to thin. His principal chore was to prepare the Cohoes page with a padded-out puff piece or two, a few rewrites from the *Record*, and a column bylined Jack Spinner, in tribute to Cohoes's faded past as a textile center. Not always soberly, which was the source of Frank Collins's perpetual worry.

I Nearly Fire Myself

The Cohoes officials strove mightily to protect Hayes, as I learned, almost at the cost of my job, when I was sent to replace him one Friday when he was too hung over to work. The people I talked to at City Hall had nothing to say except "Hello" and "Who?" and "Where's Hayesie?" I returned to the office nearly empty handed, and Frank Collins berated me for my inability to fill the Cohoes page. I responded and he responded and so on, till I ended the discussion by shouting, "I'm not going to put up with your shit any more." I stomped out. Markley, who had heard the discussion from the other side of the floor, met me at the front steps. With the air of someone who had seen and heard even worse discussions, he advised me, "Just come in tomorrow and start working. Act as if nothing happened. No apology, no explanation." I did, and Frank also acted as if nothing had happened, and I worked there until I decided, much much later, to quit. That was probably the only success Markley achieved in Troy.

Though I was unable, even for a day, to replace Gene Hayes in Cohoes, I found it easy to succeed him as *de facto* sports editor of the *Observer.* All I had to do was to offer to take some work off his hands. The *Observer* had two sports sections: two pages in the eight-page section that was printed on Friday and two more in the main news section printed Sunday morning. So I offered, for a start, to put the Friday pages together and Hayes quickly agreed. He didn't care much for sports anyway, and now he could pad out his Cohoes work to cover all of Friday. Soon I extended my offer to the two pages in the main section. No sooner said than done. My career as a sportswriter was born. Though really, I was more a desk editor than reporter. Oh, I still had time to read scads of galley proofs, both newspaper and legal.

An Offer I Could Refuse

I also went out on a kind of beat every Saturday morning. That included, as war neared, the Navy recruiting station, and one morning I browsed among the color acuity charts (making sure I was not colorblind) and the recruiter, mistakenly concluding that I might be a prospect, offered me a waiver so I could become a yeoman. A what? I thought. I graciously refused his offer: "too much to waive," I mumbled. I had been 4-F from the first physical I took. Dr. Silcocks looked across his desk at me, then walked over and ran his fingers up and down the back of my neck as if counting vertebrae. He grunted the doctors' ambiguous grunt and wrote, in his tiny cramped hand, two lines describing my condition. I never asked about it, but it convinced the draft board.

The *Observer* had no space for hangers-around and barely enough for droppers-in. The latter were few but important: undertakers bearing paid death notices (and unpaid obituaries). John Tower was the most important, as he ran the highest price funeral home in Troy and used the longest paid notices. He was tall and distinguished looking in the gray Chesterfield topcoat he wore most of the year. John had such a sincere voice that he could say Hello and make you feel that he had just conferred a blessing on you. He was doubly welcome because, as a local Democratic party leader, he could be counted on for some classy gossip. Another frequent visitor was Joe Malone, who ran a blue-collar undertaking business out of his home on Ida Hill, near Hayes's house. On each visit, he would taunt his neighbor, "Hayesie, I'm gonna make a lot of money on you: I won't have to embalm you and I can put you in a cigar box." (Hayes may have had the last laugh; he outlived both Joe Malone and the *Observer*, which perished in May 1954. Hayes dropped dead while walking in Cohoes in 1959; he was sober.)

Despite Hayes's activity, the only drinking on the *Observer's* premises occurred late each Saturday night, really Sunday morning, after the last copy had been sent to the composing room and before the press started running. Someone was sent down Broadway to Eddie Leitgeb's saloon to fetch roast fresh ham sandwiches and a quantity of bottled Piel's beer, which was cheaper than any of the three local brands. They kept the news staff around to read proofs and to handle the occasional late local story and such major wire service stories as the Cocoanut Grove fire in Boston that killed four hundred and eighty-five people, and the first U.S. troop landing abroad, in North Africa, in World War II.

❑

While I was still working at the *Observer* and just starting at the Record--that was the spring of 1939--the NLRB handed down its decision in the *Knickerbocker News* case. It found that the company had unfairly fired three Guild activists and ordered them put back to work and paid any salary they lost in the interim. As the ruling went against the newspaper, the story was terse. Nothing said about the NLRB's reasoning. The big story seemed to be that the Press Co. would appeal to the courts to reverse the decision. It left me wondering if my talk with B.J. Lewis was still *hmm, interesting, but . . .*

❑

It had taken me a bit longer to land a job after hanging around at the *Record*--longer than at the *Observer*. As I had done before, I made myself useful, though the opportunities were limited. The *Record* had a copyboy who was supposed to do the grubby chores that I had done in my earlier career. Soon, however, one of the editors invited me to help in recycling the news from the afternoon *Times Record* to the morning paper. That involved clipping stories, pasting them to large sheets, and changing the time element, and then rewriting the headline to fit the morning paper's type. Messy, boring work. Then I was allowed to take dictation from correspondents in Rensselaer and Glens Falls. Messy, boring work, until I decided to rewrite stories directly from the same out-of-town papers they were using.

Busy, but No Pay

Those city room chores left a lot of time to hang out in the sports department and further my sportswriting career. That hanging around led to chores that were not messy, boring. I had learned in hanging around that people would be glad to let you do what you wanted to if they didn't have to pay for it. So I got into good stuff, like covering college basketball games at RPI and professional ones at the Troy Armory, and, in the summer, the Albany Senators of the Eastern (Baseball) League. Not for pay, of course. But covering those games at the Armory provided me the opportunity to boast that "I went through RPI". As I had, after each game. It's not on my résumé.

Paying My Way to Work

To cover the Senators' games, I paid my own bus fare, a dime each way, to Hawkins Stadium, where I paid my nickel for the scorecard, until the club owner Tom McCaffrey noticed and made sure that I got one free. That was another great career move that I failed to recognize at the time. I got to know the sports editors of the two Albany papers, Charles Young of the *Knickerbocker News* and Dick Walsh of the *Times-Union*. So there we were, two veteran sports editors and a kid still not on a payroll, sharing the long, narrow press box on the roof of Hawkins Stadium, thirty feet or so in the air. A perfect place to watch the game. Except that Young and Walsh didn't always pay attention. Young had lots of other things to do: he wrote a daily sports column, prepared a bunch of Notes of the Game, and worked on a weekly report for *The Sporting News*. Walsh had little to do, and little interest in doing it. I had nothing else to do and kept watching every play. Several times in a game, Young looked up from his portable typewriter and asked, "What happened?" At first, I waited for Walsh to answer; when he failed to, I offered Young my version: a hit, an error, a fielder's choice, whatever. He marked it so in his official scorebook. My relations with Walsh prospered in another way. Soon he began to call on me to cover sports events around Troy, for which I was paid space rates, though I sometimes had to press him or the business office to send my check

A Grin, and a Job

As I expected, hanging around the *Record* led to the payroll. I became a substitute for the sports editor and his assistant on their nights off. It was an informal hiring: no interview, no résumé, just the sports editor saying, "Doc, you want to work a couple of nights a week? You know, when Leo and I are off. OK, Kid?" Of course it was OK. The night city editor Al Sliter, who was in charge of the morning paper, had to endorse the hiring, but that was just a grin and a nod.

The sports editor was a South Troy Irishman named Jack McGrath (pronounced McGraw) and subtitled Peerless. His brother Cornelius (Neil) was city editor of the afternoon *Times-Record;* another brother James was the Troy City Clerk and had been city editor of the *Troy Times* when it folded. (All three were Democrats and each exercised more political influence than all the Republican pontifications of the editor Dwight Marvin.) Jack had started as an office boy, right out of school--at what grade level was never clear--and became sports editor at a time when editors gave sports coverage a low priority. Jack picked up his nickname as a byline when real names couldn't be used. Its origin was not clear. Peerless was then about forty years old, fairly tall, tending toward fleshiness yet his large boned face and baldish skull gave him the vague appearance of a death's head. Peerless and his assistant each had Saturday and one other night off, officially.

Peerless was a generally placid man, a friend to everyone he knew and a lot of people he didn't. Though he had only two nights off, he spent part (or all) of others in various nearby saloons. While Peerless and others drank heavily off premises, the *Record* premises were generally dry. The main exception was the period from Christmas to New Year's when many of Peerless's friends and clients sent in bottles of good stuff. Every drop was drunk in the office, and so were we.

With the Two Abes

The sports department room had enough space for visitors, who usually filled it, except on Peerless's night off. Two chairs generally were occupied by the two Abes: Morton (Abe) Silver and Abe Freedman. Abe Silver was in his thirties, bulky, smelly, dull, and with a large nose further distorted by the continual occupancy of an index finger. He was a perpetual copyboy, whose pay was reputedly furnished indirectly by his father. Abe Silver regarded himself as Peerless's personal copyboy--a regard Peerless did not discourage. Abe Freedman was a few years older, always natty though not in the fashion *du jour*, and he suffered from the drooling-swearing form of Tourette syndrome. (At the time, Tourette syndrome was not a household word, and most people considered Abe just a wacko.) After I began working full-time at the *Record*, Abe covered the Senators' games. He kept his scorecard unconventionally, but accurately, and he could be counted on to recall, with highly complex swearing, every play that mattered, so I could write about the game.

❑

Abe Silver's view of his role, as answerable only to Peerless, had led to a discussion that led to my banishment as *persona non grata* for a few months early in my hanging around at the *Record*. One Sunday afternoon, I asked Abe to take some copy to the Albany bus, as part of a deal Peerless had made with the golf writer for the *Knickerbocker News*. But invoking Peerless's name when Peerless was off did not influence Abe. We talked about it a while, then push came to shove and Abe, outweighing me by at least seventy pounds, shoved much more strongly than I could push. I swung at him and connected not with my fist but with a paste jar I was holding. The collision of two hard surfaces caused blood to flow and the squabble to end. The incident gave rise to a myth that I had thrown the paste jar to hit Abe. That gave great unearned credit to my throwing accuracy.

I served out my exile by hanging around the Union
Hotel, a restaurant just around the corner from the *Record*,
and at the taxi stand up the street, across from the Union
Station. Jerry Murley, who ran the restaurant, asked me to
keep his books, a job I had no training and less aptitude
for. My bookkeeping would give him more time to put
moves on the female musicians he had hired to draw more
business. I did better at my enterprise than he did at his.
Jerry also gave me an opportunity to make my only visit to
a whorehouse. Oh, not that way. The restaurant delivered
meals down the street and when no one else was around,
Murley asked me to deliver some dinners to Gene Cottrell's
place, the only storefront on the line. I opened the door and
there were four or five good-looking, well-endowed ladies of
the evening wearing very showy pastel-colored nightgowns.
I looked at them in awe. They looked at me--a twenty-one-
year-old who could pass for fifteen—in anticipation. To spare
them disappointment, I decided to scram.

At the taxi stands, I met an assortment of colorful
people: Johnny Drzozd, the cab driver who sometimes tried
to ensure Pa's safe arrival home; Yock Feyl, a three hundred
pound beer salesman; a tiny old guy named Ace (for Asa)
who answered the phone for Drzozd, and Ed Murphy, late of
the Paddock restaurant in Albany. Once Murphy learned my
name, he recalled times when he had worked in hotels with
my Uncle Art, who also was called Doc. The memories were
pleasant, he said, especially about Uncle Art's response to
the sound of high heels rhythmically clicking and clacking
across the hotel lobby.

After serving my penance, I returned to the sports
desk as a visitor, hardly noticeable among the other visitors,
and quietly worked my way up to becoming the part-time
sportswriter. Peerless was host to a varied group, ranging
from the sublime of Johnny Evers, the baseball (and
doggerel) star of decades past, to the ridiculous of a retired
and rather goofy trolley car conductor named Augie. We
always hoped that Evers would tell some stories of his days

(thirty years and seventy pounds ago) as the Chicago Cubs' hundred and twenty-five pound second baseman or as the more recent general manager of the Albany Senators of the International League and his successful effort to secure a place in baseball for a paroled holdup man named Alabama Pitts (who, it turned out, couldn't hit a curve or much of anything else). Likewise, we hoped to learn much about the early days of basketball--right after Prof Naismith invented it--from Ed Wachter, a giant of the early game at six feet two, who had become the city recreation commissioner. But no, they talked about old times in South Troy, and Peerless, being a generation younger than both, often was a generation out of phase when they waxed anecdotal.

A few of the visitors talked sports. Ed Conners, who was taller than any of the players on his Troy Haymakers of the American Basketball League, explained how easy it was to lose money in a major league that included places like Troy, Kingston (NY), and Scranton and Harlem and South Philadelphia and Bay Ridge. Later Paul Sahagian offered similar tales about his team in the New York State minor league in cities like Saratoga Springs, Cohoes, Glens Falls and Mohawk, yes, Mohawk. A few others, such as Alva Kelley, the All-America end from Cornell and wartime football coach at the Watervliet Arsenal, and Simon Boardman, an all-America basketballer from New York University, were too new in town to talk politics.

❏

By then, I had resumed my athletic career, as manager-entrepreneur-futility player for the Green Island Monitors, which I entered in a Troy area amateur league. The age limit was sixteen. I was twenty-one, but no one cared. If I hadn't owned the team I couldn't have played. At bat my only weakness was a pitched ball; in the field, a batted ball. I managed to get uniforms, financed by some local merchants and a bingo party that raised fifty-seven dollars.

In the fall, I branched out to basketball with similar results. This time, I bought the uniforms: gold jerseys and purple moleskin shorts. The first time we worked up a sweat, the purple ran faster than any of us could, and I did not complete paying for them. Despite our limited ability, we were booked for prepreliminaries to the Troy Haymakers games in the Armory, where we warmed things up for the first few fans.

The Umpire Strikes

In the meantime, I became a baseball umpire, working high school games alone at five dollars each. A few years into my career, I established a standard that is still practiced today by all umpires. I was umpiring at Prospect Park in Troy. Late in the game, the Troy High team had runners on first and second when a batter singled to right field. I awaited the normal play, a throw home. But the fielder sensed an easier play and threw to third. I was stranded, sixty feet away, but when the runner from first slid behind the third baseman, I called him out. Eddie Picken, the Troy High coach, stormed out to protest: *You couldn't see the play; you can't call him out* and many more words, rendered with high dudgeon. When he paused for breath, I said, "Eddie, a guy makes a play like that look close, he's got to be out." It's standard umpiring practice now; just watch closely on tag plays of an attempted stolen base. The ball gets there first, the guy's out, tag or no tag. Picken came back to hire me for his next game.

❑

During my part-time employment at the *Record*, I also worked full-time at the Observer, thus packing a total of seven shifts into five days and earning almost a living wage. Once again I gained a mentor: Peerless's assistant Leo Curley, who had started newspapering right out of Catholic Central High School in the mid 1920s. He was about ten years older than me, heavyset and invariably pleasant. He was soon promoted to telegraph editor.

A Matter of Method

Curley's methods differed vastly from Peerless's. Leo improvised dummies of the sports pages and kept track of the stories he sent to the composing room, and, at the end of the night, he had only a few small items left over. Peerless had a primitive style: send up just about every piece of copy that came in and let the foreman of the composing room select the right amount to fill the pages. Peerless furnished some guidance. He marked many items Must and then, to indicate the order of mustness, he marked Very Must (a few were Very Very Must). There were other degrees of mustness: ! or !! or !!! or (sometimes and) an underscore, or two, or three.

After Curley was promoted, Peerless had a succession of young assistants, who also moved on to better things. Ed Hogan got a job with United Press in Albany. J. Steele Gow, a graduate of Williams College, Marvin's alma mater, proved too quiet and too talented for the job, and soon left for his native Pittsburgh. (I met him there in 1951, when I was a delegate to the Newspaper Guild convention; he was news editor at the Pittsburgh Press. Last I heard about him, he had--sad fate--become a journalism professor.) Finally a young reporter named Bob Sheeran from South Troy became the full-time assistant. He was about my age, and had come to the Record right out of high school. He operated in the Curley style and we both enjoyed working for Peerless, especially on our leader's night off.

❑

The chronology has come to 1941, and the Associated Press reported that the U.S. Supreme Court upheld the NLRB's decision in the Guild's case against the Press Co., issued two years earlier. The Court ruling meant that the *Knickerbocker News* must offer jobs back to three men fired in the Guild purge of 1937. Two of them, Austin Scannell and Henry Christman, had since moved on to the much better jobs, so they accepted reinstatement and resigned a day later. The third, John Wanhope, came back to stay. The story still was adverse to a publisher, so little detail of the Court's decision or any of the prior rulings was published. The case was over and I still could not learn if my testimony had proved to be anything more than *hmmm, interesting, but . . .*

❑

Bob Sheeran and I were working the Sunday Pearl Harbor was bombed. By the end of the week he had enlisted in the Marines.

A Raise, Then a Job

I saw a fulltime job coming. First I had to be interviewed by Dwight Marvin. It wasn't like that interview for high school correspondent in 1933, an interview that neither of us mentioned. Getting the job was easy, and I even got a raise before I was hired. Nobody had done that before; not many people at the *Record* got raises after they were hired. Marvin was a political conservative and an economic tightwad. He made an exception for the police reporter Johnny Mack (né McNamara), giving him a reproductivity award of two dollars a week for each child he sired, thereby making Johnny, the father of six, or was it eight, the highest paid reporter in town.

So how did I got a raise before I started work? Marvin suggested, "about twenty-eight dollars a week." I responded, "As long as we're talking of about, I think we should talk of about thirty. When Bob Sheeran was leaving, he told me he was making thirty and that if I took less and something happened to him he'd come back and haunt me." Marvin had never heard anything like that before. He thought about it a moment and said, "Well, we wouldn't want that to happen. And it probably would be easier to start you at thirty than to try to get the War Labor Board to approve a raise later."

(After the war, Sheeran thanked me for having kept the faith and the thirty-dollar standard.)

At full-time, I saw perhaps less of Peerless. He was off on Saturday and Sunday nights, I was off Saturday and Monday. That was official. But when I went to work at 7 p.m. on many a Tuesday, Peerless greeted me effusively as if we hadn't been together in weeks. Within a few minutes, never more than an hour, he began his departure: "I got to go out for a while, kid. OK, Doc? Take care of things. If anybody calls, I'll be back. OK? I won't be long. See you later." Sometimes, "later" was Wednesday. Sometimes, Tuesday would be reprised as the week wore on.

Whatever days he was out, I'd take care of things. If he hadn't had time to clip out a Harry Grayson column, I'd do it, freshening up the first couple of paragraphs. Or, if inspiration struck, I'd write a colyum by Peerless from scratch. No one ever seemed to notice Peerless's absence, not even Peerless. Not even the time in 1939 when I delved into the Record's sparse library to produce two scholarly columns "**By Peerless**" deflating the Abner Doubleday myth just after a major induction at the Baseball Hall of Fame. There was one occasion each year when a story "**By Peerless**" appeared on Page One--the morning the Saratoga racing season opened. The year I wrote it, Peerless implored me to include a favorite phrase of his: "The magical, mystical cry of 'They're Off' at Saratoga," His other ghosts had had to use that phrase ever since a reporter named Jack (Smitty) Manion had dropped it into his lead a half dozen years earlier and caught Peerless's imagination.

Making My Mark on Makeup

With a war on, there was no thought of having a part-time helper on our days off, so on Sunday I was free to follow Leo Curley's style. (The Sunday night foreman in the composing room was used to it.) All went well until one weeknight when, in Peerless's absence, I tried the Curley style on the regular foreman. A near disaster. He kept watching for the degrees of mustness on the copy and put aside all that was not so marked. At midnight, he called the sports desk. "Better get up here," he barked. "You're in trouble. Nowhere near enough copy to fill. What the hell you been doing?" I assured him that if he set all that copy on the desk he'd have just enough type to fill the sports space. He did; I was right. Never any trouble after that. Not even when I began using the Rivett style while Peerless was in the office. Of course, I took care of all of Peerless's friends and clients.

In the spring of 1943, I went further, emulating pages I had perused in the Oklahoma City *Times* and the Louisville *Courier-Journal* among the "exchanges" the *Record* received. I was unaware that I was doing alone what those papers had several sports desk editors to do. Peerless never objected. But then I never asked his approval. The sports pages looked beautiful, with related stories grouped under horizontal headlines of four, five or six columns. They vexed the printers, who were used to the old-fashioned vertical wraparound makeup that the rest of the *Record* continued to use.

Looking for a Job in Vain

Early in 1943, I did something I'd never done before: I applied for a job. I saw an ad in the trade paper *Editor & Publisher*: for a sports editor in Glens Falls, about fifty miles to the north. My application brought an invitation to talk to the managing editor Ralph Knight. He was not a total stranger. I had enjoyed a couple of his short stories in the *Saturday Evening Post*. They were set in Central Park in New York City in those Depression days, when Central Park was safe and friendly.

Not one of the job interviews I had before was more complicated than, *Want to cover a tennis match?* or *I've decided to put you on two nights a week. OK Kid?* So I was not prepared for what happened in Glens Falls. I tried to dress well for it, with my best, my only, suit, one of Pa's neckties, and, to ward off the chill, my kind-of-shopworn loden green car coat. The bus arrived early in Glens Falls, giving me time to case the joint and to chat with the incumbent sports editor, a friendly young fellow named Don Cunnion who was leaving to join The Associated Press in Albany. Cunnion impressed me; the plant did not. But then I was there to impress Ralph Knight. My turn at that came over dinner in a nearby restaurant. I thought I was doing pretty well with the knife and fork and conversation. Knight kept his counsel and said he would write to me. In a few days, his letter arrived. Seven pages, single spaced: you did not do well at knife-and-forking, your car coat was something an RPI freshman would wear, that gap where an upper front tooth should be looks terrible. All in all, a devastating critique, though intended to be helpful. I should have kept those seven pages; they'd have made a great chapter in the kind of How-to-Be-Interviewed books that have proliferated lately. I still had a job as assistant sports editor on a staff of two at the *Troy Record* and maybe that was--well, surely it was--at least as good as being sports editor on a staff of one in a smaller town.

❏

I didn't have much time to make comparisons like that. Not long after I received Knight's critique, Dick Walsh called me in May with a silly question, "Would you like to come to work here?" Knight had hired one of Walsh's sportswriters, a skinny, fortyish pain-in-the-ass named Frank Garcin, as his sports editor.

A Different Interview

I set out for the next interview prepared for anything. I had absorbed all Knight's criticisms; I'd know just what to do at the dinner table, and it was too warm to worry about a car coat. At the *Times-Union*, I found that interviews were more Peerless's kind than Knight's. George Williams, the managing editor, was there, so was Con Heffernan, the city editor, who used to be the baseball writer. Con introduced me to Williams with lavish praise of my ability, especially as a baseball writer. A cordial and short talk. We settled on my starting in two weeks at forty-two fifty a week.

It was time for another interview with Marvin. I told him I had taken the job at the *Times-Union* and offered him two weeks notice. He then allowed that he couldn't match that forty-two fifty, but "maybe we could get a five-dollar raise through the War Labor Board." I told him, "Thank you for that offer, but I came in to resign, not to hold you up for a raise." He had never heard talk like that before. He knew about Glens Falls and told me, "It was too bad that you didn't get that job in Glens Falls, I think that would have been a better professional opportunity for you than the *Times-Union*." I didn't think so but I kept still. We parted amicably.

I spent those two weeks toning down the makeup style so that Peerless and whoever came on in my place could carry on in the old way. Peerless said he was sorry to see me go. He probably would have emphasized that with Very, Very Must!!!! And three underscores. The printers weren't sorry to see me go. They meant it too. And on May 19, 1943, we all said goodbye.

❑

Throughout this brief history of my second hanging around, I have reported only what I knew contemporaneously about the progress of the NLRB's case against the Press Co. Inc. My reports have been sketchy, but no less complete than the newspaper reports at the time.

Lately, though, I have had the opportunity to read some of the original documents--the NLRB's findings and the court decisions--and I have a better, if not clearer, grasp on what happened. I must say "if not clearer" because the proceedings before the NLRB appear to have stumbled and bumbled along. The Guild initially had sought the reinstatement of several reporters and editors. That's where clarity ended. As the case progressed, the NLRB counsel struck off some names, but added Cameron Hyde, the managing editor, who wasn't in the bargaining unit, and a copyreader named Frank Mohan who was still working. The record also cleared up how Mary Freeman knew that I had talked to the NLRB? The answer was supplied by a former secretary of B.J. Lewis's. He had fired her, and she testified that Lewis had been brought in to break the Guild and had established an elaborate spy system.

Finally, I found the answer about the value of my testimony about my May 1937 conversation with B.J. Lewis. It was far more than *hmmm, interesting -- but . . .* There it was, in the NLRB's final decision. B.J. Lewis had known of the coming merger and accordingly had shuffled staff to put an innocent look on his purge of Guild leaders, as shown by "the unrebutted testimony of witness Rivett." Ah. Still a Hero of the Working Class.

A Job Full of Promise

My new job as a sports writer on the *Albany Times-Union* was full of promise. A promise ("it's in the contract") that I'd get a raise to fifty dollars a week in another year. A promise (it wasn't in the contract) that "you'll be doing a lot of baseball writing." The promises were made by George O. Williams, the managing editor of legend. I'm sure he believed his promises at the time in May 1943. So did I.

I was not much concerned about the future. The present was bright enough: new paper, new city, new boss, new salary. But not all really new. In some ways it was a reprise of Troy. The city room, a larger, scruffier *Observer-Budget*, right down to the wire cage and clothesline rope device that carried copy up a floor to the composing room. The sports desk, like the *Record*, presided over by a sports editor who drank a lot. Home sweet home!

None of that was a surprise, though. I knew the look of the city room from visits as far back as 1939 dunning the sports editor Dick Walsh. Each time he told me, "It's the business office; they just hold things up all the time, I'll try to push it along." Next day, I'd call the business office and hear, "Oh, we can't do a thing right now; Dick hasn't sent the voucher through." I never learned who was exactly lying, but a couple of days later the check arrived, and it never seemed large enough to cause the business office to hold it up. Three or four dollars at most.

I also knew Walsh drank a lot and smoked a lot, but not exactly how much. When I covered Eastern League baseball for the *Record*, a groundskeeper toted a pail full of iced bottles of Hedrick's beer to the rooftop press box during a double header; a half dozen bottles for Dick, one for me. I never kept count of Dick's smoking. Now, at the office, barely two hours into the day's work, Walsh already had downed two quarts of Hedrick's draft at his desk and was working on a third. The empty waxed cardboard containers were on the floor behind his chair. He had overfilled a large ashtray with the butts of a full pack of Pall Malls. Walsh, I soon learned, started every day by sending a copyboy out for four packs of Pall Malls, no easy task with a war on. The copyboy also had to fetch, one at a time, as many quarts of beer.

2 for the Price of 1

I was replacing not one but two sportswriters. Not to brag: the war limited sports and the space to put them in. I had helped create one of the vacancies: the departure, to general approval, of Frank Garcin to become sports editor of the Glens Falls *Post-Star*. The Army created the other by drafting Stanley Levine, a hustling recent college graduate. He was missed by many not only for his sunny disposition but also for his supply of lending money, available at a heavy interest rate and subject only to one question, *when do I get it back?*

The first time I met Stan, in the fall of 1938, I knew he'd be a success. We were covering the same football game. I prowled the sideline; Stan sat on the bench of the Philip Schuyler High team, for which he was third string quarterback. The coach felt Stan was more productive as a reporter for the *Times-Union* than as a player at (generously) five feet one and a hundred and twenty pounds. Stan had gone on to graduate from Siena College, which had no football team but offered equal opportunities for a hustler, as a hustler was defined in the thirties and forties. He had begun working for the *Times-Union* at space rates, and picking up extra dough at chores like taking care of the bases for the YMCA softball league. When he went on the payroll full time, some folks said, he took a pay cut.

My life on the sports desk started with some confusion. Walsh had emphasized one immutable rule: don't give any racing results on the phone. Not to anyone. The rule seemed silly--the results were put on display promptly at the private off-track betting parlors all over the city--but I obeyed. When, that first evening, a sultry whiskey contralto named

Ethel asked for the sixth at New York, which was Belmont, I said, "Sorry, we can't give out race results." The voice asked to speak to Dick, and he told me, "It's OK to give results to Ethel." I never learned who Ethel was, though I heard from her often. An afternoon or two later, another call: a furtive baritone named I asking "Whatta you got on the fourth at Chicago?" I tried again with the same result.

The Late First Edition

Another emphasized rule: the first edition must be off the composing room floor by 7 p.m. No exceptions. But it was like the race results. Within a few days, when I was overseeing the closing of the sports pages and seven o'clock had come and gone, Lou Schaefer, the head makeup printer, assembled a group of us before an incomplete page, folded a sheet of proof paper into a clerical collar around his neck, lighted a candle, and called for bowed heads and a moment of silence in respectful memory for the late first edition. Not every night. Some nights, the lateness was too much to be funny.

❑

The *Times-Union* plant at Beaver and Green Streets was a museum piece. The city room, squeezed into a low-ceilinged second floor, looked much as it had when the paper moved in in 1891, but with a lot more telephones, newer typewriters, and a greater volume of tobacco smoke. The few windows extended from floor to ceiling, but only the top half (of some) could be opened. Decor was nonexistent, unless you counted the accumulated dirt and smoke residue, and the wooden posts and beams and the sprinkler system pipes, a couple of calendars and a wall clock. The sports department, four clustered wood desks, was in an airless corner just inside the city room. A few feet beyond, the city editor presided over a similar cluster. At the Green Street corner stood the homemade horseshoe shaped copy desk. The night office of the Associated Press, one row of desks and another of Teletype machines, ranged along the Green Street wall. Desks for other Times-Union editors and reporters were arrayed in the dim interior. On the far inside a small alcove housed Teletypes of Hearst's private wire and the International News Service and served as a hideaway for the copyboys. The copyboys had pinned up photos and notices, including one dated 1941 in which Chief (as Hearst called himself) warned his editors never again to mention the name of the actress Dorothy Comingore; she had played the mistress in *Citizen Kane*, a movie that Hearst took personally. By late afternoon, the air had been replaced by smoke from cigarettes, a few cigars, one or two pipes and a bunch of smoldering ashtrays.

In 1912, the editor-publisher-owner Martin Glynn had bought the Elks Club building next door and for the next thirty years the combined building, plus an extension to Hudson Avenue built in the nineteen-twenties for new presses, housed all the departments of the paper. In 1941, the other white collar departments were moved to a building several blocks away on North Pearl Street. That move brought the morgue, the darkroom, and the art department out from under the stairs and other hidden places, and gave the managing editor a private office.

I Become the Real Doc

Promptly at six o'clock, Monday through Saturday, the staff of The Associated Press, carrying the files in a couple of well-used sample cases, trooped in from the day office at the *Knickerbocker News* in the next block. And so I again met Don Cunnion, whose job I didn't get. We exchanged greetings and mutual congratulations. A few weeks later, we became, initially, doppelgängers. That is, whenever I came to the rescue of a late-night (woman) staffer by writing a sports roundup--Eastern League baseball then, college football, college basketball later--she credited the assistance to "DOC--the real one," as distinct from "DOC"--for Donald

O. Cunnion. (After several months, Don left to join his old boss Ralph Knight at Curtis Publications in Philadelphia. I remained "DOC--the real one".)

Shortly after six each weeknight, Mike the Candyman appeared, carrying his stock of goodies in two large covered picnic baskets--mostly cigarettes, some snacks and candy bars, fresh fruits like apples, oranges, and bananas in season--from which he scratched out a living of sorts. Mike must have had a last name, but no one knew it. He might have been any age from forty to sixty. Mike was a Middle-Easterner, perhaps a Syrian, with a swarthy (and perhaps dirty) face, albeit a pleasant one, who seemed always in the same clothes, except for an added jacket in cold weather. After touring the city room, he went upstairs to the composing room, and then on to the many other enterprises that worked evenings in downtown Albany.

Meet Nat Mann

That first week, I met another sportswriter, Nat Mann, whose byline on stories about the Old Timers' track meets and such, had puzzled me, because I thought I knew all the sportswriters in the area. Puzzle turned to pleasure. Nat was short for Natalie, who was also short--under five feet. I was chauvinistic male enough to note that she had beautiful: burnished blonde hair, hazel eyes, an Ipana smile, and a sublime, if slightly zaftig, figure and a squeaky little-girl voice. I was smitten, like everyone else, but quietly. My Tuesday and Wednesday nights off so certainly negated dating her that I never asked. Nat's beautification of the city room was short-lived. She had just graduated from the Milne School and was off in late August to Cornell. (Thirty-five years later, while in Ellenville for a radio talk show, I phoned Nat; who lived there. She still had the bubbly little girl voice I remembered. She had been married for several years to a well-off entrepreneur. Her zaftig had added more zaftig, according to the folks at the radio station.)

I joined the Guild as soon as possible, that is, after my first payday provided the initiation fee. Six years had passed since I first applied in the Troy office of the *Knickerbocker Press*. It still didn't come easily. The shop steward wanted me to wait six months. Something about a probationary period. To which I said something about *bullshit! I've waited six years already.* My language was convincing.

Still No Baseball

The summer passed and so did the second promise of my hiring: the one about covering baseball games. I wrote about some games that I hadn't seen. Several times I rewrote the paltry and home team slanted prose that arrived on the Eastern League cooperative wire. Some times, I picked information off the radio broadcasts of Senators' games in such exotic places as Williamsport, or Elmira, or Hazelton or Scranton. I also gussied up Walsh's version of games as he dictated them from Hawkins Stadium, usually first games of doubleheaders. Whenever he interrupted himself to ask me to read back a passage, I read, from memory, exactly what he had dictated. He must have known what I was up to, but he never said a word.

Several weeks passed in the fall of 1943 before I was able to clear enough space for the *Scholastic Sports Forum*, the column I had taken over from Levine. It was a column by title, not by space, consisting of five or six paragraphs, all short ones, two hundred, maybe two hundred and fifty, words. Finding space for even that small a "column" was difficult. The only things that warranted a full column of space were Dick Walsh's column and his story about the Albany Senators' home baseball game. Large or small didn't matter; the *Forum* was my creation. As a new guy in town, I was not bound by the tradition that reverence had to be shown to every coach. Some of the people I wrote about adjusted slowly to the change and they beefed to Walsh who beefed to me. I kept doing what I had been doing.

In the fall, I also began covering high school football and, in season, high school basketball, both of which were among the many sports Walsh did not care for. Covering football was not always fun. There was no press box, no shelter of any kind, at any of the stadiums. The sportswriter shared the weather with the fans and the sidelines with the players. The weather and the sidelines came together one weekend in the mid-forties. Walter Scanlon, the large and competent football coach at Vincentian Institute, was falling out of favor with the people who mattered, and, unasked, I came to his rescue. The powerful Albany High team figured to beat Vincentian by a couple of touchdowns, but I picked a score of 73-0, figuring that anything less might help Scanlon keep his job. On game day it rained, it poured, and the Bleecker Stadium field, which had been a city reservoir, held all that water. Vincentian played over its head; Albany under its. The Vincentian fans saw me on the sideline and chanted, *Ri-VETT, Ri-VETT, he's all WET,* time after time after time. They were right. Albany High won by 7-0 and Scanlon kept his job long enough to leave under his own power.

No Raise, Either

In the spring of 1944, the promise that was in the contract came unglued. On the payday I was scheduled to move from fifth year experience at forty-two fifty to five full years' experience at fifty bucks, I got the same old check. Same the following week. So what the hell's going on, I asked. George Williams offered the same answer Walsh used to offer: the business office. He explained, "Somebody there noticed that the same pay, forty-two fifty, applies in the fourth and fifth year of experience and they said you'd have to stay at forty-two fifty another year." I asked the Guild to press a grievance. When the grievance was argued, I attended. A mistake. I was outraged at the story management told, and I said so vividly, and stormed out.

A few minutes later, George Williams met me outside and advised me, "You shouldn't have lost your temper, it didn't help any. You have to remember, when you're dealing with sons-of-bitches, you've got to be a son of a bitch yourself." It has been hard but I've forced myself to follow his advice.

That grievance prompted me to become active in the Guild. If the other people couldn't do a better job than to put such an ambiguity into the contract, I ought to take a shot at it. Soon I was given the chance to help present our contract demands to the publisher. I accompanied Edgar S. VanOlinda, the columnist and reviewer of cultural events. Williams had hired him years ago on the strength of his tenor voice and his tenure as an officer of a fancy retail store. I deferred to his seniority and learned how disastrous that could be. VanOlinda, who was a pleasant man, overdid his pleasantness and tried to give away many of our proposals before we could even discuss them. That was the last time VanOlinda took part in negotiations. And the last time I deferred to seniority for its own sake.

No Raise but More Money

Though I hadn't received the contract raise, my income rose abruptly that summer. Overtime, thanks to Walsh. He figured a way for him to get an evening off and for me to get paid overtime for working on my nights off when the Albany Senators were scheduled for a home game. Walsh told me to come to work regardless of the weather. If the game was on, I had to work at overtime. If it was rainy, Dick waited till I punched in on the time clock before he called the ballpark to learn there would be no game. Then he told me, "As long as you're here, you might as well stay; I'll take the rest of the night off." I averaged seventy bucks a week, maybe more, that summer.

❑

I used some of those extra bucks to repair the front tooth gap Knight had criticized, at the further urging of Sam

Markson, the Saturday night news editor. Sam had been a fulltime newsman for years, but now sold stocks and bonds weekdays. Sam urged me to go to a dentist; I said I just couldn't. He kept telling me to go, a persistent sales pitch, and I went. I had stopped going to the dentist in my early teens, after Doctor Horan, in Troy, had placed temporary filling after temporary filling in the upper front tooth that had started to come apart. Bad enough. But he also sang, loudly and badly, stuff like *When Francis dances with me, holy gee,* and, less personally, *He walks with me and He talks with me and He tells me I am His own.* I found another dentist that spring of 1944, Doctor McRedmond, a large man who did not sing. He told me, "That bad tooth has to come out, so do several others on top, you were born with faulty enamel. So many extractions you might as well have them all out; a partial plate is just asking for trouble later." I said go ahead and, in weekly clusters, out they came. Several weeks' wait for healing, during which I toughened my gum to solid food, and, finally, the full upper denture. The new look, a wide and pleasant smile, also altered my social life and led to a love life, but that, like so much more, is another story, told in the chapter *A Long Life with Shorty.*

Baseball, Finally

Two years passed, until the summer of 1945, before I covered a baseball game live. Walsh decided he had to have a night off, probably to show Williams (and anyone else) that he was indispensable. Williams might have thought so, too, but he had the features editor John Bowen stay late and take care of some of the routine material while I was at the game. It was an exciting game, but a terrible one. The teams took turns trying to give victory to each other and the score wound up at 10-9 after nearly four hours. On the bus ride back to the office, I composed the story in my mind. When I reached the office I nearly lost my mind, or that part of it. Bowen had long ago caught the bus home. Fortunately, the printers had sensed the problem, and picked up the box scores and other standard materials, and laid out the wire copy in some order on my desk. The late final edition was not much later than usual. Walsh, on learning he was not quite indispensable, never missed another home game. I never covered another one.

❑

In early 1946, Johnny Evers, an Albany resident whom I had known in Troy, was selected by the Oldtimers' Committee for the Baseball Hall of Fame. So were his old Chicago Cubs teammates Joe Tinker and Frank Chance, all of them stars in F.P.A.'s famous doggerel of the early nineteen hundreds. It was customary to seek comment from someone so honored, but I knew Evers had suffered a stroke and was not likely to be responsive. What to do? The answer was provided by Harry O'Donnell, at the AP. He called Peerless McGrath and Peerless called back with a quote from Evers: "I'm tickled to death that Joe and Frank made it too." The AP used it; so did I, although I knew that *tickled to death* was a favorite phrase of Peerless's and I never heard Evers use it.

Mourning Morse

In the wartime years, Walsh was a friendly boss. In the many lulls between editions, he told me the stories of his life. I was a new and captive audience. He was a Newfoundlander. (I hadn't yet learned that the Canadians regarded Newfies as an ethnic joke.) He had learned telegraphy as a kid and had gone to work for the local railroad. Somehow, and he was always vague about it, he had come to the States and become a telegrapher for the United Press. In 1930, he was, as he told it, struck a bitter blow by fate: the Teletype machine displaced telegraphers. Of his fate, he spoke more in sorrow than in anger, "I could handle a hundred and forty words a minute, and they replaced us with a Teletype – forty-four words a minute. A hundred and forty words. And we could break into the wire and send items ourselves. The Teletype can't do that. And we could just omit stories we knew the local paper wouldn't be interested in, or trim stories to fit the local papers. The Teletype can't do that." When Teletype took over, George Williams offered Walsh a place on the *Times-Union* copy desk. He had advanced to handling the late final baseball extra front page in the afternoon. When the sports editor departed abruptly, Walsh became sports editor.

❑

Back in 1943, when Nat Mann left for college, we were not without women, just without beauty. Marie Avery Myers (Mrs. Myers) the society editor always wore a dark man-tailored jacket and a skirt, with her white blouse collar draped outside the jacket collar, the uniform of the 1920s career woman. She had been a sobsister for a time; she covered a notorious murder trial in the late twenties. Marie also smoked incessantly and was not always patient with the dear society ladies who phoned in their great stories. There also was Noretta Smith, who kept the paper's morgue and who wrote a pet column under the byline Tipper (for her dog)--a name applied to her by everyone--and who wore a horrible perfume that wafted news of her arrival when she opened the front door, a long way from the sports desk. And finally, Jo Leonard, already an old-time reporter who looked like a favorite aunt but could report and write and drink with the best of the men, but never competitively. Wartime had brought some women to The Associated Press staff, like Margaret Owens, Toni Adams, Bea Patrick Maas, Cay Parker (later Jones) and Eileen Rowe. Margaret and Eileen almost made up for the lack of Nat Mann.

Call for Copy, Not for Boy

The war also brought women to serve as copyboys, and changed our vocabulary. When a copyboy was a boy, we caught his attention by shouting BOOOOOOOOY!!! My shout once summoned a boy from the morgue, fifty feet and two corridor twists away. When the copyboy was a girl, however, we caught her attention by hollering CAHHHHHPYYYY!! Though some of us thought we ought to call–to the prettier ones–OH BOY! Long after the war, Jeh Jackson became our first Negro (now African-American) copyboy and we removed BOOOOOOY!! from our lexicon.

As the forties moved along, Sam Markson contributed to the lore of the Beaver Street building. One Saturday evening, past press time for the first edition, and with no papers in sight, Sam went to remonstrate with Herb Campbell, then the city editor. Words flowed about who had sent the copy boy out of the building when it was time for him to fetch the papers. Herb was somewhat shorter than Sam, and, as words escalated, he reached up to take off Sam's glasses. Sam, whose brother Harry was the boxing director at Madison Square Garden, promptly landed a right fist on Herb's mouth. Herb's gold-plated bridgework popped out. Herb and Sam cancelled the pleasantries and knelt to pick up the pieces. Just as the copy boy brought in the papers and said, "they're kinda late."

Sam also introduced his son David, to the newsroom in the summer of 1944. His first assignment: the Albany-New York outboard boat race. David continued to worko summers while in college. Not long afterward, he became a writer. Highly successful too. His first book, *The Ballad of Dingus Magee*, a sendup of the Western, sold pretty well, and was made into a movie with Frank Sinatra. Real money. Since then David has settled into a career of editing and writing. His latest books have been sendups of the post-Moidern novel, or post-Modern novels; it's hard to tell the difference.

What little space we had in wartime–under a page and half weekdays, two pages on Sundays–usually had to be filled twice: once for the first edition, then, with night baseball and the like, for the final. To save typesetting–Linotypists were scarce and not always competent–we often filled much of the first edition with preprints of large patriotic cartoons and war stories by Burris Jenkins Jr. Readers of the first edition never complained about being shortchanged of sports news. They couldn't without seeming unpatriotic. Space was particularly tight on Monday mornings in the baseball season; every Sunday brought doubleheaders in the major leagues and the Eastern League. With very short leads and box scores, two double headers filled a column. If a team used many players, desperate measures were required. The most desperate was one -the printers had never heard of it--squeeze blocks of box score type in a vise to compress the ridges on each line. It made room for an extra line or two

As a patriotic gesture, Williams devoted a corner of one page each Saturday to a day-by-day review of local news, so that a reader could clip it and send it to someone in the military service. I contributed a sports news summary of a couple of hundred words. The mother of one former Albany High athlete, a retired teacher, told me she clipped the weekly review from scores of papers (which I hope were returns she got for no charge) and sent them to the young men she had met through her son's career and hers.

Even with all his drinking, Walsh usually took his load home with him. One evening, however, he came back to the office rather drunk and earned a behind-the-back nickname. I was in the art department checking a layout of the All-Albany football team dominated by a picture of Jim Murphy, a very good running back. Walsh looked at it, put an index finger on Murphy's photo, and said, "thash our man, thash our man." A couple of times more. His work done, he lurched on home. From then on, the artists always referred to him as *thash our man*.

No Doubt About Drought

The founder of the *Times-Union* had, with great foresight, located his paper so that no one ever had to go more than a block to get a drink. In any direction. Across Beaver Street was the Capitol Hotel, a bar noted, in the early days of Repeal, for its twofers: one martini a quarter, a double thirty-five cents. Just a block down Beaver was the Plaza Grill, which became my favorite as I could drink there and still watch for my bus home to Green Island. Across Green Street from the plant's side door was Steve's Grill, favored by some printers and Walsh. Up the block on Green Street toward State was Keeler's Men's Bar, attached to the city's greatest restaurant, and high-priced. To the west on Beaver Street was Myron and Ray's, favored mainly by ad salesmen.

I considered Steve's to be Walsh's saloon and avoided it unless he invited me to join him. The few times I was there, I found the atmosphere intriguing. Besides the usual denizens of newspaper bars, Steve White had attracted some neighborhood characters. Among them were an odd couple. Ann Clark, tiny and postmaturely black-haired, who walked with a mincing step that some fellow-drinkers insisted was to keep from falling through herself, had retired, for age, as a madam. Her often companion was John (Froggy) Farrell, who had retired, for disability, as a gangster/gambler after an associate carved a new mouth in his throat, leaving him with a facial and vocal resemblance to a frog. (John Farrell died in the fall of 1948, under spuriously suspicious circumstances: the *Times-Union* cloaked his demise in mystery but it turned out to be an ordinary coronary attack. I learned from his obituary that his nickname was supposed to be Foggy. Froggy was better suited to his looks and voice.

I kept my drinking out of the office, except for a carton of beer on an occasional summer night. I made up for that good behavior outside the office. I had fallen in with good company: the aforesaid Lou Schaefer. He introduced me to the Moon Tavern on Northern Boulevard and the Ranch Tavern on North Lake Avenue, both since deceased. At the Ranch, in 1946, I won one of the longest-shot bets I ever made. I put up six dollars on the St. Louis Cardinals against the barkeep's twenty on the Boston Red Sox in the

World Series. Lou and I drank a good part of the winnings right there. Schaefer also introduced me to a blind pig in a basement at Green and Schuyler Streets in the South End, an area which even then was regarded as unsafe in the wee hours. I walked a couple of nights a week down notorious Green Street with never an incident; it was often daylight when I walked back.

Not long after I acquired journeyman status—that five years' experience level—in the late spring of 1945, I thought I was ready for bigger things. Joe Reichler, whose work on the Binghamton paper I had noted, often with disdain, had been hired by the AP in New York. If he can do it, I can do it. Hubris again. I managed an appointment to see the AP sports editor Orlo Robertson in New York, and Norris Paxton, the Albany bureau chief, gave me a letter of introduction: a missive that said, in substance, "Doc Rivett is well-regarded as a sportswriter by those who regard him well." Robertson was cordial. He asked, "What sports have you covered?" I said, "Practically everything." Robertson said, "Not court tennis." I said, "No, but I know the world champ is Pierre Etchebaster." Robertson said, "Not many people know that." There followed a long and pleasant conversation. Cordiality had to be its own reward. Robertson wound up the conversation by saying, "You picked a bad time. Now that the War in Europe is over, I've got a lot of people coming back soon to claim their jobs. And I'm leaving in a couple of weeks, anyway, to work for Colonel Matt Winn at Churchill Downs." I was disappointed, but as soon as my ego recovered, I realized that I could not have survived New York City then.

❑

In the fall of that year—on the Saturday of the World Series, which Walsh had declared a holiday for himself—I won a little barking contest from George Williams. He was leafing through the first edition and called to me, "Doc, you're wasting a lot of space; look at that cut on Page Two, it's just shit, and the one on Page One ought to have a mortise instead of all that gray in the corner." Just as loudly, I told him, "George, this is just the first edition, for Chrissake; that picture on Page Two is a plug for the composite box score, and I've already ordered a mortise for that cut on Page One. Now just let me get these sports pages fixed for the next edition." George nodded and grunted, "OK, as long as you know what you're doing." He never again questioned my makeup of the sports pages, but often praised it--just between us.

The *Times-Union* people were coming back from the war and asking for their jobs back. One was Stan Levine, who insisted on having his title of assistant sports editor restored. It did not change my status, nor his (there was no extra pay for the title) so I did not object; I just continued acting like the real thing.

Stanley was the most naïve—and trusting and sometimes least successful—hustler I knew. Sometimes, even, a *nudnik*. Stan ran into a problem in 1947. He was assigned to chaperone a couple of local high school baseball players in the Hearst National Junior All-Star game in Yankee Stadium. He found the company's expense allowance inadequate and claimed more than he could document. His explanation: a couple of receipts blew out the cab window. That's not even as good as *the dog ate my homework*. A grievance ensued that gained him naught, but enhanced my reputation. As I argued the grievance, the publisher Fred Archibald suddenly said, "Stop waving your finger at me." I said, "I'll stop waving my finger at you when you stop pounding your desk at me." Archibald looked sheepishly down at his hand; he stopped and I stopped. Stan told the story often; he seemed almost as happy as if he had gotten the money.

A Golf Promotion

While Stan was handling the baseball promotion, I was in charge of the local qualifying contest for the Hearst National junior golf championship. (An enterprising sports editor named Ralph Cannon had convinced Hearst management that it should not just cover sports but promote them, through national competitions; national, at least, in the dozen or so cities with Hearst papers.) What a promotion! We had the use of a classy country club for two days. To juice up the deal, I asked a prominent member of the club to prepare a daily hole-by-hole description of the course, a hundred words or so. The prominent member was a former *Times-Union* sportswriter named Gene FitzPatrick and I wasn't aware that Walsh had fired him several years earlier for, of all things, drinking on duty. The tournament went well, with a couple of exceptions. The promotion department skimped on refreshments and I had to send someone out for more sandwiches, twenty of them, which cost me ten dollars. No reimbursement. On the first day, several of the younger entrants achieved phenomenal scores with their pencils. To make them honest for the second day, I paired each of the pencil phenoms with a good golfer and their spurious seventies turned to nominal nineties. The next year, we repeated the tournament, and our local winners went off to a national tournament that was dominated by a kid from the Pittsburgh area, Arnold Palmer.

Controlling the Desk

After the war, sports coverage slowly returned to normal. Space became available, and the staff expanded. A couple of young fellows, at separate times, came to work and left quickly. They quit—officially. But I'm certain that Walsh's demeanor hastened their departures. In 1947, Walsh learned that Johnny Jones, a sterling writer, especially about golf, had been required to leave the *Troy Record* abruptly because of something he had written. Or maybe had done, since he was an equally sterling womanizer. "Should I hire him?" Walsh asked me. He was concerned about keeping Johnny under control. With a straight face I advised him, "Yes, you can control him all right." That was about the time that Walsh asked me to start work at 4:30 instead of 5 p.m. I didn't bother to tell him that already was my starting time; my appearance at 4:45 was not early but late. Talk about control.

Jones, it turned out, did not require controlling. He was a versatile writer, including his penmanship: he wrote with either hand. Jones also had a talent for needling. When he took a call asking for resolution of a debate, Jones would tell Debater A he was right, then in turn tell Debater B he was. None of the debaters caught up with him. Jones also was a meticulous record keeper. Once the basketball coach at an inner-city high school complained that Jones had failed to give his team credit for all its victories, Jones pored through his records and declared, "You're right, you beat West Coxsackie"--a youth prison--"but we don't count alumni games."

About the time Jones came to the sports desk, George Williams hired Martin P. Kelly, a recent college graduate, as a copy boy. Marty was too talented to stay a copyboy, and, after he wrote a rather schmaltzy letter to Williams, he was promoted to the sports desk, where he became Red (for his hair) Kelly. He had a blessedly short stay in sports; Walsh did not like to have someone else, even the managing editor, select his staff. So Kelly went to the city staff, again Martin P. After a reasonably long stay there, he went on to bigger and better jobs in government and public relations, but continued for decades to serve as a part-time drama reviewer for the *Times-Union*. (Long after Marty's claim to Red had shifted to his face, I asked about his *nom du sport*. He said, "I figured that in a crowd with Dick and Doc and Stan and Johnny, Martin P wouldn't stand a chance.")

Rigging the Poll

During one basketball season, when Siena College had enlisted a group of superb athlete-students, Stan Levine asked me how he might gain wider recognition of his favorite team. It was a time when The Associated Press put out a weekly rating of the teams based on a poll, open to all sports editors, that gave equal weight to *The New York Times* and *The West Overshoe Buckle*. I told Stan that he should call all the sports editors in the area and ask them to vote for Siena for second or third, no greedy firsts. The first week, Siena gained enough votes to be ranked in the top twenty-five. That ranking attracted more real votes the following week and the week after and Siena moved into the top ten. Stan was ecstatic. The glory vanished soon; Siena lost a couple of games in a row and even the local editors couldn't vote for it with a straight face.

Ethical? Maybe not. But "newspaper ethics" in those days was in short supply, especially in the sports department. Dick Walsh, for example, received five dollars a home game for not being the official scorer for the Senators baseball team, and other amounts for not being the ring announcer at boxing or wrestling shows, and for not writing publicity about other athletic endeavors. He even allowed Al Dufty, a 57-year-old railroad machinist and baseball nut (who kept a few hens), to give him a dozen eggs at various times for running one-sentence items about the Al Dufty All-Stars. (I gave Al a bit of fame, for no eggs, when I wrote a short like this: *Forget the first robin. Forget the start of trout fishing. The true harbinger of Spring arrived today. Al Dufty, who taught Abner Doubleday how to play baseball, came in to issue a challenge to local baseball teams to play his Al Dufty All-Stars. Call him at 555-5555.*)

Pure? Or Simple?

Stan Levine also had outside income, but for services rendered. He not only covered Siena College basketball but also hustled ads for the game programs. Somehow, I managed to remain somewhat pure. After the season of the polls, Stan Levine passed me a five-dollar bill--from Siena College, he said. I calmed my conscience by dashing right out to buy a

78-r.p.m. album of Paul Robeson's *Songs for Free Men*. I also accepted a couple of freebies from the Saratoga Raceway, which I considered reasonably ethical since each was *quid post quo*. One was an invitation to bring my wife and another couple for dinner on the house. I shocked the waiter by leaving him a reasonable tip. And there was the time in 1949, shortly after I had selected a kid named Müller for the high school all-star basketball team, when a messenger arrived at the office with three superb pies—one for me, one for Dick Walsh, and one for Con Heffernan—provided by the star's father, who was the pastry chef at the DeWitt Clinton Hotel.

The year of the poll success also brought Siena's basketball team an invitation to play in a new National Catholic Invitation Tournament in Denver. Again the next season. Neither was a great success. But Siena fared better than the tournament director, a Denver sportswriter named Tommy Thomas. His artistic success was not matched financially and he cast about for a more hospitable venue. He moved his tournament to Albany, where Stan helped with fulsome publicity. On the eve of the tournament, I had Stan write a banner headline and a one-column readout for his story. He wrote a decent banner followed by **Meet Head/Arrives**. I asked if he knew what he had said; he said he did, so we used that head. Next morning at breakfast, Thomas told me later, he opened his paper to the sports pages and noticed the phonetic Meat Head/Arrives and nearly choked on his coffee. That was the last National Catholic Invitation Tournament and Tommy Thomas, broke, became a newspaperman in Troy.

❑

When rassling was revived after the war, I covered that too, more as theater than as sport. Ted Bayly, the impresario, and the touring rasslers did not mind how or what I wrote. But the rasslers did object to some writing. While Johnny Jones was still working in Troy, a pair of rasslers took exception to what he had written and one of them, awash with sweat, managed to get thrown out of the ring right into Jones's lap. It did not hurt Johnny, but his suit needed a cleaning. Bayly asked me once if I'd give a couple of his stars a ride to the Albany train station. They had just finished a show in which one, standing outside the ring, held the other by his legs and was pulling his tenderest spots into the ring post. They crammed into my Hillman Minx and expressed concern that some of the fans might see them so closely together and develop a cynical view of rassling. I assured them nobody would believe they could fit into my car.

Among the many other things Walsh did not like was interviewing people. I found it a lark. In the late 1940s, a promoter named Charley Strong brought a sportsman's show and Jack Sharkey, the old heavyweight boxing champion, to Albany. Sharkey had a different *shtick*: flyfishing. Sharkey proved to be a fascinating interview. I began my story like this: *When you interview Jack Sharkey, you just say hello and then sit back and listen.* It's a wonder that I remember anything about that interview. After the show that night, Strong invited me to show him Albany's attractions and we drank our way through a number of sleazy bars. At the last one, we admired too openly one of the young lady patrons and her escort mumbled some sinister mumbles. The bartender—an old welterweight boxer who learned I was a sportswriter and had covered some of his early fights--came to our rescue. Our tour over, Charley feared I couldn't find my way home, though I had been drinking nothing but dry sherry which everyone knows is harmless. He invited me to use the spare room in his suite at the TenEyck Hotel. He was right about my ability to find my way. During the night, I couldn't locate the toilet and threw up on the floor of one of the bathrooms. Retribution for any lapse in ethics continued the next evening when the intense hammering in my skull collided with the clamorous chatter of kids bringing in scores from a city youth basketball tourney we were promoting.

Interviewing Mildred

A couple of years later, I went to interview Babe
Didrikson Zaharias, the renowned athlete, who was
playing in a benefit golf match at Wolfert's Roost, and her
husband George, a retired rassler of nearly three hundred
pounds.I walked part of the course with George. He was
so enthusiastically enamored of his wife—he called her
Mildred--that he didn't say much about his old career. When
I met Mildred, she turned out to be a lovely and gracious
person, a real woman. As we parted, she asked if I'd let her
know who won the major national golf event that was ending
that day. She was pleased to learn that the winner was an
old friend.

Later Jim Thorpe, the old Indian hero of the 1912
Olympics whose medals were shorn away because he had
been paid for playing a few baseball games, came to town
and I interviewed him. Poor Jim! He was one of the greatest
athletes of his time and a lot of other times, and here he
was, sick and reduced to acting as a rassling referee. He
was the opposite of Jack Sharkey: a man of few words. But
someone put him in touch with a guy in Colonie who had
played baseball with him and I managed to make a story of
our conversation.

Most of my interviews were with local guys—not
famous, but fun to talk with. Bill (Country) Morris, the coach
at Albany Academy who spoke at Teletype speed, told me
of his problems with a pitcher named Tom Dewey Jr.: "His
trouble is he can't unbend at the hips . . . but I guess that's
a family characteristic." (I didn't use it.) Nick Budnowski, a
city boy just back from the war, told me about his troubles
coaching at a new suburban high school: "I told my football
players I wanted them to show me some piss and vinegar
and some kids told their parents and they got all over me
for my language." (Didn't use that either.) Father Hearn,
who was starting a basketball team at St. Ann's Academy
in the South End, said, "First thing I have to do is teach

them the dirty tricks that Father Dammann's boys at St. John's already know." (I did use that, jokingly I thought; my Catholic readers didn't see the joke.) And Dave Manwiller, the football coach at Philip Schuyler high, told me of his plan to cope with a superstar halfback on a visiting team, "If he's that good, I'll use a four-four-four defense on him." (I used that in a pregame story.) After the game, Manwiller told me, "I used the four-four-four once and it worked." (I didn't put that in the post-game story.)

When I began rolling in dough in 1944, it wasn't all take-home: I had discovered the weekend poker game and soon became a contributing editor. The game generally began about nine o'clock on Friday night, after the final edition copy had closed, and went on, with various changes of cast and venue and a work break on Saturday and Sunday afternoon, till Monday morning. The ante was a dime, and betting could begin at a nickel, though the limit usually was five dollars a bet. The dealer's choice games ran the gamut from five-card stud (or draw) with or without wild cards, to six- and seven-card stud and six- and seven-card high/low (in which it was possible to win the entire pot, high and low), to baseball, a form of seven-card stud in which threes, fives and sevens (or sometimes fives, sevens, and nines) were wild and had wildly disparate functions depending on when they were dealt. With the infinite variety and a run of luck a patient player could win a week's pay; a hopeful player could lose one. I was not a patient player.

The most patient player was Charley Davis, whose successful strategy was to fold an unpromising hand and give up a few cents on early bets, and to cash in on the good hands, which he did with annoying frequency. Charley was a formidable man, something over six feet and two hundred fifty pounds, with rotten teeth, a hiatal hernia, a whiny voice, and, we learned later, epilepsy. Charley had come to the *Times-Union* in 1937 after Hearst folded his Rochester paper, where Davis had been managing editor.

At the *Times-Union,* he was the late-shift copy editor and put together the Monday paper. Weeknights, while waiting to take over the late desk, he would go to one of the several downtown movie houses (on a pass, of course) to kill a couple of hours. When asked if he wasn't concerned about punishment for taking those extra hours off, he replied, "I'm in the business thirty-five years, I'm working five to two, I've got Tuesday and Wednesday off; what are they going to do to me?"

The game attracted a memorable group, mostly insiders. The news editor Bert Bearup usually took a drink break of an hour or two between work and poker. So did Bill Glass, a printer who had put in many summers as an umpire in the old Eastern baseball league. Glass often told stories of his exploits, and some of them caught the ear of the national columnist Bob Considine when he was in town on other business. Considine made another column out of them. Bart Coughlin, a hunchback telegrapher who had become a Teletypist for the AP, also was a regular, even when working (he could punch out fifteen minutes worth of perforated tape in five minutes). Henry Leader, the state editor for AP, often returned to the office for the poker game; he was a serious and sober player. After the war, Stan Levine took part, so occasionally did his wife Shirley. Her presence did not create enthusiasm; she was a math teacher who soberly calculated the odds in every hand (of course, her presence limited the male vocabularies). Ben Cilwick, a burly man who was the pressroom machinist, always found time, if not talent, for poker.

As a measure of my contributions to my poker pals, I should note that, after I quit the game in honor of my impending marriage, I was able to save a thousand dollars in less than six months. Charley Davis honored those contributions and my bride's charmful effect on him by giving us a large circular mirror as a wedding present. He bought it from his wife, he said, for twenty-four dollars. [The games continued, without me, for many years. The night in

1956 when the Soviets began shelling Budapest, I sat at the far edge of the copydesk editing the story while the poker game went on.]

We had no real hangers-on and few visitors at the sports desk. The closest to a hanger was Ben Lowenberg, an Army captain during the war and a teacher and the first basketball referee in the area to wear glasses in a game. He developed a loudly expressed aversion to Jones, but kept a good attendance record anyway. The visitors included three basketball coaches: Larry O'Neill, a wartime Navy blimp pilot coaching at Philip Schuyler High, who often reported on prospects he was scouting in the fourth or fifth grade; Dan Cunha, the taciturn tactician at Siena, and Nate Sutin, of Albany High. Cunha and Sutin each often continued his monologue by inviting me to an all-night cafeteria, where he could marshal enough salt and pepper shakers from several tables to illustrate his tactics and complaints.

A Very Quiet Battle

My cordial relationship with Walsh fell apart gradually. The first crack likely occurred in the spring that the Albany Senators resumed their southern spring training camp after the war. Walsh sent back a roll of film of the players and telegraphed his column from camp. I broke with decades of practice by spreading the column, along with a picture layout, across the top of the page. He learned of it when the paper arrived in Brunswick, Georgia, several days later. He let me know he didn't like it, but it was done and George Williams had praised it.

Our relationship was not helped by some other things I did. When the Albany Senators won the Eastern League pennant in (I think) 1949, I asked one of the editorial artists to paint a pennant the right size to fit into a banner headline. During one baseball season, to celebrate the third or fourth time that one of the pitchers had been stopped by rain, I asked the artist to adorn a file photo of the pitcher with rubber boots and an umbrella. When a star player at Siena was temporarily disabled with a troublesome knee, I used a photo not of his face but of his knee. And, on a report of a fight in which the loser retreated constantly, I spelled his name sdrawkcab in the headline. Walsh particularly did not like that.

Welcome to Russell's Beach

The paper moved in August 1950 to Sheridan Avenue, a much drier area than Beaver Street: only one drinking place that suited newspaper people. But it had four names. Officially, it was Ed's Bar, named for Ed Russell, the license-holder of record. But it was also known as Duke's Place (a nickname of Ed's), or Joey's (for Ed's brother who actually operated it), or, more colorfully, Russell's Beach.

Joe Russell was a slight-looking guy with black slicked back hair, thick glasses, and a talent for scrambling words. To him, a Negro was "black as the ace of coal." And when a guy was floored, he "went down like a count." He served sandwiches if someone insisted, but no fancy drinks (in his phrase "no damn lady drinks".) There was another bar, Sad Sam's, further up Sheridan Avenue, but it had little attraction for the *Times-Union* people.

There came a time when Walsh and I spent a few weeks not talking to each other. That was difficult, since I was handling the page layouts and makeup as well as covering stories from time to time, duties that should have required some consultation. Stan Levine broke the silence by asking me to talk to Walsh, and I said that I would if he would talk to me. So Walsh spoke first. No apologies, no explanations

We had a more severe break early in 1952, when I was the local Guild president and asked for leave on a Saturday night to attend a regional Guild meeting. Walsh said I couldn't have it because we were changing our headline typography that night. Changing typography was no big deal; I had done it many times without consulting anyone. So I took Saturday night off. Sunday I found a note on my desk, telling me I was suspended for taking the leave. I left a counter-note: I was here, available for work and will come to work on Monday. I also told someone from the national Guild what had happened. When I reported for work Monday, I learned that Hearst's labor office in New York had spent half the day on the phone telling George Williams in various ways that you can't do that. Williams, who had been nearly apoplectic, was apologetic, but asked me, "Next time could you give us a little more notice?" I was a good winner; I said, "Sure."

A few months later, I gave adequate notice that I was taking a leave of absence to work for the American Newspaper Guild. In September, I left the sports desk for good, also for better.

A Long Life with Shorty

Christmas Eve, 1949. 48 South Logan Street, Denver, Colorado.

Shorty and I cuddling on the living room floor. Shorty wearing her long simple black velvet dress; I in my usual rumpled attire. The record player playing.

. . . My eyes look down on your lovely face,
And I hold the world in my embrace . . .

Ah. Lieutenant Cable, I know how it is. But I'm one up on you, Lieutenant Cable. I'm going to marry the girl.

. . . some enchanted evening . . .

Oh, Emil DeBecque, you are right. Enchanted. But no stranger, no crowded room. Coco and the Sarge snuggle on the sofa. But not so enchanted.

. . .I'm gonna wash that man
right out of my hair
and send him on his way . . .

No! Oh no! Nelly Forbush, get out of here. She has washed me out enough already.

❑

The record player rolls through the original original cast album of *South Pacific*. The 78s play on and on, changing and changing, until the last record on the stack keeps playing and playing and playing till someone rises to the occasion and restarts the records. It must have been Coco or the Sarge.

It had taken Shorty and me five years–off and on, mostly off–to reach this state of grace. We owed it all to Ruth Rainier, who had brought us together the first time and now again in Denver. Ruth was there when Shorty (née Elena Margareta Elisabeta Puccio; Helen for short) and I became kind of engaged. Ruth and her friend, perhaps fiancé, Lew were walking with us in the shirtsleeves weather that nature sometimes gives Denver as a Christmas present. Weakened, no doubt, by the thin air of the Mile High City, I suggested to Shorty that we should get married. She, perhaps also a victim of the high altitude, did not say no. Lew overheard my suggestion and said, "A great idea! You could drive over to Kansas, no waiting time there. I'll let you borrow my car."

That was not what Shorty had in mind. There were certain formalities. She explained, "You've got to ask my father for my hand in marriage. And you've got to meet my mother. And pass her test. You'll have to wear a white shirt and a tie, and you'll have to show a good appetite. She's a very good cook and she expects people to show their appreciation by eating." The eating part sounded easy, but I was concerned about that necktie. I was always concerned about a necktie. All that would have to wait, though, until Shorty returned to Boston in the spring. For once I understood what it meant to wait till next year.

That Harmless Sweet Wine

We celebrated our engagement at dinner, Christmas dinner to everyone else. The girls who shared the rented house were there: Ruth, Shorty, Coco, officially Vincenza Scoca, and Pinky Crooks. And Pinky's parents from Iowa. So were Lew and I and the Sarge, Technical Sergeant Norbert McCafferty of the Air Force Intelligence. It was a great dinner; the girls were good cooks. The wine flowed. Pinky's father, who didn't drink, found the Mogen David so sweet he knew it could do no harm. It got him pleasantly drunk. His wife remained unpleasantly sober.

❏

Shorty and I had been apart for, oh, let's say a long time when I got the first hint that the off-again might be on-again. Ruth, who had gone to Denver about a year earlier, sent me a note that Shorty was now rooming with her on Williams Street. Shorty had fled to the hills to escape the heat and humidity of Boston and was now quite lonesome, Ruth reported, and added, "Why don't you write to her?" I wrote; she replied. Another note, maybe two, with replies to match. Came early September and I was on the train to Denver, day coach all the way.

Seeing the Sights

A whirlwind recourtship ensued. I stayed at a hotel downtown and rode the narrow-gauge trolley the two miles to Williams Street. Just a quick stopover. One day, I rented a car so we could drive to Central City, an old mining town that was flirting with a touristy revival. A small but picturesque scandal there had made the national news wire: the sheriff had raided a friendly card game in a curio shop and the woman-owner had retaliated with a scurrilous window display. We found the display still there. On the way, we made a brief pit stop at a grand brick building, labeled HOTEL in the gold mining ghost town of Black Hawk, along Clear Creek where some well-financed entrepreneurs were dredging for overlooked ore. At first, the hotel seemed deserted though open, but Shorty found the water closet. As we were leaving we stepped into the parlor and found an upright piano. Shorty sat down to play a few bars; the piano was badly out of tune, which matched her playing. The sound roused the owner from somewhere out back and he greeted us cordially and told us, "That was the first piano to come to the Colorado territory, the long way, shipped around Cape Horn and brought here from San Francisco." No wonder it was out of tune.

The next night, we all went to the Ringling Brothers-Barnum & Bailey circus. It was the first circus Shorty had seen. Five rings; something spectacular going on in each. Shorty was on the edge of her chair, she occupied no more than two inches of it. "If I'd known you were going to sit like that I wouldn't have paid full price for your ticket." She thought I was kidding. Our cultural ramble also took us—just the two of us--to Ellitch's Garden, an amusement park just outside town, where we attended a summer stock performance of a farce called *Clutterbuck*. The punch line that followed a loud burp--"Just be natural!"--become part of our vocabularies

❏

Later in the fall, Ruth and Shorty moved to the house they rented on South Logan, sharing it with Coco and Pinky. No more letters. I phoned often from the Plaza Grill, borrowing quarters for overtime from the friendly bartender. All the girls were nurses; Shorty at a VA hospital in Fort Logan, down the road a piece; the others in town. It was a modest place in an aging neighborhood, with just enough rooms for them. When I visited, they arranged for a neighbor to rent me sleeping space on a porch. Earlier, I had contributed several autographed photos of rasslers, Argentina Rocca among them, that the girls tacked on the kitchen walls. (The inscriptions were authentic; I wrote them.) There also was a decorative touch in the bathroom: a rear-view naked photo captioned "Shorty, don't forget your vitamins."

Meet Ruth Rainier

Ruth Rainier, née Jenkins, was a country girl from East Chatham, New York, a graduate of State College for Teachers, briefly a defense worker, then, at our first meeting, a student in the Cadet Nurse Corps and part-time secretary for the Tri-City Newspaper Guild. Ruth was a blue-eyed blonde, not quite beautiful, but sparklingly close enough, and she had just a tiny rasp in her voice, the result, she said, of a minor throat defect. Her uvula, she explained, but I've hesitated to be precise for fear of transposing a couple of the letters. As Ruth told me later, it was my voice, its volume, that led her to introduce me to her apartment mates. She was impressed by my ability to talk louder than John Wanhope (I was too) at Guild meetings. [Wanhope was truly a Guild martyr, as I have explained. The Guild meeting was the only chance he had to speak. John died in 1952.]

Ruth invited me to meet several classmates one afternoon in September 1944 in front of their quarters at 357 Morris Street. She had lined them up in ascending order of height and introduced me to Shorty, Betty, Pantas, Pete, and the tallest girl whose name escapes me. No matter. I glanced at each in ascending order, at their faces and at their legs, of which Shorty's looked best. I looked again, or yet, at Shorty. Seriously. Her blue eyes shone with (I thought) a message; I tried to send her one, too.

The names that went with the others were Betty Regan, Helen Pantas, and Gloria Peterson. The girls lived in adjoining alphabetically ordered suites in the former apartment house. All wore dress uniforms, designed by Mainbocher, and perhaps the best tailored of all the women's uniforms in World War II. The skirts were hemmed fifteen inches off the floor, which explained the superiority of Shorty's legs: more of them to be seen.

Tickets to The Game

The girls all were pleased at meeting a real sports writer. Could I get them into the RPI-Union football game next Saturday? Sure, I said, then found that I really could. All they'd have to do is get to Schenectady, sit on Union's side of the field and root for the home team. All six of them, in uniform, thumbed a ride. The same man gave them a ride back. All he asked in return was that they write to his son in service. They enjoyed that too.

I had had practice, a few weeks earlier, in cadging tickets for a group of student nurses to attend a game. The student nurses were about to graduate from training at Memorial Hospital, a seedy downtown institution. I had met one of them, Christine Bayreuther, at the Mid-City Park swimming pool, often enough to become friendly. I had developed a big hello acquaintance with some of her classmates. We all visited the pool regularly that summer, on passes. Her class, she told me, wanted to celebrate graduation but had no money. What could I suggest? A ball game, maybe. I talked with Tom McCaffrey, who owned the Albany Senators, and he set it up for the group to come free and even made sure they received free refreshments: hot dogs and the like.

I had a few dates with Chris that turned out brotherly (her idea, in which I concurred). She had entered nursing in her mid-twenties, inspired by the care her father had received after surviving the wreck of the Lake Shore Limited in Little Falls in 1940; he was a supervising locomotive engineer for the New York Central. (After that summer, I didn't see or hear from Chris until 1948. She called me at the paper. A frenzied call for help. Her brother, recently married, had collapsed and died outside his new home, and his wife had frantically carried him back into the house. Neighbors scented a scandal and called the authorities and the paper. Chris asked, could I get the paper off the case? It took some effort, but I did. Her brother had suffered a brain aneurysm, no scandal.)

Dating with Difficulty

Those first-day eyeball exchanges with Shorty were mutually and well received. We dated. Not easily. I was living in Green Island and working a 5 p.m. to 2 a.m. shift with Tuesday and Wednesday off. She was going to class days and, as cheap labor for the Albany Hospital, most of whose professional nurses had gone to war, was working various shifts with unpredictable days off. Often when I called, she was not in the dorm and I asked the girl who answered when she might be back. That caused some friction. I was simply trying to find a convenient time to call the only phone in the dorm; she thought I was prying and that led to some of the off-agains. With whatever other dates, we managed to meet one Sunday a month, for a while, after Ruth enlisted Shorty as a part-time low paid treasurer for the Guild. After meetings, we'd go to brunch, with others, to the coffee shop in the New Kenmore Hotel, across the street from our office. The Kenmore was out of bounds for all student nurses, but only if they got caught. Shorty's job ended when the elected treasurer, Paul Lyman, became the father of triplets and was rewarded with a stipend, a larger one than she'd been getting.

While my calls to Shorty sometimes caused a bit of friction, her calls to me, at the sports desk, sometimes turned out even worse. Some of the printers, being friendly guys, had begun calling me "The Greatest . . ." leaving the variable noun often unsaid. I was pleased by the adjective, and occasionally, when taking a handoff on the phone would say: "This is the Greatest." (That was a time when the Greatest in sports was Art Shires, a first baseman of limited ability and unlimited ego, not Mohammed Ali.) She received the greeting with great coolness. And that was not a transient feeling; she still mentions her dudgeon more than fifty years later.

Aiding the War Effort

It had taken a generous reading of Shorty's height to qualify her as five feet tall and thus eligible for the Cadet Nurse Corps. She was from Oneonta. She had worked a year in a defense plant at Sidney, the next sizeable town down the road. She had offered to become a lathe operator, which she liked the sound of but knew nothing about, and the personnel people sized her up as a payroll clerk and hired her. When we met, her parents had moved to Boston and her father was working in an engineering office on wartime projects.

Several months after we met, she had to undergo a mastoid operation while at a vulnerable time in her training. It was a major operation and required a long recuperation in the hospital and afterward. To cheer her in the hospital, I brought her a frilly black lace pajama set. (She now recalls it as a gift from Ruth Rainier. I recall the difficulty I had in finding something frilly in such a tiny size.) That day, a

Lutheran pastor also visited the other patient in the room. He noticed the pajamas, and lugubriously intoned, "We must pay for our sins." I hope he had to pay for that sin. As she continued her recuperation at the home of a brother in Mount Vernon, I arranged to take her on a date to New York City. We went to a movie, *Caesar and Cleopatra*, with Claude Rains and Vivien Leigh. We went afterwards to Lindy's for a snack. It was a wonderful evening but a lousy night. We missed the last train out of Grand Central and wound up taking the subway and a cab to get her home exhausted at 2 a.m., or maybe later. And very chilly. Off again.

And There Was Red

When I began courting Shorty, I was also dating another student nurse, Carolyn Curran, who also had been introduced to me by Ruth Rainier. Ruth was forgetful or was thinking of me as a philanderer. Carol, better known as Red, was partway through her course at Memorial Hospital. She was a bit taller than me, and she had blue eyes and red hair, both colors of unmatched brilliance. We dated for several months, mostly in the off-agains. Carol's father was a restaurant (that is, saloon) cook; her mother kept house and a firm restraint on Jack. One Christmas, I stopped with seasonal greetings at their apartment in Troy on my way to work and Jack asked Carol to pour me a drink. All he had was Southern Comfort. All she had was a water tumbler, it was a large drink. Well, it being Christmas, I downed it none too slowly and went on to work. The lights came up blinding bright, and the spaces between the typewriter keys turned enormous, so my fingers often fell between them.

Red and I kept dating for a while after that. Red had built up an image of me that I knew I couldn't match. Our romance, such as it was, came to a quiet end; I just drifted away. All my fault. I heard later that Red was--I hate to say it, but I can't think of another word--heartbroken and blaming herself. It was much too late for me to say otherwise.

In 1945, Ruth Rainier stopped being married. She discovered that her husband Clint was doubly double-crossing her. Not only had he taken up with another woman, he had financed his romance on Ruth's credit and money. Ruth reacted by bundling his tailor-made clothes off to Bundles for Britain, and sending his customized golf clubs to the Army hospital at Plattsburgh, and filing for divorce. The divorce case was heard in Cleveland, where Clint, a tall handsome cad, was serving in the Coast Guard. Ruth took Shorty along to serve as a character witness, and no judge could or did resist two such obviously innocent babes in such patriotic uniforms.

And a Bunch of Others

During our off-agains, Shorty and I dated others. My dates were eclectic and usually fleeting: Most of the time, I felt that I was a wartime replacement. Even after the war. Dates were mostly movies, or dinner, or drinks, or some combination. Some were different. With Margaret Owens, an editor at Associated Press, for example, the first date was a kiss and breakfast. She was working the early early desk- -8 p.m. to 4 a.m.--and I was still contributing editor to the poker game. I asked her to take custody of some of my money, no matter how I pleaded to get it into the pot, and offered to reward her with a kiss. Louder than I meant; I heard snickers from the copy desk. That night, I won. I gave her a kiss and we went to an all-night restaurant near the railroad station. We had several dates, a few breakfasts, some nightcaps. One night, when I might have had something else in mind, she told me that she had been at the Guild's formative Empire State District Council meeting, a delegate from Utica, when I resolved a near-fatal deadlock. "I thought," she told me, "that boy is very smart." That boy was a year younger than she was. She also told me that, while studying architecture at Cornell, she had enjoyed an idyllic summer with Bill

Atkinson, the Troy High graduate and fashion designer. I settled for one idyllic night with her.

I dated another girl who thought I was just the type to smoke a pipe, which she bought for me. I had given up smoking years earlier, but I tried the pipe. I was still allergic to first-hand smoke and nearly set myself afire by sticking the hot pipe into a coat pocket. I soon gave up the pipe and her. Then there was the time I went steady with *Hamlet*: saw the Laurence Olivier movie seven times. My devotion was rewarded when the theater manager noticed I had paid three times and told me I didn't have to pay any more to see it. He extended that invitation to other movies.

Shorty has told, in my hearing, about a couple of her dates. One young man who was in the Navy managed in the early postwar days to get a call patched through from Japan to her and a bunch of avid listeners at the nurse station in the hospital. Another fellow she dated met her once for breakfast when she finished work, took her horseback riding, then bowling, then . . . Well, by then he had worn out her and his welcome. That tale reminded me of some of my early–and early in the day—dates with Shorty. She and Ruth had befriended a retired river barge captain who had opened a boat livery at the Yacht Club basin, and a young veteran named George Holbine, who offered flying lessons there with his pontoon-fitted Piper Cub plane. I met Shorty and Ruth (and others) at the Yacht Club and accompanied them to a swimming place on Patroon Island, a mile or so upriver, sometimes in canoes, sometimes riding on the pontoons of the Piper. The girls all had been vaccinated against so many diseases that they could safely swim in the Hudson. I engaged in unsafe swims.

Learning About Blawis

While visiting Shorty at her dorm, I became acquainted at very long distance with John Blawis, formerly a copyreader at the *Schenectady Gazette*, and then the military mayor of a small town in liberated Germany, which I phoneticize to *Yemke on Flowerslaben.* Ruth and John had been friends for years pre-Rainier and she wrote to him frequently. He wrote back and returned her letter each time, carefully and thoroughly edited. She said rather crude things about his letters. Once she sent him a paper she had written for class; he edited that too. Her apartment mates said crude things about Blawis. I thought poorly of him at first, but concluded that he was just so desperate to practice his editing that he'd have done it to a whiskey label.

Blawis, unmarried, returned to Albany after the war and found Ruth, again unmarried, and a sort of courtship ensued. John had a saturnine look, a complexion we used to call olive, and a noticeable scar on his chin. That scar lent him a devil-may-care look, a memento perhaps of the war, or even of a duel. It was really a souvenir of his face's colliding with the rear-view mirror in his car when he forgot where the brake pedal was. I didn't meet Blawis until 1947 when he was hired, then abruptly unhired, by the *Times-Union.* Someone had discovered that he had worked briefly as an organizer for the Guild but gave the official reason that he had not taken a required physical exam. Since nobody had ever taken a physical exam, the Guild filed a grievance that resulted in Blawis's being ununhired. There was an unexpectedly sad outcome. The Guild's national counsel A.J. Isserman who had argued our case, had such a bad heart that his doctor forbade him to carry even a briefcase. As he returned to New York, however, he found no redcaps at Grand Central, picked up his suitcase and carried it several feet, and dropped dead.

❑

In 1947, Shorty and I and Blawis and Rainier, among hundreds of others, walked past rows of gimlet-eyed and flag-waving war veterans, lined up on the long sidewalk into Philip Livingston Junior High School, to attend a concert by Paul Robeson. The concert had been the subject of suits, countersuits and counter-countersuits, and the veterans were there in force to demonstrate their solidarity against both Robeson's left-wing politics and the judicial process that, in a Solomonic decision, allowed Robeson to sing but not to give a speech. We were there to support Robeson and the process. Shorty and Rainier emphasized their message by wearing red silk scarves. Robeson's voice no longer was at its peak but no one cared. His program left less doubt of his political views than a speech would have: *The Four Insurgent Generals* (anti-Franco and pro-Democratic Spain), *Joe Hill* (pro-labor unions); *Joe's Birthday Party* (a plea for the downtrodden). Plus some spirituals and other songs that had always been the hallmarks of his magnificent bass voice. After the concert we went to Joe's, the famous delicatessen on Madison Avenue, and there we encountered the warden of 357 Morris Street. She also had attended the concert and, still warmed by Robeson's singing, told the girls not to hurry and not to worry. An unexpected amnesty.

A Long Detour

In the summer of 1948, Ruth and Blawis seemed on their path to marriage; his sister-in-law was busybodying their romance. But life is full of complications. John also was dating a girl in New York City, quietly. One day, he began driving his red Lincoln Zephyr convertible to visit her. It was not a good day for him to drive. He had spent the night drinking in a blind pig on Monroe Street, where a wartime blackout curtain kept the passage of time at bay. John pulled the curtain aside and remarked to Joe O'Heaney, one of his drinking companions, "Joe, look at that, it's daylight already." Joe said, "That's OK John, just stay here and keep drinking, it'll get dark again."

John did not reach New York; he ended his trip in the middle of a cornfield off Route 9H in the town of Claverack. Inured against pain by his night before, he made his way to the road and hitched a ride on a milk tanker back toward

Albany. A few miles and few remarks later, the truck driver left him by the side of the road. A State Trooper found him, and asked, "Is that your car–the red Zephyr--in a cornfield down the road?" John said it was. The trooper asked, rhetorically, "How did you get it there, and how did you get here?" John often said "I'll be dead in a ditch," which was rhyming slang for "I'll be a sonofabitch," and he had two good shots at being dead in a ditch that morning. When he got back to Albany, a neighborhood doctor found he had some broken ribs and scrambled insides and sent him to Memorial Hospital. I went to visit him and found Ruth and Shorty at his bedside. It was a hot night–except around Ruth–and I volunteered to fetch John a cooling Tom Collins from a friendly nearby bar. His romance was dead in a ditch. Shorty and I were still off-again.

Ruth left Albany soon after that–for Denver, it turned out. Shorty returned home to Boston. John stayed in Albany, reading copy at the *Times-Union*, drinking with O'Heaney, and, in the fall, campaigning for Henry Wallace for president. John was rooming at the home of Mrs. Irene Fay, whose husband had died suddenly several months earlier. ("He was at the bank," she explained, "and said I feel terrible, I've never felt like this before, and he just died.") John had to pass her room to reach his and, he reported, "She kept her door open and she was lying on the bed bare-ass naked; the poor woman seemed awfully lonely." A euphemism, no doubt. [A few months later, she answered an ad in a lonely-hearts magazine and received a call from a suave Latino named Fernandez. He and his three-hundred-pound friend Martha Beck came to Mrs. Fay's door. They took all her money and her life. The law caught up with them and both went to the electric chair in Sing Sing.]

A few days before Election, I met Blawis near the Plaza Grill. We had been drinking before our paths crossed. We had another commiserative drink or two together and he told me that he was leaving the paper, going somewhere to take a job where he could advance himself through civil service exams. He was, of course, feeling sorry for himself. He had been handing out Wallace leaflets to the workers leaving the West Albany railroad shops that day and he felt guilty about showing up in suit and tie to meet these tired, dirty workers who were heading home. He offered me a ride home to Green Island. An interesting ride. John stopped at several street corners and waited patiently for the traffic light to turn green. There was no traffic light.

A Neat Coincidence

When I next heard from John, he too was in Colorado, but not near Denver. He had gone to the State employment office to cash in on the 52-20 club (the postwar program that guaranteed unemployed veterans a twenty-dollar-a-week dole for fifty-two weeks). In the job interview, John said he had been an artillery surveyor in the Army, so he was offered a job, in lieu of 52-20, in a road surveying crew in Weld County, an arid place that also was dry. I didn't meet John again until my second visit to Denver. We met at the bar of the Albany Hotel; John had taken a head start to overcome months of legal dryness. We went back to 48 South Logan. Ruth was at home, but not to Blawis. Shorty and Coco and I entertained him in the kitchen, where he occasionally stirred the large pot where *bracciola* simmered in tomato gravy. In his enthusiasm, he splashed some of it on the wall near the rasslers' pictures. Seeking to save Ruth's privacy, Shorty and I announced we were going to the movies; John offered to drive us. The marquee signs indicated the program was lousy so we returned, hoping John would go somewhere else. He didn't. Ruth, tired of hiding in her room, called the cops. They took Blawis in for public intox and towed his car. Next morning Blawis called, contritely, from downtown. He was puzzled (why did she call the cops?), offended (those bastards threw me out of the lockup before breakfast), and broke (could you lend me ten dollars?). I could, and did. Blawis returned it by mail, accompanied by a poem in the style of

Robert Service that he considered a paean to Weld County;
the locals didn't.

Ruth was not to be taken lightly. One night, as she
emerged from work at Children's Hospital, a man accosted
her and demanded her money. She replied, "If I had any
money I wouldn't be walking." The man took a hint and left.
Afterwards, the girls asked Ruth why she had said that. That
was taking a big chance, they suggested. Ruth explained,
"The silly bastard asked me for money. Such an insult. What
did he think was wrong with *me*?" Other nurses had been
harassed by men who hid in the bushes outside the hospital.
Now Lew took action. He enlisted a pal who was a Denver
detective and they stalked the stalkers, beating up one of
them seriously enough to be an object lesson for the others.
The bothering ceased.

Before Shorty returned to Boston in the spring of 1950,
she came close to making us parents prematurely. Perhaps I
could have phrased that more felicitously. In that last week
or so, she had succumbed to the blandishments and high pay
offered by Denver General to work in its premature nursery.
Within days, she had found a five-month old preemie, up for
adoption, that she fell in love with. "So homely," she said in
a phone call, "Can I bring it home with me?" My view was
if she thinks it's a good idea, I think so too. Fortunately, she
mentioned it to the resident in pediatrics, who gave her two
good reasons not to adopt that preemie. First, Colorado law
didn't allow kids under six months to be adopted out of state.
Second, you've been out here nine months and you're going
home with a five-month-old baby? The law and the logic won
out.

When she reached Boston empty-handed, she took
her new résumé to Beth Israel Hospital. The nursing office
looked at that nine months in Denver, raised a leering
eyebrow and hired her. I soon went to Boston, wore my white
shirt and necktie, asked her father for her hand in marriage
(he seemed glad for the chance to say yes), and ate copious

amounts of her mother's cooking. I enjoyed her cooking and she enjoyed my eating. All went well and Shorty set a June date for our wedding.

Ma Objects; I Reject

I had had a tougher time when I returned to Green Island from Denver and broke the news to Ma. She said "You're not going to marry that girl, are you?" Despite the question mark in her voice, I understood. She was telling, not asking. I said, "Yes I am." That ended the discussion. As she had done when I disappointed her in grade school, Ma turned her energy to becoming mother of the supporting actor, the bridegroom.

Shorty and I began our preparations for the wedding. I had quit playing poker and begun saving money. Good apartments at reasonable rent were scarce, but I signed a sublease, at eighty-five dollars a month, on the third-floor rear of a row house on State Street, across from the Capitol. The location sold me: a liquor store, a couple of drinkeries, a deli, and a market, all within a block. When I took Shorty to see it, she had a different view: the dark green walls repelled her. But we were stuck with the sublease, so she made the most of its attributes: a living room that accommodated a double dresser on each side of a fireplace, plus a dining table and four chairs and a sofa; an eat-in kitchen in which, sitting at a small counter, we could reach the range, refrigerator and sink, and a bedroom taller than it was wide. I set about cleaning it, with help from John Tenczar, the bartender who had advanced me quarters for my Denver calls, and John Bolger, a counterman at an all-night restaurant I visited every work night. Tenczar cautioned about leaving the door on the bedroom: "That will make it her room." Bolger said we were wasting our time: "She'll look at it and say 'Clean! You call this clean?'" Both were right.

Enter Walt Mordaunt

As so often happens, I have gotten ahead of part of the story. Back in 1948, the newsroom was shocked by a rumor that a new college graduate named Walter Mordaunt had been hired to replace Leo O'Brien on the Hill, as Capitol correspondent. This report caused great grumbling among the reporters, each of whom felt it a personal affront to be passed over for the Hill, even if only in a rumor. As a sportswriter, I had no thoughts of the Hill, which left my mind open to Mordaunt. Only the first half of the report was true; O'Brien was to remain on the Hill four more years until he won election to Congress.

In late May, Mordaunt arrived. Walt was an impressive six feet five. He was a bit old for a new graduate, twenty-eight, because he had served in the war and used his GI Bill benefits to go to journalism school at Syracuse University. He was smart enough to be not a journalist but a reporter. He became active in the Guild and (although married) in Tuesday night pub-crawling, two endeavors I also favored, so we became friends. By 1950, Walt had become picture editor, a title that George Williams dragged out every so often to give the paper a big-city tone. Of course, he met Shorty when she came to inspect the apartment and on a couple of other occasions. As our wedding date approached, he and the other Tuesday night groupies told me what fun it would be to set up a couple of pregnant ladies to parade in front the church bearing some additional explicit signs. They were kidding, I hoped. None the less, I asked Walter to be my best man. Shorty asked her sister Dorothy to be maid of honor. No ushers, no bridesmaids.

❑

Late in May 1950, Shorty phoned me at work. Her mother had died unexpectedly. A major operation had turned fatal. Next day I went to Boston, to West Roxbury, to 2 Hastings Street, to the typical three-decker house the Puccios owned. Shorty had been dry-eyed until I arrived. We embraced and her grief poured out in tears. I hardly knew Mrs. Puccio, but I felt that she'd have become a friend, not just a mother-in-law. I stayed for the funeral. Our wedding was postponed.

Soon Shorty picked a new date: Saturday, July 8. I already had bought a gold wedding band at Al Smith's pawn shop on Green Street, but Shorty decided she'd wear her mother's wedding ring. So it became a double-ring ceremony. I arranged to rent the proper uniform and to get a week of vacation time for the honeymoon. I had to tell Mordaunt where the wedding would be, but not early enough for the Tuesday-nighters to arrange their wedding treat or threat. Walter had time though to arrange—thanks to his position as picture editor—for the Hearst Boston paper to photograph our wedding and send a picture by wire to the *Times-Union*. In Boston, the photo of us leaving the church took up a third of the picture page in the *Sunday Advertiser*; in Albany, a replay of the ceremony, heavily retouched, occupied a shallow, three-column space on the sports pages.

Marrying a Family

Shorty had advised me that I was marrying not just her but her family, eight siblings and uncountable other relations--a shuddering thought. Her brothers considered it high sport to mess up the newlyweds' traveling clothes, as they had done to Shorty's sister Annina and to some cousins. The day before the wedding we packed our clothes in a single suitcase and asked her brother David to drive me to the hotel we'd stay at, explaining that it contained the best man's uniform and Pa's best suit. We got away with it.

On the way to the wedding, I bought the only barbershop shave of my life and joined Mordaunt for the cab ride to the church. I expressed trepidation--not unlike many a bridegroom-- about the impending event. He said "Look at that sign." The back wall of the driver's seat read "Sit back, relax and enjoy the ride." What else? When we stood at the altar of the Stratford Street Baptist Church, Walter enjoyed the ceremony and his role in it. As he told us later, "When Dotty was coming down to aisle, she threw me a look" (It must have been quite a look with her thick glasses magnifying her large eyes) "so I threw one back to her, and this guy in the third row intercepted it, brightened up and looked 'Who me?' I shook my head no."

The wedding dinner for family and a few friends in lieu of the usual fancy reception was a good distance away, at the Lord Fox restaurant in Foxboro. En route, the wedding party stopped at a cemetery in Canton to pay homage to Shorty's mother. The Lord Fox had spacious grounds, with lots of trees, but people insisted that Shorty and I stand out in the sun so they could get a good picture of us. They got squinty looking images and we got thirsty.

When it came time for us to leave, the Dentons, who lived upstairs in the Puccio house, offered to drive us, including Walt, there so we could change to street clothes. Frank, the oldest of Shorty's fun-loving brothers, hopped on the running board with some malice in mind. Mr. Denton said: "Are you planning to stay out there all the way to West Roxbury?" Frank took the hint and stepped off. After all three of us were in civilian clothes again, we called a cab. We instructed the driver: "Stop at the Back Bay station, and then on to the Statler Hotel." At the station, Mordaunt got out to catch a train to Connecticut to join his wife. The cab driver stared in disbelief, but took us to the hotel.

Setting Off Fireworks

Shorty and I had the leisurely Tom Collins or two we had missed at the Lord Fox, reclaimed the luggage we had checked the day before, and, escorted by a bellman, went to our room. At the door, the bellman stepped aside and said, "OK, carry her in." I had almost forgotten. Thanks, young man; an extra dollar on your tip. We leisurely dressed for bed. No rush; we were married. We nuzzled, fondled and explored, and the fireworks went off. Fabulous fantastic fireworks! Chinese flowerpots. Roman candles. Pinwheels. Roaring rockets. Boston was celebrating its rain-delayed Fourth of July. The fireworks over, we went to bed.

Next day we took the trolley back to Hastings Street to visit with Dad Puccio and Dorothy. And by Monday, after flying on American Airlines at the family rate (one full fare and one half, for a total of thirteen dollars and forty-five cents) we moved into our apartment. Broke. All my savings of eleven hundred dollars had gone into our furniture and the deposit on a week's honeymoon in June. No refund; death was not a good reason. We also had spent the twenty-dollar bill that Shorty's father had given her as get-mad money in case the wedding didn't take. That evening, I called Johnny Jones to ask if he could lend me twenty dollars; he did.

Congratulations, Kind of

We received some unusual greetings. A congratulatory telegram from Tex Zangrando, a sterling student athlete who had just graduated from Christian Brothers Academy. And, on July 21, a message from The Editorial Staff, forwarding a setting of our silver flatwear pattern. The note, on a green *Times-Union* Memorandum sheet, read, as follows:

> DEAR HELEN,
>
> AS A SIGN OF OUR UNITED ADMIRATION FOR YOU, AND TO HELP YOU IN YOUR ENDEAVOR TO MAKE A GENTLEMAN OUT OF THE RAW MATERIAL YOU HAVE MARRIED—WE HEREWITH PRESENT THESE UTENSILS— WHICH WILL BE STRANGE TO YOUR SPOUSE WE KNOW— WITH THE HOPE THAT AT LEAST YOU WILL ENJOY THEIR USE,--AND THAT PERHAPS IN THE DISTANT FUTURE EVEN YOUR HUSBAND WILL XXXXX GAIN FACILITY WITH THEM AND STOP EATING WITH HIS FINGERS.

Another message, not dated, was in the form of copy for a sports page story, complete with a typed headline, Rivett Riveted/Or Doc's Demise, to be set two columns in thirty point ultrabodoni. It reported the comments of various sports figures and others, and presented a list, decades before David Letterman. Some samples:

The marriage of Francis (Doc) Rivett, Albany Times-Union sports writer, termed the dean of area sports cynics, excited varying comments although most leaders termed the Boston "Tea Party of 1950" a great thing for the game.

"He should have little trouble on his honeymoon," said Ted Bayly, Troy wrestling promoter. "As a regular Monday-nighter at our shows, Rivett should have picked up plenty of fancy holds. I recommend Argentina Rocca's dropkick for post-honeymoon difficulties."

"I hope the Rivetts have a telephone," commented Tom McCaffrey, owner of the Albany Senators. "It would give me great pleasure to call Doc at 8 a.m. daily for about a week." . . .

Among the unusual wedding presents received by the Rivetts were:

1. Rubber-covered unbreakable chairs, specially made for kicking and throwing at timely moments.
2. Swinging doors, equipped with electric eyes so that they open just before contact with a foot. . . .
9. Three hand-me-down sports shirts, compliments of Stan Levine and Johnny Jones.
10. A bunch of grapes, from Mike [The Candyman].
11. One ton of black coffee – no sugar. . .

❏

On Labor Day, Shorty's brother David got a measure of revenge (probably unpremeditated) for the con job we pulled on him the day before our wedding. He showed up unannounced with his wife and four little kiddies in various stages of house-brokenness. It was about dinnertime. Shorty had a big pot of veal and peppers stewing on the stove. But what else could we serve? The refrigerator held a bottle of Scotch; nothing else. Location paid off. One of the neighborhood stores was open, and I managed to buy milk and cereal for the kiddies and spaghetti and so on for us grownups. David and his family left for home with copious thanks. Their youngest, whose diaper was not leakproof, left a damp remembrance. After that I had a Scotch. Cool.

❏

We had become friends with another Ruth and John couple. Ruth was Aunt Ruth, the aunt of Shorty's roommate Betty Regan; John was John Allard. We met Ruth first; John was in the Army. Ruth and John lived in the basement apartment at 321 Hamilton Street. They took care of the apartment house for their absentee landlord, Benny Cilwick- -the same Benny who was so important to the *Times-Union* poker games.

We Attend a Wedding

Ruth and John, who each had day jobs, enjoyed their relationship We thought they'd never change. But one Saturday night in the early fall of 1951, when I was home for dinner, the phone rang. It was John Allard. "Ruth and I are going to get married," he said, "and we'd like you and Shorty to stand up for us." When? In a half-hour. Sure. So I called Stan Levine, told him what happened and asked him to finish up the sports pages on a dull night. Shorty's father was visiting so we took him along to Hope Baptist Church to serve as the audience. After the ceremony, we all went to the DeWitt Clinton Hotel to celebrate. The newlyweds were taking a late train to New York City, and seemed intent on keeping the party going until train time. Dad Puccio expressed concern that we might be keeping them from--you know. Afterwards we explained the facts of their life to him.

We remained friends until Ruth's death some forty years later.

We spent our second wedding anniversary apart, and that led to unusual developments. I was in Portland, Oregon, for three weeks, for the national Guild convention and Hearst negotiations. While there I gained a new job and twenty-five pounds. Ralph Novak hired me as the contracts analyst. Hospitality rooms provided the weight. Shorty was home alone. Except for our downstairs landlords who had rented us the improvised second floor flat in their originally one-family house. During my absence, our landlady, Dottie Friedlander, continued preaching to Shorty what fun it would be to have a family. Her Exhibit One was her toddler son Richard, whom she sent clambering upstairs, shouting Shor-Tee whenever we left our front door open, which was whenever we were home When I brought home the good news about my new job, Shorty had news of her own: she had decided we should now start a family. With great efficiency, we did.

And Baby Makes Three

We fared well enough through Helen's pregnancy; Came the first weekend of May in 1953 and I went off to Buffalo to perform a dog-and-pony at a regional meeting. It seemed safe enough; the baby was not due for another two weeks. But when I came home I found that Shorty had spent much of the weekend doing heavy cleaning, pushing furniture around, and unknowingly encouraging labor. We consulted her doctor and on Tuesday morning I took her to the hospital. The doctor assured me that nothing would happen right away, so I went to work. I was back in the hospital waiting room when our son Guy arrived at 1:20 a.m., May 6. Helen was scheduled to work that day and her boss came up to ask why she wasn't at work. That afternoon, after work, I completed shopping for baby essentials. When Shorty and Guy came home, her sister-in-law Carmela volunteered to be mother's little helper each work-day for several weeks. Helen went back to work weekends when Guy was a few months old. Even as fulltime Daddy on weekends, my title ranked behind *train* and *bus* when Guy began saying words.

In Mount Vernon, our first apartment was at 49 Ehrbar Avenue, in the cold half of twin buildings (the city health officer lived in the other, which stayed warm). After several months, Shorty's brother Jim moved his family to Buffalo and we moved to his flat at 415 Cedar Avenue, as next-door neighbors to Bella Abzug, whom neighbors referred to as that adjective Commie lawyer. Our new landlords were Charley and Lena Mazzarelli; Lena was a sister of Jim Puccio's wife Phyllis.

Many Happy Returns

While we were in Mount Vernon, two old colleagues bounced back into my life for an evening or less. One evening on the train I met Sid Grapp Chertok, little changed after fifteen years. He had become advertising manager for Sprague Electric in North Adams, Mass., where he had put out a calendar illustrated with a pinup babe, captioned "Built the Way You Like Them." He also had two daughters. Another evening, Blawis visited our apartment on Ehrbar Avenue. He was between jobs, he told us in the course of a dinner and drinks. Next we heard from him was a letter from Venezuela: he was working on a survey for a railroad into the mountains, and had just returned from a trip, in a Renault 2CV, with a colleague who was getting married after his family had reached ten children. He also expressed a desire to save enough bolivars to follow Joe O'Heaney's footsteps; I never heard how he made out.

❑

In two more years, back to Albany where we rented in quick succession two floor-through flats, only to find that each was infested with carpet beetles. So we went to an uncarpeted garden apartment at 41-B Picotte Drive There we were favored by good neighbors, most of them around our age with kids around Guy's age. One evening when a fire flared in our oven I called the firemen, and our next door neighbor, a child psychiatrist, solicitously took Guy, then four, into his apartment to limit damage to the immature psyche. By the time the fire engines arrived, I had the fire out, but Guy still reveled in the event. "Fire engines come to my house," he chortled, his childish psyche intact.

❑

By the time we returned to Albany, Mordaunt's marriage, which had been fraying at the edges, had come apart at the seams. There was a divorce, with considerable bitterness from Verna Mordaunt. Walt had, in the meantime, become deputy press secretary to Gov. W. Averell Harriman. Like my job at the Guild, it turned out to be a short-termer. He went on to various public relations jobs: with the State Bar Association, until some highly-placed members objected that he wasn't a lawyer, and with the State Court of Appeals, where he was highly valued, perhaps because he was not a lawyer. In the meantime, he courted Peggy Ann Smith, whose sister Roberta was a Times-Union photographer. When, much later, they married, Walt chose Roberta as his best man; Bobby was a lesbian. Walt died, of stomach cancer, in 1994.

In 1960, we bought a thirty-five year old house at 48 Parkwood Street, partly because it was only two blocks from the school Guy attended. I will spare everyone the travails that home ownership entailed; all of you know how it is. The Puccios often had proclaimed religiously, "The Lord will provide." I sometimes proclaimed the same, but with a different accent. Someone did provide: a few months after we had struggled to meet the down payment on our house, I was promoted to acting news editor with a hefty pay increase.

Even before we were married, Helen and Ma (my bride called her Annie) had become great friends. When Ma visited us at 192 State Street, she learned to bring sugar for her coffee; we never had any. When we moved to Mount Vernon, Ma visited us and Shorty took her shopping, in stores Ma had never even dreamed of. She especially enjoyed lunching in the Bird Cage restaurant in the Lord and Taylor store in Eastchester.

1961 a Year of Sadness

Nineteen sixty-one was a sad year. Helen's father, oldest brother and uncle died. Dad Puccio had given up in mid-1960 the massive house he built on Moosic Lake, Pennsylvania (near Scranton) to live with us. He put his experience as a builder to our benefit by supervising some major changes in the house. At age seventy-five, he was still active though slowed down, so we were shocked when our family doctor, making a house call on our son, told us he had noticed the extreme yellowness of Dad's eyes. He arranged a consult with a surgeon, and tests showed Dad had a serious liver ailment. An operation showed massive damage, the result of an early unnoticed attack of viral hepatitis. Dad Puccio died a few days later.

In early summer, Helen's oldest brother Frank, who had helped us with a significant loan disguised as a gift, became ill at his home in Hawthorne. He died after an operation; he was fifty-six. In late summer, Helen's Uncle Nick, who had boarded with a family on Oneonta some fifteen years, came to live with us. A few months later, he complained, but not strongly, of pain in his abdomen. Then he vomited what looked like coffee grounds; really blood, a sign he had suffered an intestinal blockage. An operation. A fatal outcome.

❑

A few years later, Helen developed puzzling symptoms but not disabling ones, nagging things that she attributed to the fact "I've never been this old before." She was about forty. In late 1966, she experienced difficulty walking. Still no clear-cut diagnosis, until she went to our family doctor,

Leon Feltman, in January 1967. He promptly and quietly diagnosed her ailment as "multiple sclerosis or a tumor on the spinal cord" and referred her to a neurologist. Tests showed that she had multiple sclerosis and she spent three weeks in the hospital. When the neurologist discharged her, he said she could return to work, but take it easy. "There's no devil driving you," he said. He did not know Helen; she was her own devil. After a very short trial in which she was unable to regain her full physical prowess, she retired from nursing. For some twenty years after that, she put her skills to use as a one-day-a-week volunteer at the Red Cross blood bank.

Ma Wins Last Bingo

After we moved back to Albany in 1955, Helen often drove to Green Island with Guy to visit Grandma. By that time, Ma was enjoying poor health. She often told, with a laugh, of getting conflicting advice from my "sugar doctor", who had prescribed insulin for her type 2 diabetes, and my "pressure doctor". She did not seem dangerously ill and she continued her three-night-a-week bingo schedule. Right to the end. She died in her sleep in 1969, after a winning night at bingo. Her wake, at McNulty's, attracted friends from all over, including each of the bingo halls, and there was hardly a damp eye, as her pals told affectionate, usually funny, stories about Ma.

❑

I had lost track over the years of my classmates who had graduated in 1935 from Watervliet High School, so I was surprised to receive an invitation to the first class reunion, "zackly fifty years" after graduation. Adam J. Simonian had arranged for a dinner at the Officers' Club in the Watervliet Arsenal. A goodly crowd was there and I recognized several of the men I hadn't seen for so long: Charles DerGurahian, Bob Holmes, Art Kershaw, Irv Goldstone, Marty Pemrick, among them. Only one woman, Bernice Kiskis, who had come in from California and still looked like a high school senior, clicked in my memory We have had reunions every five years since. At the sixty-fifth anniversary, only a handful of us could attend.

❑

In 1997, Helen organized the fiftieth anniversary reunion of her Cadet nurse class. About a dozen classmates found their way from California, Texas, Florida and closer places. The formal reunion took place over dinner at a hotel. We provided nametags, which proved a big help; only a couple of the girls--besides Helen--still had their nurse-school figures. That one night seemed hardly enough get-together for fifty years, so many of us assembled again for lunch Saturday and we invited everyone to dinner at our house. Baked salmon with lemon and pesto--a house specialty. Except for two people who couldn't stand fish. We stopped a nearby deli, bought a few real thick slices of roast beef and a can of beef gravy--voila! a roast beef dinner. They praised it. The girls suggested that I should be an honorary member of their class. I told them it was too late: I had been for fifty years.

❑

We come now to 2000 and our fiftieth wedding anniversary. We planned a big party in a downtown hotel, but not on the exact anniversary. Helen's sister Dorothy, who lives in Augusta, Georgia, couldn't make that date. So we changed it to July 29. But we couldn't let the exact date go unmarked. Ottawa, particularly the Chateau Laurier, where we had celebrated earlier anniversaries, beckoned. The city and the hotel lived up to their promise. And, on Monday, as we prepared to leave, exceeded their promise. I looked out the window of our room and there was a beautiful morning rainbow, all its colors as sharp as a TV test pattern, hovering with one end just above ground, and only a hundred feet or so away. I looked carefully; no pot—of gold or anything else.

Our formal party in Albany was a great success: about fifty family, friends and neighbors, not mutually exclusive categories. As the party ended, and many of us stayed to chat (and gossip), a marvelous fireworks show erupted, within sight, on the waterfront. Just like our wedding night. And, as happened fifty years before, when the fireworks ended, we went to bed.

Through all these years since 1967, Shorty has, through sheer willpower , remained able to walk unaided. She also has dome all the housework as if the devil were chasing her. Her own devil. Lately though. She has begun complaining, "I don't know why I feel so tired; I never used to." She never was eighty years old before.

No Experience Possible

When Ralph Novak began talking about the job he had in mind for me, he scoffed at experience as a criterion. "All experience means is that someone has done something for a long time," he said, "it doesn't mean he's been doing it right." What made his view remarkable was that the American Newspaper Guild, of which he was the executive vice president, set great store by experience and required that it be recognized, up to a point, with higher pay, in all its contracts.

However heretical his view of experience in general might seem, it made sense for the job we were talking about. It was something that hadn't been done before in the Guild, and perhaps not in any trade union. To put it in positively negative terms: no experience possible.

❏

By that time, I had accumulated experience of a sort: general, not particular. I had become active in the local grandly named Tri-City Newspaper Guild after an ambiguous contract provision deprived me of a raise for a year. After my first negotiating experience convinced me that I, if not the guild, needed better representation, I ran for office in 1949. I won election as secretary on a runoff ballot, after tying with Hugh Tuohey, a young reporter at the *T-U*. The following year, I was elected president: not even close. The year after that, likewise.

Even before that, in 1945, I was selected as one of Albany's delegates to the formative meeting of the Guild's Empire State District Council at the TenEyck Hotel. It drew an impressive array, representing locals from New York City to Buffalo (and Hudson County, New Jersey). The debate, however, was petty: how will votes be allotted, and how much will each local have to pay? The little locals—Albany, Newburgh, Utica, Rochester and Buffalo—wanted to keep the leftish leadership of New York's ten thousand members from dominating policy. New York's leaders wanted to insure that they wouldn't have to pay a thousand dollars a month into an upstate slush fund. It seemed to me that a limit had to be put on voting power and on cost. So, late in the afternoon, I moved to set a limit of about a hundred dollars on monthly payments and five hundred votes per local. It was just what everyone wanted, and the district council was born.

An Early Lesson

Early in my negotiating, I learned again the need for analysis. The *Times-Union* contract included "display ad salesmen–junior." A slot for a young man just breaking in, I thought. But no, the only man in that group was sixty-five years old; "junior" was the company's euphemism for "handling small accounts." We threatened to tell the salesman's clients that they were considered minor while being charged major rates. The category was eliminated; the salesman gained a substantial raise.

I brought myself to Novak's attention early in 1950 by writing him an impolitely critical letter complaining about the slow course of negotiations on the Hearst National Memorandum. He replied with an invitation--more like a challenge: see if you can do any better--to join the unpaid group that sat with him in the talks.

Possibly I had been brought to his attention even earlier by Bill Bade, then the editor of *The Guild Reporter*, who had often come to Albany to lead negotiations in which I took part. Bade volunteered his time, so we had to pay only for his expenses. He compensated for the lack of compensation by browsing in John Scopes's second-hand bookstore, where he bought, for a quarter each, copies of *Godey's Ladies' Book* and similar magazines from the mid-1800s. He harvested several hand-tinted steel engravings from each and framed them for gifts. (He framed a print depicting Albany in the 1850's and gave it to us as a wedding present.)

More About Bill Bade

Bade, pronounced body, was about six feet four with a formidable torso mounted on remarkably long legs. He delighted in betting that he could kick a light fixture considerably higher than his head; he always won. He also delighted in needling Tom Brennan, the company's principal negotiator in Albany. He always won.. (By the time Novak hired me, Bade had gone back to his hometown, Minneapolis, as paid executive for the local. Bade was generous to the end; he dropped dead the following winter after helping to push a friend's car out of a snow bank in St. Paul.)

On my first day in the Hearst talks in the summer of 1950, I sat quietly nearly all morning while the Hearst people, particularly the chief negotiator Harvey Kelly, muddied up a definition we thought had long been settled. An esoteric but important subject. The word was "special." We had always agreed that the word allowed management to avoid seniority in rehiring someone who had been laid off only if the job opening required special–that is, greater-- skills than the laid-off person had. Now Hearst was arguing that "special" meant lower skills. Just before lunch, I said my first words of the day, "Mister Kelly, you've spent the whole morning trying to turn the meaning of special on its head. It's time to stop this nonsense and move on." The meaning of special remained as special as it had been. Mr. Kelly changed the subject in the afternoon. I said many more words from then on

The afternoon introduced me to a tradition of Hearst negotiating: the Children's Hour. From Longfellow's poem: *a pause in the day's occupation known as the children's hour.* After we had negotiated with the usual lack of agreement for a few hours, Kelly sneaked a look at his watch. Four-fifteen. The conversation became even more desultory. Another look. Four-thirty-five. A clearing of the throat and Mr. Kelly announced in his basso profundo voice, "Gentlemen, I think it's time for the Children's Hour"--a nod to one of his minions–"Call and have the cart brought up." Soon a room service waiter appeared with a cart full of various potables, prominently including Chivas Regal, Kelly's favorite.

Once Kelly had left, the chief Hearst labor lawyer, Bob Bassett, tall, pink-faced, pink-haired (cropped and curly), in his early forties, announced (an opening day ritual) that we were welcome to come upstairs in the Warwick Hotel to his suite for more. We went. Then out to dinner on Hearst. Then back to an encore of the encore. The purpose of all this, I learned later, was to find a weak member of the Guild team. That purpose might have kept the Hearst accountants happy, but the only Guild guy who mattered was Novak and he had long ago left for home in Ossining, an hour away. That night we sort of reversed Bassett's procedure. Al Dipman, a picture editor from the San Francisco *Examiner,* who tried to wash away his vocal tic, *I mean, that is, I mean, that is, that is, etc.,* proved unable to do so, and, by 9 o'clock, someone had to escort him to his room where he promptly fell asleep. Hours later, as the rest of us were stumbling toward bed, Dipman, refreshed, reappeared and kept Bassett and his colleagues company until dawn. None of them weakened.

Later that week, the all-male Guild negotiators invited my wife and Eva Jollos, the Guild's contracts committee secretary, to attend. When the Children's Hour came, Kelly took Novak aside and said, not entirely jokingly, "Damn it Novak, you took away eighty per cent of my vocabulary today." Harvey's language wasn't bad, just colorful. He called preposterous reasoning *masturbation of the intellect,* talk without end *nifnaw,* idle threats *cat-hopping,* and circular argument *rabbit-tracking.* He also viewed some of our proposals with the disdainful sentence: *That chills the blood.*

A Question of Drink

As the negotiations continued and I commuted between my job and the talks, we all met over dinner one night and

Novak asked me, "Why haven't you ever come to work for the Guild?" I told him, "Because nobody ever asked me to." Not that night either. The Hearst talks continued and continued. So did my talks with Novak. Ours got down to cases. Novak suddenly asked, "Do you drink?" I responded, "What have you got?" That wasn't what he had in mind. He explained, "Anyone who doesn't drink wouldn't have the imagination required for the job." I thought: Yeah, and, really, if you don't drink now, the job will drive you to it. Really prescient.

About the same time (I learned years later), the Hearst chain was interviewing a prospective new lawyer on the same subject but in a more practical way. The question there was, *How much can you drink without falling over?* Their question was not theoretical. The lawyer involved, Ed Landergren, told me about it--over drinks, naturally. He had passed the law-type interviews with the lawyers, but had to be interviewed at last by Harvey Kelly. Harvey was not a lawyer, but a seat-of-the-pants negotiator who had learned his way in the rough, sometimes lethal, timber industry in the Pacific Northwest. When Ed met Kelly for lunch, he already had been advised–no, warned--of the nature of the test. Kelly ordered a Chivas Regal; Landergren ordered a Martini. Make it a double, said Kelly; likewise, said Landergren. So they said Scotch and Martini and double and likewise several times during and after lunch. Kelly used to say his doctor would let him have one drink a day and he was, in 1950, up to September 25th, 1974, and gaining. Landergren passed the test by surviving, and he was hired. He also learned a valuable lesson: never try to match anyone Martini for Scotch. And that goes double for doubles.

❑

Grievances and negotiations kept me busy in Albany. We did not always win, but we tried to have fun even when losing. When we pushed a grievance, alleging a pay cut, on behalf of a young classified ad salesman whose bonus the company had slashed, the publisher argued that he had changed the rules because the salesman was making more than his boss. I said, "He deserved to. He's bringing in more money than his boss does. And you could take care of it by giving his boss a raise." We did not prevail, but we enjoyed the dismay of the classified ad manager. He didn't get a raise, and he lost a highly productive salesman, who left to start a publication of his own.

A few years later, we issued the most memorable news bulletin in local history. Deep in negotiations, the *Times-Union* made its usual flourish. "We're scraping the bottom of the barrel," the publisher Gene Robb told us. And a few sentences later, he offered a package of pay and conditions in an effort to settle the contract. We did not accept it. After the meeting, Walter Mordaunt and I drafted a bulletin to our members explaining the developments. Mordaunt composed the headline, which read: T-U 'Scrapes Bottom;'/Offers Us a Package.

A Contracts Analyst

Novak hired me in July 1952 in Portland, Oregon, at a time when I was sure we would not be starting a family soon. I agreed to a salary of a hundred and fifteen dollars a week, about twenty more than I was making at the *Times- Union*. Enough, I figured, to enable us to maintain our standard of living, which was not very high. When I returned home, however, I found that Shorty had changed our mind about starting a family.

By the time I was to start my new job in September, Shorty was pregnant. My proposed budget did not account for a third mouth to feed. Could I, should I, try to repeat my feat in Troy of getting a raise before I was fully hired? Before I could act rashly, I learned that the answer was no. Novak originally hired a woman from the Midwest for the analyst job, but dropped her when she upped the ante.

❑

I had been in the office on the fourth floor of a grimy building owned by the Textile Workers Union at 99 University

Place barely long enough to locate the men's room, when Novak sent me to Bethlehem. Pennsylvania, to find out the truth about a strike at the *Globe-Times*. The Philadelphia local had called the strike to help it gain a contract with the Atlantic City paper, where the *Globe*-Times publisher Rollin Adams was also the publisher. The Philadelphia local decided that it could enlist the twenty thousand members of the Steelworkers union in Bethlehem to support its effort; Atlantic City offered no union base.

Striking Out in Bethlehem

In Bethlehem, I found that the Philadelphia local had won a representation election at the *Globe-Times* newsroom, by a total of four votes to three, and called a strike for recognition. I met the four members who had walked out. They said a mediator told them they had lost the strike; the paper was still coming out. Dave Schick, the paid executive of the Philadelphia Guild, told me that the Steelworkers had reneged on their offer of aid. I met C.D. Newell, the Steelworkers' regional vice president, and asked him about it. He said, "When the Guild asked us for help, we said sure. We thought they could do what we do, shut the place down, and we'd help out with strike benefits and the like. Instead they wanted us to shut the plant down for them. The first day we sent a big semi flatbed over and parked it across the loading dock so they couldn't get the papers out. But we couldn't keep doing it and I told them so."

Back in New York, I wrote a report to Novak that started like this: *This is the wrong strike by the wrong people in the wrong place for the wrong reason.* And went on to detail what I had learned.

My report was accurate but not correct, not politically correct. I was the wrong guy in the wrong place and at the wrong time to say such things. I was too young, too new and too Novak. My report grated on Schick, and on Bill Farson, the secretary-treasurer, who also was a member of the Philadelphia local. I knew little about the politics of the Guild. Novak and Farson had been elected in 1949 as successors to the first anti-Communist slate that took office in 1941. I soon learned they were running mates not friends, and by September 1952 were wary colleagues. Novak, an auditor from the *Detroit Times,* was short, pear-shaped and a lively thinker. Farson, an ad salesman from the *Philadelphia Inquirer,* was taller, slender, athletic (he played tennis) and thought mainly about his ego.

❑

Pleased at my report, I set about analyzing contracts rather haphazardly. Novak had planned to have an analysis in a local's hands before it prepared its contract demands. So did I. In the event, I was sending analyses to locals that already were in negotiations. The analyses were still helpful; negotiations always took months, even years. Within a few weeks, I decided to skip past several locals, and to concentrate on those getting ready to negotiate, with longer-range and longer analyses.

It was not long before some local officers took offense, naturally. Any time someone reads *your contract needs fixing,* the subliminal message is, *you did a poor job of negotiating.* The letters and phone calls became personal: *who are you to tell us how to negotiate?; you ought to come out of your ivory tower; when did you ever negotiate a contract?; we did the best we could.* And so on. What could I say? Nothing. So I didn't.

Leuchter's License

One writer accused me of practicing law without a license. I asked our general counsel Irving Leuchter about it. He said, "Of course you are. Anyone doing your kind of work practices law in some way. But don't worry. I'm giving you a license to practice law without a license." I've used Leuchter's license ever since. Irving came to Albany once to argue a sticky arbitration involving a military leave case; it ended early and badly. But, so it shouldn't be a total loss, I invited him home for lunch, and Helen drove him to Williamstown that afternoon, so he could indulge his passion for art at the Clark Institute.

To get a little ahead of chronology, it took me nearly two years to reach the New York local's contracts. There were, as I recall, ten of them, all nearly identical. My analyses became directions for whatever fixing was needed—not much really--times ten. The reaction of Tom Murphy, the local executive, was outrage times ten, at the thought that anyone might learn of his shortcomings, real or not. He accosted Novak and me at the International office and accused us (particularly Novak) of trying to sabotage his stewardship. We hadn't even thought of that.

How to Lie by the Mile

Between analyses, I found time to write some segments of a collective bargaining manual that Novak wanted to issue as a sort of generic analysis: a how-to-get-more booklet. The most helpful section was the first. Inspired by Darrell Huff's then-current book *How to Lie with Statistics,* I developed arguments that justified a car-mileage allowance far above any in existence. How plausible it seemed! Local officers ate it up. Getting an excessive allowance for car mileage was better than a small raise; it didn't count on the income tax. And publishers found granting higher mileage rates preferable to higher salary rates. I wrote a few other sections, but the manual never was finished.

❑

For some time, I was the newest member of the professional staff in the office. (There also were several—the count varied—international representatives, IRs, in the field.) The inside staff, in order of importance, were J. William Blatz, from Columbus (Ohio), director of organization; Ellis T. Baker III, from Baltimore, director of research and education, both of whom Novak had hired, and, from an earlier era, Eva Jollos, secretary of the contracts committee, and Charley Crissey, from Jersey, editor of *The Guild Reporter.* Bill Blatz was built like a linebacker (circa 1950) and his jaw—my, what a jaw—signaled his aggressive nature. Baker, called E T B Three, was taller, crew cut, and softly padded with a layer of pomposity. Jollos, an unhandsome graduate of the University of Wisconsin, spoke with the accent and undeniable authority of her native Austria. All four of us were in our mid-thirties. Crissey, several years older, had been an IR. All of us, save Crissey, joined Novak and Farson on the contracts committee, which, as the need arose, debated the meaning of every word, semi-colon, and comma, in deciding whether to give a local contract its imprimatur.

The Bounding Buffoons

As director of education, Baker had organized a group—Baker's Bounding Buffoons to the rest of the staff—to give training courses at regional Guild meetings. I was one of the buffoons. We conducted a course in Buffalo the first weekend of May 1953. I returned from it to find Helen in labor a couple of weeks ahead of schedule.

We staff members were to receive a small raise in 1953; we had to depend on the largesse of each year's convention. So, at the convention in Boston, the IRs sang their plea. Each verse, to the tune of *Battle Hymn of the Republic*, was a paean to an IR (or two). And the chorus was:

> *Glory glory to us eye-ahhrs!*
> *Glory glory to us eye ahhrs!*
> *Glory glory to us eye ahhrs!*
> *We deserve a substantial raise!*

We inside staffers offered to take the same salary as the IRs. I raised my voice in their song. Novak sardonically endorsed the raise for me, telling our chorus master, "Rivett is one of

you guys, he's an IR–Ir Responsible." We did not achieve pay
parity

A month later, in July 1953, bad news came from
Albany: the *Knickerbocker News* had fired Janet Scott, one
of the Guild pioneers and an old friend, after she took the
Fifth Amendment at a local Congressman's hearing into
Communism. The Albany local was reluctant to come to her
rescue. I thought the Gannett people were using her non-
answer as a good reason to get rid of her. In 1935, she had
written, anonymously, a scathing piece about B.J. Lewis, the
editorial director, for the *Guild Reporter*. She had escaped
the purge of Guild people when the papers combined in 1937,
when firing her would have been obviously revenge. Scott
had been accused several times of being a Communist and
always evaded a direct answer. On the other hand, her editors
showed their trust by assigning her to cover an election law
court case in 1950 in which she was involved as a potential
candidate of the once-leftist American Labor Party.
    Novak asked me to draft a letter imploring the local
to fight. I wrote from the heart, an inspirational appeal to
fight the good fight for the Guild's sake, not just Janet's. All
in vain. The *Times-Union* coverage of her appearance before
the Congressman, with large headlines, had poisoned the
well of public opinion. So the Congressman had a prominent
victim to go with the handful of mid-level State employees
and restaurant workers he had exposed.

❑

    The negotiations on the national Hearst agreement
that I had joined in 1950 were completed in 1954, but not
yet signed. After we had reached agreement, the New York
local gained four more weeks of alternate benefits than the
fifty-six weeks we had negotiated. Novak promptly asked
Kelly to meet again. The three of us met in Kelly's suite in
the Gotham Hotel, a pricey place at Fifth Avenue and 55th
Street. The meeting took only a few minutes. Kelly scolded
Novak for asking for more when the new agreement was

ready to be signed. Novak told him, "Harvey, I warned you that we had to get whatever you gave anyone else; we have to have sixty weeks, too." Kelly grumbled a bit, but agreed. It was too early for the Children's Hour, but not too early for him to extend his one-drink a day regimen another few days. He called room service for a Chivas Regal, doubled and redoubled, and looked at us. We each nodded. We savored the Scotch and relaxed conversation the rest of the afternoon.

By that time, Novak had taught me about the power of preventive procrastination. I was earnestly typing a response to a local officer who had written for some bargaining advice; an *emergency*, he said. Novak came into the office to talk to his secretary, with whom I shared space, and casually asked what I was doing. I told him. He said, "Don't bother answering him. It's not an emergency; if it was, he'd call. Just wait for him to call and then you can find out exactly what he wants to know. He's probably asking you the wrong questions now. And, if you don't write, there's no record." I stopped writing. The guy never called.

Lost battles, in addition to analyses, soon became part of my assignment; battles, that is, that other people had lost or wouldn't even fight. For instance: the battle of the Jamestown (NY) *Sun,* which the printers union had started after striking the *Post-Journal.* The printers' national union had hired Jim Higgins from the editorship of the progressive York (Pa.) *Gazette and Daily* to run the paper and Higgins had given a newly-hatched Guild local the model contract in all respects except pay. After a year, the printers union, whose local members were working for strike benefits not real pay, replaced Higgins with a tough bottom-line manager, Ed Byrne. He sought to junk most of the contract. Various IRs tried and failed to negotiate a new agreement. Novak finally told me, "Go out there and do anything you can to get a good contract, anything short of a strike."

The Jamestown negotiating committee was not impressive. With one exception—an attractive busty young woman whose intellect didn't matter. At a local strategy meeting, I suggested having her sit directly across from Ed Byrne, to occupy his mind. A great idea, but a little late; I was told that she already was Byrne's girlfriend. At a rare weekday session, the International Typographical Union sent in one of its vice-presidents, Toby Lyons, who invited me to breakfast, and then spent the whole time moaning about how much his stock in Bethlehem Steel had declined. Several weeks later, he phoned me at New York and announced, "We're closing the paper." I said, "That's all right, just give our people their pay in lieu of notice and pay them severance pay and all the other things they have coming." He hung up.

The paper continued. So did my negotiating. We filed charges of impropriety with the state Labor Relations Board. Novak told me, "Remember what I told you when I sent you out there? Well, forget the last part." A strike against a strike paper just couldn't happen, but the printers union eventually found its publishing strategy a waste of money and the *Sun* set.

Next came the *Pawtucket (RI) Times*, where others had negotiated and given up. Only one major issue was left: keeping the additional pay for desk editors. One issue left unsaid: being nasty to the management negotiators. The local folk considered nastiness necessary in a good negotiator; I didn't. Without forethought, however, I fulfilled their desire. One afternoon, as we nifnawed about some minor issue, the hereditary publisher Stanley Black rose from his seat, mumbled "I can't stand any more of this" and left the room. I saw tears. At a local meeting that night, my unintended nastiness was applauded. We also kept the desk differential.

Eeriness in Erie

On to Scranton, for the last quarter of bargaining. Literally the last quarter–of a dollar. The local bargainers wanted help to close the contract. I gave them more help than they wanted. I insisted that they finally bring photographers and women reporters to the same pay level as men reporters. I succeeded but the local folk were tougher to convince than the two co-publishers. And the hospitality of one member was almost disabling. I had visited the newsroom and Tommy Phillips, the city editor, invited me to come back after work (about 2 a.m.) and chat with him and friends. We talked in his kitchen where a refrigerator was loaded with bottles of Stegmaier beer. (His wife kept the food in a separate refrigerator.) The visit ended at sunup. Negotiations began at 1 p.m.

As I was wrapping up affairs at Scranton, Novak telephoned: "Get to Erie right away. They're in arbitration over a bunch of dismissals." I caught a plane that afternoon and landed in a situation I knew nothing about. The Erie publisher Ed Lamb, a generally liberal sort, had notified the Guild that the paper was in dire straits and that he would dismiss twenty-one people in various departments in reverse order of seniority. The local Guild was claiming that no dismissals were warranted. I looked at the publisher's numbers; they looked bad. I cross-examined a company witness; the numbers sounded worse.

As I waited after lunch for the hearing to resume, the arbitrator came by and said, "I'm surprised to see you here; I thought you'd be trying to saw this off. Every time you ask about a number, your case gets worse." . When we resumed, I asked him—without consulting the local—to issue a directed verdict saving a few of the jobs. He wouldn't. The two local leaders expressed outrage. Nothing more to do there, so I dashed to get a plane home. I didn't have time to call Novak until I reached the Newark airport. The Erie guys had called him first and had accused me of selling them out, among other things. Novak was livid—at them not me. I calmed him down. I learned later why those two local guys were so angry. They weren't concerned about what happened to

the other people. They wanted to be among the dismissed so
they could collect severance pay; they already had secured
jobs elsewhere. They went back to negotiating and got what
they were seeking. Two other people kept their jobs.

.   At each Guild convention, the most popular committee,
by the delegates' choice, was collective bargaining. In each
year's budget, however, the best-supported activity was
organizing. Each convention re-endorsed its predecessor's
supply-side theory that high spending on organizing would
bring in so many new members that they would support
further organizing efforts that would . . . as if it really
might. In the meantime, nothing for collective bargaining.
The big locals hired an executive to negotiate; the small
ones called on the international for help, at a price. Blatz
was pleased to send one of his IRs to negotiate, provided the
local defrayed the IR's salary and expenses. That procedure
kept Blatz's accounts in the black and enabled him to build
a strong organization among those locals.

I Stick with Novak

In 1955, as a Guild election approached, the rift
between Novak and Farson widened; Farson was going to run
for the top office. Charles A. Perlik Jr., a reporter from the
Buffalo Evening News, who had joined Blatz's crew shortly
after I was hired, was Farson's candidate for secretary-
treasurer. Staff members began choosing sides; I was one
of the few who stuck with Novak. He began planning his
campaign as a benefactor to the many locals that couldn't
afford their own negotiators. He asked me, by default,
to help him plan and explain a revolutionary program: a
fulltime national staff devoted to local bargaining. In a two-
page spread in the *Guild Reporter*, we broke out a map of
each region and that should have scared us off. There was
little except empty space in the Southwest, the Northwest,
the Rocky Mountains, the Great Plains and the Southeast.

Expenses for traveling the hundreds, even thousands, of miles would far exceed the negotiator's salary.

To Novak's foes, his revolutionary bargaining plan was merely revolting. We had offered too much detail, too many things that people could pick apart. Along with the wide expanses of countryside, the maps showed that at least one local in each district already was paying its own staff to negotiate. Those locals hollered dual taxation. The plan went down to defeat at the Albany convention. So did my job; no money for it in the budget. The subsequent election removed Novak. As my third anniversary at the Guild neared, I headed back to the *Times-Union*.

I had one last assignment: handling a contract arbitration for the York (Pa.) local. Guild rules forbade such an arbitration, but there was no alternative; the York Guild had thirty (or so) members, all in the newsroom of the *Gazette & Daily* and could not have called an effective strike. The paper, run by the Gitts father and son, had won prizes and the loyalty of its writers and editors for its editorial liberality, but its pay levels ranked near the bottom of all ninety-nine contracts. The Gitts had offered the Guild no wage increase, pleading poverty—they did not accept alcohol or tobacco advertising. But they had granted the printers a four-dollar-a-week raise. The Guild local sought a similar increase. After hearings, I submitted a brief that convincingly justified our demands. Weeks passed, and I was back in Albany, when the arbitrator awarded the Guild an increase of two dollars and a quarter a week. I thought I had done better than that.

Active Again in Albany

Back in Albany, I resumed my unpaid activity in the local. I was elected a delegate to conventions in St. Louis and San Jose in the fifties and, among others, Washington in the sixties. Business was business, but pleasure was more memorable. In St. Louis, the local hosts took us to

Grant Farm, where the Budweiser people showed us their Clydesdales and fed us cookout food and Busch Bavarian beer. In San Jose, then a small pre-silicon city, the big attractions to me were Original Joe's restaurant, which served outlandishly large portions, and the Falstaff brewery hospitality room. As I drafted the collective bargaining committee report for that convention, I was inspired by a half-sandwich from Joe's and a steady supply of half-bottles of Falstaff. Neither interfered with my three-finger typing.

At one of those conventions, I came to the rescue of the Hearst negotiations. Tom Murphy claimed that the Hearst national agreement handicapped the New York local's negotiations and moved to drop the small appropriation for the Hearst talks from the budget. New York was big enough to hold the national gains. But I was worried that the smaller locals might give away some of the national provisions, perhaps even the union shop. I rushed to Murphy, told him of my concerns, and asked, "If we set up a way for the smaller locals to continue the Hearst agreement and pay for it through a special assessment, would you support it?" He said he would. I took the floor and dictated a motion that established a Hearst chain council financed by a per capita assessment on the locals involved. With New York's support, it passed easily.

The Hearst negotiations had, in 1956, produced another memorable occasion, though, as usual, no result. We met in Chicago, at the Ambassador Hotel, on the Gold Coast, and observed a real Children's Hour in Bob Bassett's grand duplex apartment across the street. A real child, his six-year-old daughter, served drinks and reported, "My mother loves to make drinks." Her mother made them in oversized glasses, doubles if not triples.

When the Hearst talks resumed on their own, Don Ball of the Detroit local became the chief negotiator. As the negotiations continued, Ball left the Detroit *Times* and, by default, I became chief negotiator. Again, we talked and talked and talked. Most of the talk consisted of management—by this time it was Tom Brennan, also by default—insisting on changing the alternate benefits section from pay-as-you-go to funding on an actuarial basis. Brennan kept saying, "We've got to have some way to get control of the costs." I kept telling him we'd go for funding, but "We won't take any less than we have now." Brennan threw in another condition, "We want to get the benefits in line with what our competitors give." So I asked, "Which competitors?" And he answered, "Scripps-Howard." I said "Bullshit, Scripps-Howard is only in two cities you're in, that's not competition." This nifnaw melded into rabbit-tracking into masturbation of the intellect with some overtones of cat-hopping. And for negotiating session after session, in New York and Boston and wherever. Nothing came of it; and the Hearst agreement continued in force. And alternate benefits continued unfunded.

Back when Novak was talking to me about a job, I had told him that I felt I had no aptitude for organizing. He told me, "If you can negotiate, you can organize." We let it go at that. In the late 1950s, I brought a lot of people into the Albany Guild, but I can't take much credit for it. The truism that managements do more organizing than unions turned out to be true.

Easy Organizing

My first organizing effort was unintentional. At the request of the Wire Service Local, which had no members in Albany, I asked Norris Paxton, the Associated Press bureau chief, to put up a bulletin board for the Guild. "Nothing personal," I assured him. "We just want to let people know how negotiations are going; we're trying to increase the minimum salary rates." He responded, "It certainly is personal. The minimums don't mean anything. If I have anyone here at just the minimum, it's because he's a nice guy and I like him." When I reported the conversation to some AP staffers, I learned, and so did they, that there were a lot of nice guys (and girls) in Albany AP. They all signed Guild cards.

Next came the circulation departments of both papers. For more than twenty years, since the early days of the Guild, they had been represented by independent, meaning company, unions. The *Times-Union* circulation district managers and truck drivers had begun their union in self-defense. Ken Moore, a photographer and Guild leader at the *Times-Union,* had discovered in the 1930's a pattern of dishonesty that permeated the circulation department and was making loud noises about it. The *Times-Union* was an afternoon paper and the drivers distributed papers from a loose bundle. In a report I read in the files of the Albany Guild, Moore claimed that he had trailed some drivers and found that they were shorting newsstands–a paper here, two or three there—and collecting for the full number. With forty or fifty stops per edition, that sort of shorting could add up. He insisted that their bosses were sharing in the proceeds. Naturally the circulation people did not believe a Guild leader with that attitude would represent their best interests as they saw them.

The culture had not changed much; a charge of dishonesty led to the company union's conversion. For years, the company had rewarded its carrier boys for adding customers–awards like a basketball, a football, a baseball glove. The awards sometimes were picked off by district managers. In 1958, the *Times-Union* fired the president of the company union, Bill Fineman, for taking a large supply of such awards to use in a summer camp he operated at Schroon Lake. He wanted to fight back, but the company union couldn't pay for arbitration. He came to me, as the Guild president, for help. He could bring the entire union– around fifty-five people–into the Guild if we would pay the twenty-five hundred dollars for arbitration. I thought it was a great bargain. So did the international Guild, which spent an average of several thousand dollars per net new member. I made the deal quietly, even secretly, which caused some opposition in the Albany local when I revealed it as a *fait accompli* at a meeting. Jim Gallagher, a vice president, objected that the deal was not only secret but also immoral, that we shouldn't be protecting someone charged with dishonesty. I expressed my displeasure at his second-guessing by offering to quit right then so could become president; he didn't take me up on it. [A few years later, Jim, who was an avid Episcopalian, took part in a forum on the ordination of women priests. He spoke against the practice, sat down and fell dead. Some felt that She had taken revenge.] We lost the arbitration, but kept the members.

The conversion of the *Knickerbocker News* union–around thirty-five members--was a different matter. The management began mistreating some of the older district managers, who looked around and saw no protection, and no prospective leaders. They talked to Chris Cunningham, a display advertising salesman at the *Knick* who had become local president. He asked me to help. The paper insisted on a formal proceeding through the National Labor Relations Board. The international Guild picked up the tab and considered it another bargain.

As a local bargainer, I had set two short-term goals: first, moving the top minimum salary for reporters and so on up to and even past the printers' scale, and second, starting a pension plan. The Guild convention mandates set much higher goals for salaries, and we always included them in our proposal for a new contract. Once though, I told management we would come down from that high request: "We'll settle for a living wage." Robb asked, "What do you consider a living wage?" I told him, "Oh, not much, just enough to pay the bills and have a little walkaround money." He reacted in mock (?) horror, "My God, we could never afford that." Thus ended our little levity. In the meantime, we concentrated on closing the several dollar advantage the printers enjoyed. The current state, I argued, was like paying stenographers more than their bosses. I don't know how well that went down with the printers. Persistence paid. Eventually, we also achieved a pension plan that was paid entirely by the company. It didn't provide much of a pension because it didn't have much going into it. [Some time after I left the paper, a real pension plan for all employees was put into effect. It was a true benefit plan, whose payments were based on years of service and final average salary. My first payment, in 1983, was sixty dollars a month. When my fellow reporter John Maguire heard about it, he told me, "Christ, Doc, that isn't even wine money for you." He was right. The payment has since grown to about two hundred eleven dollars a month; my wine bill has dwindled.]

Late in my stay at the *Times-Union*, Herb Haas, a crusty old-timer whose lexicon did not include charm, retired as business manager and a young man named Roy Anderson succeeded him. Anderson just overflowed with charm of the Dale Carnegie variety. The first time we met, he expressed pleasure at meeting me, and said, "I've heard you're a near-genius." I replied, "Thank you, Mr. Anderson, but I wouldn't say that." I paused while he marveled at my modesty, and added, "I wouldn't say near."

A Kind of Reunion

At another of our friendly get-togethers, Bob Danzig, who was being groomed for something big—hereditary successor to Gene Robb, it turned out—chided me when I kept referring to his side of the table as "management." In the best Dale Carnegie manner, he told me, "Doc, you have to remember that there is a man in management." In my best Italian, I said, "Yes, Bob, and there's a *managg'* in management too." Dale Carnegie did not teach a damn word in Italian, so Bob did not understand me. [In August 2002, while I was standing on a ramp at the Saratoga Performing Arts Center, a fleshy, tanned man greeted me, and quickly added, Bob Danzig. Good thing, for he didn't look like the Bob Danzig I remembered. He introduced me to a companion, Time Union Publisher David White, as "an active Guild president and an honorable one. An honorable one, that's important." Thank you Bob.]

❑

Not all my efforts had been successful. In the late 1950s, when the easy-going old classified ad manager at the *Knickerbocker News* retired, the paper replaced him with a younger man, from out of town, who instituted strict procedures. The telephone solicitors (an odd title for a bunch of mostly young women) plotted his early downfall. One of them, a pretty little brunette, who should, in homage to the cliché, have been a blonde, asked for an extra day off. To observe Yom Kippur, she said. The new boss wouldn't permit it. A grievance ensued, and then an arbitration. We were doing well with our portrayal of the boss as a mean man who arbitrarily refused to grant an employee time off to worship on the holiest day of her faith. Until I asked her a key question: "What was the occasion for which you wanted the day off?" I knew the correct answer would make our case. Her reaction was a blank stare. Seconds passed, and so did our case. She batted her eyes and said, "I don't remember." That's all she said.

In 1964, the strike we had so often prepared for materialized. I had been diselected as local president, and I was not involved in the negotiations, so the imminence of a strike caught me by surprise. The Guild had set up a strike fund and rented a strike headquarters and all the reporters boycotted bylines, as we had done before. We did it in the spirit of Harvey Kelly's tenet: "I can't give you anything; you've got to take it away from me." Planning publicly for a strike was usually enough to "take it away." The closest call I remember was a year when only a couple of issues remained on the table and I went out to the newsroom to rally the troops, while management recessed to reconsider its position. Management came back with a concession we could agree to. Very fortunate. I had trouble keeping a straight face about calling people out on a night when the temperature already had fallen to seven degrees.

We Lose 1964 in 1962

The seeds for the 1964 strike were sown in negotiations in 1962 for the prior contract. I entered them at the last minute, as an observer. Just a few loose ends remained, principally deciding when higher minimum salaries would take effect for a few jobs that had been reclassified. Fred Jones, an IR from Toronto who was our chief negotiator, insisted that the increases had to go back to the end of the prior contract. Joe Casey, a local lawyer whom the *Times-Union* had inherited in its purchase of the *Knickerbocker News*, misread his notes and said that had been agreed to. Robb sat at the end of his table, fuming over Casey's mistake. I had a foreboding that Robb was going to get even if he lost that issue and I whispered to Jones to pull back. He did not, so we won our point.

When the 1964 bargaining began, the *Times-Union* had a new lawyer, Robert L. Jones III. Robert Jones the Turd was a large man who had a reputation for seeking not just to out-bargain a union, but to destroy it. He lived up to his reputation. Fred Jones returned as the Guild's spokesman. The talks dawdled on, as usual, well into the fall. Finally, on the Saturday before Thanksgiving, the strike was to go to a vote. The meeting was delayed a couple of times, and most of the members present prepared for the vote at Russell's Beach (officially Ed's Bar). So intense were the preparations that the cash register broke down and the bartender Mike Quain was compelled to pile the cash on the back bar. The vote was spiritedly unanimous: strike NOW. So, as the Sunday paper started rolling off the press, we mounted a picket line. We interfered with the paper delivery but didn't stop it. Our timing was impressively lousy. By that time the paper had in house all the ads that plumped up the Thanksgiving Day issue beyond belief.

It was not until we were out that everyone became aware that we had no support from the other unions for reasons that we should have known all along. Incidents a year earlier, in Albany and in Toronto. In Albany, the stereotypers had staged a wildcat strike during the workday, then asked for support from the Guild. The timing made it impossible for us to vote. I assured the strikers, though, that we would not permit the company to put out a paper. The company had not been prepared for the wildcat, so the stereotypers won their point, whatever it was. In 1964, they did not remember my assurance. In Toronto, the printers union had struck the two major papers and the Guild local there had been unable to respect the picket lines, because of Ontario labor law. The Albany printers remembered the lack of support, but not the Ontario law.

We were out alone, but we acted tough. That first night, we resorted to belly-to-butt picketing to mess up distribution of the Sunday paper..

Block that Paper Truck

On Monday, the second full day of the strike, I was at strike headquarters when a call came for reinforcements: "They're trying to move in a truckload of newsprint." All of us dashed down the hill to line up belly-to-butt three or four across in front of the delivery door on Sheridan Avenue. The truck driver, a member of the Teamsters union, was about to back the load into the plant. It was a delicate move at best, because a telephone pole across the street limited his maneuvering. The company had called on the police to clear a path, but we would not be moved. I found myself in the front rank as the driver backed the truck a ways, then unbacked it, time and again. As he did so, I came into contact with one of the cops. I kept my hands in the slash pockets of my jacket and kind of bellied him. He bellied back. He said, "If you keep this up, I'll have to arrest you." I said, "Arrest

me if you want to, but we're not going to let that paper in."
We repeated our frank and cordial exchange several times,
until the driver, pleading frazzled nerves, pulled his truck to
the opposite curb and walked away. The cops departed too,
and one of my comrades told me that my adversary was John
Cody. Damn! John Cody was fists-down the roughest cop on
a world class rough force. (That evening a nonunion boss at
the trucking company came, the cops cleared a path through
a few pickets, and the paper was delivered.) We never tried
another blockade.

A night or so later, we received unexpected help
from the fire department. Moments before the four delivery
trucks were ready to leave the dock, a hook and ladder truck
rolled up, and parked spang across the trucks' exit. The
firemen left it there while they conducted the longest search
in the history of local bomb scares. That took care of one
day's *Times-Union* deliveries. A few nights later, a couple of
striking ad salesmen took care of part of the circulation by
following a delivery truck on its rounds and picking up every
bundle it had dropped off.

All these dustups were cited as Violent Incidents
by Robert Jones the Turd when he sought a court order
limiting our picketing; the judge issued the order. A few
days later, on Saturday night—the end of the second week—
we were reinforced by a large group of Papermakers' Union
members, who set up an automobile picket line and took part
in a massive snake dance in the middle of Sheridan Avenue.
The visitors' leader, Crazy Frank Mendez, brandishing a
linoleum knife, asked "Where are the fucking scabs' cars?"
We had no idea.. All our activity was in vain; the *Times-
Union* had shifted its delivery operation to the Union Station
baggage room, where there were no pickets. We certainly
were lacking in intelligence. Information too.

We also were lacking in bright moments. The brightest
occurred while we were in court. Our lawyer Art McGinn
was seeking information for a counter-attack. Robb had been

keeping out of sight, afraid he might be required to produce information about the American Newspaper Publishers Association's strike preparation. McGinn's process server gave Robb's people the impression that he was from the ANPA, and was ushered into the gleaming white office. Robb greeted him and couldn't avoid the subpoena. Instantly, Robb shouted, "Who let that man in here? Get him out of here!" We played and replayed that story all afternoon. It took some of the pain from the injunction.

One more Violent Incident occurred after that. Late one night, two reporters, Bill Hogan and Johnny Cowe, sneaked through an alleyway off Columbia Street, on the hill behind the plant, and came within a stone's throw of a pressroom window. They threw the stone, or two, through the glass, and lit out. As they ran back through the alleyway they shouted "Get those kids! Get those kids!" Tom Rourke, a regular maintenance man who was working as a security guard, was nearby. He told them, "There aren't any kids; now get your asses out of here." Tom did not get tough with us; he was also a city alderman. That incident inspired the *Times-Union* to build a new plant a few years later on a more secure site in the suburbs. Robb told several people, *that will never happen again.*

I had not been involved in negotiations, and I was unaware of the flimsy nature of the strike issues: mainly work shifts for circulation drivers. A few other issues, but not enough to strike for. Our real motive was the buildup of unassuaged detestation of several layers of management.

Without asking anyone, I phoned a State Labor Department official who had been a Guild member in Buffalo, and asked him to assign a more aggressive and more labor-oriented mediator to the settlement efforts. The man he sent was very helpful in achieving a settlement close to what we might have had without a strike, if we also had been without Jones the Turd and Jones the Fred. (The state official left town before the strike was settled. So did his secretary. His wife stayed behind.) The meeting for the vote to approve the settlement was momentous. Among the reporters it drew was the new Albany correspondent for *The New York Times*, R.W. (Johnny) Apple Jr. The strike inspired the reporter Bill Kennedy to make his debut as the novelist William Kennedy with *The Ink Truck*. It was not a very good novel, but then it hadn't been a very good strike.

Even after I left the paper in 1967, I remained in touch with the Guild. The Empire State District Council, which I had had a hand in founding, held a commemorative meeting in Albany. I attended and found only a couple of familiar faces. In 1983, the local Guild celebrated its fiftieth anniversary with a dinner. Janet Scott was a guest of honor, in tribute to her being present at the creation. No one—not even I--mentioned my role in the Guild's successful stand against Gannett's forces of evil back in 1937.

My final involvement—well, so far—was in an arbitration case about leave for Guild service. Despite the clear language of the contract, the company had denied a request by the local president for leave so he could help organize the Glens Falls *Post-Star*. Those people needed a union; many were paid so little that they qualified for food stamps. When I responded to a subpoena, the only people I knew in the room were Tom Brennan, by then in his eighties and still looking like V.M. Molotov, and Larry Goddeau, also over eighty, the resident controller in my time. I greeted them rather warmly. Then, for the first time, I met the Guild people who had talked to me by phone. The hearing already had dragged on for several days. I testified that I had taken leave for Guild purposes several times, for conventions, for the council meeting that had led to my suspension, and to work three years as contracts analyst. The arbitrator ruled for the Guild. By the time he ruled, no prospects remained at the Glens Falls *Post-Star*.

Encountering Fame

My Guild career led me to brief encounters with fame. Not my fame, but the reflected fame of others. And for even longer than the fifteen minutes that Andy Warhol said each of us could expect. I enjoyed a whole evening of fame in 1945 in New York City, thanks to Howie Weiman, a copyreader for the *Times-Union*. Howie, a New Yorker who also had Tuesday and Wednesday off, talked me into joining him, and a couple of hundred paying guests, at a party the New York local was throwing to raise funds for a leftish candidate for national Guild president: an editorial writer from Boston. His rightish opponent was an entertainment writer from Memphis. What a choice! The New York local had no trouble enticing an all-star cast of entertainers and potables to match the notables. Performers like Danny Kaye (or an impersonator thereof), Susan Reid, the zitherist/folk singer and a beauty, and Jan Clayton, who had the second lead in *Carousel*, recently opened on Broadway.

Jan apologized briefly for not having been provided a blockbuster song in *Carousel*. Then she sang a ditty whose refrain was *It's not that I wouldn't; Lord knows it's not that I couldn't, I'm just the laziest girl in town.* A great performance. She added a couple of her songs from *Carousel.* As soon as she took a break I was at her side. The dance band was playing. I don't dance because I can't dance. Except when I have had enough drinks to forget that I can't dance. I had had enough drinks, so I asked Jan to dance. She was in my arms. Closely. She danced beautifully, making up for my deficiency. Between dances, Howie joined us. Jan and I danced and talked and Howie just talked. As the evening ended in early morning, Jan told me, "I enjoyed meeting you. I haven't been fed such a line since I was in high school." She sounded pleased. I assured her that what I said was real; I wouldn't even know how to spin a line. She still looked pleased, but not convinced.

The next time I saw Jan Clayton was on television twenty-five or thirty years later. After a life of much travail she had found a new niche, playing the mother on *Lassie*. She still looked quite danceable.

In 1952 at the Guild convention in Portland, Oregon, I next got close to fame. Not as close as to Jan Clayton, nor as much fun. The convention's featured speaker was the president of the Screen Actors' Guild and he gave us the full five-ninety-five oratorical treatment about his exploits in recently driving the Communists out of leadership. in his union. The American Newspaper Guild had done so in 1941. After dinner, I joined the reception line and shook hands with him and murmured some ambiguous comment about his talk. My only encounter with Ronald Reagan.

Fame and glamour crossed my path again in 1954. at the convention in Los Angeles, just a few streets from Hollywood. Among the movie people who came to the opening cocktail party was Kim Novak, accompanied by a male starlet named John Smith. No place to dance, so I had to be content just to talk. Nothing romantic; I was a married man. I offered to buy her a drink from the champagne fountain. I took a couple for myself. I had a brief conversation with John Smith, who was almost as pretty as Kim. I asked him what name he used when he registered at a hotel with a woman not his wife. He gave me a pretty look, but blank.

On balance, my time in the Guild was a success and fun. But I missed out on something. In my early years, my elders warned me against the Communist leaders of the New York local. "They have young women who try to use sex to subvert people like you." It never happened. Damn!

My Career of Note

Newspapering ain't what it used to be. Some of us think it never was. The immediate cause of this cliché, and of my getting ahead of the story again, was a visit by a reporter for the *Times Union* to interview me about my life and times when I was about to retire in 1989 as a public relations officer for New York State, after a career of twenty-plus years on top of a couple of other careers. He plopped a tape recorder on my desk--"you don't mind, do you?"--and whipped out a spiral bound notebook and began asking questions.

When I was a reporter, a lot of us didn't take many notes, just enough to be correct about spellings, or addresses, or numbers, or fancy words. I felt, as Yogi Berra did about hitting, you can't think and take notes at the same time. I also felt that if you can't remember it, it isn't worth using. I had role models for my non-notetaking: the sports columnist Frank Graham, who used to write all those sparkling pieces about the repartee around the batting practice cage, and *The New Yorker* writers John McNulty and A.J. Liebling and Joseph Mitchell, who found all those delightful, typical but unusual characters in places like Bellevue Hospital and Madison Square Garden and McSorley's Old Ale House. Think they could have got those beautiful quotes if they pulled out a tape recorder and spiral notebook? I knew the answer to that. (It turns out that I was wrong. At least about Joseph Mitchell. I've just reread his *New Yorker* pieces in the book *Up in the Old Hotel*, and he keeps mentioning his notes and even refers to opening a file drawer. Damn! Is there no legend we can trust any more?) Oh, these notable memories aren't quite as dependable as I recalled. Now that I have gone looking through some of my old stories on microfilm, I find that I must have taken more notes than I cared to remember, or to recall.

One of the first stories I covered when I reresumed reporting in 1961 proved that you really can't think and take notes at the same time. It was a messily complex story about a family that detected strange sounds and smells and general goings-on in their home that was directly opposite (but some distance from) a General Electric site where some secret research was in progress. They had complained about the strange stuff and some engineers and technicians from an Army research unit came to look into the problem. I took notes, lots of notes, about hearing (the family could detect sounds in the dog whistle range) and ozone and various other stuff. When I began writing, I had a large number of facts but no clear idea what they meant. The story wasn't very good.

Trusting Memory, Or Notes

In other stories, I also tested my theory that if something is important enough to use, I'd remember it. This proof consisted of taking some notes, not many, and starting to write without referring to them, and then, after a sentence of so, sneaking a look at the notes. Invariably, I had remembered stuff that was worth using, but it didn't always mesh with my notes. Memory was much more colorful. Which to use? I tried to do the right thing.

A few colleagues took copious notes. Dick Lewis, for one, earned most of his living as a shorthand court reporter and moonlighted as a reporter for the *Times-Union*. He took verbatim notes, all in shorthand, just as he did in court. That was just reflex for him. One year, when the office provided him with a wire recorder--a primitive predecessor of the tape recorder--he used it for a series of weekly Q and A interviews. The machine was too big and heavy to carry on routine stories and just as well. The verbatim stuff Dick produced was accurate. But his subjects were often dull. The machine gave out just about the time the managing editor's attention span did.

We didn't have fancy spiral bound notebooks, either. We could have had the notebooks, but the paper wouldn't buy them, so we didn't. What we took notes on was a handful of copy paper. (Copy paper, for the benefit of those brought up in paperless offices, was produced by chopping the unused ends of rolls of newsprint into roughly eight-and-a-half by eleven-inch sheets. The chopping did not always produce neat oblongs; we held the oblique paper for, we joked, slanted stories. We also occasionally had yellow copy paper for, of course, yellow journalism.) A bundle of those sheets, folded three ways to fit into a coat pocket or the palm of a hand, was our notebook.

So, What Goes Where

Some times, we would write notes for two or three stories--a whole afternoon's work--on the one bunch of sheets. When we began writing, what notes went with what story? I ran into a problem that way when I went out to get comment on a couple of wonderful education reforms that Governor Rockefeller had just proposed. When I sat down to type the stories, I got one comment about a complicated teachers' salary proposal (bad) into a story about expanding state aid for schools (good). The copyreader magnified my mistake by writing a bold type crosshead **Proposal a Monstrosity** just above a boldface paragraph about an official's unofficial criticism of the salary plan. Next day, the Education Commissioner issued a bland statement that the quotation didn't reflect official policy. I was assured that he wasn't upset by my mistake.

We never preserved a file of our notes; at least nobody I knew did. Sometimes we retained a day or two's notes for more worthwhile purposes. Like keeping the jelly in jelly doughnuts from oozing onto the desk, or, for the more fastidious, keeping the desk from contaminating the jelly. I also found a pile of notes on my desk useful in avoiding stories I'd rather not write. "I'd love to do it, Wes," I'd tell the city editor, "but I've got all these stories to put together for the first edition. Sorry." That would send him off looking for a reporter with a clean desk.

My main reason for not filing notes was that I didn't have any place to file them. Desk drawers were too valuable for that. One time when I had to clean my desk in preparation for moves by a new city editor, I found mine crowded with valuable things; much more valuable than notes on a story already written. Such as a pair of cutdown long pants in case the air-conditioning failed, a twelve-year-old appointment book with no appointments, a three-year-old state Executive Budget, a couple of leaflets about the Wicks Act governing public construction contracts (still valid forty years later), a turbid booklet on teaching reading by the phonics method, a couple of file folders labeled *Fertilizer* and containing some speeches by Governor Rockefeller. Most important: a beer stein souvenir from an American Newspaper Guild convention and two anonymous shot glasses, all of which expressed my version of the law of beverages.

Take Notes? You Kidding?

We found--we often used that plural pronoun to spread the blame when we meant I--lots of good reasons for not taking notes. Often it wasn't smart to. One summer's evening, for example, I dashed to the scene of a reported shooting, a fatal one, in a neighborhood so tense that the night chief detective spoke to me only in passing. No notes in public view, but I wandered about the crime scene, listening to the cops interview the perpetrator about how many shots he had fired and why. The answers were "two" and "he threw something at me; I thought he was trying to get me." (One of the shots went right into the middle of the victim's forehead.) Then I went around the corner under a streetlight and put down a few words. Afterward I wondered whom I thought I was kidding: except for the cops, I was the only white guy in the block and I didn't look like a cop.

Even in friendlier surroundings there often were notable reasons not to take notes. It might be just too dark, as when a university president spoke with unaccustomed candor before a student gathering in a coffee house where the only illumination came from a tiny candle in the middle of each table; if I held the paper close enough to read I might set it afire. Or the paper might be too wet to hold the pencil marks, as I first learned when covering high school football in the rain, and confirmed when invited by a fire chief to inspect the ruins while the hoses were still splashing the vicinity. Or I might just have dashed out with a photographer, but no pencil, when the fire bell rang (the photographer probably had a pencil, but he was always somewhere else), Or to protect a source from reprisals by the TV news crews. That happened in 1965, on a hot night in a long hot summer of racial strife in Troy. The city manager Bob Stierer had announced that he would not give TV interviews. I met him as he patrolled the streets, and he said No interview. I said, No interview; I just want to talk to you a couple of minutes. We talked. When a TV crew approached, I said, "OK, if you don't want to be interviewed, I'll get the information somewhere else." The TV crew believed me. Until they saw the paper in the morning.

There was another pretty good reason, you know, of course, for not taking, like, comprehensive notes for quotes. We just couldn't take down every one of the yuhnos and uhcoses people said. That is, like, I mean.

Oh, Just Make It Up

Some of my colleagues in those distant days didn't need any notes; they just made things up. When assigned to be The Inquiring Reporter, Al Rockefeller, a reporter I had worked with in Troy, often went, with a photographer, to a grubby drinking spot called the World's Fair, and, while sipping at the bar, invented the answerers and their answers. Oh, the former were real in a way; Al just fancied up their titles: a former porter (janitor) became an exporter, a bartender a wine merchant, a snow shoveler a pathologist, and so on. Dick Powers, who relished The Inquiring Reporter assignment--it was his entire day's output--had a different technique: he used real names and real identifications, but he made up the answers, being careful to phone each person to read the answer. Since his answer always was classy, the answerer never objected.

I'm not sure how much faking Johnny Cowe engaged in, but one sample is instructive. Johnny came to us from England by way of Jamaica and became, for a time, the transportation writer. He wrote a piece quoting a truck driver as saying in substance "I'm a Republican from Georgia and I've driven a lorry for twenty-five years. I really enjoy moving the wreckage from the homes of all these Democrats." Republican from Georgia? In the sixties? Lorry driver? The diligent copy editor let the full quote get into the paper!

No Notes, No Problem

None of the people I wrote no-notes stories about objected that I had misquoted them. To the contrary, they uniformly praised my stories, sometimes lavishly so. Perhaps they really felt that way. But I often had the sneaking suspicion that they were loath to object, for fear that I'd then begin quoting them exactly. That sort of thing happened recently (in the nineties). A reporter accused by a politician of misquoting him retaliated by meticulously reproducing the complainant's speech, the garbled grammar, the skewed syntax and the mixed metaphors, but to no avail. The politician never noticed and most readers thought it was the reporter who was deficient in English. The people I quoted knew the difference.

Back to Reporting

I resumed my reporting career–if I may count my experience in Troy in the 1930s--in the fall of 1955, when I returned from my tour with the Newspaper Guild. There had been some changes made during my absence. After George Williams died in 1952, Bert Bearup was named managing editor as a nearly final act by Fred Archibald as publisher. Gene Robb came from Hearst's lobbying office in Washington to succeed Archibald and inherited Bearup, among others. (Shortly after Williams died, while I was working for the Guild, I visited Jerry Walker, the old city editor of the *Knickerbocker Press,* at his office as editor of the trade paper *Editor & Publisher.* We had a cordial talk and Walker told me, among other things, that he had urged Archibald to leave the selection of a managing editor to his successor. Robb quickly established a base as a power in Albany civic circles, brought in circulation and advertising directors, but it was to take him seven years to put his man in as managing editor.)

Bearup greeted me with the news that he was moving me to the city staff. He didn't say why; I didn't ask. Later, I learned that Walsh had given Bearup an ultimatum: *it's him or me as sports editor.* I showed a little *pro forma* displeasure, but I had decided that I did not want to become a latter-day Dick Walsh or Peerless McGrath or Charley Young. Bearup made me feel right at home, with the same shift I had had on the sports desk: 5 p.m. to 2 a.m., with Tuesday and Wednesday off. The work was mostly dull puttering, except on Saturday and Sunday when Ray O'Connor, the night city editor, was off.

O'Connor had been the hero, twenty-five years earlier, in the coverage of the Legs Diamond murder. The years had treated Ray badly. His wife died young; he was drafted by the Army despite his chronically sore feet (he soon was undrafted); he drank a lot. By 1955, he had lost a few teeth which enhanced the lantern jaw, and, though generally lean looking, he had developed a paunch. He was irascible at best, and was not at his best after a lunchtime spent at Ed's Bar. I had little to do: update some item left hanging by the dayside, check the police at 6 o'clock and again around midnight. If the late police rounds turned up a crime short of murder or a car crash short of fatal, O'Connor usually asked, *white or black?* White, maybe a paragraph or two; black, forget it.

A Historic Decision

[O'Connor achieved more city room fame in 1961, after Governor Rockefeller's oldest son Michael disappeared while on an anthropological study mission in New Guinea. The Governor decided to fly there to supervise the search for his son and the press office called the *Times-Union* to ask if someone wanted to go along. Without asking anyone, without a second thought, probably without even a first thought, he said "Nobody gives a shit about that." The Governor's office took it as a show of no interest.]

Weekends, when he was off, I could cover a story or two. I even wrote an editorial for Bearup in which I urged a hit and run driver whose car had killed a young girl to give himself up. Beautiful writing. Compelling. A few days later, on a Sunday, he gave up. A successful appeal? No. He hadn't even seen it. Dick Lewis covered the final chapter and called in his story to me; we shared a byline, but I'm not sure why I got credit. Another Sunday, the police had an interesting story: a motorist had tried to flee the scene of an accident but left a trail of leaking radiator fluid that the cops followed to make an arrest. The desk sergeant explained, "That should take care of people who say we couldn't track an elephant with bleeding piles in a snowstorm." I sanitized it to *a bleeding trunk*. It made a neat light item for the bottom of Page 1.

On Election Night, I was called in to cover the voting in Troy, at Republican headquarters, because that party was expected to win. Unaccustomed to such matters, I made myself at home amid the party's vote counters, the only reporter on the inside, and learned quickly that the Republican had lost the mayoralty by two hundred fifty-eight votes. Another night, I made a call to update a story John Maguire had written about Governor W. Averell Harriman's proclamation of National Poetry Day. I had to ask how the governor spent the day; he had read prose. Maguire won one hundred dollars in that month's Hearst national writing contest, and he gave me a bottle of good five-dollar liquor as my share. Other weekends, I took advantage of the laxity of a colleague and wrote *The Roamer* column, mostly about Star Boarder.

Star Boarder was not a figment of imagination, but my son Guy, age two and a half. He inspired the columns which I wrote with no advance notice to fill a void left when the real Roamer, a reporter named George Murphy, failed to turn in his column copy on time. After the first couple of columns about Star Boarder appeared, George filed an objection: "All my friends know I've got two daughters and they can't understand why the column refers to a son." I offered a simple solution, rather two of them. One: turn your stuff in on time, or, two, tell your friends you're using your imagination.

An Award-Winning Editor

Six months passed, and I was getting used to the boredom of the city desk, so Bearup told me he wanted me to move to the copy desk. Just for a few months, he said, to strengthen the desk. Having observed the copyreaders, I felt that working there must be duller than working with Ray O'Connor. I explored my options and found there weren't any, so in the spring of 1956 I became a copyreader. One consolation: I'd be on the 2 to 11 p.m. shift, which meant I could go home for dinner each night. The few months ended in September 1961.

Bearup had brought Ed Nowinski from Syracuse to succeed him as the slot man on the copy desk; in practice he was the news editor, with responsibility for selecting the local and wire stories, determining the headline play, and designing the pages. (The slot man sat in the opening of the horseshoe shaped copy desk; the copyreaders sat around the outer edge and were known as rim men. No women on our copy desk.) A copyreader edited the material and wrote headlines. By lunch break at 6 o'clock, I generally handled thirty to thirty-five items, some of them short ones, for the first edition; after lunch, somewhere between eight and twelve. No one else handled as much.

Nowinski had been out of newspapering for a few years. He held a couple of jobs—running a candle factory and being a bagman for the ruling Republican Party in Syracuse. The latter job got him into trouble with the IRS, which claimed that some of the money he collected had stuck to his fingers and he had not declared it as income. While his case was in court, Ed asked me about local banking practices, specifically about the charges for a checking account. I told him that anyone who carried a minimum balance of a couple of hundred bucks got free checking service. He snickered; he carried a minimum balance of a couple of thousand, right in his pocket. When he appeared in court under a plea deal, he paid his fine in cash, right out of that pocket. Several thousand.

Forecasting an Air Crash

I had been on the desk only a few months when on a Saturday afternoon—it was June 30, 1956; I looked it up the Associated Press carried a short out of Los Angeles about an airliner being overdue on a flight east. In minutes, another brief item: a plane out of San Francisco for the east also was overdue. I dug out the office atlas, a smudged and dog-eared volume, and applied a ruler to what I figured was the flight path of each plane. They crossed near the Grand Canyon. I told Nowinski what was coming. Within minutes, the AP filed a new report: a TWA Super Constellation and a United DC 7 jet had collided while circling to give everyone a better view of the Grand Canyon; a hundred and twenty-eight dead. Nowinski gave me the story to handle. And a lot more followed.

The quality of the articles I handled grew to match the quantity. Nowinski began to hand me, every day, the wire service reports of two or three major stories, and to ask me "What's the best story?" At the outset, I'd say, "Depends on what else you've got." After a couple of such responses, he made it clear that I had all the top stories and would get all the best stories, and he left it up to me to grade them for him. I became assistant news editor without portfolio and without extra pay. I loved it.

One Memorial Day, Nowinski left early and told me to take over the final edition. He had selected two photos of the collapse of photographers' scaffolding at the Indianapolis raceway and placed them on Page 2. My first move was to expand each by another column and move them to Page 1, in the spirit of George Williams and William Randolph Hearst. That move required other changes and I added a few that were not required. Next day, Nowinski complimented me and said, " I was going to move those pictures out front for the final." I told him that I had figured he would. I think I was as truthful as he was.

In the fall of 1959, I received an invitation about a new job. I was not unhappy at the *Times-Union*, but it seemed an opportunity for a raise of twenty-five dollars (or more) a week. John Thompson, an old Guild colleague (he had been an international vice president) met me at a Guild function and asked if I knew anyone interested in a tryout (for pay) at the Boston *Traveler* copydesk where he worked. I told him, "Yeah, I am." He got me an invitation to try out on my days off. One catch: the shift started at 6 a.m., an hour when I was more used to getting home than getting up. But John invited me to stay at his house in Quincy and he drove me to work each day. Made breakfast for me too. It was like the desk at the *Times-Union*. The first couple of hours were hectic--I logged thirty-five items for that period--but the rest of the day was relaxed. It was fun.

In. Out—Four Sentences

About midway of the second day, Al Williams, the copy desk chief, and I set a speed record--four sentences--for entry to exit interview. He said, as he had the day before, "It's great to have a pro over there," and added, "I'd like you to come to work for me." I thought of the prospect of a quick raise, of two nosy brothers-in-law living near Boston, of our nine apartments in nine years, and said, "I'd like to, but I want to talk to my wife first," Al snorted and said, "I'd be damned if I'd let my wife decide where I worked." I took that as a withdrawal of the offer. I stayed at the *Times-Union;* the *Traveler* folded a few years later.

In the meantime, I had become a prize-winning headline writer. On Thanksgiving Eve of 1958, when I was filling in on the late desk, I came upon an AP story about the birth of a boy on a vessel that plied the St. Lawrence River between New York State and Ontario; the mother had named the child for the boat. I dropped the story into a small spot at the bottom of Page 1, with the headline: **This Little Boy Has/A Ferry Godfather.** It turned out to be a profitable Thanksgiving. Bearup entered it in the Hearst writing contest. The judge found it worth a hundred bucks. The pun, he noted, "was not strained." But I had had to look to the final paragraph for the headline.

Mission Implausible

On November 2, 1959, Nowinski handed me another opportunity to become a prize-winning editor, but I didn't appreciate it at the time. He pushed over the usual sheaf of copy and asked, as usual, which was best. No question. That was the day Charles VanDoren, who had been unbelievably successful on the television quiz show *Twenty-One,* admitted in court, after many denials outside, that his performance had not been believable, that he had been given the answers and coached in his suspenseful responses. Nowinski already had drawn the dummy for Page 1 and had left space for a five-column two-line headline on the main story—one that allowed only seventeen and a half units of letters and spaces to a line. How did he expect anyone to crowd all that into thirty-five units? But what the hell! If he wants that kind of head, I'll give it to him. I didn't even think of words like VanDoren, or quiz show, or admits guilt. Too many letters. After a minute or so, I visualized a couple of lines and wrote: ***VanD at Last Gives/The Right Answers.*** It fit. I handed it to Nowinski with the edited copy. He barely glanced at either.

Bearup did more than glance and entered it in the monthly Hearst Newspapers writing contest. The judge noted the "sardonic" nature of the head and awarded me the top prize of one hundred dollars, just in time for Christmas. (That wasn't the most sardonic head I wrote. I favor the one I put on a story about a false alarm of the death of Nikita Khrushchev. That read: **A Good Story Is Spoiled by the Facts.**)

Nearly a year later, I got another check, for five hundred dollars, for the year's best headline, about VanD. Gene Robb sent me the official notice of all the annual awards and wrote on it: "I couldn't be more pleased if I'd won it myself & I need it. Congratulations."

By the time I received that annual award, I had become officially the acting news editor. I received the news of my promotion in mid-September 1960 in Washington where, on vacation time, I was handling media relations for the newly merged United Papermakers and Paperworkers Union. Dan Button, who had been editorial writer when I left Albany, phoned and said "I've just been appointed executive editor, and I want you to come back as soon as you can to take over the copy desk." I flew back the next day. Bearup and Nowinski also had been on vacation when Robb gave Button overall control of the newsroom and named Jack Leary managing editor. Leary had been editing miscellaneous pages: real estate, youth activities, and the like. Bearup became the associate editor with unspecified duties. Nowinski became the dayside copy editor, handling canned features and other junk.

A Sunday Paper, for Sure

I came directly to the newsroom from my evening flight from Washington Thursday and stayed. Not a line of copy had been processed for Sunday's paper. I started right away. By the end of work Friday, I knew there would be a Sunday paper. It turned out to be a different paper, right from Page One. The AP moved a human-interest story about a woman who had clambered down a well to rescue her child and I played it above the main story. Robb, Button and Leary thought it was great. So did I. But the news pages were still wrapped inside the comic section.

Though my title was acting, Button told me to take charge of getting the paper out. My salary also seemed to be acting; I got a substantial raise, but only as simulated overtime. In the event, I worked most of the time anyway. A week or so into my new job, Button and Leary invited me to join them for a Sunday breakfast at a Howard Johnson. They planned to change city editors and asked my opinion of their prime suspect. I gave them an honest, and unfavorable, evaluation–in confidence, I thought. A few days later, the guy involved told me what I had said about him. He was most unhappy. I had to pay for my breakfast too.

In my evenings on the rim, one of my colleagues noticed that I was handling all the big stories and, between editions, said, "You ought to be in there"–he pointed to the slot. I did not disagree, but I said, "The trouble with my being in there is that I wouldn't have me out here." How prophetic! Button brought in a friend of his from Troy to be a copyreader. A nice guy. No doubt bright. But he couldn't write a headline right. When I asked for a three-line head, he wrote two lines, and vice versa. I told Button his guy was not cut out to be a copyreader; Button made him the editorial writer. Another young man had difficulty writing even the one-line or two-line headline on a short item; each time he looked upward, as if for heavenly guidance. I looked up too and told him, "I hope you can see the headline up there; I can't." He stayed and improved under my not divine guidance. Still looked upward though.

The Knick News Cometh

Within a couple of weeks after my ascension, Hearst bought the *Knickerbocker News* from Gannett. A general moving around and the *Knickerbocker* people moved into the *Times-Union* building on Sheridan Avenue. Now that he was right nearby, Hal VanLoan, the *Knick* news editor, complained, "You aren't leaving me any stories. It's tough finding something to lead the first edition with." I was not sympathetic. Van Loan eventually left to become an editor with *Pacific Stars & Stripes* in Tokyo. Took up with a Japanese lady too.

The presidential campaign dominated the news in the fall of 1960 and Button was worried that we might be accused of favoring one candidate over the other. Especially when the candidates, John F. Kennedy and Richard M. Nixon, appeared in our area a few days apart. He instructed me to be sure that we had a precise balance in space, down to the inch. I did not measure the coverage that closely. What they did was what they got. It turned out fairly even after all.

On Election Night, I nearly pulled a *Chicago Tribune*– you remember: **Dewey Defeats Truman**. The 1960 race was extremely close; on Election Night, no news organization was projecting who'd win. As the deadline for the regular final edition neared, Jack Stein, the circulation director, insisted that we had to have a winner in our banner headline, no matter what. With minutes to spare, the Associated Press carried a bulletin: the *New York Times* was calling Kennedy the apparent winner. So I gave Stein his winner, hedged with a kicker line: New York Times Projects. Then the long wait for our Sunrise Edition that went to press about 2:30 a.m. I don't know where Button and Leary were; they hadn't come to the desk and I was too busy tracking the shifting margins to go to them. A little after 1:30 a.m., I closed the Sunrise edition with a big, black and bold: **Kennedy Elected**. I had written the lead story from wire service reports. It had a Washington dateline, and a positive flair in bold type:

Senator John F. Kennedy swept to the presidency early today.

At 1:30 a.m., EST, he had nailed down 272 electoral votes to 132 for Nixon.

It takes 269 electoral votes to win the White House and The Associated Press scorecard showed Kennedy was leading in states that would make him a winner with plenty to spare, 325 to 198.

I went home, looked at the television for a while, noticed that Kennedy's margin was not as substantial as it had appeared. It was, in my mind, still in doubt when I went to bed. I slept well; it was too late to change anything. When I got up in late morning, I went back to the television. At 11 a.m., the unofficial count was complete: Kennedy Elected. For real. No *Chicago Tribune*. The official Electoral College tally was three hundred and three to two hundred nineteen.

1956 Was Different

My tribulation in the 1960 election was partial compensation for the easy time in 1956, the only other presidential race when I was on the copy desk. Dwight Eisenhower had assumed such a lead over Adlai Stevenson (in their second matchup) that we had the winner in the regular final. That final tally was four hundred and fifty-seven to seventy-three. But we had to stay around to sew up all the results in the Sunrise Edition. Bearup was in the slot and he asked me to stay, along with King William IV*. We passed copy, headlines and King William back and forth at the desk. I noticed that, on one trip to the composing room, Bert was so burdened by King William that he had difficulty stepping over the lines between the floor tiles. I volunteered to handle the composing room chores. He took care of the good king.

A Series of Disasters

With the 1960 election out of the way, life on the desk settled into a series of catastrophes, to which I applied tabloidish display. On December 16, a TWA Super Constellation and a United Airlines DC 8 collided over New York City and killed a hundred thirty-four people in all. One boy floated down, still in his seat, into a snow bank in Brooklyn. A great photo of people trying to help him. I played it big with a caption: **Miracle in a Snowbank**. Not a true miracle: the boy had been deeply burned and lived hardly a day longer.

A month later, another plane crash and another miracle. Maybe two miracles. A Mexican Airlines DC-9 taking off from Idlewild (pre-JFK) in thick fog crashed and burned a few miles beyond the runway. Just minutes before the deadline for our limited mail edition, the AP carried a bulletin reporting that rescuers had reached the crash site and found no signs of life. That meant everybody was dead, no? With a few more short paragraphs of wire copy, I sent in a new Page 1 with a banner proclaiming a jet crash with all aboard dead. Just as the press run ended, AP sent a new lead explaining why there had been no signs of life: nearly everyone had walked away from the crash. The death toll was four, not a hundred and some. So I sent in a new headline for the final edition, two lines deep: **Idlewild Miracle/102 of 106 Survive Jet Crash.** The second miracle was that no one was aware that I had resurrected about a hundred people.

All that happened on January 19, the day before the inauguration of John F. Kennedy, the preview of which I covered in a three-column headline below the crash: **Storm Perils Inaugural.** No one mentioned the short shrift I had given the quadrennial wonder story. The storm passed and the inauguration dominated Page 1 the next day. Amid large Hearstian photos, I used ribbons of reverse print (white on black) to present some cadenced quotes from Kennedy's speech.

An Alarm From Box 32

A few weeks later, just after midnight on March 3, the Executive Mansion caught fire while the Governor and his first wife were upstairs in separate bedrooms. The alarm rang in the city room while I was on the phone with Ray Joy, a photographer who was telling me that a two-alarm fire he covered was just out and asking if we needed his pictures right then. I counted the rings on the alarm and heard the police radio announce, "Transmitting an alarm from box thirty-two, a working fire at the Executive Mansion." Ray heard it too. He beat the firemen by climbing over a locked gate, and shot pictures of the Rockefellers stranded on a portico roof with a framed painting of Nelson's father and of firemen helping them down a ladder. All this was too late for the regular final edition, but I stopped the presses after a few hundred papers had run, and waited for a fire extra. Leary (at home), rounded up a photoengraver. We produced a very good fire extra. Later on, though, Button chided me for using Ray Joy on such a big story when management was trying to get rid of him. I didn't bother explaining that Rivett's choice was a Hobson's choice. Ray lasted several weeks more. That was longer than the Rockefeller marriage lasted; the night of the fire was the last they spent under the same roof. But no one knew that for a long time.

Later in March, I put together a couple of refers—Page One items, usually a paragraph or two, that refer to long stories inside—that must have set world records for size. Early in March, the Mayor, Erastus Corning 2nd, announced plans for a grandiose urban renewal of more than three hundred acres; I played it on Sunday with a hyperbolic spread that took up the top half of Page 1, and referred to a longer story inside. A few weeks later, Governor Rockefeller asked for an appropriation of a hundred fifty thousand dollars to plan a new government center; that refer, wrapped in a photo of Albany up hill from river, was good for the top third of Page One and was larger than the story inside. The Governor's plan became a billion-dollar undertaking; the Mayor's nowhere near as big.

A Reporter for One Story

Early in the summer, the only person on the city desk told me that four young men had been killed in an auto accident, but he couldn't get the details. The final edition deadline was near, so I asked, "Why don't you go to the hospital"—where the bodies had been taken—"and get the information? I'll take care of your phones." He said he couldn't leave the desk. I was alone, too, but I went. Right at the hospital door, I met a departing State Trooper who read me his notes, all the details about the four dead teenagers and how they died: they were riding on a running board and the driver veered off the road and crushed them between the car and some trees. I phoned the city desk and dictated a story, then a headline. By the time I returned to the office, all the type had been set and I put together a new Page One. I have forgotten who was on the city desk that night. On purpose.

In running the copydesk, I was guided by experience: don't ask if you can do something, just do it. With the aid of the St. Petersburg (Florida) *Times,* I devised a couple of news spots: for small developments in long-running big stories, a corner called Continuing Stories; for mostly trivia about people, Who's News. And I set aside the whole news space on the first page of the second section for a local Feature of the Day. To make life easy for the rim men, I allowed adequate space for headlines, even to the extent of running a banner headline into several columns of a second line. In mid-summer. I heard that my old boss Dwight Marvin had said "Rivett isn't putting out a newspaper, he's putting out a daily magazine." Good analysis.

Why We Never Met

We never had editorial meetings. Seldom any kind of meeting. When we had one, it illustrated why we didn't. One afternoon, for example, Dan Button and I went to a meeting with the advertising director and the circulation director. We wanted to get fewer ads on Page Two and Page Three, so we could get more news up front. *Fuhgedaboudit!* The ad chief was not listening. The circulation director had brought his own agenda. Once it became clear that we were wasting our time, I returned to the copydesk. Button stayed a bit longer. He showed me his report on the meeting. A score by innings:

Business   **1 1 1 1 1 1 1 1 1 -- 9**
Editorial   **0 0 0 0 0 0 0 0 0 – 0**

I thought it was worse than that.

Life as acting news editor was not all stress. One slow night, I handed a long piece—four or five feet--of Hearst service copy to Jim Davey, on the rim, and asked him to cut it in half. He assiduously blacked out a word here, another there, likewise a sentence and a paragraph and more words and sentences and paragraphs, and proudly handed it to me; it had half as many words as the original. "Very nice," I told him, "but you should have done what I told you: just cut it in half." Using my scissors, I showed what I meant: lengthwise. He looked sick.

I had found that one of the many compartments built into the homemade copydesk was just the right size to hold a gallon jug of Paisano, the red wine that started the Gallos toward their fortune. Even then, I was not impressed by its quality, but it was cheap and copyreaders would drink anything, especially if it was free.

At the end of the summer, after we returned from our usual vacation visit to my wife's sister and her family in Oak Ridge, Tennessee, my career as an actor slowly came to an abrupt end. Jack Leary gave me an assignment I thought was pretty silly, unless he was sending me a message. He wanted me to revamp the typography but keep the same type fonts. I went along with the silliness and drew up a couple or three alternative treatments. In the slot, I had been trying to do more than I could with the staff I had, and, as a result, the paper was often late with one edition or another. No one had told me to change my ways, but someone must have been keeping score.

A Self-Inflicted K.O.

Whatever Leary had in mind, I inflicted the final damage. The climax was the result of an unexceptional event: the classified ads exceeded the space estimate, and that required finding new space for some paid death notices. I was engaged in a running dispute with the guy who laid out the ad space and, as a result of my trying to make him look bad, I omitted two paid death notices. Next day, I was no longer acting news editor. Herb Haas went further; he wrote that, inasmuch as I had left out vital notices, I was not ever to have a position of responsibility at the paper.

I panicked. It was too close a resemblance to that day in 1937 when Julius Heller fired me. I still had a job this time, as reporter, but that put me back where I had been in 1955, nearly as bad, I thought, as being fired. I decided not to ask the Guild to enter a grievance; management might show it had good cause to do what it did and I might wind up really fired. I went back to the Papermakers' Union to see about a fulltime job as editor; they had just hired one. I asked Gene Robb—I pleaded with Gene Robb—for reinstatement. My plea was in vain.

I'm a Reporter – Again

So, after another day, I reported, as a reporter, to the city editor Barney Fowler. With some trepidation, for we had had several frank and cordial (as the diplomats say) conversations while I was the news editor. And with more concern for my pay, because much of it was based on simulated overtime. Fowler had forgotten or (less likely) forgiven my frankness. And my pay remained at the news editor level. Had Haas also forgotten or forgiven? More likely, we Guild negotiators had convinced him that when the contract said no pay cut it meant no pay cut, even if the job changes.

.   I had one more editing chore. Stan Levine, who had succeeded Dick Walsh as sports editor, succeeded me in the news slot. Leary gave him a vote of confidence by asking me to draw up some Page One layouts. Laying out a page before you knew what was going into it seemed nutty. But I drew up a dozen or so, Stan slipped them into his desk drawer and used them, in some order, for several weeks. We never let Haas know.

The only trouble I had with Fowler was that he insisted on my using my given name Francis instead of my taken name Doc as a byline. Doc's old sports readers probably didn't have a clue about Francis. Barney, who also was known as Spec—for Spectator, an old columning byline—handed out a few assignments, but mostly left his reporters to find and cover their own stories. Barney had a few foibles: he had grown fond of bears (the result of working in the state Conservation Department), and he hotly pursued stories about public workers abusing their job-related cars (while he often borrowed the company car overnight).

I tried to fit in on a staff that included John Maguire, tp whom I devote a chapter; Bill O'Brien, who went on to the Rochester *Times-Union*; Pete Bowles, a florid-faced

Southwesterner who went to *Newsday*; a collection of less-talented reporters, and a young man named Art Plotnick who had been disinvited from State College for Teachers and who augmented his measly salary by writing stories, at a hundred dollars each, for a weekly soft-porn magazine.

A Loss for 'Hot Nuts'

Fowler sent me to the Albany Democratic headquarters to cover the 1961 election. Button had taken a personal interest in that campaign, throwing the paper's editorial support, for the first time, to a non-Democratic candidate, a Presbyterian minister running on a fusion ticket. I suppose Button thought the race might therefore be close. It wasn't. Erastus Corning 2nd piled up the usual margin, three to one. The only drama came when, not long after the polls closed, a Western Union messenger arrived with a telegram of concession for the mayor. Perhaps he would now, for the first time, mention his opponent's name. He declaimed the telegram, and, reaching the end, peered archly over his reading glasses and said "Robert K. Hot Nuts." The pun remained nearly private. Dick Weber of the *Knick News* reported that the mayor had mispronounced the name of the Rev. Robert K. Hudnut; I chickened out and wrote only that the mayor finally said his opponents' name.

Later that month, I offered to work up a feature on the twentieth anniversary of Pearl Harbor, and Fowler gave me enough time to do it right. I found several interesting participants in that date of infamy. One was a sportswriter at the *Troy Record,* a round young man named Perry Wood. I had known Perry for several years and had steered him to the Troy job when he came home from the Navy. But I had forgotten that he once was slender and graceful enough to get through hatches and gangways on a submarine, as he had done at Pearl Harbor. An Albany firefighter told me— the first time he ever spoke of it, he said—of his harrowing experience, trapped below decks under the turret of one of the stricken battleships for hours. He was in tears at the end. To round out the story, I talked to Pete Dalessandro, who won the Medal of Honor in the 1944 Battle of the Hürtgen Forest. He had not been at Pearl Harbor, but I wondered, where were you? He was in a training camp in North Carolina, he said, and the MPs rounded up him and other GIs to get back to base because Pearl Harbor was bombed. Pete had to ask, where's Pearl Harbor? Right in my lead.

A New City Editor

After a building-wide search, Button and Leary found their new city editor right next door in the *Knickerbocker News* city room. He was, at first glance, an unlikely choice, for Walter Hawver[1] was the television columnist. He was fairly tall, slightly padded, and walked with the mincing step of Gil Hodges. He turned out to be an excellent city editor. Especially for me. He let me continue to pick out my own assignments and to expand the range of my coverage, and, eventually, to regain my taken name Doc.

When an Albany police sergeant was murdered, late in February 1962, I learned the value of Being There. Hawver gave me the chore of writing the main story, even though it had occurred hours before ·I came to work, The other reporters on the story were due to go home at 6 p.m., and I would Be There as the evening wore on. I shuffled together notes and copy from other reporters, including John Maguire, who was a great writer, and did a little reporting. The murder was horrible: a paroled thug who had been holding a family hostage in their house on well-to-do Manning Boulevard got the drop on the sergeant, fired one

---

[1] Hawver left the paper after the 1964 Guild strike to be the news director of a local TV station, moved on to a similar job in Houston, and later taught journalism there. He moved back to the Albany area in retirement. He died May 30, 2001, after a siege of Parkinson's and Alzheimer's diseases.

shotgun blast into his chest and then fired the second barrel into the wound. Most of the hostage family saw the deed. The killer walked away and left the shotgun box behind. Quickly we learned who he was, but where he was became a mystery. My bit of reporting cashed in on my sportswriting days. The family's cleaning woman had escaped the house and called the police from a nearby dentist's office. The dentist had been the last person to talk to the cop, but he wouldn't respond to reporters. I called him, reminded him that I had selected him as an all-Albany football player and promised not to use his name. He gave me some helpful information.

The authorities caught up with the killer several days later, after he was hurt in a car crash in Chicago. He still had the shotgun in his car. While the guy was en route back to Albany, Button asked me to check on a report that the killer was an ex-cop. (I was puzzled since we already knew he was on parole.) So I asked Police Chief John Tuffey and unleashed the full panoply of his tics—shoulders, jaw, eyebrows and cigar—and the full force of his vocabulary. I was pleased to hear such combinations and permutations. I told the editors just what Tuffey had said, and settled down to write all about the capture.

A couple of years later, I was in the office when word came that a young man was on the roof of the DeWitt Clinton Hotel, sitting on the parapet and threatening to jump, while a crowd gathered in the street below. Tom Wilkinson went to the scene and I was the rewrite. The police and a priest went to the roof to try to talk the man out of jumping; the crowd began to chant "Jump! Jump! Jump!" The higher powers prevailed. The man let himself be rescued. But the story was about *Jump! Jump! Jump!* So was the headline. The man became an afterthought.

In late July 1962, I fell into my biggest story by Being There. I was calling the police rounds about 6 o'clock, when the Rensselaer County Sheriff's office reported, "A gas truck blew up on the Plank Road in Berlin, We've got a mutual aid fire alarm, a lot of people hurt." Hawver promptly sent reporter Sean Ryan to the scene. I volunteered to go too. I came upon a scene of desolation, smoking ruins of perhaps a dozen houses, some still aflame. I talked to the county fire coordinator for the official facts, then to an old man who had lived in one of the houses for personal stuff. He explained who lived in each of the houses that were no longer there. I drew a rough map on my note paper, not sure what I'd do with it. (It provided a caption for an aerial photo that Bernie Kolenberg took.) Then I ran into Johnny Mack, an old colleague at the *Troy Record*, who told me what a local girl told him about driving home from work, following the truck, its brakes afire, down the Plank Road hill. I couldn't find her, but her parents verified her story—especially about the front of the propane tank hitting a tree and splitting open. That was the lead, of course. (Much too late, I wondered how she had managed to drive around the stricken truck.)

The pressurized liquid propane poured down from the roadway into cellars, some turned to gas and formed a cloud that billowed northward a half-mile or more. A pilot light in a cellar set off a firestorm that engulfed everything. Only one man died right away: the driver of the tanker. (He got to Berlin because he had lost his way to Bennington, Vermont.) Many others, badly burned, were taken to hospitals, primarily the nearest, in Bennington. I was supposed to phone notes back to the office, but the local phone operator was holding her two trunk lines to Troy for emergencies, not news. I found Ryan, asked him to check on a few unresolved questions, and drove back to Albany. Hawver had called John Maguire back to rewrite from what Ryan and I called in. John was a little put out when I appeared. Too bad, John. I banged out, in short takes of a paragraph or two, about seven or eight hundred words. They made the 10 o'clock mail edition, which was delayed only a few minutes. For the final, I inserted some details that Ryan called in. Only one death that night (the toll rose to ten) and a bunch of injuries, but the story got second-coming treatment. (The story won the hundred dollar award in the Hearst writing contest; Ryan and I split it evenly. I became the only Hearstling of that era to win awards for headlines and writing.)

The story was still a big one for several days. I went back to do a Sunday feature that ran about forty-five hundred words, did another feature about the Bennington hospital, and wrote obituaries as the death toll rose.. In that Sunday feature, as on the night of the accident, eyewitnesses insisted that the prow of the tank swung out over the roadway and hit a tree. Several weeks later, the official verdict: metal fatigue and poor construction caused the tank to split open; it hadn't hit anything. So much for eyewitnesses.

Cops and Firemen

Another dinner-time call: three teenagers killed by a car in Hampton Manor, a probably drunk driver. I learned the names of the victims and a survivor, some of the circumstances, and phoned in a story. I went on the town justice's home-office to await the appearance of the driver. He looked so shaken and abject that the judge offered him a cup of coffee and asked me to fetch it from the kitchen.

Weeks later the owner of a carwash in Rensselaer, closing business for the day, shot his wife and himself. They were taken to Albany Hospital, dead on arrival. I went to the hospital in time to meet the coroner's physician, Dr. Leon Feltman, who read me all his information—nearly everything. All I needed from Rensselaer was the names of the cops investigating the case. Dr. Feltman was also our family doctor.

When the *Laurentian*, the Delaware & Hudson passenger train from Montreal to Albany, derailed near Waterford, some ten miles away, I dashed off with the photographer Joe Higgins. Joe also worked part-time for the Cohoes police and carried a portable red flasher that we used to ease our way through rush-hour traffic. The derailment was not spectacular: the rails had spread and the train came to an abrupt halt. An express messenger who had been standing in the doorway of his baggage car was thrown out to his death. The passengers had been led up an incline from the tracks to a cemetery. I nudged Higgins into shooting a picture of an old woman sitting on her suitcase next to a gravestone, with the train as background. It made the national wires.

Not all the police beat stories were so weighty. One afternoon, a young man walked into a branch bank at New Scotland Avenue and Morris Street, strolled behind the counter and helped himself to a large bundle of money. When he walked out, some neighborhood kids followed him. A couple of off-duty cops who lived nearby followed them. The quiet chase went slowly through backyards, over fences, through gates, and on to the young man's home. He was widely known for his mental handicaps. I wrote a light piece about the incident, and attracted letters of denunciation from avid mental health advocates.

It wasn't exactly police stuff, but one night, I went off, with a photographer—Joe Higgins again—in quest of a harbor seal that had been seen on a riverbank just north of Albany. We found him, or her, and took a picture as evidence. The State Conservation Commissioner Brown Reid suggested, "John Lomenzo should be here. He'd know what to do. He's the keeper of the state seal." Lomenzo was secretary of state.

On Education

Another example of Being There: No one was available to cover a school board meeting, so I gave up my dinner hour. After the meeting at the board president Neile Towner's law office, as board members, staff, and reporters strolled down a long corridor to the elevator at 112 State Street, Mr.

Towner told a couple of stories about his school days and added, "Some people say I'm one of the great minds of the nineteenth century." I said, "Mr. Towner, the way I heard it, it was fifteenth century." He guffawed. We became friends for life, which was not very long. Mr. Towner, already in his nineties, fell a few months later and never recovered.

I went on to cover all kinds of education stuff. One Sunday in November 1962, for example, I had three bylined stories in the same issue: on team teaching in the lower grades of an Albany school, on a study of the judicial powers of the state education commissioner, and on the progress in adding a doctoral program at the University at Albany. Not that I wrote them all the same day. I kept them in my desk for days. No chance of being scooped. The education people didn't send out press releases. So contacts counted. Some of the public school principals had been coaches in my sports writing days. And the people who counted at Albany State and the Education Department didn't believe me when I told them I was schmoozing around just to get out of the office; they insisted on steering me toward good stories.

We had a spurt of education reform, a word that covered any kind of change, in response to the Soviet launching of Sputnik: the new physics, two new chemistry curricula, language labs and the New Math. Nearly every school chief was in love with the New Math, which dealt in sets and subsets and bases, like twelve and ten and two, and installed it from kindergarten to grade twelve. At the fad's height, I happened to meet one of the inventors and asked him his reaction He said he was surprised and baffled. "We developed it for specialists in mathematics," he told me. "We never expected to see it used in the early grades." The story didn't get much play. The New Math passed away long ago.

In the midst of a torpid 1965 mayoral race, Button asked me to write a series of pieces on the condition of Albany's old schools. Suspecting that he had a political motive in a city election year, I turned in each story just in time for the day's paper. Mayor Corning also suspected a political motive, and he capitalized on my series. I had to enlist a school official as an escort and, to my surprise, he showed me things I never could have found alone. While the series was running, the school board announced the selection of a site for a new high school, and a new grade school to replace two old buildings in Arbor Hill. Button was displeased by my series; he said I should have analyzed the teaching and so on. I told him he had never mentioned that before. So he asked me to go out with the Republican candidate for mayor who would show me what I had missed. The story I wrote was so bad it never saw print.

Some of the education stories took on aspects of cold war diplomacy. Early in 1962, Bob Maas, a young publicist at RPI, offered me the chance to interview three Soviet Union engineers who were studying there. As I entered the interview room, the youngest of the three, who spoke English with a perfect pitch, held up a cigarette pack and intoned, "Weenston tests goood like a cigarette shoood." The oldest smiled through steel-capped teeth and told of his service in the Great Patriotic War. The middle one—the spook?--said almost nothing and in a low voice. A few weeks later, they went to Williams College to debate three American students: another two-column story.

A year later a couple of Soviet theoretical physicists came to RPI for some courses and I interviewed them. Nothing like the first three. They were not at all sociable and complained at length that RPI lacked equipment they needed. To which an RPI professor said, "What equipment? I'm a theoretical physicist and all I need are pencil, paper and a few books." Neat balance.

Even more of my education/Cold War reporting involved Latin America. The Center for Inter-American (CIA) Studies at Albany State was host to students from the Dominican Republic, Costa Rica, and Mexico. The Mexicans, particularly from the Autonomous University of

Guadalajara, came for longer stays, which included a week's immersion in English. That made interviewing easy; no need to wait for an interpreter. As one group was leaving, I was invited to the farewell party and they gave me a pony skin wallet. It was too good to carry around. I still have it in a dresser drawer.

Then there was the day the Education Commissioner, James E. Allen, issued two orders about *de facto* segregation. One required a specific district to transfer–bus—some pupils; the other warned districts to watch out for growing concentrations of Negro students. Most reporters combined the two, making it appear that widespread busing was imminent. I kept them separate. Allen's misunderstood orders created a flood of mail to his office, where it was segregated in a closet. After a while, Walter King, who spoke for the commissioner, gave me access to a number of them. The gem: from a family friend of the Allens, expressing concern that such a nice Presbyterian boy could perpetrate such an order.

Someone in the Education Department asked me to review, for a fee, the curriculum for a community journalism course to be given in Brazil. The material had been translated into English, and, since the course was supported by a Rockefeller fund, I was told, I did not have to be too critical. So I reviewed it—favorably, of course—and added a few non-binding comments. I got a check for seventy-five dollars. I had worked about an hour.

Politics

In the early spring of 1962, the day after St. Patrick's Day, I went to Schenectady to cover a testimonial dinner for a local politician. Ho hum. But Being There paid off: Ted Kennedy, making his first campaign for his brother Jack's old seat in the U.S. Senate, was the guest speaker. Teddy, whose main asset then was his family name, breezed in by plane from a parade in North Adams, breezed through his stump speech, and breezed on out. I was not impressed. I breezed through the story.

That fall, I talked Hawver into giving me time and expenses to spend two days covering the efforts of Sam Stratton, of Schenectady, to retain his seat in Congress. .He had been—in his word—Rockymandered into a new district that was shaped like a bloated submarine and was heavily Republican. It stretched from Amsterdam to Canandaigua and from Binghamton to Lake Ontario, with very little of his old district. The incumbent in most of the new district, John Taber, had retired, and the Republican candidate was Janet Hill Gordon, a member of the state Assembly. What contrasts! Mrs. Gordon drove up to meetings in a convoy of new Fords, with a covey of Republican officials; Sam drove up in his wife's battered station wagon with one aide. Sam introduced himself as "Congressman Stratton, and I need your help." Janet stuck pretty much to scripted meetings. My stories didn't run until Sunday and Monday, a week before election; budget problems.

Being There again. On Election Eve, Hawver asked me to write the Election roundup. (We must have been between Capitol reporters.) I noted that the race for Governor had reached "a climax—of a sort," a qualifier that had never been used before. The big question, I wrote, was what Rockefeller's victory margin would be. Not that Robert Morgenthau, the Democrat, would have much to do about it. The Conservative Party had entered the race and its candidate might cut into Rockefeller's margin. He did.

On Election night, I returned to the Stratton-Gordon race, the only reporter in Sam's headquarters at the Sleepy Dutchman Motel outside Amsterdam By the time a dozen election districts had reported, I phoned the office and dictated a short story for the first edition, declaring Stratton the winner. His principal aide had, right at the start, observed an omen in the name of the adding machine: Victor. Sam won by about twelve thousand votes.

In the summer of 1964, Being There, I answered the phone just as I was heading home for dinner. I didn't get there. The caller was R. Peter Straus, a New York City radio magnate, who had won a U.S. Supreme Court case that changed the way the state elected its legislators. He invited—no, ordered—me to the Capitol, where he was installing a set of private guards to protect the maps used in setting legislative districts. A funny go-around: there already were state guards at the scene, so Straus's guards guarded the state guards. The building superintendent, a Colonel Blimpish sort, contributed no light at all on the proceedings, but he made a funnier sidebar to the main story. When Straus wrote a book about his success, he included my sidebar. The book is long out of print. I never read it.

That September I covered the state convention of the Conservative party in Saratoga Springs. The party had been formed for the express purpose of ousting Governor Rockefeller and U.S. Senator Jacob Javits. In 1964, it nominated Henry Paolucci, a Fordham University professor, for the Senate. (He did not oust Javits.) I must have been irked at someone on the city desk, for I wrote the main story, a Man in the News, and a long sidebar on local reaction. The only times I overproduced like that was to punish the desk.

A few days later, I went to Glens Falls to cover the first triumphant campaign tour of Bobby Kennedy for U.S. Senator. Though a carpetbagger, he had won the nomination over Stratton just a week earlier in a boss-dominated convention. Kennedy was scheduled to reach Glens Fall at about 6 p.m. after stops in a couple of other upstate cities. A couple of thousand people—and I—were waiting. And waiting and waiting. Each half hour, someone announced a new and later arrival time. A power failure about 9 p.m. killed the soft-drink vending machines. Shortly after midnight, Bobby arrived. The crowd was still there, and even

more people lined the streets to the city park, where some
four thousand gathered. In his talk there, Bobby invoked—
blatantly, I reported—the name of his brother, the martyred
president. I wrote a fairly long spot story for Friday's paper,
then a Saturday feature about Bobby's returning a pen he
had borrowed in the 1960 campaign (for his brother) to a
Glens Falls kid, and, for Sunday, a piece about the public's
adoration of a Kennedy, but was it Jack or Bobby?

Intelligence & Counter

In the mid-nineteen-sixties, when war raged on the
college campuses against the war raging in Vietnam, I wrote
several stories about protests at Albany State University.
One morning, I received a phone call at home. A State
Trooper, a counterintelligence operator (with considerable
counterintelligence) asked about something, "I think they
call it a teach-in." I told him, "There are signs about it
plastered all over that part of town. Why don't you go look?"
I never heard from him again.

By that time, I had had a brief encounter with the
FBI. I was following up a story about an out-of-town postal
worker, a Negro (in the term of the times), named Sam
Clark who had been arrested on some minor charge over
Memorial Day weekend and claimed that the Albany police
had roughed him up. Words followed words and a Grand
Jury cleared the cops. Then Mr. Clark's supporters claimed
the county didn't allow Negroes on the Grand Jury. I walked
to the Courthouse to interview the Commissioner of Jurors,
Mrs. Elizabeth Pinckney, who had earned life tenure many
years earlier by selecting the proper grand jurors to hear
local government scandals. We had a pleasant chat, almost
noteless. She told me "I don't have any coloreds on the jury
list any more. I used to have Doctor Robinson and his wife
but they asked me to take them off. But all the judges know

that. They see the juries. And they never said anything." I wrote it.

The usual two FBI agents came to the *Times-Union* office a few days later to talk to me. Very cordial. They never asked for my notes. Not even if I had notes. They had talked to some other people, including the Commissioner. At the end, they told me they had concluded that she just didn't like the idea of adding anyone to her list.

A couple of times, while I was covering Albany State's Center for Inter-American Studies (CIA), word came back to me that the CIA (the real one) was upset about a couple of stories I had written. No official complaint. Just an offhand comment by a third-party that the local CIA spook (posing as a businessmen in Schenectady) couldn't understand how I got a couple of stories from scholars who had visited the Dominican Republic before he could debrief them. I sent back word: tell him it's just class.

A Primary Concern

In 1964, the Noahic principle—two by two—guided our political coverage. It started with the County Democratic nominating meeting in the old Polish American Community Center on Sheridan Avenue. George W. Harder, who two years earlier had entered the primary against Assemblyman Frank Cox, one of Democratic leader Dan O'Connell's favorite favorites, was going to try again. Leary asked me to go with Ed Fennell, our city hall reporter. Probably I was supposed to keep Fennell honest. It turned out to be a dull meeting, over in a few minutes. Too early to return to the office, so Fennell and I stayed to chat and have a beer or two. I noticed Dan O'Connell, the fabled party boss, standing, back to bar, holding court for several old timers who approached him one by one, leaned close to talk into his ear and let him talk in his hoarse whisper into theirs, and waited while he reached into one pants pocket or the other to peel off a bill—a five or a ten?--as tribute to old times. That was the only time I saw O'Connell; he was then nearly eighty.

Fennell and I decided we owed Leary a better story since he had stayed so late. As we entered the city room, we were staging a loud argument. Fennell shouted, "For Christ sake Doc, you can't use that stuff." I shouted back, "The hell I can't. All those people saw it. They all heard what Cox and Harder called each other. I got to use it." A few more exchanges brought Leary out of his office. He was a slight, sandy-haired fellow who was given to gnawing at his fingernails. (Fennell had dubbed him The Harmonica Player.) I began typing. Leary said barely audibly, "We'll have to run this by Mr. Robb." Typing furiously, I snarled, "Not we, Jack. This is my story." He sat behind me as I banged away: no fights, no harsh words. At the fourth paragraph, I heard a groan. I didn't look. I hate to see a grown man cry—or an editor.

On Primary Day, another Noahic expedition. This time, Hal Kallenburg accompanied me on a tour of polling places. At School 8, in the Italian neighborhood, a committeeman told us, "We got a language problem here. A lot of these older people don't know English good. We tell them vote in November. They don't know vote in September." Further into the South End: "Nobody knows primary. See that block: know how many families live there? Forty-eight. Know how many get a paper? One." A few more stops, a few more variations. Hal and I wrote what we had seen and heard. Kind of funny. Button asked, "But what about the election law?" We said, "What about it; we don't have a copy." Neither did Button, who decided that if he couldn't get a scandal story, he didn't want any. Our afternoon went into the waste basket.

Building Blocks

The refers I had written, as news editor, in the spring of 1961 began catching up with me a year later. In March 1962, the Governor's commission announced at a press conference its site selection and initiated the land-taking of about ninety-nine acres for a "multi-million dollar" project. Thus I began a mini-career, covering what was first called the South Mall (Mayor Corning dubbed it Brasilia) and later the Empire State Plaza. After a while, editors asked how many was "multi". I could not get an official answer, so, with the help of some industry sources, I arrived at "$250 million". The Governor's office never disputed my guess. The mechanics of the land-taking, the court room follow-up, the relocation of thirteen thousand people, the unveiling (in March 1963) of the model of the project, and the dickering and bickering over its financing provided story after story. I managed, with the help of photographer Bernie Kolenberg, to scoop the Governor on the unveiling.

I had already scooped Rockefeller, with his unwitting help, a year earlier. In the summer of 1962, he made a speech on Friday about the new University at Albany campus, promising to make public a model of it the next week. That gave me enough time to locate one man, the head of the art department at the university, who gave me a lot of good information that I published the morning of the unveiling. The governor excoriated his staff. He may have been dyslexic, but he had no trouble speaking with colorful emphasis.

When the South Mall model was unveiled, I tried to confirm my estimate of the cost. I asked the chief architect, Wallace K. Harrison. He kind of agreed: "There's five hundred thousand square feet of office space and, if you take fifty dollars a square foot, it would come to two hundred and fifty million dollars." Several minutes later, in a news conference, he amended that to say that the total cost would be about two hundred and fifty million dollars, but only about half would be spent early. I used his latter remark in my story. He didn't exactly lie, as he omitted the cost of excavation, and of the Egg and the Cultural Center. The cost wound up at nearly one billion dollars (before interest on the bonds). As the cost mounted, I wrote about each new increase, to the consternation of state officials, who thought their numbers were secret. Eventually, one of them asked Mayor Corning how those numbers had leaked. The Mayor told me he answered: "An enterprising young reporter reads your legal notices about each new bond sale." The ads stopped mentioning price.

To carry out the expansion of the university and the mental health system, Rockefeller established two new bureaucracies. More for me to cover. Retired Army General David Traub built an elaborate hierarchy to oversee university construction, from the individual campus plan to the universal lettering for signs. On the other hand, Milton Musicus, a longtime state bureaucrat, put together a barebones organization to supervise the mental health building program. Not even a public relations officer.

Rockefeller also endorsed a switch from very large mental institutions to very small ones. When I heard of the proposal, I called Hyman Forstenzer, the top administrator in the department, and he came from home in Schenectady on a Saturday to walk me through the encyclopedic new program. (Next time I saw Mr. Forstenzer, I was with the Public Service Commission, whose offices shared a building with mental health headquarters. He was still working, mentally alert, though Lou Gehrig's disease had forced him into a motorized wheelchair that he controlled by his breath. He died not long after.)

Medical Economics

A routine press release from the Teamsters Union early in 1962 led me into writing about medical economics. The

Teamsters reported that a study they commissioned found that twenty-eight percent of one type of elective surgeries paid for by Blue Cross in New York had been found medically unjustified. A makeup editor had wrapped the story above an ad for the local Blue Cross. That afternoon Fred Bond, the public relations officer for Blue Cross, called to invite me to join him for dinner so he could explain such matters to me. That was my first lesson in medical economics: a health insurance PR man can eat a lot free if he has the proper guests.

Bond also introduced me to Ralph Hammersley, the Blue Cross CEO. He displayed candor beyond the call of duty in explaining how he took advantage of the hospitals' figures to keep his payments low. He also introduced me to some hospital directors (the bosses, that is), and people involved in health care planning.

When Medicaid came along, our Capitol reporters' disinclination to cover complicated matters again allowed me to expand my beat. I covered meetings and hearings, where mumblers masqueraded as experts and experts clearly voiced their thoughts. Among the former was Marion Folsom, one of Eisenhower's secretaries of health, etc. The latter group included state Senator George R. Metcalf and George Wyman, the social welfare commissioner, and Hugh R. Jones, head of the Social Welfare Board. I also received letters from several actuaries, who offered for print their versions of the likely cost of the program. Everybody— mumbler, expert, actuary—was wrong on that: too low.

Finally, Ned Waterman, a lobbyist for the Conservative Party, tipped me off to a major story. "They haven't filed a fiscal bill"—a required estimate of the annual cost for five years—"only a sheet of paper with numbers that don't add up," he told me. I went to the Senate finance committee office and asked for it. After some embarrassed minutes, Gus Poleto, an old Green Islander and secretary of the committee, showed me the sheet. It didn't add up. I wrote the story and

Bill Rising, a copy reader whose forte till then I considered to be his ability to nap in a tilted-back chair, wrote a perfect banner headline: **Medicaid Gets Blank Check.** Sharper than my story.

I wrote several stories about the state's effort—largely fruitless—to close unnecessary hospitals. And, in 1966, I wrote nearly a full page about the factors that were pushing hospital costs, and patients' and Medicaid's bills, ever higher. Much of it is still valid today.

It was about then that I sat in on a couple of meetings to plan a large new addition—now the main building—for St. Peter's Hospital. Nothing off the record, everyone agreed. After the first meeting, I wrote that one of the architects, explaining the need for larger obstetrics accommodations, said that the birthing facilities at the Brady Hospital, which were to be replaced, were second-rate and thus not drawing as many customers as the new one would. At the second meeting, the good sisters in charge of St. Peter's voiced indignation that anything of theirs might be called second rate. They wondered aloud if I should be allowed to stay. A consultant quickly rose to my defense and, I suppose, his. He assured the sisters that my reporting reinforced their justification for the new facilities. I figured that two such stories were all the readers could bear and quit while I was ahead.

In the Courts

Some case—it must have been important—came up in the Court of Appeals one day when no one else could or would go. The usual result: I went. I don't recall the nature of that case. But I loved that day in court, and took the beat as mine. Covering the court was fairly easy. At arguments, the judges asked a lot of questions and the lawyers answered most of them. I was, I feel sure, the first to report the answers along with the questions. Several cases were momentous:

ensuring the right to publicly provided counsel in minor cases, redefining kidnapping, and others. But the cases that my recall found easiest to dig out of memory were minor, even trivial.

After John DeGraff (who had been the Guild lawyer in the 1937 case I was involved in) had argued the Albany Country Club's suit for more money from the State for its property (taken for the new university campus), I complimented him. You seemed to know every tree by its first name. "I should," he said, "I think I've hit every one of them." Not so pleasant was the outcome of a case in which an Albany man, not a lawyer, had floundered about as he argued his own case. At the end, the opposing counsel sought to shake his hand as a sign it was nothing personal. To the flustered non-lawyer, it was personal; he responded with a few forearm thwacks across the lawyer's back. The court was aghast.

One day, the court calendar provided a light piece, which I wrote thus: "Among the motions on the Court of Appeals calendar yesterday was Matter of Lazarus—death benefit." That was it. Nowadays, a story like that, if it got into the paper at all, would require great research, comments from all sides, and a half-column of copy to distinguish this Lazarus from the original..

I didn't cover the lower courts much. An exception was Election Day 1964. I went to a hearing in Police Court for about twenty people, who had been arrested in twos and threes for picketing outside a polling place in a firehouse. Their supporters crammed the courtroom. The judge lectured them for having caused an arresting officer to have a heart attack. A bit of hyperbole, if not a lie. The stricken cop, as I reported, had been involved with a single picket about two miles away from the firehouse. The pickets—mostly University at Albany students, with a few members of The Brothers, an activist black group--were set free with no penalty.

At the Capitol

Though I never became a Legislative Correspondent—
an exalted rank that required some attendance at legislative
sessions—I covered events at the Capitol from time to time. In
early 1963, a story I picked up at the State University led to
the Capitol. Governor Rockefeller planned to begin charging
tuition to pay off bonds for his monumental new building
program. It turned out to be a Rube Goldberg scheme; the
students would pay tuition, the state would appropriate
matching dollars for general university operations. The device
pleased bond buyers who viewed tuition as a more certain
payback than annual appropriations by the Legislature.
Student organizations thought poorly of paying tuition for
any purpose and their protests made it a continuing daily
story.

In March, I covered the Governor's Executive Budget,
and attended the customary "budget school," a briefing for
reporters at the Executive Mansion. When one reporter
asked about the tuition plan, a budget official said, "Talk to
Doc, he knows everything about it." The reporter didn't. That
school was memorable for the presence of the mansion butler,
who served the reporters drinks all afternoon—mine was
dry sherry, very dry. That also was the budget that raised
cigarette taxes ten cents a pack. To help improve the public
health, the tax commissioner told me. The Commissioner
Joseph Murphy was a heavy smoker; he died several years
later of lung cancer.

At the Capitol, I also covered some of the lobbying,
which the Correspondents haughtily brushed off. The
lobbyists were more interesting than the lawmakers they
were lobbying. Three young lawyers—George W. Harder,
John Boehner and Ed Bogdan—laughingly insisted they
defended Truth, Justice and the American Way. They lobbied
against repeal of the Wicks Law, which required multiple
contracts for public construction. Since the mechanical
contractors they represented (and their employees) provided

more votes and more donations than the general contractors, they preserved the Wicks Law—in effect even now. Not so lucky was Francis Boardman, the Lonesome Brakeman, in his efforts to preserve the Full Crew Law, which required a specified number of workers on each train. He didn't have access to so many voters or donors; the law was repealed. Another colorful lobbyist was Nick Kisberg, who represented the Teamsters Union with considerable success since he could offer a legislator more support than even the defenders of the Wicks Law could. He also was a great gossipist and often provided leads to non-lobbying stories.

Investigations

I was asked in 1964 to cover some hearings of the State Investigation Commission, which seemed to have a permanent set of targets in Albany. This time, the subject was Albany County's purchasing practices. The hearing started at 10 a.m., four hours overtime, so of course I took the assignment. I had some misgivings about keeping up with the flow of testimony. No need to worry. The investigators called a recess after each telling revelation, invited the reporters into an inner sanctum, handed out rapid transcripts of the Q and A, and told us just what the testimony meant. It was great stuff: one paving machine purchased under three separate descriptions on three consecutive purchase orders; two sons of a prominent politician, young men who had probably not worked before, hauling in huge orders for janitorial supplies from the county and so on. A few days later, Robb sent me a check for a hundred dollars for my excellent coverage.

In the early sixties, the Internal Revenue Service provided reporters with a fishing expedition. Send us a list of names, the IRS said, and we'll tell you if anyone on the list failed to file an income tax return. Arvis Chalmers scored first: an upstate Assemblyman on his list hadn't filed. Let's match it, Hawver said. I submitted a list of local people, including, on a whim, the county welfare commissioner Marsh Breslin. Bingo! He hadn't filed. I went to his office to talk about it. He pleaded for us not to use it; he hadn't filed because of a family problem, but he didn't owe any tax. I told him it was up to the editor; Hawver said we'd run it, including his explanation. After a decent interval, Dan O'Connell, something of a Puritan, sacked Breslin. His three sons grew up to become a state Senator, a state Supreme Court justice, and the Albany County Executive.

I also investigated something I had wondered about for some time: who gets the lowest license plate numbers? At my request, the Motor Vehicle Department gave me a list of the first hundred plate numbers and the names to go with them. I wrote a short lead and tacked on the list. It caused an uproar among the legislators and judges who had failed, completely, to break the hundred. They probably didn't do too well on the next hundred either. Soon, the state set up a bunch of license plate categories, for judges, legislators, and so on, each starting with a 1.

Covering the Weather

Early in Hawver's tenure, I became the snowstorm expert. Each January, it seems, the Albany area was engulfed by a major storm. In 1964, it was a true blizzard—deep snow, high winds and low temperatures—that required more than a column to detail. The next day, I wrote a follow about the city's new snow tire law: the law was a success, the tires weren't. (That day also brought the murder of Clarence Valenti as he sat at the bar of his restaurant in Colonie. I had to wade through hip deep snow to reach an outdoor payphone to dictate my story.) Another January: a snowstorm all in short sentences. Real short. Someone must have criticized my long sentences in other snow jobs. Still another January, a three-inch snowfall. I wrote: "It snowed yesterday. Big deal. It's supposed to snow in January." And on for a couple of hundred words. All the snowstorm stories were bulked up by tales of stalled traffic, in the same places in each storm. Since the sixties, I've noticed, traffic moves better in the snow most times. Is that nostalgia or better snow removal?

Covering Whatever

Then there was, in Bob Dole's immortal word, whatever.

The whatever included, once each, a drama review, a TV review, and a sports story. I became a drama reviewer by invitation of the Albany Civic Theater producer, who .after the performance, asked if I could please write something because the regular reviewer hadn't appeared. Next afternoon, I turned in about three hundred words of honest praise. Later, Hawver asked me to extend my lunch hour at home, so I could report on a Public TV show about urban affairs, in which Button was to appear. Another three hundred words or so, concluding: "Dan Button was moderator of the show, which needed no moderation." When the sports editor Tom Cunningham found himself short-handed, he asked me to cover a Siena College-Albany University basketball game, a local classic. The game ran well into overtime and so did I. I wrote something like: *The object of basketball is to put the ball through the hoop, but for 17 minutes last night. Siena and Albany State refrained from doing to. State's Roger Casey finally recalled the object of the game and State won in three overtimes.* Nobody told me when to stop, so my story was nearly as long as the game.

After Hawver

Walter Hawver left soon after the Guild strike was settled in 1964 and gloom descended on the city room. Wesley

Keeler, a copy reader who had hidden, or simply lacked, any talent, became city editor. Maguire and I seemed to be the principal butts of his stupidity. When a colleague asked Maguire why we put up with such treatment, he said, "Doc and I don't mind how much he dumps on us as long as we're the best paid guys in the room."

On November 9, 1965, the lights went out, and Keeler seemed further in the dark than most of us. The way it happened—the lights flared bright, then dimmed, flared again, and, finally, went out—made me think it was a major occurrence. I suggested to Keeler that we ought to have someone out covering reaction; it might be dark a long time. Keeler asked, "Are you volunteering?" I grabbed a pack of notepaper and headed out on the street. Downtown was dead dark. But I encountered Joe Higgins, who had nothing to do. We set out in his car, equipped with a good radio that could bring in WCAU Philadelphia, outside the blacked out area. We toured the area: police headquarters, the Veterans' hospital, the Albany Medical Center hospital, state Civil Defense headquarters, the airport, the bus station, the railroad station, and back to the police station. Good stuff! The CD spokesman assured us, "No sweat." Volunteers directed traffic. A doctor heading for a conference wrote his speech at the railroad station, thanks to light supplied by a fire truck. The woman station master announced the train arrivals through an acoustic megaphone; just like the old days, she said. The police and firemen were using walkie-talkies for dispatching. Another stop: a bar near police headquarters to learn how the drinkers were coping. Only whiskey available. On my first drink, the lights began blinking on. Back to the office. "How much do you want?" I asked Keeler. He still hasn't answered. I just wrote as fast as I could as long as I needed—about a thousand words. Everything but that last stop.

❑

In September 1966, Keeler posted a notice assigning reporters to races in the election campaign. My name headed the list: to cover the campaign for Chief Judge of the Court of Appeals. But there was no race; all four parties—Democrat, Republican, Conservative, Liberal—had endorsed the same man, Associate Judge Stanley Fuld. I asked Keeler, "Are you sending me a message?" He said, "No. I thought you should cover the biggest job, the one at the top of the ballot." I took his word. He was too dumb to send me a message.

I covered the race in one interview. It was supposed to be a short talk; it stretched to more than an hour. Judge Fuld mentioned at the outset that his election would mean the end of Saint Stanley, the name by which convicts referred to him because of his supposedly favorable action on their pleadings, and quickly added, "But that's off the record." So it stayed while we talked about the predilections of judges, new threats to privacy, skiing in the Alps, his grandchildren, proper courtroom couture (including neckties for reporters), and so on. As I prepared to go, I asked about Saint Stanley: could I use it if I don't attribute it to you, to court attachés, perhaps? He said OK. I used it without attribution to lead a two-column story.

Most of this memoir has been about what I did. Now a paragraph about what I didn't. I didn't throw a typewriter. Especially not out the window. I did throw an adding machine—but not very far; the electric cord caught it up short. I did tip---just tip—a typewriter into a large wastebasket. However my reputation as a typewriter thrower started, it became embellished. The typewriter went out the window, specifically the second story window. That meant it happened, mythically of course, in the old building on Beaver Street. But the typewriters there were bolted to the desks. The typewriter I flipped stood on a pedestal of the copy desk while I was news editor. I used it to write captions or refers or whatever. One night it refused to write what I was trying to write, so I tipped it into the wastebasket, inches away.. I fished it out, tried again and it worked fine.

The Old Reporter

As time passed and I became one of the old guys—I was over forty—in the newsroom, younger reporters like John McLoughlin (now a big guy in local TV news) sometimes asked me for advice on such matters as writing a lead. Usually, I responded by asking, "What do you want to say?" He mumbled something that led me to say, "That sounds pretty good, why don't you just write that down?" He did, and found that the rest of the story flowed naturally from there. One night, though, at a seminar in Ed's Bar, a real young reporter from the *Knick News*, asked it differently: "How do you write a perfect lead?" I thought a few seconds. "You don't. You don't even try." I advised him. "For one thing, if you write a perfect lead, you have to write a perfect story. For another, if you write a perfect anything, the desk will expect you to do it every time—provided the desk can recognize what you've done. Just do the best you can. It will probably be better than the desk deserves."

With Levitt, No Levity

A couple of suits hang in my closet as they have for the last thirty-some years. One is navy. The other is banker gray with pinstripes. They have been in and out and in and out of fashion. In or out now? I don't know. Or care. I seldom wear them--only for wakes, weddings and court appearances. Wearing is not what I keep them for. They're mementos of my midlife career change from reporter to public relations expert.

I did not own even one suit the day Arthur Levitt hired me to continue the burnishing of his official image as State Comptroller. In all my years at the Albany *Times-Union* and the American Newspaper Guild, I seldom wore a suit or even a necktie. Most of the time at the paper I was on the sports desk or the copy desk: shirtsleeve jobs. Even at the Guild, a sport coat sufficed for dress-up. At the Comptroller's hiring ceremony, I wore a sport jacket and a tie, both as conservative as I could find. But I was out of place. The next day, I went downtown and bought those two suits. A couple of neckties, too, and a few white shirts.

❑

That hiring ceremony was the climax of interviews that started in late 1966 when I was forty-eight years old. I had worked in the same place long enough, ordinarily, to feel comfortable. But I felt uncomfortable working for a city editor who sent me messages without knowing he was.

Though uncomfortable, I kept doing what I had been doing: picking out the stories I wanted to cover and staying out of the office as much as possible. One afternoon in the fall, I walked into the State Comptroller's office, a regular news stop, and, to my surprise, a deputy named Martin Ives, who had become a friendly news source, greeted me thus, "Doc, our PR man Hank Paley is leaving. Why don't you take the job?" I was flattered even though I knew he could not really offer me the job. I said, "Oh, that would be great.

Thanks." About two weeks later, I bunked into a lobbyist (for S&H Green Stamps) named Bill Schecter, who had been the Comptroller's PR man before Paley. He said, "I hear you're interested in my old job. If you really are, I'll talk to the guy who can make you an offer." I took him up on that offer, the best I'd ever gotten from trading stamps.

Looking for Someone Else

The offer--well, the indication of an offer--came a few weeks later. A telephone call at the office, asking if I could come up the hill and meet Bill Volet, the Comptroller's executive assistant. So I went the next day. Paley, an old friend, was waiting for me. I had followed him (as a part-timer) into another job several years earlier after he left the editorship of the AFL-CIO Papermakers Union newspaper. This time Hank was going to start his own PR business. He ushered me into Volet's office and sat in one of the leather upholstered armchairs.

After introductions, I plopped into a leather easy chair matching the one Paley picked; Volet sat on a leather sofa. I had just landed when Volet said, "Rivit,"--he always had trouble saying my name right– "We don't want a newspaper guy for this job, we want a real PR guy." I began pushing myself out of the chair, saying, "Mr. Volet, if that's the kind of guy you want, then you don't want me." He said "Siddown" and emphasized it with a pushing motion from afar. Then he said, "What we're looking for is somebody like Harry O'Donnell or Warren Moscow or Leslie Slote"--names to be conjured with in government PR circles–"you know, this is an important job." I started to rise again and said, "Mr. Volet, if you're looking for somebody like that, you'd better hire one of them; I'm not like them at all." Another "siddown" and the interview resumed. For a few minutes, Volet still was talking about wanting someone else, not Rivit; and Rivit was talking about you'd better find someone else. Then the talk turned to what a PR man ought to be doing, like speech writing and making sure that the Comptroller's image kept shining brightly. Abruptly, the interview ended. I was baffled. Paley walked out with me and, as soon as the door closed on us, he whispered, "You've got the job." I was still baffled.

❑

Whether they wanted me or someone else, they took their time. Weeks passed. Along came another call for another interview. Sure, I said, but my wife had just been diagnosed with multiple sclerosis and the interview would have to wait. A couple of days later, I saw Volet again. "You still interested in the job?" said Volet. "As much as I've ever been," I replied. A little more talk; no offer. Weeks passed. Then I received an urgent call from Paley, "Bring in some clippings of your stuff, any clippings; I guess they want to see if you can write." I had never kept clippings--too indolent or too diffident--so I had to raid the newspaper morgue, where all dead news is kept, for a half-dozen or so clippings. Among them was a piece I had written after the 1966 election, explaining why Levitt, despite his election to a fourth term, could never be a power in the Democratic Party. It was truthful, thus unflattering, but this was no time to be picky. (The story also mentioned the presence and power of Volet in the same manner.) I gave the few clippings to Paley the next day, and never heard about them again.

'You've Got the Job'

So it was a surprise when, a few weeks later, I was called again for still another interview with Volet. This time, I delayed the meeting a day so I could help my wife with her physical therapy. The interview started like all others, "Rivit, you still interested in this job?" And "As interested as I ever have been." Suddenly: "Well, you've got it. You're our man. We're going over and tell Arthur."--I was agape —"Before we go, I got to ask you something. I want to pay you what we're paying Paley. So I got to know: how much are you making now?" I hated to say how little, not how much. So I stretched it a bit. "You know, with a little moonlighting, I'm clearing about thirteen." Volet said, "Not enough. We're paying Paley nineteen. Look, when we see Arthur he's going to ask you the same question. Tell him about sixteen. That's close enough." We entered the Comptroller's mahogany paneled office, and Volet began the routine. When Levitt asked me how much I was making, I said sixteen--and kept a straight face. Volet said, "See Arthur, we've got to pay him what we been paying Paley." And I was hired. At nineteen something.

First I had to visit the personnel office and, for the first time in all the jobs I had held, I filed my résumé. In it, I mentioned my days, thirty-plus years earlier, at the Albany Collegiate Center--on the résumé it could have looked like years. Nobody cared anyway. So I was hired but not yet working. After all the hurry-up-and-wait, I decided that I ought to stick around the *Times-Union* for another month to close out my tenure as local Guild president and get started on contract negotiations.

A Grand Times 19 Job

On my first day in office, I was determined to Make a Good Impression. I wore the navy blue suit, a stylish number with side-vent jacket, a new white shirt and an unremarkable necktie. My vanity was in vain. That first day of work, April 20, 1967, was a Thursday, the day the State pay period began. The Comptroller already had called it a week in Albany and was back in New York, close to home.

Levitt had announced my hiring in a neat two paragraph release of my authorship. At the end it noted that the salary was nineteen thousand a hundred twenty dollars. That was not a mark of immodesty. Every notice of a state hiring had to mention salary, so that editors, who often were paid less, could publicly deplore the high State salaries, and reporters, whose pay was even lower, could privately grouse about that lucky sonofabitch getting all that money and I deserve it more.

The salary got into the headlines and I enjoyed those first few days. People called to offer congratulations; other people wrote their felicitations, often with a gentle chiding for having left them to deal with some reporter they'd have to train all over again. One of the calls came from Bill Skirving, my first mentor, who, more than thirty years later, was still a reporter for the *Knickerbocker News*. I was glad to hear from Bill; I thanked him for the kindness he had shown me in those early days. He complimented me on my new job. Then he complained, not exactly blaming me, that he should have gotten the job. He told me he had a good sponsor. But, after a long interview, Volet told him to come back the next day with a ten-minute speech for the Comptroller. "I didn't bother," Skirving explained, "Such bullshit!" I said something like *uh huh*. Sometimes, I wondered just a little bit who had been my rabbi, my anonymous godfather. The Mayor, perhaps? Or even Gene Robb, the publisher? I never asked.

A Leave on Leaving

I left the *Times-Union* in stages. I kept a foot in the door by asking for a six-month leave of absence, as provided in the Guild contract. Near the end of those six months I resigned by letter to the managing editor Jack Leary and to Robb. My grace note to Robb was the more cordial. I was going for good, I told him, but I might come back "if you'd ever be interested in my talents and if you could keep me in the style to which I'm likely to be accustomed, or reasonably close to it. . . In the meantime, I hope you'll leave a light in the window for me." His (as usual) gracious reply said "We've got a lot of windows and they'll all be lighted; take your pick." That was four or five publishers ago and fortunately I have not needed to go back. Fortunately, because the new home of the *Times Union* is surrounded by a wall; I wouldn't be able to see a window, lighted or not.

The job with Levitt was not my first shot at government public relations. For a good bit of 1966, I had sunlighted, while a reporter on the evening shift at the *Times-Union,* in the public relations office of the State Health Department. I was on the payroll under a Federal grant to publicize the research laboratories, but spent most of my time composing press releases in which Governor Nelson A. Rockefeller could point with pre-election pride to the success of the billion-dollar Pure Waters Bond that the voters had approved the year before. We were announcing merely the doling out of grants for planning to various localities, some barely on the map, but we made it appear real. I also wrote a few pieces about the research efforts, to justify my payroll slot, for the monthly house organ *Health News.* One of them is still valid. It was called *Sewer in the Sky* and reported on the finding by Vincent Schaffer, the cloud-seeding scientist, of the presence of lead from auto exhausts in the air, coast to coast, which upset rainfall patterns by naturally seeding susceptible clouds. The material is different now but it still fills the air. (Job crossover activity, now deemed a sinful conflict of interest, was not discouraged then. One of my *Times-Union* colleagues, who covered medical news, also wrote speeches for the Health Commissioner. And the chief PR guy at the Health Department moonlighted on the *Times-Union* copy desk. He enlisted me for sunlighting.)

4 Terms, 5 PR Men

Levitt was in his fourth term and I became his fifth public relations officer in that twelve-plus year period. One of my predecessors had served eight years, skewing the statistics; the others no more than two. The think-piece I wrote after the 1966 election pictured Levitt as a quiet man who would rather sit on a hotel lobby sofa and pore over *The Daily Bond Buyer* than mingle with other politicians. As a worry wart, who, on Election night, could question why his vote total in some remote county was so low; had he done something to alienate those voters? (Overlooking, of course, that said county was and always had been overwhelmingly Republican).

Much of the information in that piece, which I attributed to unnamed but highly placed sources, had come from Paley. This was the third time, going back to 1959, that we exchanged jobs and by far the most profitable to me. The other two times, I had become or stopped being the low-paid sunlighting editor of the monthly paper (and sometime press officer) for the International Brotherhood of Paper Makers, AFL, whose headquarters was in Albany. Each time, I was paid not by the union but by Gene FitzPatrick, a former *Times-Union* sportswriter who operated as Gene FitzPatrick Associates. (I was his only associate. He got the job because he had once worked for the union and was a golfing buddy of the union president; I got the job because Gene disliked work and I was willing to take the pay he offered, a small fraction of what he received.)

Hank Paley Arrives

My job was supposed to last until the Brotherhood, an old-line AFL union, completed a merger with its CIO counterpart. Officials from the CIO union came to Albany in 1959, but the merger had to be affirmed by a convention in 1960. One of the CIO officials was Paley, and his arrival meant my departure.

Some CIO officers soon announced that they planned to seek election to the same offices in the merged union. The Brotherhood officers had no intention of letting that happen. The split widened in the late spring of 1960 when the Brotherhood officers or refused to come to the rescue of seven workers in a can-making plant in New Jersey after they had been fired for trying to organize a CIO-type local. Paley resigned in protest and published a manifesto for industrial unionism.

So, for the first time, I succeeded Paley, under the same terms as before but with a little more pay and a lot more work: writing and publishing the officers' report to the convention that was only six weeks away. Then came an invitation to use a week of vacation to handle press relations at the convention in Washington in September. Paley was there too, and we remained on friendly terms. Which was better than my relations with the press. The reporters, all specialists in labor matters, were more interested in the unseemly rift--which I tried to avoid talking about--than in official pronouncements. Just before the closing day, when the rift opened even wider, Dan Button urgently called me back to Albany to be the acting news editor at the *Times-Union*.

I continued at the Papermakers for another issue or two, and struck a blow for freedom of the press. The blow knocked out the only CIO candidate elected to office. All the new officers, following custom, had sent official biographies for the paper, but the good-old-boy president Paul Phillips objected to using the dissident's. I argued that we had a duty to run it, and Phillips gave in. The CIO guy revealed that he had not been a union member long enough to qualify for office.

A New Role for Paley

Paley remained in Albany and we stayed in touch. He became press officer for Joe Carlino, the Republican Speaker of the Assembly. He kept the job until, in the Johnsonian sweep and the court-ordered reapportionment of the Legislature of 1964, his boss was diselected. (Paley was still there when the Guild went on strike, and he offered me a place on the payroll for the duration. With great gratitude, I declined.) Hank's next stop was the Comptroller's office, which he left under his own power. He also left a sardonic message, in inch-high Cheltenham type, neatly framed and hung in several offices: **Some Things/Are Best Left/Said Undone.**

I inherited Paley's secretary and his assistant and a large, well-appointed office. What a change from the *Times-Union*! From a battered steel desk with barely elbow room to the next one to a space fifteen feet square, a wooden executive desk, a conference table, even a coat rack, and windows--but no view. There was a catch or two. The office had been designed so that visitors could be checked and incoming phone calls screened. My secretary and gatekeeper was Ceil Schutzman, an older woman from Brooklyn, a devout believer in good office practice. As I was used to answering my phone I told Ceil I'd pick up all calls on the first (of four) lines. She lectured me that it was not good office practice. I prevailed.

Ceil also was den mother to three other girls--when *girls* was not politically incorrect--only one of whom was on the public relations payroll and only one, a different one, was still a girl. So many people and so little to do led to a lot of make-work and chatting, which I decided was none of my business. Occasionally, though, I had to tell the girls to close their office door so no one passing by would notice that one of them was standing on a desk while having her hemline changed by another.

My assistant was Ron Tarwater, an earnestly formal young man who had been managing editor of the Norwich *Sun*, until Volet hired him the summer before. He had, for a time, an assistant, a woman whose tenure was so short I never really knew her, who clipped out-of-town newspapers for favorable mentions of the Comptroller.

MeetingMeetingMeeting

On my first Monday on the job, I was introduced to the Comptroller's staff meeting in a paneled room toward the far end of the sixth floor of the Alfred E. Smith State Office Building. Levitt sat at the head of a large mahogany conference table, flanked, in some order of rank, by the several deputies and a few other senior staff members.

Volet sat off to the Comptroller's right, over the shoulder of Al (for Alfred) Haight, the first deputy comptroller and speechwriter for Levitt. My seat was at the Comptroller's left, at the far end of the table, outranking only Egon Plager, a sociology professor who was a part-time adviser to Levitt, and Kay Minnock, an administrative specialist who served as secretary. She was the only woman in the room.

I thought the staff meeting would be a fine place to learn quickly what was going on. I was disabused of that idea by the second or third Monday. Most of the discussion seemed to repeat matters from the week before. And, as time marched on, the discussions repeated the week before the week before the week before, and so on like a hall of mirrors. The Comptroller seemed pleased with the repetition and, in fact, often fostered it.

The absence of an agenda did not mean the meeting lacked focus. The participants usually focused on the shortcomings, actual or perceived, of a colleague. They might have focused on me, but realized that Levitt and Volet were doing that daily. Most often the focus was Leon Braun, an amiable, diffident man who was in charge of the retirement system. Leon took the criticism calmly, for he knew, as did his critics, that he was indispensable to the Comptroller. Leon supervised the retirement system's investments and thus provided Levitt entrée to a circle of influential brokers and bankers. He also was the key to support by the Liberal Party, a decisive factor in Levitt's first and second elections. Sometimes, the focus was Tom Whalen, the department's highest ranking civil service employee, who was as secure as Braun. As head of the cash management unit, he also made Levitt feel at home with still another group of bankers and brokers.

Old Acquaintances

I had known Braun and Whalen for a few years. I had first met Braun when I was a reporter interviewing a group of Dominicans who were visiting the Albany University. He slipped into the small conference room in the Wellington Hotel, his home in Albany, and, after listening a while, asked some enlightening questions. Afterward, he told me he had often visited the Dominican Republic and thought its people were lovely. Whalen had known me from my sportswriting days in the forties, when his son Tom III was a high school quarterback. In 1969, Tom III ran for city court judge, as a Democrat, and his father asked if I would help him. I dashed off a six-point program for his campaign and he beat the Republican candidate, a backslid Democrat, by a three to one margin. My advice had little to do with his success.

[I digress, as usual, to report on some other political consultations I undertook in the Levitt years. All on my own time, of course. Larry Novak, the shrewd Columbia County Democratic leader, asked me for some help with his candidate for State Assembly, running against a long-term incumbent. My first advice was "Get your Great White Hope out of sight, way out, until Election Day." Couldn't do that. So I put together some material he could use. The Great White Hope lost but did far better than I or Novak expected. Volet asked me to help a friend of his who was running for a judgeship in Sullivan County. He too might have done better in absentia but I didn't dare suggest that. Instead I advised him to capitalize on the only thing that set him apart from his opponent: he had learned law as an apprentice. "Be the people's judge," I advised. He couldn't do that; people wouldn't respect him. He lost. Jacob Herzog, a friendly lawyer who had never run for office, asked me for help in his 1968 campaign against Congressman Dan Button. I tried, but not very hard. He was swamped. One success: in 1969, Albany Mayor Erastus Corning asked me to do some research for him. He could have won by the same margin without me.]

Same Speech Many Times

Al Haight, a gray-faced outwardly-calm man, came from a distinguished line of upstate lawyers (one ancestor had served on a high state court) and, theoretically, he ran the operations of the department. In fact, he ceded that power to Volet, who had a keen eye for political advantage. As speechwriter, Haight supplied the Comptroller with sincere-sounding essays on topics like *What's Right with America.* Whatever the title, it usually was the same speech cut and pasted to look fresh but not so fresh as to be uncomfortable for the Comptroller. Since Levitt spoke almost exclusively to non-political groups--the Masons, DeMolay, high school classes, and Rotary, Kiwanis, the Lions--he could safely take a low key approach.

Levitt generally was addressed as Comptroller--and the *compt* had to be carefully sounded. He also did not mind being called Colonel, a reference to his World War II rank in the Army's legal corps. (He also had served in World War I, as a private, but that information, along with his birth date, had been eliminated from his official biography. Elected officials never grew old.) Only a few really close, and longtime, associates addressed him as Arthur. He did not encourage familiarity and had trouble coping with excessive displays of it. One time a news photographer arranging a group shot repeatedly addressed him as *Artie* to his noticeable discomfiture.

One of the Arthur group was Theodore Spatz, the general counsel. Teddy Spatz, a short, disheveled chain smoker from Brooklyn (Levitt's home base), was also our lobbyist to the Legislature and to the Constitutional Convention of 1968. His mumbled cryptic references to laws and people seemed to have meaning to Levitt and Volet, which was what really counted. Another who was close to the Comptroller--his office was between Levitt's and Volet's--was Buster (really Maurice) Fleischman, a tough politician who served as the deputy for administration. He came to Albany from a remarkably long tenure as City Manager of Long Beach. He retained, or re-earned, good standing after a scandalous affair with his secretary that ended one marriage and started another. The other deputies were younger than I was: John J. (Jay) Feeney, from Rockland County, in charge of municipal audits, and Martin Ives, from the Army Audit Agency, in charge of state audits. A step lower in official rank, but of great importance to Levitt, was Harold (Hap) Conroy, who managed operations of the retirement system. Conroy was not a lawyer, but Levitt marveled at his encyclopedic knowledge of the mystifyingly complex retirement laws.

❑

None of the other participants seemed to notice the repetitious nature of the meetings. They displayed a pokerfaced calm. I couldn't. One day, when Plager mumbled along about a topic we already had heard a couple of times, I glowered and snorted something about "I thought we had covered that last week and the week before." Silence. Someone--Al Haight, I think--changed the subject. Afterwards, Volet called me in to his office and said, "You shouldn't have picked on an old man like that; I heard you have an attitude; you gotta control your feelings." I assured him that whenever my attitude took control, it led to more than just a glower and a snort. Less than an hour later, as I passed his office, Volet beckoned me in and said, "It's nearly lunch time; let's have a Martini." He opened the tiny refrigerator and made the drinks, though there was not a drop of Vermouth on the premises. He did it a few more times during my career there.

Down the Hatch

That was the only on-premises drinking I knew of. Ah, but what a lot of off-premises drinking the employees engaged in. I had a drink *with* lunch; several colleagues had drinks *for* lunch. One auditor also managed to get off to the Towne Tavern, two blocks up the street, for a drink on his morning and afternoon breaks, as well as lunch, and before work and after work, and chivvied the barkeep if he was a few minutes late in opening. He tried to stop but each time he found that he couldn't function non-alcoholically. Another auditor, highly valued for his ability to develop the year-end fiscal data overnight pre-computer, drank not as often but more vigorously; every so often he would reach the building, enter the revolving door, spin around it two or three times, and emerge, not to be seen for a week or more.

One afternoon when I had stopped at the Bleecker, a nearby bar, several acquaintances came by. "A tough day at the office," I explained. "Do you have to have a reason to drink?" said one. I replied, "Of course; you don't think I'm an alcoholic, do you" It was a rhetorical question. But the answer wasn't clear. A drink for lunch, a drink going home, a drink before dinner, and other drinks here and there. The lunch routine was so settled that one legally dry primary election day, when I stopped at Shaughnessy's for lunch, the waitress put a teacup before me and said, "Here's your usual cup of tea." It was my usual whiskey sour.

❑

At last a new topic arose at the meeting. Levitt announced with evident pride, "The Governor has asked me to be treasurer of SPAC"--the Saratoga Performing Arts Center—"and I'd like to offer some ideas for increasing their revenues. Do you boys have any ideas?" Right away, Marty Ives said, "Herb Alpert." (It was at the peak of Herb Alpert's popularity with an unusual musical group. They were often on the Tonight show and had sold zillions of records and would have packed SPAC.) The Comptroller said, "Who?" Ives: "The Tijuana Brass." Levitt: "Oh." End of idea. The Comptroller had another idea: he put the arm on all the boys to buy tickets for a Philadelphia Orchestra performance. I've been going ever since.

Learning Volet's Ways

Some of my old newspaper colleagues, who had seen my attitude at work and knew second-hand of Volet's brusqueness, asked me, in less elegant terms, "How in hell do you get along with that sonofabitch Volet." I explained, "We both speak the same language." Not entirely. I kept him off balance. Like the Monday morning when I arrived about 9 o'clock and Volet was standing at the bullpen railing outside his office. He said, "Rivit, you're late. I came up from the city and I got here ahead of you." I smiled and said, "Yes, Bill, but you got up earlier." I kept walking. Another morning, after he had read a story in which I was quoted, not quite accurately, he came storming into my office. Before he could say a word, I said, "Stupidity, Bill, sheer stupidity." He responded, "Dammit, Rivit, you don't give me a chance to bawl you out."

Actually, Volet and I got along fairly well. Our occasional pre-lunch Martinis led to relaxed talks. Sometimes he told about growing up in a section of Brooklyn surrounded by Irish and other *goyim*. One story went like this, "Those Irish kids'd catch us going through their territory and they'd gang up and threaten to knock the shit out of you Jew bastards. You had to be ready for a fight, because if you said we're not Jews, they'd say, OK, show us your cock, and nobody but Jews were circumcised in those days." Another time, I mentioned my frustration about getting press releases approved by the Comptroller. Volet explained that this happened all the time, and added, "When Ollie Pilat was here he said, Bill, you got to do something, put a gun in that guy's hands, maybe that would help us get in the papers." (Oliver Pilat was Levitt's first press officer; he had taken a six months leave from the old *New York Post* and, just before the leave expired, he went back.)

'Just Saving You Work'

Volet sometimes vexed me by strolling through my office, without even a nod, to assign some project to Tarwater. In a calmer moment, I mentioned this to Volet, and he said, "That don't mean anything. I just didn't want to bother you about it. I figured you'd ask Ronnie to do it anyway." I probably would have. Ron was young enough for Volet to treat him almost as a son, a kind of love-hate relationship. (Many years later, a personnel officer of that era told me, "Volet would come up and say, 'we gotta take care of Ronnie, he's doing a good job, get him a raise.' So I'd start doing the paperwork, but before I could complete it, he'd come up again and say, 'gotta fire that Ronnie, put through the papers.' Never any reason. Luckily, I didn't, because a few days later, Volet was up again wanting a raise for Tarwater. This stuff went on for a couple of years.")

Although Volet usually left Albany on Wednesday, he could not put up with anyone else leaving early. When he sensed that some employees were sneaking out, he stationed a personnel officer in the ground floor elevator lobby. A few people were caught the first day, but none after that. The early leavers left even earlier, before the personnel guy reached the lobby. Volet also made a bed check each Friday afternoon, calling various offices, including mine, with some trivial question. There were times, on a Thursday or Friday, that I had to talk to the Comptroller in New York. Each time, he was at the Health Club and his secretary would get him on the phone. When I picked up, I would hear very labored breathing, a frightening gaspy snort, a second or two of silence, another gaspy snort, and so on. While I worried that each gaspy snort might be the last, I was consoled by the thought that the Comptroller had to keep his conversation to a word or two at a time in contrast to his usual logorrheic style. When in good breath, he was able to stretch out an answer to a reporter's question for four or five minutes, without saying anything.

Getting Out a Release

The Comptroller loved favorable mention in the press, particularly *The New York Times*, but his operating methods made it difficult to grab the *Times's* attention. Anything we sent out had to be *professional,* he said, which meant dull, *and make sure all the boys have a look at it.* As there were six boys involved, securing the necessary approvals might take a whole day. No E-mail then, not even a high-powered photocopier, so it was necessary to walk a single copy around to each of the six, in a careful order to avoid any outburst of jealousy. There was one very early model Xerox, which had a tendency to serve up charbroiled paper in lieu of a copy, and was surmounted by a sign--No Reproduction Without Permission--that evoked snickers from the reproductable secretaries. Volet offered a loophole: "If it's something routine, just be sure to have the proper deputy look it over." Most of our output was routine: announcements of distributions of various funds to local governments, listings of municipal audits available for examination. And a monthly packet of light pieces based on legal opinions rendered to local governments; since these offered the only opportunity for levity or creativity, I wrote them. I added another routine item, a brief monthly statement of the State's tax revenues and expenditures, as compared with Governor Rockefeller's budget. Most of the Capitol reporters failed to understand the subversiveness of a true report each month on the state of the State's finances.

On the occasions when the *Times* picked up one of our releases, the Comptroller was pleased, but not entirely. If the story landed anywhere but Page One, he would complain to me. And when the Governor or the Attorney General would appear on the *Times's* front page, Levitt was certain to complain again, like, "Rocky and Louie always get on the front page, I think Rocky has some influence there and gets them to favor Louie, too." I said nothing. During the legislative session, when the special interests filled the nights with receptions, Levitt would sometimes exhibit a mild anxiety about Lefkowitz, as the two nearly met at reception after reception. The next day, Levitt would complain to Volet, "Bill, did you see Louie coming into the Legion reception last night? He does that all the time. He must have someone feeding him my schedule."

Levitt's rivalry with Lefkowitz was long-standing, and, as far as I could learn, one-sided. It was based, I surmised, on title envy--people addressed Louie as General--as well as envy of the ease with which Lefkowitz generated stories that interested the *Times;* matters like real estate financing and ticket-scalping, for instance. The two men were opposites in many ways. Levitt was a reserved, almost shy, man with polished diction, TV-anchor white wavy hair, and a carefully tailored wardrobe (his shirt cuffs seemed stitched to show just the right amount of white beyond his jacket sleeves). Lefkowitz was effusive, balding, spoke to his Lower East Side origins, and was undistinguished in his haberdashery.

Different Approaches

Arthur and Louie had come to office in different ways. Levitt was an accidental candidate in 1954. The Democrats had to select someone in a hurry after their original candidate for Comptroller got caught with his hand in a till. They needed a Jew from Brooklyn, to provide balance, with W. Averell Harriman for governor. Levitt was the unpaid president of the New York City School Board, whose reputation was unsullied. Harriman won by a couple of hundred thousand; Levitt by about sixty thousand. Next time around, in 1958, Harriman lost to Rockefeller, and Levitt barely squeaked in, by about eleven thousand votes over James Lundy, whom Rockefeller rewarded with the chairmanship of the Public Service Commission. That year marked Lefkowitz's first campaign for attorney general--he had been a State Senator--and he won by a plurality of nearly six hundred thousand, the same margin as Rockefeller. That turned out to be the last tough battle Levitt had; Rockefeller offered high consolation awards for the losing candidates. (One Republican who tried too hard to win, Edward Regan of Buffalo, was left jobless when he lost. Regan eventually succeeded to the Comptrollership after Levitt retired and long after Rocky had, too.)

By the time I joined his staff, Levitt had engaged in a couple of electoral misadventures, but Volet still insisted he was a logical candidate for governor. In 1961, Levitt had agreed to run in a primary against New York Mayor Robert F. Wagner, Jr. Though he had by then been elected twice as comptroller, Levitt displayed no campaigning skill at all, and permitted Wagner to label him the candidate of the bosses which he was. The vote was not close. In 1965, Levitt was about to announce his candidacy for the State Court of Appeals when he backtracked. He had discovered, he said, that a couple of other Democratic high officeholders belonged to his political club in Brooklyn and it seemed unseemly for one club to be so dominant. (He didn't feel that such a plenitude of pals as pols affected his eligibility as comptroller.) The real reason he turned down the judge candidacy, most people felt, was that he would be running against Kenneth Keating, an Upstater whose hair was whiter than Levitt's (though unwaved) and who had made a valiant losing run against Bobby Kennedy for United States Senator in 1964. In his court campaign, Keating received the sympathy vote that had gone to Kennedy the year before.

At least one other person held Levitt in high esteem. After I advised Gene Robb that I would not be returning, his response complimented me on working for "one of the very finest public officials the State of New York has ever elected. I am glad he hasn't run for Governor because I would have a terrible time deciding to vote between him and Nelson Rockefeller."

A Day at the State Fair

That first summer I became acquainted with another ritual: the State Fair exhibit. Levitt, like the other Constitutional officers, had a special day and a special place in the State Fair in Syracuse. In mid-summer I was dispatched, with Tarwater, to confer with Chester Gore, an advertising expert in New York who had handled Levitt's campaigns. Volet (and probably Levitt too) considered Gore a genius. For 1966 he had devised two television spots, of thirty seconds and sixty seconds, that used the same pictures and same script. The thirty-second spot went like this, "A nickel here, a quarter there, a dime here, a dollar there "--and several nickels and dimes and quarters later-- "Comptroller Arthur Levitt has saved the state's taxpayers one hundred thirteen million five hundred and forty seven thousand six hundred and eighty nine dollars and sixty-three cents." The sixty-second spot went more like *a   nick el   here a quar   ter   there* and so on. What was good enough for 1966 would be good enough for 1967, with just a new number, I suggested, "More than a hundred and twenty-five million." Gore said, "No, people don't believe a round number like that, it has to be specific." I offered a specific, something like a hundred and twenty-five million, four hundred and seventy-six thousand nine hundred and thirty-five dollars and forty-two cents. Gore said it sounded good, but "Last year it took weeks to get the number confirmed, how about your number?" I was thinking *who gives a damn?* but I was saying, "That number will stand up, no question." We put it into the display; no one ever asked about it.

Safe, not Solvent

Tarwater and I nearly didn't get to New York for that meeting with Gore. As I drove down the Thruway, the State car reacted poorly to the rain-covered surface. It slid out of control. A figure-eight, another one. I stopped counting, but it probably was a figure thirty-two before the car came to rest, heading south again on the right side of the road. As we got out to survey the damage, Ron said, "We almost made our wives solvent that time." We left the Thruway at the next exit. Better slow than solvent.

Another year, I was permitted to devise the display and livened it up with a rear-projection slide show with narration by me. It wasn't supposed to be me--I had hired a wonderful voice--but the device developed a bug and we had to remake the show at the last minute and no one else was available. The following year, I advanced to a movie of the Comptroller and wrote a neat one-minute script that I thought was pushing anyone's attention span. Levitt complained to Volet, "Bill, I don't like that, I want to say more." Volet, of course, told Levitt to say as much as he wanted, which was five minutes. I happened to be at the Fair that year when Levitt came to celebrate Comptroller's day. He paused about ten seconds to watch himself, smiled in satisfaction, and walked on. That was the day a Fairgoer stopped and watched for a couple of minutes, and said "Mister Levitt sure is a fine attorney general."

Some Creative Efforts

An outlet for my creativity was preparing the *Preliminary Annual Report of the Comptroller*, and a booklet on school financing, and a recruitment handout. In the 1969 *Report*, the covers carried photos of every comptroller from the beginning of time, with Levitt the most prominent by a wide margin. In the 1970 edition, I put together a set of graphs depicting the rise of State expenditures (and revenues) of various kinds since Levitt took office, thereby providing an odious comparison of Rockefeller's taxing and spending. Nobody noticed.

Later in 1970, Volet asked me to supervise the publication of a history of the Comptroller's Office, by Arthur

Levitt, of course. The manuscript had been prepared by Dr. Plager in densely academic prose. I rewrote it to general approval, even Plager's. Then I consulted a book designer in New York. The publication was in sight. A few weeks afterward, the comptroller decided that someone might raise a fuss if he spent six thousand dollars of State money to publish his book in an election year. It really was not a political puff piece.

One source of safe publicity and a bit of patronage was the State's abandoned property fund, which was controlled by the Comptroller. The fund inspired occasional feature stories of national circulation about the putative accounts that W.C. Fields, the comedian, had stashed away under names like Snavely Whiplash and then forgotten. The names in question never could be found but we did not let that discourage the writers. The patronage resulted from a requirement that each year any financial firm holding abandoned accounts must advertise their existence in a newspaper of general circulation. The big banks and insurance companies usually chose a paper like *The New York Times* for its prestige. But there were many smaller accounts for smaller papers to seek, among them New York City weeklies like *The Chelsea-Clinton Times* and Catholic diocesan papers. The requests came first to me, and I took them to Volet. He told me, "Do the best you can for the Catholic papers, the Catholics in New York City won for us the first time. We didn't get much of the Jewish vote. The Jews didn't like Arthur naming his kid Junior, that's not the Jewish way; but they do have different first names." Aaron and Avrom, as I remember them.

'Did Willy Okay It?'

Information often was treated as a form of patronage. The first time I received a request from a reporter for details about someone's salary, I took the question to Vince McArdle, head of an audit unit (whose son later became

Albany corporation counsel) and he had a question of his own, "Did Willy okay it?" He hadn't, so I had to go ask. Volet's question was, "Who wants it? Is he a friend of ours?" I had to tell Volet and Levitt many times, "We've got no friends, they're all reporters, but maybe we could make them **enemies**." It took a long time to convince them. Occasionally, and especially when the asker was Arvis Chalmers, the *Knickerbocker News* columnist, Volet was pleased to have me get the answers. Arvis would share, with some glee, the gossip that led him to ask--even when he couldn't print the full story--and Volet relished having the inside dope. His favorite--mine too--was one about a young woman in the Governor's office who had worked her way up the payroll very swiftly, because (Arvis said) of Rockefeller's interest in her performance; Rocky handed her off as a protégé to a high-ranking official who already was married. That official soon became unmarried and then wed the protégé. Another time, when an investigative reporter for the *New York Herald-Tribune* came to dig into transactions involving the sites of drug treatment facilities, Volet gave enthusiastic approval; one of the reporter's targets was the lieutenant governor, Malcolm Wilson.

Wasting His Time

In the early sixties, Levitt had brought in Marty Ives to establish a unit to conduct management audits of State agencies and its reports should have provided powerful and positive public relations for the Comptroller. It didn't work that way, mostly because the process that allowed the audited agency time to respond to findings resulted in lapses as long as two years from study to report. On the few occasions Volet allowed me to leak a report to a newspaper--usually *The New York Times*--it was so far out of date that the reporter made some unfriendly remarks, with participial adjectives, about my wasting his time.

Ives prevailed on Levitt to take one daring step: a public review of the Governor's proposal to lease one of the two proposed World Trade Center towers for state offices. Ives thought that review would lead to rejection of the lease, if not the towers. To study the cost of the project and its benefits, if any, Ives retained a world-famous consulting firm. Right on schedule and in keeping with its past practices, the firm concluded that the World Trade Center would be a marvelous financial success and the State would get all the best from its lease. Just the opposite of what Ives was looking for. The consultant, though, was always able and willing to meet a client's needs. Change a couple of pages of text and the conclusion and Levitt had what Ives wanted. The public hearings generated favorable ink: the public's watchdog was barking again. After a reasonable period, the Comptroller concluded that the deal was all right.

In 1970, Levitt had become the longest-serving Comptroller in history and many of his friends in the financial world, headed by David Rockefeller, threw a big party in his honor at the Waldorf-Astoria. It was not our party, but Volet gave me a small list of newspapermen to be invited as guests not reporters. One of then was Arvis Chalmers. It was a black-tie event and I suffered through it in a rented tuxedo and a starched shirt collar. After several long congratulatory speeches, the longest and most congratulatory by Levitt, the dinner was over. I sought pleasant company and found it: Arvis and The Mayor Erastus Corning 2nd and his--how inadequate the word!--confidante Polly Noonan, and her boss State Senator Jeremiah Bloom. A bit of sexual persiflage among Arvis and The Mayor and Polly. Then Senator Bloom said, "Did you hear him go on and on thanking everybody in the place except the people that made it possible in the first place, the Democratic Party?" Arvis said, "Doc's his PR man," as if that should alter the Senator's views.

Levitt's name generated wonderful publicity out of trifles. A one-paragraph notice to local officials urging them to forgo mortgage-burning ceremonies, to avoid air pollution, got Levitt's name in headlines across the State. So did a brief directive that the cost of airplane trips by state workers between Albany and New York City--then twenty-four dollars a round trip--would no longer be reimbursed. Another little item that generated large coverage was the rejection of the State University at Albany's order for a silver flute for its music department; the Comptroller--really one of the accountants who knew something about music--ruled that a brass flute would be adequate and a couple of hundred dollars cheaper.

Killed with RFK

In June of 1968, we had a great achievement to announce: the Comptroller had installed a new computer system that would give his New York and Albany offices instant access to all sorts of information. For once, everyone signed off promptly on the proposed release. The whole package was sent out for use in afternoon papers of June 6. On the night of June 5, Senator Robert F. Kennedy was assassinated in Los Angeles. Not a word of the computer system saw the light of print.

I managed to get into trouble with the Comptroller a couple of times as a result of my inelegant responses to reporters. When the Comptroller abruptly cancelled the sale of some State bonds because of the interest cost was too high, I told a reporter who asked about a new date that "It'll be when we guess conditions will be favorable." The next morning, the Comptroller chided me severely: *we never guess about such things.* Months later, during State budget time, a reporter for the *Times* called for comment. I thought I made it clear that we had no role in initiating any budget or tax matters. But the story came out the other way, that the Comptroller was considering higher taxes. Levitt did not chide me; he laid me out in lavender, to use an old family phrase. He was perhaps more upset that I was described as "spokesman for the Comptroller"–*I don't have a spokesman--* than at the content of the story. What saved me from a worse fate was that I had arranged, far in advance, to be in New York City that day, helping administer oral exams for PR types for the Civil Service Department. Perhaps those were occasions to say "Stupidity, Comptroller, sheer stupidity," but I didn't try it. Levity did not go well with Levitt.

"You Sure You Want the Job?'

After I had been at the Comptroller's office a couple of years, Volet decided that he would add another professional to our PR staff. This time, it need not be one of the super-types,. just someone off the civil service list. Though the list had been around for a couple of years, I found one young man who was bright, articulate, a good writer, and a sincere interview. Before I could get Volet to hire him, another agency grabbed him. Now we were down to people I had to find a way not to hire. That is not easy. I found ways, though. To one applicant full of enthusiasm for an obviously high-level position, I described the job as one of dull detail that would keep him in the office so the rest of us would be free to travel. He declined. Along came a fellow who let me know he would prefer a quiet role in the office; to him I described a job that would require a great deal of travel. He declined. And so it went through the rest of the four or five people on the list. Once we had exhausted the old list, Volet somehow found some new candidates that we interviewed in New York City. Much better prospects. A young woman seemed alarmingly capable; at least, she turned on an alarm in Volet's mind. Then a young man with adequate attributes. No alarm to Volet, so we (meaning he) hired the fellow, who stayed several years in State service.

I had been the subject of another interview a year or so earlier. A graduate student in poli sci or something asked me why I had left the newspaper to become a press officer for the Comptroller. I gave him an honest answer: the money. He gave me a hurt look and said, "Didn't you consider the importance of public service?" I didn't bother answering him. What did he think newspapering was?

Working at the Comptroller's office had turned out to be an interesting career. Interesting in the sense of the ancient Chinese curse: May you live in interesting times. Working there often resembled being interviewed there: everything was hurry-up-and-wait and both Levitt and Volet lived up to the characterizations I had written in 1966. So it continued until the day after the 1970 election. Buster Fleischman came to my office with bad news: "The Comptroller is planning to make some staff changes; well, one staff change, in the public relations office. But be calm." I was.

'But You're Not Fired'

A week later I heard the official word, directly from Levitt. I had envisioned a rather abrupt exit, probably with no formality. The only thing I could think of was an anecdote I had run across years before in which a college football coach explained his departure thus: "After you're hired in a job like this, the next thing you can look forward to is being fired." I said something close to that and, to my surprise, it was the right thing. Levitt took pride in never having fired anyone (he didn't count those fired by Volet). He told me, "Now, Doc, you're not being fired. No, no, I don't want you to think that way. My, you're much too valuable. You know more about State government and finance than . . . than anyone . . . than, than Norm Hurd" --I enjoyed the flattery; Dr. Hurd was Governor Rockefeller's top aide--"I want you to get together with Bill and Buster and write up a job we can put you in. I want you to stay." After a false start, we wrote a job description under which I became Fiscal Research Consultant to the Comptroller. Despite the lofty title, I took a five thousand dollar annual pay cut, back to my original nineteen something salary. But I still had a roof over my head and the time to look for more permanent employment. (Some years later, I learned the real reason for my defrocking. Levitt had made a deal, during his campaign, with Governor Rockefeller to hire the PR man of the New York City comptroller as a reward for that worthy's endorsement of Rockefeller. A preposterous reason, but not for Levitt.)

My career as Public Relations Officer came to an end on December 31, 1970. My new career began on January 1, 1971. Though that new job was not supposed to include writing, I spent fun-filled days, hiding in the library, writing special reports to the Comptroller. The first was a detailed analysis of the 1970 election returns that demonstrated to Levitt that he had really outperformed Lefkowitz, a little legerdemain I had learned from Darrell Huff's famous book *How to Lie with Statistics*. Then there was my analysis of the Rockefeller proposal to buy Stewart Air Force Base for sixty-five million dollars, an odious comparison to the State's purchase a couple of years earlier of the Long Island Rail Road for the same amount. Neither of them affected the Comptroller's actions, but I hadn't expected them to.

Some Pleasant Letters

Shortly after I was defrocked, I learned that two of the most potent reporters in the Capitol had written to Levitt expressing their dismay. I know because they sent me blind copies. The letters gave my self esteem a great boost. Charley Holcomb, chief of the Gannett Newspapers' Capitol bureau, told the Comptroller that I was "the most helpful and knowledgeable pubic relations person in state government . . . He was unfailingly responsive with facts, figures and essential background when asked. . . a great help in our efforts to understand and interpret the complexities of state finance . . . ." Charles Dumas, head of the Associated Press

Capitol bureau, was equally complimentary, saying things like, "At all times he was competent, courteous, responsive and extremely helpful." Oh, in the letter, he disavowed "any impulse of personal friendship." On top of the copy he sent me, however, Dumas wrote "This is locking the barn door after -- . And it probably won't help much. But it makes me feel better, anyway." Me too.

My new job as Fiscal Research Consultant was, in a way, a reprise of Hanging Around, but with a place on the payroll. A few weeks passed and then history sort of repeated itself. On lunch-time one day, I encountered Gary Perkinson, the PR guy for the Teachers' Retirement System, and mentioned that I had probably saved him a few minutes' work by answering a reporter who called me rather than him. He thanked me and, as we parted, asked if I knew anyone interested in the PR job at the Public Service Commission. I blurted "yeh, me." I told him of my changed circumstances. He said he'd call a friend who was personnel officer at the Commission and see what could be done. Well, it had worked once before.

In the Public Service

It was like turning the calendar back a quarter-century, give or take a couple of years. Back to the days when getting hired was no more complicated than answering *YES!* when someone asked if you'd like to go to work. Oh, slightly more complicated: three guys asking instead of just one. And each asking in a slightly different way, a week or so apart. Not one suggesting that he wanted someone else. That was my introduction to the Public Service Commission.[1] The first interviewer was Arnie Prindle, the personnel officer. The gist of his questions was an answer! "Gee. I've heard a lot of good things about you. We'd like you to come work for us." But of course I'd like to talk to his boss who would be mine, Sam Madison, the secretary to the Commission. I met him a week later; more of the same: an invitation not an inquisition. And so on to Eric Rubin, the assistant to the Chairman, whose bureacratic bearing rose to the occasion: "The final decision is the Chairman's." As I knew all alnog.

Thus, I came to meet the chairman Joseph C. Swidler, who had been brought in the year before by Gov. Nelson A. Rockefeller to clean an Augean stable of troubles--failed phone service, an imminent collapse of the electric power system, a shortage of natural gas, struggling water companies--and now, very low on his agenda, to hire a new PR man. With all those big troubles ahead of me, I had to wait past the appointed hour. I sat in the lobby, watching various microminiskirted secretaries (or whoever) sashaying back and forth. When I was ushered in, Swidler offered a *pro forma* apology for the delay. I said, "Oh, I didn't mind waiting. I was enjoying the scenery." Swidler was an appreciator too. He said, with a big smile, "Fine, we wouldn't want people to think we were foolish here." What a lovely start!

On the Job, not Payroll

At any rate (a phrase I soon learned to avoid), the chairman acted as if I had already been hired. He told me how important the public relations job was and that I would not be heavily involved in speech writing. He asked me about my wry neck; the first time any interviewer had noticed, or at least had brought it up. I was hired. No résumé, no mention of salary, no question about technical matters, which was a blessing. All I knew then about electric power, for example, was that when you flicked the switch up, the light went on.

I went to work again--on the fourth anniversary of my hiring by Levitt--but not yet on the payroll. Two complications. First, the Rockefeller administration had come on hard times and a "job freeze" was in effect. (The idea of a "job freeze" was so unusual the phrase was always put inside quotation marks). Second, I heard that someone in the Governor's office had expressed concern, as I was an enrolled Democrat and had worked for Levitt. I mentioned this to John Maguire and he had a sardonically comforting thought, "Christ, Doc, if Levitt didn't mind your being a Democrat, why should Rocky?"

A Tragic Beginning

My first day in the office was unlike any other: a party, then a tragedy. The party was a farewell to my predecessor Bob Shillinglaw, who had already left the office for good. I met a lot of people; another friendly start. The tragedy affected Donna Pidgeon, who was Shillinglaw's secretary, now mine. As one of the first to return from the festive lunch, I was greeted in the office by a middle-aged couple garbed in black. Messengers of death. The man asked, "Where is Donna?" I told him, "She'll be here soon." And I asked who. Her father, at work in GE. A moment later, she walked in. She understood at once; the messenger was her uncle, her

father's brother. She wailed her grief. I walked out, closed
the door and left her to her sorrow.

❏

Still not on the payroll, I was asked to come in on
a Sunday—a Sunday!--to prepare a Very Important Press
Release. Swidler had convinced the Governor that, in order
to overcome the pervasive threat of an electric system failure,
the State must take control of the planning and building of
new power plants and new power lines. The release I worked
on was about a plan to match the power supply in New York
City with the likely (higher) demand that summer. It also was
part of a campaign to convince the Legislature of the need
for proper planning. One of the commissioners, Ken Jones,
had issued a report recommending twenty-three steps in all
to balance supply with demand, and the twenty-third was
to run the subways at half-speed. Politically powerful, as
was soon confirmed. On Monday afternoon, Swidler called
me to his office and I met Hugh Morrow, the Governor's
super-PR man, for the only time. Swidler had edited my
draft. Morrow read it over the phone to Bobby Douglass, the
Governor's chief of staff. Morrow told Swidler, "Bobby says
it's OK, Joe; now Doc and I will get it out." While we walked
to my office, Morrow said, "We'll give Joe his changes in
the first paragraph, then pick up the rest; it's fine." I told
him I was worried about not being on the payroll. He said,
"You've got nothing to worry about." (Next day, I read, in all
the papers, that Jones's report had caught the Rockefeller
administration by surprise.)

Morrow was right about my job, but it still took a while
to get my first PSC check. While I waited, I was involved
in new interviews. Whenever I met Prindle, or Madison, or
Rubin, he had a question: "Have you heard anything from
the Governor's office?" Each time, I answered, "You know, I
was just going to ask you that." It was June before I was put
on the payroll at the same nineteen thousand one hundred

twenty dollars I had started with in the Comptroller's office. And ended with too

I was one of hundreds of people Swidler hired. The others came from all over the country, but mainly from Washington. People who had worked for Swidler when he was chairman of the Federal Power Commission (1961-65), or people he knew from his lawyering for utilities. They replaced about two hundred and fifty people Swidler had transferred to the State Department of Transportation, ostensibly to follow a change in function. Swidler moved some people just to get rid of them. He also found new and sometimes less important assignments for some who stayed, but he did not cut their pay. Most of the new people came with thirty thousand dollar salaries and enthusiasm, as the parking lot showed on Saturdays and Sundays. Swidler also brought a spirit of openness and collegiality to a department that always had operated stealthily.

A Philosophical Question

Rubin soon left for a job in Washington, but not before he had posed another question: what is your philosophy about public relations? I thought about ten seconds. I couldn't say, as I had to some colleagues in the Comptroller's office: "Don't exactly lie." Too flip to tell an "assistant to" someone. So I retreated to: "We can't expect people to love us, so I'll try to get them to understand us." When, a few weeks later, Eric left us, I neatly folded my philosophy into the same package that held my résumé, never to be flaunted again. Rubin's successor was Charles A. Zielinski, a young lawyer who had been assistant to a maverick member of the Federal Communications Commission.

❏

Before I could get people to understand us, I had to understand what was going on. Everything that happened or might happen was put on paper and a copy turned up in my office. Everything: notices, orders, recommended decisions, staff testimony, company testimony, briefs (legal not literal ones), agendas, and party invitations. A ream of paper every few days. Much of it filled my briefcase each evening and, yes, I read it all. Getting those documents was sometimes a mixed blessing. The openness was often obscured in lawyer language, and, even worse, in engineer-imitating-lawyer language. To get out a press release that could be understood, I had to get the approval of only the person who originated the material. Some authors, though, had fallen in love with their pseudo-language and retranslated my English. I then commented on their editing in some Anglo-Saxon words and stuck to my version.

A Learning Curve

For an advanced course in regulation, I turned frequently to Maynard Ugol, the chief of the Office of Special Assistants—the opinion writers—whose office was one door away from mine. Maynard, several years younger than I, was brilliant and patient and soft-spoken. He also was tall, slender and not handsome, and a fashion plate who always was color-coordinated right to his shoes: light blue to match his summer slacks, for instance. I never learned his sartorial splendor.

Ugol had enlisted an unusual corps of opinion writers, only one of whom—Ed Murphy, an engineer—came from the pre-Swidler force, Joe Klovekorn, an unlawlerly gay young lawyer, had grown up on Cedar Avenue in Mount Vernon, a couple of houses away from where I lived in 1952-1955, and we shared memories of our neighbor Bella Abzug. (Joe went to the Pennsylvania commission and died of AIDS at age 49); Dan Schiffer, whom I once described as the "comparative of Schiff"—general counsel Peter Schiff. Schiffer mumbled when possible, including in his handwriting. A later addition, Herb Brown, drove an original SAAB, and, when I broke a leg in 1974, bootlegged a half-pint of Scotch to my hospital bed; I had to refuse it.

In the Commission's quarters at 44 Holland Avenue, I shared a double-sized office with my secretary, and with Margery Temple, the reports editor, and her assistant, whose identity changed quite often. Miss Temple, whose desk was behind me, was afflicted with shattering coughing spells and each time she stopped I was wary of turning around: I always wondered if she was still with us. The odd mixture in my office and even odder layouts elsewhere in the building were the result of Swidler's determination that this was to be just a brief stop on the way to a complete building in the Empire State Plaza, just across the street from the Governor's office. (Joe didn't make it; the move did not take place until 1975.)

Swidler was a compact wiry well-tailored man of non-Herculean proportions who took his exercise each morning in our office building by walking upstairs from the ground floor to the top, then back to the third, where his office was. He was more than sixty years old, so our official biography dropped mention of his birth year which was 1909. It still noted his service in high office with the Tennessee Valley Authority from 1933 to 1957.

Changes for the Better

Swidler had also wrought changes in the Commission. He brought in Ken Jones—Professor William K. Jones of Columbia Law School—and Carmel Carrington Marr, the first black and first woman to serve on the Commission. Jones had the reputation, probably merited, for dictating his decisions starting with the table of contents and working on through. He also had a uniquely horrible sounding laugh, as if he had learned it from a poorly-edited soundtrack for *Laugh In*. Mrs. Marr, who came from an old Brooklyn family of Republicans, had little to say in Commission meetings; she felt no compulsion to repeat what someone else had said:

a rare trait. The other Commissioners were old Republican wheel horses: Edward P. Larkin, and John F. Ryan. Larkin had been presiding supervisor in the Town of Hempstead in Nassau County and Rockefeller appointed him to the Commission in 1961 because the Republican leaders were afraid that Larkin (and they) would be voted out of office in the fall. Ryan just needed a job in 1971. Larkin was sympathetic to New York Telephone Company; Ryan to Niagara Mohawk, the power company, and to telephone users in his home county. Swidler played on their preferences to guarantee votes for his pet projects.

❑

Along with reorganizing the Commission staff, Swidler had directed it to represent the public in all cases before the Commission. In an effort to show customers that someone was taking their side, I issued a couple of press releases describing the Staff's opposition to a New York Telephone Company request for a four hundred million dollar rate increase. It had never been done before. A day or so later, Swidler told me that the company was upset because it had not been offered a chance to comment. I told him, "They've already publicized all the reasons they should get an increase; they can always try it again." He kind of agreed and added, "Just be sure you don't embarrass the Commission." I replied, "Chairman, only the Commission can embarrass the Commission." He grinned and nodded. A decade passed before a chairman again mentioned that I should avoid embarrassing the Commission.

A Show of Support

Swidler showed me support above and beyond the call of duty. Early in that first summer, I erupted in anger and vulgar language when a woman reporter at *Newsday* accused me of lying to her. She called the Chairman. He phoned me (his office was twenty feet away) and said quietly, "You'll have to remember to control yourself; we need all the good public relations we can get." I was amazed by his mildness.

Some months later, when I brought him a draft of the 1971 Annual Report for review, he read the introduction, no more, and said, "You make it seem that we've taken care of all our problems; my God, if we did that, there wouldn't be any need for us. Rewrite it to say we're making progress. That's good enough." I was a bit upset and mentioned it to Ugol, who told me, "That's not bad. Last year, when Shillinglaw brought in the annual report, Joe looked at the first page, said 'That's shit!' and dropped the whole thing in the wastebasket."

❏

The natural gas shortage worsened–the country was using gas faster than new supplies were being discovered-- and the Commission investigated what could be done about it. After many hearings in which the Staff described the problem and offered solutions, a hearing officer recommended, to my astonishment, that nothing need be done. I was still the new kid in the office, but as soon as I discovered this odd outcome in an advance draft, I told his boss Isador Crade about it. He saw the disparity and assigned another hearing officer to make it right

Hearing the Public

The Commission was beset in the early seventies by the disruptive tactics of various left-wingers at our public statement hearings and by bomb threats in the office. Swidler did not give in to either. A Maoist group in Buffalo was particularly nasty and when word came during a Commission session that a hearing examiner had kept a hearing going through the disruptions, Swidler said, "I wish there were something special I could do for him." Someone suggested, "Give him this weekend off." Everyone laughed. The examiner did not get the weekend off. The bomb scares all were made in phone calls to the telephone operator at one of the downtown department stores, and our building was emptied each time. When someone had the effrontery to phone in a bomb scare while the Commission was meeting, Swidler moved the proceedings out to the parking lot. He sat on the fender of a car to preside; nearly everyone else had to stand. When a bomb threat was reported when there was no session, many of the staff sought safety in the Elbo Room, a nearby bar.

The public statement hearings had been designed to give customers a chance to blow off steam. At one hearing in Albany, Sandy Jacobs, a reporter for *The Wall Street Journal*, found the lead for a Page One article about a New York Telephone rate case: a little old lady in tennis shoes, the cliché come to life. He asked me, "How did you manage to get her here for me to see?" I kept my secret. For the most part, though, the hearings were dominated by amateur (or semi-professional) advocates, whose intentions were much better than their effect. Janet Stebins, whose address was a post office box, represented a large number of small consumer groups; grandmotherly Mrs. Florence Rice was the Harlem Consumers Education Council; Carl Jones always looked toward heaven (or the ceiling) for inspiration as he spoke. Two local folk—Earl Fraley, a large man of limited intellect, and Joe Petnel, a self-styled inventor from Troy—insisted on being sworn as to the truth of their comments. George Levine and Ellie Martell added some pseudo-evidence to their testimony and took their show around the state, offering to hire out to interested parties. When they sought financing from Erie County, a reporter in Buffalo asked me about their achievements. I told him the truth, which spoiled their chances. When Ed Larkin saw the reporter's story, he told me, "You shouldn't have said that; they're just a couple of poor souls trying to make a living." George and Ellie remained cordial.

Larkin's comment was true to form. He had been in politics all his adult life and was, anyway, kindly disposed to his fellow man. A belief widely held in the office was that Larkin's salary was no more than walkaround money, as he reputedly had acquired a stake in the course of his earlier office-holdings. Ed owned a yacht, well, a large cabin cruiser, and one time, as he eased it out of a mooring, it brushed its neighbor, inflicting some superficial damage. Ed apologized to the other yachtsman and offered to pay for the repairs. The other fellow continued to rant, so Ed suggested, "Would you feel better if you poked me in the nose?" Which the other fellow did. Ed complained of chest pains, but the real injury was to his dignity.

In July 1988, Larkin, in Albany for a Commission meeting, complained of a pain in his gut. It must have been a terrible pain, for the gut was globally large. Folks urged him to go the emergency room at Albany Medical Center. No way, he said, can't tell what those doctors might do, But the pain grew worse and Mrs. Marr's entreaties prevailed. On July 20, he went into the hospital. The doctors operated and for a time he appeared to be recovering, but he grew worse and, on August 30, he died. He truly was mourned.

Death in the Evening

In response to popular demand, mainly from politicians, the Commission held some public statement hearings in its offices in the World Trade Center in Manhattan. It was not an easy place to reach, but the politicians brought in busloads of old people from the Bronx. They filled the hearing room, usually expressing only concern for how long will we have to stay, and when do we get lunch? Once a politician organized a people's hearing and took over the proceeding; it was nearly lunchtime, so the hearing officer recessed his hearing. The people's hearing did not last long: no TV cameras.

Later public hearings in New York took a deadly turn. Not on purpose, of course. Those hearings were held in the evening, which was a worse time to reach or leave the place. At the first hearing, an old man spoke briefly, walked back

to his seat and suddenly slumped over. I went outside to call
the security people to help. He was beyond help, but they
quickly moved him, chair and all, into a side room, then to a
hospital. Months later, it happened again. That ended night
hearings. No one wanted to see if death came in threes, or
where the third one might fall.

❑

For an old bureaucrat, Swidler did not always
understand the workings of the bureaucracy. After the
Legislature had passed the laws that gave the State full
authority over the placement of electric power plants and
major power lines, the staff had to put together regulations
for the procedures. Staff lawyers produced a book-length set
of rules to carry out Article VIII covering power plants. Too
long, said Swidler, try again. A few weeks later, Staff came
back with revised rules, even longer. Swidler quit while he
was behind. Talking to a hearing officer, I referred to the
plant-siting law as Section Eight. He corrected me, "That's
the one about mental discharges from the military; this is
Article Eight." I said, "There's a difference?" (By the time the
plant siting law had run its course, several chairmen later,
the one-stop procedure had become a full-stop procedure. Of
eight plants proposed, only one was licensed and built. By
then, I had written hundreds of press releases and answered
thousands of questions from reporters and I was more certain
than ever that it was all about Section Eight.)

About Power Lines

The power line success rate was considerably higher,
though not especially smooth. There were seemingly endless
debates among public and staff about the intrusion of power
lines into their surroundings. Should a line be run along the
Thruway, already despoiling the environment, or through a
wilderness where it couldn't be seen? Should the towers be of
wood or steel, poles or lattice, straight crossarms or bowed?
In the end, every line was disturbingly visible. One major

project developed questions about the effect of electromagnetic effusions on the health of people living nearby. That was a line designed to operate at the extremely high capacity of seven hundred thirty-five thousand volts and to carry low-cost Canadian-generated power toward the New York area. After extensive hearings at which experts produced testimony of every coloration, the Commission concluded that the line could be safely operated, but ordered more studies to confirm its view. The studies stretched out over years and millions of dollars. Only one of them, which concerned local household current, not extra high voltage lines, turned up evidence that the high level of electromagnetic fields near some homes in the vicinity of transformers coincided with a slightly elevated level of childhood cancers. The difference turned out to be one case in ten thousand children; from one case to two. The media pumped it up to an increase of one hundred percent. In that case alone, I wrote scores of press releases and answered hundreds of questions.

Release Gets $250,000

In late 1973, in the wake of the Yom Kippur war, the Arab oil embargo created severe shortages of gasoline, heating oil and generator fuel, and Swidler asked me to draft a press release, in the Governor's name, establishing an interdepartmental group to recommend energy conservation measures, with a fund of two hundred fifty thousand dollars (on top of the Commission's twelve million dollars a year budget). It was my most effective release. The Budget Division gave Swidler the dough with no ado. Swidler made sure that his group put forth all the recommendations he wanted, even to discarding some mushy material from the Department of Transportation and writing much stronger proposals. One of them called on Detroit to make smaller cars. That drew some attention nationally, and the Walter Cronkite news program sent one of its best reporters, Robert Schakne, to Albany to get Swidler to say it on camera. I watched as Schakne interviewed the chairman. As the film rolled, Swidler discussed the oil shortage, the need to save energy, and on and on. Every time Schakne closed in on the need for smaller autos Swidler equivocated. Every time, through a large roll of film, and, after lunch, another roll. A couple of hours in all. Finally, his day's film spent, Schakne turned off the camera and doused the lights. And Swidler said what Schakne wanted all along. No one outside the room heard it.

The oil shortage—more precisely, the ten-fold higher prices that it brought--also led to more severe increases in electric bills, because the utilities were permitted to pass their added costs. The customers beefed—often to me, because I was quoted in the media--that their electric bills exceeded their mortgage payments. I shared their pain. I never told them that my mortgage, at five and three-quarters per cent, cost only ninety-eight dollars a month.

Con Edison Gets Sick

A curious concatenation of events—the oil embargo, tighter environmental controls, and a new accounting method ordered by the Commission—caused Con Edison to omit a dividend in early 1974. Though there had been many warnings, Swidler expressed surprise and disappointment and banished the director of the Power Division, Harold Colbeth, to the hearing office. Colbeth never had been comfortable as director, anyway. But Swidler had the wrong victim. If anyone should have had advance notice of Con Edison's plan, it was Swidler. It was he, as a private lawyer, who had influenced Con Edison to select Charles F. Luce as its chief executive. Con Edison's decision not to pay a dividend sent all New York utility stocks tumbling and all their borrowing costs soaring. Hundreds of people who had bought utility stocks as a hedge against retirement wrote sad letters of protest to the Commission. To no avail then.

But within a few years, Con Edison was healthy again and its stock price rose and rose; so did its dividend.

❑

My secretary Donna Pidgeon, who had married, left rather abruptly when her husband was drafted and ordered to an Army training camp in the south. Donna made a noteworthy exit. She occasionally erred in her typing–or accurately reproduced my drafting errors--which one of our hearing officers, Tom Brady, made a hobby of telling her about. He found another error on her final day at work and came to tell her. With an overly innocent smile, she said, "Thank you, Mr. Brady, I wanted to be sure I'd see you before I left."

While I wondered about replacing her, Arnie Prindle phoned with an offer: a secretary whose boss had just resigned had to find a new place because she had been too nasty to the man who was being promoted to be her boss. A secretary is a secretary, I thought, and said OK. Karen Kohinke was at my office in a minute. As an interviewer, I acted as my interviewers had. I said, "Karen, I have one very important question"–she squirmed--"when can you start?" She said, "Right now." I told her, "No, it's four-thirty; come in tomorrow." She stayed with me for a couple of years, until a new commissioner made her an offer she couldn't refuse. She wound up as secretary to a chairman.

When Karen moved up, Norine Wellisch became my secretary. She had been well trained in secretarial school and addressed me and referred to me as Mister Rivett, to my annoyance since everyone else called me Doc. Miss Wellisch was an excellent worker but had her little touches of flakiness. She owned a cat, a gray-striped-on-white alleycat who walked with a severe stagger because of a brain injury, and sometimes brought her to the office. Kitty was well behaved, usually slept on an old sweater in the typewriter bay of her owner's desk, and ventured forth only occasionally to size up the neighborhood.

Enter: Fred Kahn

Swidler left the Commission early in 1974 to become, at Rockefeller's behest, the first director of the Institute for Public Policy Alternatives in the State University system. As Swidler was about to depart, I worried briefly about my future. Would the new man want his own PR officer? The answer, a month later, was no. Swidler had helped to pick his successor: Alfred E. Kahn, a dean and economics professor at Cornell University. Swidler knew Kahn from his days at the FPC, where natural gas pricing was a major business. Kahn, as an expert witness, had developed a two-tier pricing plan that distinguished between the costs of gas produced at old wells (low) and at new ones (high) and the FPC adopted it. Kahn took two months to move in, which he did on July 1.

Alan Roth, who had been Swidler's executive assistant, had recently become a Commissioner and served as interim chairman. Roth was a short, slight man with a back problem that led him to pace rather than sit through a telephone conversation. We were very friendly, except for part of a day. Alan had objected to my use, in a press release, of *that* when he preferred *which*. I made the change and left him a note: "In view of your objection that that that that I used is not correct, I have changed it to the which which you prefer." He was not amused. Alan's appointment as commissioner was good only till the following February 1. When that date neared, he asked me to issue a press release, announcing his decision to leave so that his votes would not be judged as a campaign for reappointment. Noble thought! But a few weeks after he left, it was announced that he had joined a public interest law firm in Washington. The spinner had been spun.

His Best Spokesman

Fred Kahn became his own best spokesman. He also put his stamp on commission sessions, turning them from crisp reviews of decisions into academic meanderings through issues. Even I offered some pearls of wisdom. The second time I did so, Ugol counseled me to desist. I asked, "Did I say something wrong?" Maynard told me, "No, you were right, but that's not the point. The point is that after you say something for a few seconds, someone else has to say the same thing for several minutes and so on." Kahn also tried to change the emphasis in rate cases from accounting results to economic effects, to marginal cost. My shorthand explanation was the cost of providing, or the saving in not providing, each additional unit of whatever. The Commission adopted marginal cost as a gospel, which was embraced also by the energy utilities since rising inflation in general was sending marginal costs soaring.

Kahn saw marginal-cost pricing as a way to curtail power use at vital times. He proposed time-of-use rates that would vary with the level of demand on the system. Since rates were based on average costs, his plan would require a substantial increase in, say, daytime charges in summer and offer reductions in the off hours. His idea was economically sound, logically impeccable, and politically disastrous. Residential customers expressed outrage. Politicians could count more votes among customers than among economists. That was the end of time-of-use billing.

Working for Kahn was fun, most of the time. He was no fashion plate and invoked no dress code. He often padded about the office shoeless, revealing mismatched socks. When he lived in a rented house near the office, he usually walked to work, making notes on a clipboard even as he crossed the streets. He sometimes handed his secretary a dictation tape that began, "I am dictating this as I drive to Ithaca and have not had the opportunity to review it." As usual, his prose was impeccable: sentences sometimes ran a whole

page, with each , each ; each (and) each – and – in its
perfect place. Also each.

The Consumers Advise

Kahn established the first formal Consumer Advisory
Council, which met periodically. Consumerists who weren't on
the council accused him of co-opting the movement. It really
worked the other way; the council advised him what problem
each member wanted solved to enhance his or her position
in the consumerist movement. The Council did not have any
real power, but claimed to speak for all residential utility
customers. The head of a large food-processing company
in Rochester took their claims seriously and wrote Kahn
repeatedly asking for a place on the Council, representing
larger consumers. Kahn replied each time, until he wrote
a letter that began, "I am not interested in establishing a
pen-pal relationship with you," and went on for seven single-
spaced pages to explain why.

Kahn's letters tended to be long and, sometimes,
impolitic if not impolite. When the Senate Majority Leader
sent a letter addressed to Dear Fred and signed Andy, Kahn
responded to Dear Senator Anderson, noted that they had
never met but he hoped that they might and he might then
be more familiar in his communications and signed off
Alfred E. Kahn. He also took critical note of an Op-Ed piece
the Assembly Minority Leader Perry Duryea had written for
Newsday and sent him a letter that began like this: "I am
glad to note your statement that your article represented
your honestly held views and was not written for political
advantage" and continued another five or six pages in that
vein.

❑

In 1975, the Commission, still fighting the last
shortage, convened a symposium on solar power, which
had just caught the media fancy as a solution to electric
generating problems: the sun would always be there.

The symposium drew a large audience: utility people by obligation, entrepreneurs by opportunity. The latter were more enthusiastic than the former and, as one of them said, "I hope the Commission doesn't let the utilities take this over." He was licking his chops; the aluminum siding spree was over and a fellow had to make a living at something. The entrepreneurs discovered what the utilities and their prospective customers already knew: the sun is always there but not always shining.

Multiplying the Talk

That same year, the new Governor Hugh L. Carey decided to expand the Commission to seven members, as the law permitted, with two "consumer" representatives, and asked Fred to invite the expansion. He did, of course, but reluctantly. Over lunch in the cafeteria of our building, I asked him why he objected, and said, "Going from five commissioners to seven will only expand the talk by forty per cent." He explained, "It's worse than that, much worse. It's a geometric increase: five times six times seven." His calculation proved closer than mine. Later, the Legislature required the Commission to open its sessions to the public, including TV cameras. Kahn said he was worried that an open meeting would inhibit the free exchange of views. It did, for about five minutes. Then the Commissioners discovered that their golden words might turn up in print and on the air. That took care of any inhibitions.

❑

The first additional commissioner was Ed Berlin, a protégé of Swidler's. On his first day in town, he was driving a State pool car when a driver came the wrong way out of a one-way street and blindsided him. Ed was not hurt, but wondered if it was an ill omen (*Infra*). Carey's second "consumer" appointee was a Suffolk County Judge named Anne Mead who broke the news herself in a phone call to Kahn. She mentioned that she was calling from Denver

and Kahn said he'd see her there next week at a regulatory
conference. She said, "Not that Denver. I'm in Denver, New
York." We found Denver on the map: a tiny dot in the hills
of Delaware County, just above Roxbury, the hometown
of the nineteenth century Robber Baron Jay Gould. [The
Commission and staff were by then housed in one of the
small towers in the Empire State Plaza, the site that Swidler
had coveted but never enjoyed.]

A Single Voice: Mine

The natural gas shortage became acute again in the
winter of 1976-7. The coldest weather in memory (and longer)
enveloped the eastern half of the country and the pipelines
weren't able to meet the demand. We were in the middle
of conflicting interests: home versus school versus factory
versus retail. And we were sharing responsibility for dealing
with it with the State Energy Office, a recent and rather
inflated innovation of Governor Carey's. Both agencies were
responding to media questions, until the governor heard a
radio news interview with the Energy Office spokeswoman,
to the background of loud laughter. He immediately ordered
all media calls to be referred to me. It was a lot more work,
but I enjoyed it. The Energy Office spokeswoman was a
former *Newsday* reporter, the one I had clashed with years
earlier.

About that time, too, the Staff, which had a sprinkling
of oddballs, flakes and dingbats, added an opinion writer who
was outstanding even in such company. Rafael Epstein—
one of Kotter's Kids, some dubbed him—soon put together
a Utility Museum in his office: a collection of utility gloves,
utility pails, utility tape, every utility except a public utility.
He also wrote original analyses of non-cases and otherwise
had fun. His wife was in medical school in Cluj, Romania,
and he took his vacations with her in Europe; once teaching

himself Greek so they could enjoy the Islands. He also was
born on June 18, about thirty years later than I was.

Kahn left in 1977 to become chief of the Civil
Aeronautics Board for President Jimmy Carter. He famously
led the deregulation of air fares. With that task done, he
became chief fighter against inflation; one of our punsters,
familiar with Fred's interest in light opera, called him Die
Fledermaus (pronounced deflator mouse). Just before Kahn
left Albany, the Commission Staff in a New York Tel rate case
objected that the company had not justified the pay increase
it had granted to installers, so it should not be allowed to
recover the added cost in rates. The Communications Workers
union put out its own spin: that the Staff was alleging that
phone workers were overpaid. (They were paid more than
junior engineers on the Staff, the people who questioned the
pay raises.) The union also told its members, falsely, that
the union had forced Kahn out. Eventually, the Commission
decided that the high salaries for installers were justified
because they resulted from union negotiations, handily
overlooking that New York Tel had no incentive to control
its costs.

The Ill Omen Strikes

Berlin became acting chairman and the ill omen
(*supra*) went to work. He was promptly assailed by the
phone workers' union, though he had had nothing to do
with the Staff's position. Even worse, while he was taking
a long-planned vacation in July, Con Edison's power system
fell apart and New York City was engulfed in lootings and
fire-settings. I was home when the power failed and I stayed
there to keep in touch with Commission staff and the press.
For a while I was as much in the dark as New York City was.
Soon one of our staff reached the New York Power Pool in

Guilderland, the central dispatch agency for the state, and I began coming in from the dark.

After the blackout, Governor Carey brought an outside expert, Norman Clapp, of Wisconsin, in to investigate what caused it. And he appointed Zielinski acting chairman. (Ed Berlin had departed for private law practice, as a partner of Swidler's, in Washington.) Clapp enlisted a couple of *pro bono* lawyers, a few outside consultants, and some of the Commission staff. I handled, in a limited way, his media relations. That was not an easy job; the media were seeking scandal, Clapp was seeking answers. At last, Jack Anderson, the Washington columnist, learned of the blackout. He had one of his aides call me and I told her all I could. Then she asked "What can you tell me off the record?" I said, "Off the record? Everything I've told you on the record." One of our staff lawyers, Dick King, overheard my end of the conversation and spread the story, making me an instant legend. In September, a similar breakdown of Con Edison became a possibility when a lightning storm knocked out some power lines. A dispatcher followed Commission guidelines, shut down part of the system, and averted disaster. Zielinski also weathered that storm.

A Peyser-Designate

After the Con Edison inquiry, Governor Carey designated Peter M. Peyser, an old and diselected colleague from Congress, as commissioner and chairman. After losing the election, Peyser had switched from Republican to Democrat, from the purest of motives: he wanted a job. He might have gotten one if the governor had designated him merely as a Commissioner; his nonentity never would have been noticed. But Chairman? The Democrats were incensed. One Senator on the committee that reviewed such nominations showed up with an arm in a sling, a signal that his arm was being twisted. Peyser still might have been confirmed had he kept a low profile. But his vanity prevailed over his sanity. He persisted in taking over the Chairman's office and dispatching notes headed "From the Desk of Peter M. Peyser, Chairman-Designate." He never made it beyond designate, to my unbounded relief. He had assured me that he'd keep me on in some role, but he was going to appoint his son as his official and personal spokesman.

With Peyser out of the way, Carey designated Zielinski as chairman, with no confirmation needed. He was the youngest chairman in history. (His father was about my age.) He also was perhaps the least likely. Chuck had advanced to executive assistant to the chairman, succeeding Roth. Carey had appointed him a commissioner in response to a campaign by a Republican State Senator from Buffalo, James McFarland, to have a Western New Yorker added to the Commission. McFarland was chairman of the Senate committee overseeing the Commission. Though Zielinski had lived in Washington or Albany since graduating from law school, he fit the profile politically: he was born in Buffalo and his parents still lived there.

Harold Jerry's Journey

Harold Jerry had become a commissioner in 1973, by appointment of Governor Rockefeller. Jerry, as a State Senator from Chemung-Steuben Counties, had cast a crucial vote for Rockefeller's tax program in 1961 and had lost a primary to an anti-taxer next time around. Rockefeller provided him a succession of jobs, including five years in environmental conservation, a field he staked out in Commission proceedings. In 1979, when Jerry's term as about to expire, Governor Carey announced that he would be replaced by a Democrat, Eric Outwater, a Federal environmental official. On hearing the news, Harold began

clearing his desk, until Sam Madison advised him to relax
and wait, pointing out that at least one past Commissioner
had served thirteen months after a governor said he'd be
replaced. Harold waited. The Outwater nomination got
lost in the hundred feet or so between the Governor's office
and the Senate. Jerry was reappointed and reappointed
and reappointed. and wound up, well after I retired, as
Chairman. Twice. That duality came about after Jerry
voted, alone, against Governor George Pataki's preference
in a meeting of an interdepartmental environmental panel.
The Governor then fired Jerry as chairman--he continued as
a commissioner--and the deputy chairman, a Democrat, rose
to the top. Pataki found that he had no other Republican
likely to be chairman, and reappointed Jerry.

Harold also was the first commissioner to issue a
dissent to a Commission opinion. That was partly my fault.
A reporter, David Schaffer of the AP, had called about some
other matter and asked why all the Commission opinions
had been unanimous; can't anyone dissent? I said there was
nothing to stop them. He relayed that information to Jerry,
and soon I had a dissenting opinion on my hands. Then
another and another, as the other commissioners realized
that they could gain recognition for their views, whatever
they were.

A Painful Episode

Life with Zielinski also was fun. In 1980, the Sunday
edition of the New York *Daily News* was running a full Op-
Ed page by a good government guy and he devoted his space
one day to an interview with John Dyson, the head of the
New York Power Authority. Dyson got off some strong (and,
to me, unwarranted) criticism of the Commission. Next
day, Paul Browne, a reporter for the Watertown *Times* and
freelancer for the weekly *Empire State Report,* phoned to
ask the Commission's reaction; I told him there was none.
My reaction? I said, "If Dyson ever gets the ailment George

Brett has"–it was hemorrhoids, as everyone knew–"his entire body will hurt." When *Empire State Report* arrived a few days later, there was the quote. Zielinski's secretary phoned to ask me to come up to his office. Hesitantly, I walked in. Zielinski was laughing, and asked, "Did you really say that?" Yep. End of episode. A few days later, Cliff Spieler, the Power Authority's PR officer and a friend from my Newspaper Guild days, phoned. He was laughing. I asked him how he could laugh about it. He said, "I've got the door closed. But, anyway, John thought it was funny too." It was supposed to be caustic, not comic.

❑

Early in Kahn's tenure, the State had given all hearing officers a new and higher status as Administrative Law Judges. And Crade, as chief judge, toured the country to recruit new judges for his staff. He promoted a couple of staff lawyers, brought in some retired judges from Federal agencies, hired a fellow with law and physics degrees specially for the nuclear plant siting cases, and enticed the chairman of the Utah regulatory commission with more money, if less status, than he was used to. Crade did not live long to enjoy his new staff. In the course of a major, but generally non-fatal, operation, a surgeon nicked his liver and he bled to death. His successor Bill Cowan enjoyed the services of several of the new judges, like Frank Robinson, a young lawyer who looked like a five foot one Abe Lincoln; John Vernieu, the Utahan; and Tom Matias, and Bill Levy, from the Federal ranks.

Some Help – Or Is It?

I had been working alone all those years, and Zielinski finally offered me the chance to hire an assistant. Coincidence intervened. A former Buffalo reporter, Bob Balme, dropped in and asked me if I knew of a job available; he had been let go at the Thruway Authority. Politics, he said. After a short PSC-style interview, I hired him. I never called to ask why he had been let go, sure I wouldn't get an honest answer. I discovered the reason quickly; Bob suffered an incurable and disabling allergy—to work. He disdained simple chores, like answering a phone. He scoffed at the Commission's actions, saying it's all politics. He had trouble writing even routine news releases. I had trouble being civil to him and after several weeks, I stopped trying. I told him he was fired. He pleaded that I should have overheard his efforts to buy a house; I hadn't been listening. He appealed to Sam Madison, who said it was Doc's decision and he wouldn't change it, then to Zielinski, who said the same thing. Days later, I received a phone call from McFarland, by then a Civil Service Commissioner, who reported that Balme had complained to him about being fired for political reasons. My response was curt: "Bullshit, he was allergic to work." McFarland told me he had come to the same conclusion.

Still needing an assistant, I began interviewing people on a civil service list, until the personnel office asked me to talk to a young woman, Pam Brown, who was working in the Health Department. She seemed trainable. I mentioned her to Madison and to Zielinski. They were enthusiastic about hiring a woman, and a black woman to boot. I hired her. She lived up to expectations.

Burstein: Bright But Antsy

While McFarland was still in the Senate, Governor Carey nominated Karen Burstein, a former State Senator, to the Commission. When the nomination came before McFarland's committee, he asked her about her marital status. That had no bearing on the job, but McFarland was hot on gossip that Burstein was a lesbian. She replied, "I have a license to practice law in New York State and I meet the requirements of the Public Officers Law. That is all you are entitled to know." [Burstein came out several years later while running for attorney general.] Karen was brilliant but antsy, like someone who had had St. Vitus Dance as a kid. She worked odd hours, mostly late at night, whether in Albany or New York. She was generous to a fault, once sponsoring a young woman who was out on parole after a few years in prison for arranging the theft and resale of road-building equipment. The woman, Chickie by name, seemed on her best behavior and Karen kept her busy rustling up cigarettes and coffee. Chickie left abruptly, arrested again, charged with taking fifteen hundred dollars to provide help (that she couldn't give) to someone in a jam with the law.

Burstein left office in 1980 to run for Congress in a district on Long Island, where the Republican incumbent had retired and a Democrat might have a chance. Karen ran a creditable campaign, but lost to a male Republican. What happened, I asked one of Karen's people afterwards. She said, "We never expected to run into a Ken doll." Huh? "A Ken doll. You know: Barbie's boyfriend." Prettier than Karen.

By the time Burstein joined the Commission, I had decided to let each member write an official biography. Karen provided such an utterly comprehensive story of her life, that I looked for a closing line: On the seventh day, She rested. [Kind of like me and this book.] The only time I suggested a change was when Richard Bower, newly arrived from Dartmouth College, noted that what he would miss most was nightly gin games with his wife. I said, "Dick, are you sure you want to say that? What will people think of a forty-nine-year-old guy missing a gin game more than anything else with his wife?" He deleted that sentence.

A Photo Finish

Along with the biographies, I had to arrange for an official photograph of each new Commissioner. The photographer usually submitted a sheet of twenty or more images for the Commissioner to choose from, after consultation with spouse or secretary or whoever. It was a smooth operation until Elie M. Noam, a telecommunications expert from Columbia University, became a commissioner. His hair was as springy as that guy in *Dilbert*, so he didn't like any of the prints. I called on another photographer. Elie didn't like those either. I expressed commiseration: "I have the same trouble, Elie, every photo of me is a perfect likeness."

❑

Zielinski left office early in 1981 to join a Washington law firm. On the way out, he became the first chairman to issue a dissenting opinion, arguing in a Con Edison rate case that the Commission had failed to recognize the company's need to recover all its investment costs. An AP reporter quoted me, not Zielinski, as saying that the company could have gotten as much as ten million dollars more, if it had only asked. It could have. That occurred a few weeks before my tenth anniversary in the job.

In that decade, I had enjoyed, in more than one sense, the freedom to operate the public relations office in my fashion. Early on, I devised a logotype for use on Commission publications: a simple monogram. (I had also devised and discarded a more complicated arrangement of symbols for the activities we regulated.) Someone objected that only the Commission could adopt a seal. But that's not a seal, I explained, it's a logo. My explanation won. One hearing officer asked why I hadn't used the colors of Niagara University, his alma mater, on the cover of an annual report. Because I hadn't thought of it. What were the colors? *Purple and white.* The cover of the next report was purple on white. When a good government group sued to force the PSC and other agencies to issue their annual reports on time— all of us were a little late, from three to twelve months—a *Knickerbocker News* reporter asked for comment. I told him the suers were on the wrong track, they ought to be trying to stop the annual reports as a waste of money, since all the material in them already had been published a couple of times. My comment ran in the early edition, which brought me praise for subversive outspokenness, and was chopped out in later editions.

❏

Somehow--I don't remember volunteering--I wound up attending various consumer forums. At one such on Long Island, someone said that Governor Rockefeller welcomed utility rate increases because the state gained higher tax payments from them. I just said, "I'm glad my mind doesn't work like that," and drew laughs. I also accepted an invitation to what my inviter said would be a friendly meeting in Brooklyn; I left wondering what an unfriendly group would be like. Later Andrew Stein, then borough president of Manhattan and looking for higher office, and Richie Kessel, his consultant, invited me to take part in a consumerist class at Brooklyn College; Stein didn't show up. Then there was a late night talk show on a local FM station when just about all the listeners, a dozen of them, called with fairly serious questions. Party time arrived, and someone asked, "What about wall rye? They'd make good boiler fuel, very high Btu content." Huh? "You know, wall-rye, the plural of walrus." I said, "Yeh, they've got a lot of Btus, but their tusks keep clogging up the grates."

'What Does This Mean?'

In spite of my best effort at clarity, I sometimes received a phone call from a reporter who said, "I don't understand your press release." Oh, and what don't you understand? "Everything." So I began going through the release almost word for word. It turned out the reporter understood everything, but he (never a she) wanted to quote me rather than the faceless Commission. More frequently, reporters called to ask about some element in the release. I was often abrupt: "If you'd just read it all, what you're looking for is in the fourth paragraph."

As the voice of the Commission, I also became its face in TV interviews. I learned sound-bites. I also learned to concentrate on the subject at hand rather than the often beautiful interviewer or sometimes more beautiful camera operator. I also learned how fleeting TV fame can be. Friends, including some from out-of-town, remarked on how well I looked and sounded on TV. I asked, what was I talking about? "Oh, I can't remember; I wasn't paying much attention. But you looked real good." Thanks.

Helping Betty Furness

Some editorial writers called me for background. And Betty Furness, the TV consumer reporter who had been Rockefeller's first head of the Consumer Protection Board, often called. She had left the state job when she realized that the Governor was using her good reputation as a front for inaction. Soon Betty and I were first-naming one another and she was praising me for what she called honest background.

I was friendly, if not real friends, with nearly all the reporters, though I remained aware that they were reporters not friends. If I had an inclination to drop names, I could mention a lot of reporters I knew—and I think helped—when they were covering Albany on their way to better things. Some names I will drop: Peter Kihss of *The New York Times,* a world-class reporter and rewriteman; Bob McFadden, another *Times* star; Bob Carroll of the New York *Daily News;* Stuart Diamond, Rick Brand and Bob Fresco of *Newsday;* Linda Greenhouse and Susan Chira, also of the Times, and Barnaby J. Feder, just beginning his career with the *Energy User News.* Occasionally, I invited a few reporters, among them Bruce Drake of the *Daily News,* home for dinner.

The *Times* for Dinner

Toward the end of my tenure, I invited the entire *Times* bureau: Betsy Kolbert, Jeff Schmalz and Karl Uhlig. They brought wine and good company. No shop talk. Just stories, like Uhlig telling about his arrival in New York City from the Midwest. "We were having trouble opening the outer door of the apartment house, so we asked a couple of cops for help. They found the reason: a corpse jammed against the inside of the door. No signs of violence. But one cop said to his partner, 'Joe, remember we had the same thing a couple of weeks ago right here.' Quite an introduction to New York."

When Zielinski left, Governor Carey selected Paul L. Gioia, his first assistant counsel, to succeed him. Gioia had joined the counsel's office in 1973, with Rockefeller, and had a relatively long career in a job that usually led early to rich opportunities in private practice. A cultural revolution began. A dress code. A curb on discussion. An air of suspicion. A high-level review of every press release. Several of my colleagues who had been hired in Swidler's first year or so were just shy of the ten years' service that would vest their pension rights, and they worried whether they'd ever get a pension. I just worried whether I'd still have a job.

My first meeting with Gioia heightened that worry. He mentioned that if what I said about the Con Edison case had been said in the Governor's office, the sayer would have been fired. A warning? A threat? I took it as both. Before that first week was out, he saw an editorial in the New York *Daily News* praising the Commission for having found Con Edison at fault for the costly shutdown of a nuclear plant. The editorial writer had misread my press release about Staff's testimony in the case. No more releases about the staff, Gioia told me. From now on, 'The Commission's going to be the hero, not the staff." He missed the opportunity for heroism by piling delay upon deferral in the investigation.

Months later, the Commission announced its conclusion: staff was right, after all.

Gioia told me to change my ways of dealing with the media: "Don't answer them right away, tell them you'll have to get the information and get back to them. Talk to me about it; two heads are better than one." After ten years of providing prompt answers, I knew the media wouldn't take wait for an answer. In those ten years, I had also written clear (I thought) and full explanations of the process and of the decisions. That too was changed by Gioia.

Trying a Positive Spin

A few years into his tenure, Gioia sought to put a positive spin on the Commission's rate decisions. As he directed, I began writing that the Commission *turned down the request of* [fill in the blank] *for a rate increase of* [fill in the blank]. *The Commission announced it would approve an increase of* [fill in the blank]. It was technically correct, but it also was a spin that reporters, including me, had laughed out of existence many years before. After I had issued a few such releases, a legislator from the boondocks, not generally considered a great mind, wrote a letter to the Attorney General, copy to Gioia, politely describing the language as deceptive. That ended the spin.

In Gioia's dress code a necktie was *de rigueur.* I was afraid it might be *de rigueur mortis* from a combination of my wry neck and a firm collar. Gioia had been brought up in Catholic schools and viewed a necktie as a sign of respect. I wore a necktie to express my feelings in his presence, a special dress-code necktie, as garish as I could find, a two-dollar special from a tie shop in an arcade of Grand Central Terminal. (He wore a kind of L.L .Bean gumshoe to protect his delicate feet, but he had no regard for my delicate neck.)

Such differences in opinion and action might have caused my quick departure. How did I survive? Probably because, as one of Gioia's top people told me later, "He was afraid the Governor would send over someone even worse." Gioia and I also were somewhat insulated from each other; the chairman's office was on the twentieth floor, he found mine on the fourteenth by accident and never came back.

My attitude placed me high on Gioia's list, but I was not alone. He dismissed the general counsel, as other chairmen had done, and the head of the utility financial audit office, as they had not. He also excoriated Commissioner Mead, in an open meeting well attended by the press, for having made public a staff report on the Long Island Lighting Company's Shoreham nuclear plant. When Governor Cuomo appointed Rosemary Pooler, a Syracuse Democrat with electoral aspirations, to the Commission, she and Gioia promptly formed a mutual detestation society. Whichever of them expressed a view first, on anything, the other was certain to express an opposing view.

A New Emphasis

From the start, Gioia sought a new approach to calming utility customers' outrage at ever-increasing bills. He established, with great fanfare, a Consumer Service Division, headed by one of his colleagues in the Governor's office, Lisa Rosenblum. She had gained fame as a tennis player who coached Governor Carey's game; she was known as Star. She built a large staff, mainly from people who had been doing the same work in the utility divisions. She reported great success in resolving consumers' complaints. Gioia also ended the long opposition by past chairmen to the Legislature's enacting as law consumer protection measures that already were in the Commission's rules. (See *The Morning After.*)

One of the people Lisa Rosenblum added was a former schoolteacher named Ed Collins, whom she put in charge of a new outreach and education unit. He was assigned to, among other things, recruit New York City media people for his staff. A futile task, since everyone above copyboy rank was making far more than Collins could offer. In the meantime, Pat Bulgaro, a friend of mine who had been appointed to run the state tax department (as executive deputy commissioner) told me he would like to hire Collins, explaining "He can write, that talent is tough to find these days." Word got back to Gioia, and he promptly worked out a trade; he sent Collins to my office and Pam Brown (now Carter) to consumer affairs. It was a trade that helped both teams and both players. (As the number two person in the office and still on the payroll as a consumer outreacher, Collins gained job security through his insulation from politics.)

❑

The future of nuclear generators—generally a Federal concern—had become a highly controversial part of the Commission's agenda. Two plants were under construction—Shoreham on Long Island and Nine Mile Point 2 on Lake Ontario—and construction costs of each wildly exceeded the wildest estimates. Under pressure, the Commission began reviewing their economic viability. The Commission Staff was not finding any economic problems. When the Staff report supporting the Nine Mile Point plant came before the Commission for a vote, a snowstorm raged in the Northeast, and two Commissioners whose favorable votes were needed seemed stuck out of town. With help from the chairman, both arrived, though late, and the deferred vote, late in the evening, was 4-3, to adopt the favorable report. The three minority votes were cast by the women members: Marr, Mead and Pooler. The votes were personal, not political.

A couple of reporters for the Syracuse *Herald-Journal,* Jonathan Salant and Erik Kriss, wrote some stories based on their theory that Gioia was carrying out Governor Mario Cuomo's agenda to ensure that the upstate plant would be built. They refused to understand that Cuomo had appointed Pooler whose contrary vote was equal to Gioia's and her voice even louder.

Mrs. Pooler's path to the Commission had been an odd one. She had been head of the State Consumer Protection Board and Cuomo wanted to put his own man, Richie Kessel, there. He offered Ms. Pooler a place on the Civil Service Commission. She held out successfully for the PSC. Hardly a PSC decision passed without her issuing a dissent. I had been mentioning dissents in releases under prior chairmen, but Gioia told me to stop doing so. Mrs. Pooler turned her scorn on me. That probably was to be expected. During her stewardship of the Consumer Protection Board, she gave a *Knickerbocker News* reporter an estimate of the amount her efforts had saved utility customers. The reporter called me for comment. I laughed. The reporter wrote that I giggled. Pooler never forgot. I wonder how she'd have felt if the reporter had accurately described my guffaw.

Gioia Loses Chair

Gioia's tenure as Chairman ended in controversy in early 1987. Governor Cuomo deposed him as chairman (a post he filled at the pleasure of the Governor) and sought to end his term altogether. Gioia threatened to sue to keep his job; he kept it. The Governor appointed Ms. Mead as Chair (her version of the title) after she had already filed for retirement. (Her unfiling was a routine matter.) Gioia stayed on for several months, but without a voice or vote; Ms. Mead had not forgotten or forgiven. Ms. Mead installed Bill Cowan as her executive assistant and, unofficially, her *alter ego*. She called me to her office; as I entered, I orated, "Free at last, free at last, praise God Almighty, free at last." Others had expressed the same view, less oratorically. She restored me to the person list and asked me to resume writing the monthly report to the Governor with the usual conciseness. (Gioia had been sending tomes of twenty, even thirty, pages and more.) The Governor's office expressed pleasure at receiving a four-page report.

Cowan, who had started as an opinion writer about the time I was hired, headed that office for a while, and also served as chief judge and as general counsel, all of them with great distinction. In the latter days of Gioia's tenure as chairman, Cowan led the negotiations that resulted in the abandonment of Long Island Lighting's nuclear effort and its recovery of nearly all its investment. [In 1995, after Pataki took office, Harold Jerry called Cowan to his office and said: "The good news is that I've been appointed chairman. The bad news is that I have to fire you." With the aid of Fred Kahn, Cowan landed a better job with a water utility trade organization in Washington. He was succeeded as counsel by Maureen O. Helmer, who, as Maureen O'Donnell, had been a paid intern in Cowan's opinion writers' office.]

For a long time before Cuomo deposed Gioia, rumors had circulated that Peter Bradford, the chairman of the Maine utility commission and once a member of the federal Nuclear Regulatory Commission, would become chairman in New York. Bradford had worked one summer in one of the Ralph Nader's operations and ever after was described as a Naderite. Many people speculated that he'd come to Albany only as a way stop on his journey to Washington; a minority view (and mine) was that coming to Albany was reward enough, a doubling of his pay to nearly a hundred thousand dollars. Ms. Mead indicated that she was content to keep the Chair warm until Bradford's arrival, which came a few months later.

Bradford was an imposing man: six feet eight, bearded. He took a dim view, even dimmer than Gioia's, of the openness of New York's processes. In Maine, he explained, if the three Commissioners could not agree on an item in their regular meeting, "we could get together a day or so later in the corridor and take care of it." In New York, the seven Commissioners had to wait until the next meeting, and give the required notice, before acting again. He was wary, too, of letting the public in on much; the published agendas for meetings were reduced to a few items for open discussion, the rest were treated as routine. Press releases grew smaller and rarer.

Bradford had been in Albany only a short time when news came from Maine that his wife had charged him with assaulting her, slamming her into a wall at home, to be precise. They were involved in divorce. When the charge was reported in Albany, Bradford told me to refer any inquiries about it to him. My pleasure.

Reassessment Times Too

In the late 1980s Bradford led the Commission into a self-assessment–a bureaucratic boondoggle newly in vogue– at the request of the state budget office. A separate staff within the staff supervised the assessment, and put forth a set of recommendations. While the self-assessment was going on, Bradford reassessed the public relations program. In order, he said, to give more responsibility to the Office of Secretary, which, he failed to note, already was in charge of the public relations office, the office would be reshaped as the Office of External Relations, with a much broader scope of duties. I understood the signal. I wrote a memo to Jake Kelliher, who had become the secretary and my table of organization boss, explaining how I would organize an office of External Affairs. Then I made a long overdue appointment for a thorough physical examination. It showed slightly elevated blood sugar, for which my doctor advised me to lose weight. I advised myself to retire.

I wanted to go quietly. No farewell party, no speeches, no nothing. But Kelliher prevailed on me to come to a retirement lunch. It had to be several days before I retired: the only time the Chairman would be available. No speeches, I insisted. He agreed. I agreed, suspecting that they might otherwise have had a farewell party without me. It was a great party–a couple of hundred people there on their lunch hours. They gave me some nice farewell gifts suited to my likes: the Baseball Encyclopedia, a museum replica of an Egyptian cat statue, a wristwatch, and money. Jake introduced me superlatively at length. An introduction, he said, not a speech. Just a few weeks before, the *Times Union* had run an exposé of some other state employees who had played in a golf tournament during the workday. So I cautioned the partygoers: "When you run into a reporter on your way out, remember: you charged your time off." They were relieved to find no reporter.

There was still time for another retirement party for all my friends on the fourteenth floor: the file clerks, the print shop hands, the messengers, and all else who couldn't afford the official rite. I asked one of the file clerks to spend my money on an array of refreshments, including wine and beer, and we enjoyed a generous lunch hour (about a hundred and fifty minutes) of farewells.

On the next day, Thursday, September 29, 1989, I set off with my wife on a long vacation (or retirement) trip.

The Golden Years

Now I am in the Golden Years of retirement. In my younger days, retirement was considered not a trip to the Golden Years, but a first step toward the cemetery. The railroad men warned each other not to retire. "Look at old Mister Hogan,"—or Mr. Corbett, or . . . the names were interchangeable--"he only lasted three months." They didn't notice that Mister Hogan (or Whoever) was already in his eighties, after a career of sixty years or more of heavy lifting, when he retired with no pension, no health plan. I was only seventy-one and my résumé was light on lifting and I had three pensions and a healthy health plan.

Helen and I celebrated by starting on our first real vacation (vacation from what? I was retired) in more than twenty years, a motoring trip to Augusta, Georgia, to visit Helen's sister Dorothy. A leisurely drive, by way of art museums in Wilmington, Delaware; Baltimore, Raleigh, and Florence, South Carolina. We reached Florence the day after power came on again in the wake of Hurricane Hugo. A week in Augusta, then home again, by way of a different group of museums. That three-week trip set the style for our future vacations, same destination, different routes, different museums.

We Strike It Rich

Our travels also included a motor trip to the Canadian Maritimes, and some flights to California to visit Helen's sisters. With her sister Annina, and using her car, I drove up the Coast Highway to Monterey, and, another time, down the coast to San Diego. Each time we also visited sister Mary (and her husband) in Banning, where the wind blows all the time. We told our grandson Joseph about our travels and he reported to his classmates in third grade, "My grandparents are rich; they go to Georgia and they go to California."

In our travels, we viewed art and practiced the art of eating. We developed that art to the highest degree in museums: the Philadelphia Museum of Art, the North Carolina Art Museum, the Chrysler Museum in Norfolk, the Albright-Knox in Buffalo, and the Memorial Art Gallery in Rochester. Outside museums, we found other artful eating places, most notably the Polo restaurant in the Double Tree hotel in Baltimore. And some that were awful. The worst was the 45th Parallel Cafe on Deer Island, New Brunswick, whose popularity with the locals reflected badly on home cooking around there.

Cooking Up a Hobby

Back from that first vacation, what to do? A hobby perhaps. Well, I liked to bake: bread, cake, cookies, the lot. But I had talked to Bill Cowan before I left and he told me, "You can't bake every day." He was right. I sought inspiration. My old colleague George Laird, who had retired to Delray Beach, Florida, had developed an unusual hobby. When he read a column he disagreed with, he dashed off a note to the writer: "Your column that appeared last Friday in the Miami *Herald* has been awarded the George Ashton Laird citation, which is as follows"—and the final word in boxcar rubber-stamp type—"BULLSHIT!" After some thought I decided not to emulate Laird; I would have gone broke paying postage on my citations.

How about hanging around? Attending a function at the Albany Institute of History and Art, I discovered there was a need for volunteers. But doing what? Stuffing envelopes? The librarian assured me I wouldn't have to push the envelope. A gradual start, reorganizing the vertical files. Then on to scrapbooks, a mighty and disorganized group; and photo albums, more and messier.

Then came the photograph files. A collection of thousands of images the Institute had bought from Morris Gerber. Sorting out the replications, organizing the good stuff by streets and numbers, correcting identifications, determining locations and dating them fairly closely. Three times through. On to about seventeen hundred pictures left to the institute a decade earlier by Mayor Erastus Corning 2nd. Most of them had been taken by newspaper photographers and had captions of varying usefulness. For the last several years, the mayor had a personal photographer, whose idea of captioning was to scrawl the date on the back of the print. My memory filled in many of the gaps. I catalogued that collection, and several smaller ones. A lot of fun and some place to go one day a week, right up to now.

A Video Payback

At another Institute function, I met Tony Esposito, then the president of Capital Cablevision, who made me another offer. I had known Tony since, as a brand-new lobbyist for the state cable TV industry, he appeared at the Public Service Commission to monitor proceedings to determine how much the cable companies would have to pay for space on utility poles. I interpreted for him. Now he asked me to help produce some five-minute videos to take up some time on the CNN Headline News. Me? Television? Why not? So I became, at various times, an associate producer, a segment producer, and a consultant, with credits on the screen. When Tony was masterminding a video to celebrate Tom Whalen's ten years as mayor, I sat through a long spell of nifnawing, then suggested that they put together testimonials from people who had dealt with Tom. I was an instant genius.

A Chance at History

In 1993, a got a phone call that almost changed my life, and the city's history. The caller was Dan Button, who had just announced that he would run for mayor of Albany though he lived in Delmar. (Living out of town had been no problem for Mayor Corning, who combined both for more than forty years.) At lunch the next day, Button asked me to be his press guy. I was interested (neither of the Democrats impressed me) but I told him that one of our long-planned vacations might take me out of town at a vital time, so could I think about it? I thought for a day, then called and left word that I would be out of town when needed most; that was the day he reluctantly gave up his quest. But just think of the fun a couple of seventy-five-year-old guys could have had. Might even have won. Might not, too.

That incident reminded me of something else that most people would have long ago forgotten. In 1966, when Button had convinced the Republicans that he would make a good candidate for an open seat in the House of Representatives, I was still angry at him for having brought some of his family in to scab during our strike in 1964. So I secured a vote by the Albany Newspaper Guild endorsing his opponent Dick Conners. I gave the *Times-Union* a one sentence announcement of same, that ran the next morning. Someone at the paper checked and a slightly longer piece appeared the next day, explaining that the endorsement was only by a vote of eight to seven. Button won the real election by a much-larger margin.

Dinner? Brunch? So?

I had begun offering a home-cooked meal for six for some benefit auctions while still employed. In retirement, I expanded the offer to raffles, and altogether raised several thousand dollars for worthy causes. With some unusual outcomes. A couple that won an auction asked to have dinner served as a Sunday brunch. OK, even though I thought the kulebiaka—a mixture of salmon, rice, mushrooms and hard-boiled eggs baked in pastry—was heavy fare so early in the day. They loved it. At another auction, I watched with pleasure as a woman frantically bid up the price, against herself. At my wife's insistence, I have retired from that that kind of cooking.

Even before I retired, I had been active in several organizations. I was one of the founding members of the

New Scotland-Whitehall Neighborhood Association, and, after several years, was elected president. The group fostered longer hours and added space and, eventually, air conditioning at the local branch library. When those things happened we took credit. After my second term, the association was killed by the kindness of the local alderman Peter Horan, who resolved our neighborhood problems before we had a chance to.

When Helen was diagnosed for multiple sclerosis, we became members of the local chapter of the National Multiple Sclerosis Society. I promptly became a director and, as usual, was elected president for two years. I remained active after that, serving a total of twenty years.

Some time back—I was still employed—I served briefly, by invitation, on the board of the Northeast Symphonic Band, which was sponsored by the state Office of General Services. After a couple of months, the band's founder, an engineer named Re, died and so did the band.

Subbing for Helen

Helen's illness, just for a day, introduced me to Vanguard, the auxiliary to the Albany Symphony Orchestra. I substituted for her as hostess—the only title then available—at its Designer Showhouse (the next year my badge was edited to host). When Helen gave up her post as a director, Vanguard chose me to succeed her. I expanded my activities in many ways, supervising mailings, and, for four years, editing the periodic newsletter. For a few years, I have been a model at the fashion show that accompanies the Albany Tulip Festival luncheon. I have showed off my legs by wearing shorts (thunderous applause). I've also modeled tuxedos..

I suppose Helen should get credit too for my election to the board of the Friends of the Albany Public Library. Jerry Flax, a friend and the Friend who asked me to serve, mentioned that I was about the most active borrower from the library. Really, it was Helen who borrowed the books;

they just got charged to my card. Which reminds me of the time I was asked to join the board of directors of the Albany Symphony Orchestra. The asker told me how much I could bring to the board: ideas, energy, and, of course, money, lots of money. Since I didn't have lots of money, I declined with thanks.

We volunteered for years as hosts at the annual New York in Bloom celebration in the State Museum and, thanks to Helen, were selected for special honors in 2000. After Helen acknowledged the honor, I said: "When I heard I was being honored, I felt like Marv Throneberry in those Miller Lite commercials: 'I don't know what I'm doing at this party.' Now that I've heard Helen, I understand. I was honored for being her husband."

A Golden Touch

I have lately discovered why these are called the Golden Years: the doctors get rich on them.

❑

That last line was supposed to be just a throwaway: a sardonic comment on the state of old folks and medical economics. I had not been contributing much to the welfare of doctors.

Then, last April (2004), I woke up about five in the morning, feeling a little uneasy – no pain, no fever, nothing but a premonition. I called 911, prepared to apologize for a false alarm. But the medics found something wrong—a heart attack Off to St. Peter's Hospital. A week later I had surgery to make two coronary bypasses, clean out a carotid artery, and replace the aortic valve. The total billed to Medicare was over a hundred thousand dollars. I paid about a hundred dollars.

.

Sidebars &
Digressions

Grandfather's Medicine

From time to time, when I was a little kid, Pa would head for the cellar and emerge with a small dust-covered bottle. "I've got to take a bottle of Grandfather's medicine to Mr. Whoever," he would explain. I knew that Grandfather the Doctor died when I was a toddler. I didn't know whether Grandfather's medicine was something he had taken in his last illness, or something he made, or just a name Pa made up for something else, as he sometimes did. As time passed, the trips to Mr. Whoever became less frequent' then stopped. The supply had run out.

By that time I had learned that Grandfather's medicine was something Grandfather invented. Years after his demise, old patients fondly asked if we had any more of his medicine at home. It was, judging from their comments, a cure for practically anything.

Grandfather was, I thought for years, a homeopathic physician, the kind that was prevalent in his era, the late 1800s and early 1900s. But, I have recently found, he was an allopath and also claimed to be an eclectic physician. A considerable difference: homeopaths used treatments that resembled the patient's symptoms; allopaths used remedies that were the opposite of the symptoms. Grandfather was listed in the Albany City Directory for 1888 and for 1889 as a member of the Eclectic Medical Society of Albany County. The directory noted that the national society was organized in 1874–the year of the doctor's marriage. He identified himself as an allopath in the skimpy information that was provided to the America Medical Association on his death. What was an eclectic physician? There are two definitions: one who depended on plant remedies or one who used a variety of treatments. Either way, Grandfather fit the definition.

The old Doctor had his moments of high eclecticism, as I learned when I was about eleven years old and hanging out at the Delaware & Hudson Railroad yard office. It was there that I met one of his old patients, by then very old, named Matty something-or-other. Matty was a small man to start and age had shrunk him--except for his nose: that was wider than his face could absorb, triply bulbous, and luridly laced with purple and red blood vessels, resembling (in a latter-day phrase) a bloodshot eggplant. He lived alone in the family home, a tiny, now ramshackle, house, alongside the railroad tracks.

Saved—by a Nose

When one of the railroaders introduced me to him as the grandson of Old Doctor Rivett, Matty straightened as far as his years would let him, smiled as broadly as his nose would permit, and greeted me enthusiastically. "Your grandfather was a great doctor, a wonderful man; he saved my life when I was a young fella working on the canal."--by that he meant the old Erie Canal, where mules pulled the barges—"A wonderful man," Matty said. "I hope you take after him. He saved my life. A mule kicked me. Could have killed me. His hoof just caught my nose and nearly tore it off of my face. It was just hanging there. Lucky for me your grandfather was only over on the next block. The other fellas I was working with took me over there and he took care of me right in his office. Sewed my nose back on. A great job. A wonderful man." I accepted his praise on Grandfather's behalf .

A great job it was for those days. What doctors do now with microscopes and tiny instruments and extremely fine threads, Grandfather and doctors of his time tried to do with whatever needles and thread were lying in their offices. Fortunately, their patients hadn't yet discovered psychic trauma, or else they knew enough to keep quiet about it, since psychic ills then led not to a successful lawsuit but to the loony bin. So Matty got along quite well for the rest of his days.

I never encountered, or even heard about, anyone else who had benefited from Grandfather's surgery, perhaps because he operated, as on Matty, only when there was no other measure available. A case of do or die, and probably mostly it was die.

All Natural Ingredients

Grandfather's medicine had survived long enough that some of his younger patients were still able to offer praise of it. I couldn't understand it then or now. I thought I had a clue when, in my early teens, I saw an old label. Ten per cent alcohol, it noted. Aha, I thought, a cure for practically anything, and a palliative for Prohibition.

I had it wrong. I recently came upon a copy of the label and part of Grandfather's formula. The label lives up to the comments by the old-time patients. It describes Dr. Rivett's Medical Discovery, prepared by Dr. F.A.W. Rivett, as "a remedy in all diseases of the blood, stomach, kidneys and liver, loss of appetite, sick headache, constipation, jaundice and all diseases of the bladder. Dose: one to two teaspoonfuls three or four times a day: before meals and at bedtime."

The formula had a formidable list of ingredients: all natural, all vegetable, all exotic (by today's standard). All allopathic, too. The magic ingredients included red clover tops, berberis aquifolium, burdock root, stillingia root, prickly ash bark, and elder (berry) flowers, cascara sagrada and senna flowers, blue flag root and poke root, and, finally, mandrake root. I looked up a few of them and found: *pokeweed*--a thick fleshy poisonous root that yields emetic and purgative extracts; *blue flag*--the dried flower is used as a cathartic and emetic; *cascara sagrada* --used as a mild laxative. Just the thing for whatever.

Grandfather must have made his concoction in a large tub. The recipe called for pounds of most of the leafy and rooty materials and large quantities of alcohol and water, among other things. Once the active--a perfect descriptive--ingredients had been gathered, they were set to steep in a precisely defined mixture of water, alcohol, aqua ammonia, and wintergreen oil. So far, I had everything in hand; perhaps I could make Doc Rivett's Medical Rediscovery. But the formula ended in mystery. The last words were "Cut the winter" and it trailed off to a torn bottom edge of the paper.

What did it taste like? I never knew. Knowing what was in it, I'm glad I didn't know. It must have been a truly wonderful medicine. Hardly worth taking, though, for the alcohol. At two teaspoonfuls three or four times a day, there wasn't enough alcohol to displace a snort of the wife's Lydia Pinkham's, twenty-five per cent alcohol and easier to get.

But Who Was John?

I also found a recipe in Grandfather's handwriting--though it seemed too readable to have been written by a doctor--for "John's Liniment". That was a surprise. I never knew about John's Liniment, so I have no idea who John was. Certainly the liniment wasn't as popular as the Medical Discovery. It might, however, have been even more beneficial to the public health. Anyone using it--with its mix of turpentine, camphire, cedar oil, hemlock oil, camphorated oil, sassafras oil, and such--certainly could not have gotten close enough to anyone else to spread an illness. Or to catch it either. Better than a quarantine.

Pa dabbled in the formulary in his turn. Not the same way that Grandfather had. Pa worked mainly on potions that needed a cure and furnished a palliative for Prohibition. Pa often brewed his own beer and less often mixed his own version of bathtub booze. When it came beer-brewing time, I was ten or eleven years old, which was old enough for me to be dispatched across the bridge to Troy to buy a large can of malt extract, a bag of hops, and, perhaps, a large box of bottle caps--the kind crimped in place by a gadget that looked like an oversized stapler.

Pa started his brewing in a large earthen crock, a very heavy crock and, after a while, it fell and broke. It might have been an accident, because the crock was so heavy that Pa had difficulty handling it empty. Or, since it fell while empty, he might have aided its fall. That crock could have been the same one that Grandfather used to concoct his magical medicine; just about the right size for one batch. Pa soon had a lightweight replacement: a handsome copper tub, lined with tin, that one of the tinsmiths next door fabricated at no charge. No money, that is, but a lot of beer flowed next door.

Birth of Cold Aging

When the brew reached critical mass, Pa siphoned it into however many bottles were needed. The amount varied because Pa's brewing was an art not a science. Siphoning was a task Pa welcomed (though he said he didn't) because each tug at the siphon hose was good for a swallow of fresh warm beer, potent and gassy. I was permitted to cap the bottles. Then the brew was aged, for anywhere from a day to a week, depending on the state of Pa's thirst. The aging took place in a little space in the corner of the dining room alongside the stovepipe, the flue from the furnace. All was well, until one bitterly cold winter night, when the furnace raced to keep up with the falling mercury. Suddenly, the family was roused by a sound like a trolley car running over a row of track torpedoes like the kind Pa would bring home for the Fourth of July. Or, as Ma said a few days later when she calmed down, like the sound Pa made after he siphoned a full crock of beer. Those popped bottles left a malty hoppy aroma that lingered all winter. But nary another bottle ever was aged there. At Ma's insistence, Pa discovered, long before an advertising writer developed the theme, the virtues of cold-aged beer.

With Iodine, It's Scotch

The more potent potion Pa made was another matter. And scarcer. He had to wait until a gallon can of good pure grain alcohol became available, usually through the good offices of the local barber, who obtained it, with some air of legality, to make hair tonic.(That was the story anyway.) With alcohol in hand, Pa would send me to Troy, to Killilea's drug store on Broadway, to purchase a tiny bottle of rye flavoring. That flavoring was enough to transform a gallon of alcohol and a gallon of water into two gallons of rye whiskey. For aged whiskey add a splash of glycerine. For Scotch, add a bit of iodine.

Looking out for my future welfare, Pa offered me a drink of his poteen. His idea, which seemed like a good one at the time, was that I'd be so repelled by the vile taste that I'd never touch another drop of hard liquor. He was right, to a point. He mixed me a drink with ginger ale. I took a sip. The taste was vile, all right. Terrible. I could still taste it, in memory, for years. And I still detest the ginger ale.

Pa's chemical career tapered off well before Repeal rendered his skills obsolete. Making beer became too much trouble when it was easier to send a son over to Ralph Morrone's speakeasy near the railroad tracks to get a gallon of genuwine home brew (made at a brewery, of course) in a jug right from the tap. Cheaper too. There were times, many of them, when Pa went to Morrone's, which was next to DeMento's grocery, but entered from the railroad tracks, to bring his beer home internally. Pa also visited often at Mike Martin's, further down the block. And Ma nearly as often sent me to one or another of the speakeasys to lead Pa home. Often, we strolled across Market Street, to George, with Pa leaning fairly heavily on my right shoulder. The Broderick girls and the Smith girls, all four of them past retirement age, sitting on the front porches, gawpingly noted our stroll and probably concluded that it was Pa's weight upon my shoulder that had depressed it two inches lower than my left shoulder.

❏

Ma took her turn at the chemistry, too, making now and then a crock of homemade root beer. Her method resembled Pa's brewing, mixing the yeast, sugar, water and root beer extract in Pa's crock. When it was just right--rightness also was an art form--Ma let Pa siphon the root beer into bottles and I capped them. Pa never swallowed any of the root beer. Ma maintained that her concoction was non-alcoholic, but I found it hard to believe that she could mix water, yeast and sugar without producing some alcohol. Later someone produced a root beer called Mom's. Nowhere near as good as Ma's.

❏

Pa had deferred the start of his chemical work till after Grandmother Rivett died. Right up to the last lucid moment she was a proud wearer of the white ribbon of the Women's Christian Temperance Union. A dutiful son, Pa had been enthusiastic as he carried out her primary tenet: Down with Alcohol. In all its forms.

Closing a Gender Gap

Gender gap. Gender testing. Gender consciousness.

Oh, such an effort to avoid using the S word. About the only way it's still used is in the phrase "to have sex", which doesn't mean mere possession but action. One other use still in vogue: the phrase is sexual harassment, not gender bending, or whatever nicey-nice phrase might be dreamed up to take its place. What I'm getting at is that most folk are trying awfully hard to mystify gender (and replace sex). That parenthesis doesn't look right. But you get the idea, don't you?

In my young youth, sex was a mystery and gender was unknown, or at least unspoken. I remember the day gender entered my consciousness. It was a sunny summery day in mid-September, not long after my thirteenth birthday. In so many ways I was young for my age, lacking in the sensual sophistication of a much later generation brought up learning the secrets of life from the underwear ads. Especially those full color numbers in Macy's ad flyers, and the *New York Times Magazine*, and the show windows of Victoria's Secret. In my day, underwear was kept undercover.

My mentor in the gender thing was an older woman. Her name was Emily Cavanaugh and she was, in her mature way, quite attractive; her brownish hair, not dark enough to be a real brunette nor light enough for a blonde, was loosely curled and errant strands of it fell over her left temple, her hazel eyes sparkled through her eyeglasses with their light tortoise shell rims, and her bright teeth were just uneven enough to add genuineness to her glowing knowing smile. It was not her looks that appealed most to me, it was her intellect. Emily Cavanaugh could speak French well, albeit with a South Troy Irish accent. And she trilled her Rs almost musically. Actually she rolled her Rs, but I have hesitated to use that phrase since I first heard the joke about the English pub waitress who mistook a compliment about her diction for praise of the pronation of her hips. It was the same Rs sound.

❑

So here I was on that summery September day, unaware of the existence of gender. I did know there was a difference between boys and girls. I learned that when I was five years old, in the first grade. Just what difference was not clear, but I knew that boys went to the bathroom on the left side of the cellar, girls on the right side. Luckily I am left-handed, so I never lost my way.

A Learning Curve

I learned a little more about the difference that same year when Ma took me along when she went to Frear's big store in Troy. Frear's was a lovely place for me to visit, especially if Ma needed something on one of the upper floors and we had to ride up on the elevator with its ornate cage-like frame inside a similarly cage-like shaft so that you could see where you were going and where you had been. This day, Ma had to go to the bathroom and she took me with her. I thought I was a little old for that but I went along. I noticed right away that there was no little gutter alongside the wall like the one we peed into at school. I never asked why.

The next time I had a chance to learn more about the difference came when I was eight or nine years old. Some of us kids were out enjoying the summer weather, trying to do some trick riding on our bikes (like staying upright on only two wheels) over on a side street near the railroad tracks where there was no need to watch out for autos. Ma did not like us to go over there; she thought the kids that lived there were not very nice. On this day one of the little girls who lived over there, maybe three or four years old, kept pulling her dress up and her underpants down. I noticed nothing.

Somehow I did get it straight that there were two sexes: boys were male and girls were female. Then, in seventh grade (I think it was) I was thrown into confusion. We were studying history--or was it English?--and we had to study Henry Wadsworth Longfellow's poem about Paul Revere's Ride. Somebody was reading it out loud and said something that sounded like: "every middle sexed village and farm." Male, female, two sexes. Now middle sexed. What the heck is that? Then I read it and it came out: "every Middlesex village and farm." Middlesex, not middle sexed, but still too much for me. (Fortunately, we did not have to get into the names of towns and counties like Sussex, Essex, Wessex, and stuff like that.)

Some Le's, Some La's

Oh, I'm getting to the point. There we were, Emily and me, on a sunny September afternoon, oblivious to our surroundings, enthralled that we could speak French to one another. And Emily looked straight at me, with her sparkling hazel eyes and bright uneven teeth and she blurted--I could never forget her exact words--"Le plume est sur la table." She repeated "Le plume est sur la table." And again, her voice rising in pitch with her excitement: "Le plume est sur la table."

Hastily she explained: "le plume--the pen—le denotes masculine gender. And la table . . .--the table—la is feminine gender. All French words have gender." The secret was out. I knew gender, not all the la-dee-le's and not all the le-dee-la's. But I knew gender. (Later I learned that some French words even have neuter gender, but I am still not sure if that is the same as middle sexed.) With that new knowledge of gender fresh in mind, I looked around Room 309 of Troy High School. My classmates--most of them—had the same look of awe and wonder.

Hoovervilles

The homeless have been a topic of considerable discussion and even controversy in recent years. Everything seems to be in dispute: from *why are they homeless?* to *why don't we provide them affordable housing?* The answers range from the ridiculous to the obscene: from *they're down on their luck* to *it's all their fault, they're dope addicts or drunks or crazy or they're just plain ne'erdowells.* As for housing, no one seems to understand that nothing is affordable if you're broke or poor and have little prospect of being otherwise. And there's always someone complaining about the cost of housing the homeless: like the government spending twenty-two hundred and fifty dollars a month to put a family of five in a motel room. Or somebody else complaining that a motel room is no place for a family of five, the poor things.

In the early years of the Great Depression, people were homeless too. A lot more than lately, yet nobody talked about providing them affordable housing, or about how much it cost to provide them shelter. Everybody knew why the homeless were homeless: they didn't have jobs, nor prospects. As for affordable housing, even a lot of people who were living in houses couldn't really afford them. Then, as now, the homeless, some of them, used ingenuity and abandoned materials to take care of their housing.

❏

The homeless men of the Depression--there were homeless families around the country, but not around Green Island--traveled in empty freight cars, and slept at night in police station lockups. Being on the road was a tough life and when it got too tough the homeless began to settle down and build clusters of homes: Hoovervilles, named for Herbert Hoover, the man who made it all necessary.

Hoovervilles must have been universal. Even Green Island had one, and it's too small now for even one McDonald's. Mostly, the Hoovervilles were built out of sight, down behind the railroad yards, or on the outskirts of the city dump, or out along the abandoned canal. In Green Island, the dozen or so homeless men who showed up in the late spring of 1932 built their Hooverville on the bank of a tidal flat of the Hudson River, alongside a disused coal trestle, right in sight of everyone walking across the bridge to or from Troy. That covered most of the people still working. The village fathers did not like it.

Affordable Housing

We kids--about a half-dozen pals--knew right away that the hobos were building their Hooverville. We used to walk, or bike, down there after school to watch the work. They used materials they found nearby: sheets of tin from old billboards, two by fours from the railroad freight yard or from an unguarded lumber yard a couple of blocks away. To save material, they butted their shacks like lean-tos, using the old Peterson & Packer coal trestle for one side. Our parents heard about the Hooverville and we heard from them. "Don't you go near there," Ma told us, loudly and too late. "Those dirty hobos. It's terrible to think they'd come to Green Island. It ain't safe any more. You stay the hell away from them." And on and on anon. A refrain that surely was sung in every home in the village. So, naturally, most of our group kept going to watch and soon to talk to the hobos. No danger that we could see, or hear. Our elders, however, prevailed. Not long after the affordable housing was completed, the assistant police chief Bill Freeman, told the hobos they were not wanted, not in plain sight. So get out of town, he said.

Quietly, the men became homeless again, picking up their few belongings and walking off toward the railroad yard in search of a train they could take somewhere, affordably. So went all but two: Irish and Stanley by name. They wanted to stay in Green Island; they never said why. They found a place, with the advice of some of us kids, that was still in Green

Island but out of sight, over on Center Island. They built just north of an old dump, years of garbage topped by years of cinders, that had been the site of a baseball park used by Troy in the old State League. That baseball park still held a place in many local memories. That was where, in 1919 or '20, our next door neighbor, a man named Ray Richardson, had struck out Babe Ruth. Really, he had struck out Babe Ruth. The Babe was on a pickup team of big leaguers who picked up extra dough by barnstorming around the country making local semipro teams look good.

Of Irish and Stanley

The site Irish and Stanley picked was only a few feet above high tide, in a cleared space among the poplars, facing Troy. Irish and Stanley built well. They used red bricks from a footpath to the old ballpark for a floor, and carefully tucked the ends of the tin sidewalls (from the old ballpark fences) under the brick to form a ratproof barrier. Very important. The enormous and ugly river rats abounded on Center Island, still feeding off the remains of the old garbage. The men located a cast-iron stove somewhere and carted it over the bridge and past the dump. Likewise an iron bedstead.

❑

Contrary to Ma's dire warnings, Irish and Stanley proved not at all dangerous. Downright friendly, in fact. I don't recall their last names, probably because I never knew them. No matter; they were probably using a different name in every town. Each of them told us the story of his life in installments. The chapters were not always consistent. One of the first stories was Irish telling us how he had once worked with Freeman in a shipyard in New Jersey. That tale was kind of a surprise to us, because we were all sure that Bill had come off the boat from Ireland directly to Green Island, married a girl whose family had political connections, and was promptly given a job on the police force.

Freeman proved friendly to them, providing a blanket and some groceries--the "bean order"--from the overseer of the poor. Pa let me give them an old papermaker's felt, a heavy sheet of boiled wool, that they could use as a blanket. Ma contributed a couple of old pans. And we kids offered help on our own, thanks to the unintended generosity of some local storekeepers. Less euphemistically, we swiped stuff from local grocery stores for our friends. Generally, we took things while no one was looking, but sometimes we made mistakes, which we corrected by splitting and dashing away.

Bobby's Sad Tale

We weren't always quick enough. One evening, while we were helping the owners of a new supermarket to be generous, we were careless. One of their guys grabbed one of our pals; the rest of us loyally ran away. The kid they caught was Bobby Graham, who was twelve years old and could pass for nine, who could, without trying, evoke sympathy from strangers. This time he tried. He went into his little boy act, complete with tears and even sobs, and a sad story about how he was starving and his family had not had anything to eat for, I don't know, maybe three or four days. (That was not an unusual happening back then.) So the store manager at last told him never to do anything like that again; if his family was that hungry, come and ask for something. And Bobby was freed and the store people never took back the half-pound Hershey bar that had been his downfall. The manager must have wondered how long a family could survive on one Hershey bar, even a large one. After that close call, we decided that we would not let that supermarket ever again help our friends.

Stanley and Irish were an odd not queer couple. Stanley was an old guy, must have been fifty, and what we called a Polack. By his stories he had traveled all over the U.S.A. Irish was much younger, perhaps in his early 30s;

he didn't admit to having been around as much as Stanley. Their stories sounded as if they had met for the first time in Green Island. Maybe.

❏

There was no welfare in 1932. Stanley and Irish had their own welfare system. Stanley would work a day or two at a time in the Goodwill Industries place in Troy. He was paid something like a dollar a day for helping to get things ready for other poor people to buy cheap. He also collected a large fringe benefit with the help of an oversized overcoat that had huge inside pockets: a shoplifter's special. Each day he worked, he found room in those pockets for a jar or two of put-up food, some underwear, a couple of pairs of sox, even shoes. Nobody seemed to notice; perhaps they didn't want to. Irish developed a different method: he panhandled some, he picked up an odd job here and there, he flirted with the unpretty sales girls at the Mohican Market in Troy and they gave him day-old buns and produce.

The Facts of Hobo Life

Irish and Stanley also earned some change by fishing. They borrowed Steve Gongeleski's boat from its mooring in Watervliet whenever they figured the owner would be unable to use it. It was pretty big for a rowboat, and it was equipped with a net, about four feet square, that could be lowered and raised by a crank. There was pretty good fishing just under the Federal Dam in Troy, and the Mohican paid a cent a pound as is or as was. When winter came and the river froze over, we kids took care of the fishing. At low tide we were able to spot very large carp and snapping turtles trapped between the ice and tidal-flat bottom. It was a simple matter to chop a hole in the ice and bring out the nearly-solid prey. Irish and Stanley sold them too, the carp for a penny a pound, the turtles for more.

In some ways, Stanley and Irish led lives not far different from the poor people who still had a home of a sort.

They heated their shack and cooked on a single wood-burning stove, they dipped a pail in the Hudson for water (taking care to boil it good before using), dashed outside (or used a chamber pot) in lieu of a loo, and took their weekly bath in the public bath in Troy. In Green Island, nearly everyone had running water, but many families had to use outhouses or share indoor toilets with other families, and heat often was in one room at a time.

We kids were allowed to stop in at the tin shanty almost any time, even if Stanley and Irish were not home. It made a neat little hideaway when we played hooky. We were even more welcome if we brought over some relief from one of the generous stores, or chopped some firewood. The shanty also was a fine place to dry off if we slipped on the rocks or fell through the ice on our way over. And a place to warm up when we went sledding down the dump hill. That sledding was fine fun in the afternoon and a real adventure when we had only the moon for light. The hill was nearly straight down and the outrun small and the numerous trees put a premium on careful steering. Which was lacking one night when I and another kid rode belly-flop style down the hill and hit a bare spot that veered us into a large poplar. I was riding on top and took most of the blow with my right shoulder and right side of my head. I was knocked out, and I was still out when the other kid rallied help from the shanty. They brought me back there, and I thawed out and regained enough of my senses so that I could be brought home. I was still so fuzzy that I couldn't hear, or remember, Ma asking me if I tore my coat, and all the things she told me about how stupid it was to run into a tree and what if you got killed and . . .

Her advice was good, but I didn't need it. The way my shoulder hurt and my ears rung, I didn't go near a sled the rest of that winter. And the rest of that winter was all that Irish and Stanley stayed. They had explained that they were just living in Green Island until things opened up a bit. No one could see anything opening at all, but early in

March Stanley and Irish packed up a few things and took off. Just about the time that Franklin Roosevelt was being inaugurated and getting ready to open things up. The fellows picked a good time to leave. A couple of weeks later, the Hudson River flooded, as it did nearly every spring. Not a bad flood. Just enough to remove nearly every trace of the shanty. From everywhere save memory.

Some Tales Pa Told

For many a year, I was convinced that the bright bright light in the western sky that I could see from our front stoop was a big big searchlight on a high high pole at the General Electric plant over in Schenectady. That's what it looked like. Especially after Pa said that's what it was. Pa had that look of excessive honesty that would have served him well as a used car salesman or as president of the United States. When he looked at you with his baby blues and told you something you believed. So I believed that it was really a big big searchlight I was looking at. After all, I was only a little kid and I didn't know how big such a big big searchlight would have to be, or how high the high high pole would have to be, to be seen all the way to Green Island. Pa said so with his blue eyes looking at me and that was enough.

By the time I was old enough to know that that big big searchlight really was Venus or Mars or Sirius, I decided that Pa's story was too good to be spoiled by the facts. Years later, when my son was old enough to hear the same story, I found that I just couldn't tell him. Oh, it wasn't an attack of honesty. The big big searchlight wasn't there. Maybe out of season or maybe the earth-glow was just too strong for the big big searchlight to shine through.

Pa also used to tell us kids other tales, which, like the one about the big big searchlight, we probably were not supposed to believe. But we were too young to know that, and, besides, the telling kept Pa and his blue eyes in practice. Those tales--the ones we found fascinating and quite believable--were about the way various places in our region got their names. There was Hoosick, for example: a place that didn't have a name until a new doctor came to town and, lacking acquaintance with his prospective patients, continually had to ask *Who's sick?* And Schaghticoke--at least Pa's tale helped us learn how to pronounce it--which was the unnamed site of a colonial inn, where the cook often evicted a resident feline from the kitchen by shouting: *Scat, I cook!* Some of the Dutchmen messed up the spelling. Not bad stuff for kids four and five years old to pass on to their friends.

❑

Pa also told an interesting story about his school days--not that he had many of those, having left school after the eighth grade, or maybe slightly before. His story was a sort of Nineteenth Century show-and-tell. About a schoolboy--sometimes Pa himself, sometimes another kid--reporting to the teacher that on the way to school, "I saw a man get hit by a trolley car." She asked, "Where?" The kid said, "Right in the ass." She said, "Oh, that's not a proper word; you mean rectum." The boy responded, "It sure did." Well, that's the way Pa told it. I can't get those blue eyes into print.

Catching a Killer

There was one tale we didn't hear from Pa until we were old enough to be tempted to disbelief: the one about Pa helping the Green Island police to solve a murder case. Only the way Pa told it or we heard it, it seemed more like he had caught the perpetrator. Either way, a great story, but not easy to believe that there ever was a murder in Green Island, and, once you got past that doubt, not easy to believe that Pa ever had a hand in solving it.

Several years later, as a young reporter, I learned that Pa's tale was (nearly) true. I was researching a feature story about the retirement of the local police chief Cap Elliott--Orlando by real name--after fifty years of service. Since I was getting paid space rates, I was assiduously reading the blotter of the early twentieth century to expand on crimes the old chief had worked on. And there in a fine copperplate handwriting, among all the other complaints and dispositions of cases involving such crimes as petty larceny, trespassing, and bastardy (siring out-of-wedlock was a fairly frequent entry), was the only murder in the book. What Pa said happened had (mostly) happened. The blotter recorded that one night shortly after the unique murder, R. Stanley Rivett, a resident of 57 George Street, while returning home by trolley car from Cohoes, had observed another passenger wearing a ring that resembled the one stolen from the murder victim. Pa knew the fellow by name. So he got off the car as if going home, walked an extra half block to the police station and reported what he had seen. So it was really the cops, not Pa, who nabbed the murderer. But no matter, his honest blue eyes had prevailed again. Honestly.

R for Rupert – Vt.

Mentioning Pa's first initial reminds me of another, yes, still another, place name story he told. But I didn't hear this one till after I was married. He told this one for the benefit of my new bride: how a little town in Vermont came to be named for him. The story went something like this: as a young brakeman on the Delaware and Hudson, he worked on a local freight that traversed the countryside from Troy to Rutland by way of tiny towns that already bore names like Eagle Bridge, and Salem, and Shushan, and Pawlet, and, of course, the neat little place that was still nameless. Somehow, in Pa's story, which took much longer to tell, the residents of that little place were impressed by the industry and efficiency of the brakeman who helped unload parcels of freight at their depot. And they inquired as to his name. R. Stanley, he said, and the R stands for Rupert. Struck by the unusualness of that first name, the residents took it for their own, and it has stuck to this day. In fact, there are now East Rupert and West Rupert, as well. Having brought his seldom-used first name out of the closet, Pa found it fitting and even flattering that, from then on, my bride addressed him as Rupert.

❏

Pa also told lots of other stories, some of which might have been true. Well, nearly true. Like the story about the malediction he used to utter when he suspected that someone, particularly one of his in-laws, had done him a minor or imagined wrong. "I don't wish anybody any bad luck," he'd say, "but I hope whoever did it shits his pants." Never once, though, did such an event come to pass. Perhaps Pa was asking too much, as even he came to think. One day he varied the mal in his diction: "I don't wish anybody any bad luck, but I hope whoever did it loses his false teeth." That very evening came the result he wished. His father-in-law, after an evening enthusiastically if not wisely spent inspecting some saloons in Troy, was walking across the bridge toward home when the evening's intake became an outrush so violent that it took his upper plate out of his mouth and into the Hudson River. That, I reflected later, must have been close to the truth. Otherwise Pa would have gone on to tell how the old man had gone fishing a few weeks later and caught a large sturgeon and, on cleaning it, found the plate inside it. With Pa's blue eyes, a quite believable ending.

A Song of Impatience

Despite his proclivities, Pa had little patience with others who tended to fabricate, or embroider, or otherwise improve upon the truth. When Pa heard such a fanciful tale from someone else, he would sing--in his fashion--to the tune of *Auld Lang Syne*, the words we so often heard:

> *Your story may be true, my friend,*
> *But it sounds so very queer;*
> *Go tell your troubles*
>   *to the copperonthebeat*
> *'Cause your bullshit don't go here*

Pa had a repertoire of other songs that were not very memorable. Neither was his singing. The only ditty I remember, and I recall perhaps less of it than Pa did, went like this:

At the bar, at the bar
Where I smoked my first cigar
And the burden of my pockets rolled away. . . .
Ummm umm ummm . . .

Pa also could be disgustingly blue-eyed generous, as on the few occasions when a neighbor who owned a flivver or a tin lizzie would invite us for a ride that involved a return across the bridge from Troy. It was a toll bridge--ten cents for a car--and the collector came out into the road. Pa generously offered to pay the toll and as the collector reached for a dime, Pa handed him a moist but not sloppy mass of B. Payn's Son's CrossPipes chewing tobacco. Fortunately, the car never stalled. Pa chewed, as did so many of his fellow workers, to evade the strictures of Rule H, one of the universal alphabetical rules for railroaders, the rule that forbade the use of tobacco on duty. As for Rule G, the one that forbade the use of alcohol: they just ignored it.

Incensed at a Mass

As a railroad man in the early nineteen hundreds, Pa often was called on to attend a funeral of a colleague who had, sober or otherwise, come to an untimely end. It was at one of those funerals of a late Roman Catholic, Pa said, that he alone heard a remarkable bit of chanting in the Latin Mass of Requiem for the dear departed's soul. He was sure no one else heard it, because they, being good Catholics, didn't ever listen to the words of the Mass, which was all in Latin and they didn't know Latin. Nor did Pa know Latin. He just felt he should listen carefully, he said, so he could tell his Methodist mother all about it. So, while the rest of the mourners sat unlistening and hearing only the cadence of *umm-de-dee-dum* followed by *dee-dee-dum-dee-dee,* Pa heard the priest, the baritone, liltingly chant *Oh, what did you do with the incense pot?* and he heard the altar boy, the soprano, respond just as liltingly *I left it in the hall, it was too damn hot.*

Whatever disbelief I harbored about this story vanished when I was going on eleven and attended the baptism of my little sister Shirley Ann at St. Mark's Episcopal Church around the corner on Hudson Avenue. With my own ears I heard a variation that convinced me that such nearly unheard messages are possible. I heard the acting rector--weekdays he was the superintendent of schools Blinky DeMille--intoning the formulistic words of baptism: *In the name of the Father . . . and of the Son . . . and of the Moon . . . ulp -- I mean, of the Holy Spirit . . . .* And I was not alone. Ma, even with her poor hearing, heard it. Pa didn't. Poor Pa! He was up the road on a railroad run.

❏

Later that year when I was starting to hang around the D&H yard office, I asked Pa how he had gotten started as a brakeman. Over someone's dead body, he told me. Not in exactly those words, but close. It happened when Pa was fifteen years old--not an unusual age then to begin work--and had just begun the entry level job as a switchtender in the lower yard in Green Island. It was his job, when a locomotive shunted a freight car, to switch it onto the right track. Over and over every night. Other crew members--the brakemen--rode the cars to a stop, controlled by hand powered brakes, and, using antiquated devices, coupled them to one another. Since the coupling operation required a brakeman to walk or run along the tracks and reach between cars, it was a job of limited life expectancy. And someone's exhausting that expectancy, Pa said, led to his advancement to brakeman. In mid-shift one night, the yard foreman called him aside with a report and an offer. The report: a brakeman in the upper yard had just "greased the rails"--a matter-of-fact way of saying he had been run over--and a job was open. Almost before the poor fellow's remains were cold, Pa became a trainman, a title he retained for fifty-four years.

How Pa Got His Honest Look

What made Pa's baby blues so believable--except when he allowed them to twinkle--was that they shone from a round, almost cherubic, unsunned face that was set off from his unsunned scalp by the merest halo of hair. Indoors, that is. Outdoors, as far back as I can recall, Pa never went without a hat of some kind: when on duty, a blue cap with a stiff bill in freight service, or a solid crowned dark blue cap with a small leather visor for passenger service; when off duty, a brown fedora, the same brown fedora for year after decade. He could have kept his hat on for a haircut. None the less, Pa directed the barber each time: "Just a trim of the sides and back. I think I'll let the top go this time." Pa's air of veracity also was enhanced by his porchly figure. Yes, porchly, much too much there to be passed off as a bay window.

Once Pa resorted to a visual trick to quiet a neighbor lady. She had a nice little garden on her side of the fence and she often commented on the contrast to the scraggly tomato plants on our side. Pa had no pretensions about his gardening, but her comments got his goat. One night he dug out some old Christmas tree ornaments—red balls— and, in the dark, attached them to his plants. He had left for work when neighbor lady spotted the beautiful fruit in our yard. She asked Ma how we had managed to grow such nice tomatoes. Ma had no idea what she was talking about. Neighbor lady knew better than to ask Pa.

A Brush with Money

Pa's excessively honest blue-eyed look wasn't always lighthearted and harmless. One time, his blue eyes got him into trouble, serious trouble, what would be jail trouble, Federal jail trouble, today. Of course, the blue eyes got him out of trouble. This chapter began when many of Pa's railroad associates and friends looked into his honest blue eyes and concluded that he was just the man--honesty personified--to be elected treasurer of Trojan Lodge No. 90 of the Brotherhood of Railroad Trainmen. And several hundreds of dollars each month found their way into Pa's hands, and into a little tin box in our downstairs clothes closet. The money stayed there until Pa got around to depositing it in the Green Island Bank, up on the next corner.

The trouble started when Pa looked into a mirror and was impressed by the obvious honesty of the man who looked back at him. So, when Pa needed a little money, he allowed the tin box to advance him the loan of a buck or two against the small monthly stipend that went with the treasurership. It soon became a five spot or a sawbuck. Just a loan till payday. Never a lot at a time. Just enough to buy a few drinks, or to pay for his room in Montreal, or even a little stake for the older son. Then older son--who had inherited his father's honest blue-eyed look--began eliminating the middle man for an advance of his own: a few coins now and then, not much, just enough for an ice cream sundae, or a magazine, or a dollar, maybe two, to play the one-armed-bandit slot machine in the sandwich shop down the street. Never much at a time, just like Pa. And both of them always intending to stop and to pay it all back. Tomorrow.

Pa found ways to cover up the difference in his books. A little ink eradicator, a borrowed typewriter made everything look fine. Until the accounts couldn't be balanced, just not enough money, and the lodge brothers felt the need to audit the books. They took Pa's books and gave him a receipt for every page--in detail--and deposited the books safely in their meeting room in Odd Fellows Hall, on Hudson Avenue kitty-corner from the old school. When the brothers gathered for the audit, they found nothing. No page, no binding. They had disappeared. Nothing left to audit and no fault to find.

Blue Eyes Save the Day

But Pa's blue eyes shone through and soon all was forgiven. He had given every brother a proper receipt for his dues, so, having lost nothing, they had no hard feelings toward him. And the Grand Lodge recovered all that was due it from the bonding company. And the bonding company, valuing repayment above retribution, settled for Pa's promise to pay some of what he had taken the same way he had taken: not a lot at a time, but for a lot of time. Thus passed the only serious untoward effect of Pa's infatuation with his own honesty.

Several years later--by then that sad episode was thoroughly forgotten as well as forgiven--Pa learned that the power of his blue eyes extended even to the written page. It was in a way a painful lesson. Pa was by then a baggage man on the Delaware and Hudson sleeper from Montreal that ended its run, after a stop in Troy, in the Albany Union Station, right across the street from Swift Mead's emporium, entrance to which could be gained after hours by rapping the edge of a quarter on the front window. That was a signal that one had the price of a drink or two. Pa always made it a point to carry a quarter or two. And one night when Swift Mead's provided shelter from a snowstorm, Pa had too many quarters. When he left, he violently encountered a cold sober sidewalk. He regained his feet as the bus appeared and he rode home, where next afternoon he woke to more suffering than usual, the pain of broken ribs.

Form 280 Slows Trains

Pa dispatched me to the local D&H yard office to obtain a Form 280, an accident report that would enable Pa to collect some pay while disabled. On that form he wrote that on the late night before, as the train snaked its way through the curves of the Willsboro Rocks along the shore of Lake Champlain, a large and heavy suitcase maliciously and viciously struck him in the ribs. No sooner had the D&H read that report than it issued a general order reducing by five miles per hour the speed permitted passenger trains traversing the Willsboro Rocks area. The honest blue eyes had worked their magic, even in writing.

Or do I mistake the origin of the broken ribs that gave rise to the slow order? It might well have been the time that Pa was taken so drunk in the dining (and drinking) car at the rear of his train that he failed to reach Albany. A taxi driver named Johnny Drzozd had noticed his condition in Troy and carted Pa home. (Someone signed Pa off duty in Albany.) Johnny helped Pa up the front steps and, as Pa opened the door, asked if Pa could make it through the house. Pa said *I'm all right*, and, as Johnny drove away, he tripped over something that wasn't there and fell ribs first into a coffee table. The coffee table didn't look so good after that, either. It was hard to keep Pa's stories about his broken ribs straight. They seemed to be epidemic. In his earlier years, he ascribed them to a switch handle kicking back. Until he realized that I knew the handle couldn't kick back unless the switch thrower had bollixed his job.

Heartened by the successful outcomes of his 280, whichever event gave rise to it, Pa told me: "If anything happens to me"--the euphemism for *when I die* --"I want you to take me over to the yard and lay me on the tracks and send in a 280. Might as well get something out of it." I nodded and grunted what Pa could have taken for an assent, but I never meant to do it. Not scruples. Something much more real: I just couldn't figure out how to do it. Pa outweighed me by seventy pounds and I knew I couldn't carry him that far.

Ashes to Ashes

Several years after that success, in July 1954, within days of his thirty-eighth wedding anniversary and five months shy of his sixty-ninth birthday, Pa died. My wife and I and our year old son had been visiting and were saying our goodbyes. Pa was scheduled to work that night. His health wasn't any worse than usual: high blood pressure, severe headaches, stuff like that. "See you later," I was saying, when Pa tumbled forward out of the easy chair in the sitting room, clapped a hand to the back of his head, and closed his blue eyes. Pa's doctor lived across the street and I ran to summon him. The doctor pushed a couple of pills into Pa's mouth and called an ambulance. The doctor met me at the hospital: "Your father had a severe stroke, blood is still flowing into his brain. I think the best thing we can do is make him comfortable." I agreed. Pa died during the night.

I drove Ma to Albany to pick out a fitting coffin. I looked at some cheap boxes, since Pa had expressed a desire to be cremated; no sense burning up a lot of money too. Ma had other ideas. She had to show the neighbors and Pa's fellow workers that she had class, even if she doubted his. It was an impressive coffin. I was never sure of it but I hope Ma just rented it.

We waked Pa at Jack McNulty's funeral home on Hudson Avenue. Uptown. A Catholic. A man whose name Pa had scorned, and whose works he detested. But it was a good wake. Jack (or someone) had provided a bottle in the smoking room. The reminiscences also flowed. An old friend of Pa's, Jim Keith who had lost part of an arm in a railroad accident years ago but kept on working, asked how Pa died. A stroke. "A funny thing," said Jim, "whenever Doc and I talked about such things, he was always afraid he'd get cancer. I was always worried about having a stroke. A funny thing. I've got cancer." Jim lived several years more.

❑

When news of Pa's death reached Montreal, the people at the Victoria station and the little lunchroom and the bar and the hotel across the street, those people who had heard him sometimes turn down a proffered drink by saying through his blue eyes *Thank you very much. I would be pleased to accept your kind offer but I must abstain so that I may partake of Communion in the morning,* those people took up collections to buy Mass cards to send south for the repose of his supposedly Catholic soul. They entrusted their missives to a colleague of Pa's, who handed me the sad final greetings and said, "I didn't suppose it would do any harm, so I never told them that Stanley wasn't a Catholic."

Getting Pa to Church

Stanley wasn't much of a Protestant either. The only time I remember that he was in a church was for my wedding a few years earlier. It was a Baptist church and we had a quiet ceremony. Pa said he enjoyed it, but I think he was disappointed that he didn't have an opportunity to hear again *What did you do with the incense pot?/I left it in the hall it was too damn hot.* The final religious ceremony Pa attended was his funeral, an observance conducted in the chapel of a crematorium, with a Methodist minister droning the final farewell.

What a blue-eyed story Pa could have made of that. He'd surely have quoted the minister as intoning one of Pa's favorite quatrains:

> *Ashes to ashes*
> *And dust to dust*
> *If whiskey don't get you*
> *Then white mule must.*

As was well-known to Pa and his colleagues, white mile was moonshine. It now is better known as neutral grain spirits or ethanol or Skreech or vodka.

Climbing in Some Family Trees

Looking back at our forebears never was a strong point for us Rivetts, and an even weaker one for the Sickleses, my mother's family. We Rivetts were content to know no more than who my father's parents were. And on my mother's side, we knew even less. Partly, I suppose, we were reluctant to look back for fear of what we might see. Especially after a distant cousin proffered a lot of information in the nineteen-twenties about my father's mother's family, the Newburys, going back to the seventeen hundreds. Right there at the beginning was the kind of thing we were concerned about: that first Newbery sired five children before he married their mother. Who knew what might lurk in my mother's family trees? Or my father's father's?

I have found out a little about the Rivett family. I had resisted the blandishments of a publisher who had offered some to sell me, at a special price, *Rivetts Since the Civil War* and *300 Years of the Rivetts in America*. I knew our family since the Civil War; as for the earlier years, I was sure the Rivetts were in France or Canada. What I had was a paper Pa had printed by hand: a very brief history of his family that went no further back than his father, Dr. F.A.W. Rivett. It provided a birth date, October 29, 1850. But not where Grandfather was born or had lived, or had received his medical training. Nor even what the A. or the W. stood for (I knew the F. was for Francis, which the doctor seemed to want to hide). We know, from the obituary that appeared in the *Troy Record* after he died of pneumonia on January 17, 1920, that, already a doctor, he married, in 1874, in AuSable Forks, New York. The *Record* eulogized him "as a man of amiable and sympathetic disposition."

While I refused to pay for a book that might have been a hoax, I couldn't resist all temptation. So I went to the State Library. In the Census of 1880, I found Grandfather listed in the village of AuSable Forks, Town of Jay, Essex County. He was identified as a physician, born in Canada, thirty-seven years old. Wait a minute! Thirty-seven years old meant he was born in 1843, not 1850, and he was thirty-one years old, not twenty-four, when he married seventeen-year-old Alice Alzine Newbery.

Degree of Difficulty

Now the question arises: where did Grandfather get his medical degree, if indeed he got one? It was not uncommon in those days, when qualifications were passed on by county medical societies, for a young man to gain the requisite medical knowledge by apprenticing to an older and somehow qualified doctor. Sometimes, I feel sure, a young man became a medical doctor by his proclamation. Which course was Grandfather's? I haven't found the answer. Perhaps it's better unfound.

Pa failed to write where he or his siblings were born, though he often said that his birthplace was Indian Fields, a hamlet long since submerged in the Albany water supply reservoir. Like many things Pa said, it might have been so. He was born, wherever, in 1885; the family settled in Green Island in 1887.

❑

Ma and Pa might have known more about their forebears than they passed on to us kids. Ma, for example, must have known some details about her family, on her mother's side as well as her father's. But we never heard even the last name of Ma's mother's family. I missed an opportunity, while I was just a kid, to learn a little about Ma's family from an old man who might have been her father, or maybe her grandfather; he looked old enough. I was too young to know what was going on, and he was too old. We met while he was spending an afternoon visiting the Sickles family across the street. He was a shrunken man who bundled against the cold even when it was warm, and he spoke rather breathlessly and he told me a story or two about his days as a mule driver on the old Erie Canal before his breath or his memory gave out. But I can't remember ever hearing his first name, or even if he was a Sickles or someone in Ma's mother's family.

That might seem unusual in these days when many people try to trace their family ties back to Adam and Eve. Our family, though, didn't even look closely at the ties of the current generation. I'm not sure, for example, how many brothers and sisters Ma had. Whatever the number, Pa held a dim view of all of them, and especially his brother-in-law Alexander Sickles, the one who lived across the street. What Pa didn't like about Uncle Aleck was that he had "turned Catholic" when he married and that he outranked Pa on the seniority list among Delaware and Hudson Railroad trainmen.

<u>Knowing Some Sickleses</u>

I knew the Sickleses across the street, of course; their son Joe, fifth of six siblings, was about my age and we sometimes played together. And Cousin Margaret, the second oldest, who was "in training" as a nurse, used to visit with Ma whenever she had the time. The only other one I knew well in Ma's family was her sister Nettie, shortened from Jeanette. (As a toddler, I mispronounced it Nennie which she liked so much she used it.) I remember her always as a short, very fat and jolly lady--the kind that gave rise to the legend that all fat people are good-natured. She was married to Warren Burt, lean and leathery faced, who worked in the Tilley Ladder factory, an occupation that Pa rated lower on the social scale than railroad track workers. Uncle Warren was a generous man, warm-hearted toward kids, but, lacking children of his own, he didn't always know how to express his warmth. He thought tickling was a fine way to do it, and he always called me "pup", which I didn't think was nice. On the good side, he took me on the trolley car to the Albany baseball game a few times, when I was about eight years old, to the old wooden grandstand of Chadwick Park, and later to the new steel and concrete Hawkins Stadium, which replaced it.

It was about that time that we--Pa and Ma and I--learned more about the Newburys than we had wanted to know. A man we knew as Dr. Smithers, a physician who practiced for a time at the Ford Plant in Green Island (his name really was Schmitter; the family changed it in the first World War) sent Pa's mother a typed copy of the family history. It really was a history, with narratives about many of the branches. We all read it, but I was too young to notice the profligate prematurity in the first Newbury's family. After that one reading, it was put away for safekeeping. A few years ago, my sister found Dr. Schmitter-Smithers's original.

Meet the Newberys

The original history provided some detail about the seventh child of Jonathan, who was the second born in wedlock, as follows:

> *JOHN NEWBERY was born June 28, 1779. He died November 23, 1862. He was a veteran of the War of 1812, tradition says he was a captain. Mrs. Alice Rivett, of Green Island, [his grand daughter] remembers seeing his old uniform and sword hanging in his room at the time of his funeral . . .[His wife] was a mid-wife and performed the functions of a country doctor in her community,*

riding astride her horse with
saddlebags and traveling many
miles thus in all sorts of weather.
[She also bore thirteen children
over twenty-four years and lived
to age eighty.]

Not one of John Newbury's nine siblings appears to have survived long enough to warrant the noting of their deaths. By the next generation, John's, life expectancy had increased. So had the thoroughness of the family narrative. Five of John's thirteen offspring lived to adulthood. The history noted that "the third child, Daniel, died from swallowing a copper cent. The ninth child, John Smith, was drowned in a spring of water." Daniel was six years old; John Smith's age was not noted.

❑

We knew some of the Newbery clan, contemporaries of Pa's mother, who lived in Clarksville, which, in the 1920s, was a half-day's drive in a Model T from Green Island. We only visited them twice that I know of. It was difficult to find a car-owning neighbor who would drive us that far. One of the Clarksville branch, Cousin Lucy, called on us more often. Not really to see us. It just seemed that every time she was nearby she felt the need to come and ask if she could use our bathroom. Her last name was Newbery, I suppose--Dr. Schmitter's history is of little help--but she was always known to us by the name Pa bestowed on her: Loosey Bowels.

An Unfinishable Job

From the time Helen and I married we shared benign neglect toward family history. Some of the current generation of our families seem to be more concerned about the past, though not always by choice. It was a Cub scout project that caused my grandson Joe, then a nine-year-old, to trace his family history back about as far as I had: to his parents' parents. He told me about his project and he asked, with noticeable embarrassment: "Grandfather, what's your first name?" He had to ask; the only name he'd ever heard me called was Doc. I told him: "It's Francis. And don't be embarrassed to ask. Why, when grandmother and I were married, I had to remind her: 'When the minister asks "Do you Helen take Francis?" don't say "Who?" just say "Yes."'"

Some time later, my wife volunteered me to assemble the branches and twigs of her family tree, the Puccios. A grandniece of hers, noting the complexity of the family, had written, wondering who her grandparents were--really were, not just their names--and how she was related to various other Puccios. Oh sure, my wife wrote back, Doc'll be glad to do it on his word processor; it shouldn't be much work. She had forgotten how much her family had grown in the years since I had married into it--more than doubled in numbers and generations. That project is still not finished and I'm using my fourth-generation word processor. And it will never be finished, judging from the fertility of the new generation.

While I was able to chronicle much of a current family history of the Puccios, I had been unable to trace them backward beyond the generations in America. Helen knew about her mother's mother, Alfonsina Leonetti Carratû, but not about the earlier Puccios or Carratûs. Helen's best memory of her grandmother was that she had outlived five husbands, a braggable feat right up there with the first Newbery's siring of five before he married their mother.

The Puccios and the Carratûs had come to the United States, at separate times, from separate towns in Italy, and they had never encountered each other until they met in Brooklyn around the turn of the century. The Puccios came from Catanzaro, a town about halfway down the instep of the boot of Italy; the Carratûs from Cava di Tirenni, right next to Salerno. Such was the code of the time that Salvatore Gaetano Puccio and Annina Carratû were never together without a chaperone until their wedding night on September 28, 1905, the day after her eighteenth birthday, three months shy of his twentieth. In the next twenty-two years, they had ten children; the third-born, Elia Moses, died in infancy, of "summer complaint," all the others survived well into adulthood. Annina Carratû Puccio died in May 1950, a few weeks before Helen and I were married; I hardly knew her. Salvatore Gaetano Puccio died in January 1961; we had become great friends.

All we had known about the Puccio family in Italy is that a couple of Helen's uncles and, presumably, their families still lived there in the early 1960s. The Carratûs were, except for grandmother Alfonsina, a blank. It was not until the early 1990s that Helen's oldest sister Mary sent us a copy of some material she had found in the old family Bible: a listing (incomplete) of two generations further back on each side of the family. The birth dates for the children, for instance, noted only month and day, not year. For the forebears, dates of birth and death were missing; so was the whole roster of aunts and uncles and cousins.

Some Hidden Branches

Some unexpected detail emerged about each of the additional past generations. On the Puccio side, the grandfather Francesco was identified as "city clerk"; his father Nicola as a "wealthy landowner". On the Carratû side, Helen's mother's father Vincenzo was listed as "ice cream manufacturer"; his father Andrea as a "shoemaker/musician". Of all the women, only Helen's grandmother Alfonsina had ventured into business; she was a "manufacturing milliner" -- a hat maker. Oh, the family Bible listing does not bear out Helen's tale of a five-times married, five-times widowed lady. Perhaps a case of Biblical revisionism.

❑

The difficulty of tracing the Puccio family tree back toward its roots is illustrated by the murkiness of some fairly recent history: how, for example, Helen's parents, married in Brooklyn, had turned up in Oneonta a dozen years later. When I asked Helen, she had an honest answer: "I don't know." She had always thought that the family moved directly from Brooklyn to Oneonta. But Mary discovered that Daniel was born in Long Island in 1910. Elia Moses also was born on Long Island. We asked Helen's brother Dan. What he recalled was a story typical of the times: someone, a Puccio or a Carratû, had gone to Oneonta and sent back word that there were jobs available, so off the Puccios and the Carratûs trooped in quest of another city where the streets were paved with gold. They found jobs and stayed; the Puccios for a little over thirty years, some of their cousins sprung from Carratûs are still there.

Some future genealogist in the Puccio family may be puzzled when trying to reconcile the Bible notes with official documents. Dad Puccio often registered birth certificates in names that his wife had never thought of. He favored Biblical names for the boys; royal ones for the girls. The first-born son, for instance, whom we all knew as Francis or Frank, was officially Francesco (with Lord knows what middle names). Later on, Dad bestowed on Joseph a couple of front names still disguised by the initials E. (probably for Elijah) F., neither of which Joseph used. Dad registered Helen as Elena Margareta Elisabetta, which she thinks was the name of a queen of Italy. The birth date of Dorothy, officially Dorotea Grace Triestina (plus other queenly names), was listed in the Bible as February 20, 1927, and she chose to be married on that date in 1953. She learned, when she applied for Social Security, that she had been born around 11:15 p.m. on February 19.

In our family, Ma chose the names. I was named Francis Stanley, taking initially the first name of Grandfather and middle name of my Aunt Flora and secondly Pa's middle name. My little brother was named Douglas Trotter; Ma said the Douglas came from a long-ago relative who was a drummer boy in the Civil War (though I suspect it was more likely for the original Douglas Fairbanks, then a matinée idol) and Trotter for the doctor who delivered him. For Shirley Ann, Ma offered no explanation; my guess is that it derived from Ma's reading of such magazines as *True Story, True Romances, True Confessions* and the like, where heroines bore names like Shirley Ann.

❑

In her Bible notes, Mary had described her father as "contractor/engineer," which estates he attained in that order. Dad Puccio had worked for a mason contractor in his early years in Brooklyn and Long Island City, and went on to set up his own business in Oneonta. He prospered in building roads, bridges, post offices, fire houses, schools and such to the extent that he was able to buy his own steam shovel, a mark of real distinction in those days, and a source of envy among competitors. Meanwhile, he earned his engineering credentials from the International Correspondence Schools. The Great Depression came and Sal's business went.

More About the Carratûs

We learned a great deal about the Carratû family from a wildly distant cousin of Helen's named Vincent N. Carratû, whom we met in 1988. He is a Briton, and he headed one of the world's top investigative agencies (that description is from *Time*, May 28, 1984) involved in tracking down product counterfeiters. That work took Vincent N. Carratû over the world, and wherever he went he also tracked down Carratûs.

Our meeting occurred because another Carratû, my wife's cousin and sister-in-law Carmela Puccio, had tracked down the detective, thanks to an intercepted document. Carmela's father was a son of the hatmaking Alfonsina Carratû. Carmela married Helen's oldest brother Frank in 1930; Frank died in 1961. The intercepted document was a cancelled check payable to Carratû International, a detective agency, in London. The interceptor was another Carratû

(Helen, widow of Peter, who was a brother of Carmela's) who was working part-time in a bank near her home on Long Island. She made a note of the name and address from the check and forwarded it to Carmela, who brashly wrote to the London Carratû to introduce herself.

He was not dismayed by the intrusion into his banking affairs. "What an unexpected pleasure to receive your letter and to hear of yet another Carratû," he wrote in response. "Yes, we are related. . ." Several paragraphs later: "My wife and I do get to the United States quite frequently, even to White Plains. We have friends who actually live in your part of the world. Perhaps we can look you up the next time we cross the Atlantic." He did and she called us and that's how we met.

When we met at Carmela's, it was certainly a larger group than he could have contemplated. Carmela had driven to the White Plains station to greet him. By the time she returned, we had gathered: Carmela's daughter RoseMarie, my wife and I and two of my wife's sisters, Annina Stout and Dorothy Webber. Mrs. Stout, whose husband had died a few years earlier, was visiting Carmela. Dorothy and her husband Brooke had been visiting us in Albany and were on their way home to Augusta, Georgia.

Vincent N. Carratû turned out to be a tallish man, getting just a bit fleshy, with thinning dark hair, and rather ordinary looking. I suppose that's a fine attribute for a successful detective. And Vincent Carratû was successful. *Time* said about him: "Among private eyes, Carratû is indisputably the king." After twelve years with Scotland Yard's fraud squad, he had organized Carratû International in 1963 in Manchester with one employee; now he had offices also in London, Rome, New York, HongKong, Taipei, and Johannesburg, with a hundred or more employees. We spent most of the afternoon talking about his quests for counterfeiters and Carratûs.

Not that he had much to say about his main business. People in that line of work don't say anything that could be used against them. He did tell how he had expanded his business a few years earlier (it had been reported in *Time*) by offering the major French perfume manufacturers a year's work on a trial basis. Most of them took up his offer and liked the results; they stayed with him.

A Gift from the Pope

As to the Carratûs, he assured Carmela, "We are all related. The name is unique. I believe it is a fabricated name, and certainly not of Italian origin. This makes it extremely easy to pursue as only descendants of the original family would be entitled to use it." He had traced the original family back to Cava di Tirenni. That's whence his father emigrated to England in 1918, right after the first World War, with his older brother Nicola. There were then (that's 1988) four different groups of Carratûs still in Cava, another in Rome and another in Turin. But the Carratûs certainly had gotten around: Vincent has found them in South Africa, Venezuela, France, and Spain. And, of course, in the United States. He had found his first American Carratûs in Flushing in 1973: Mario, Louis, Rudolph, and Dolores. His method of finding Carratûs is pretty low-tech: he looks in the local telephone books. That is why it took him so long to find the Long Island Carratûs: they had had unlisted phone numbers for several years. Carmela, though born a Carratû, had been a Puccio for over fifty years.

"The original Carratû came from Hungary or Germany," Vincent told us. "He was a mercenary and an officer in the Papal Army fighting in the Vatican wars. Most of the German and Hungarian mercenaries who came to Italy had names that were impossible for Italians to pronounce. So the names were Italianized. That's what accounts for the spelling of our name," -- the final u with a roof over it is unItalian -- "and that's why I favor a Hungarian origin, rather than German."

❑

Revising a foreign name into a new tongue was not unique to Italy, though the Italians seem to have been content to use their spelling to convey the original sound. We Americans did it differently. Some cousins of my wife are named Kelly because an American timekeeper could not be troubled to learn the spelling of their forebear's name. The real name had been forgotten, my wife used to explain. Just the other day, Helen suddenly recalled the original name as Pignatelli – said in Italian as pih-nya-telli. We were looking at *The Book of Saints* at the library, and she saw mention of a saint named Pignatelli and said, "That was Uncle Tony's name before it was Kelly." The Kellys get into this discussion of family trees because Tony Kelly fell in love at first sight with Mary Carratû, a sister of Annina, and thus became Uncle Tony to the Puccio kids.

The Carratû sisters provided an unusual branch in the family tree when, on January 20, 1925, each gave birth to a daughter (cousins, who were, to each other at least, twins) while the families' doctor shuttled the few blocks between their homes to make the deliveries.

The Sound All Depends

The Rivett family also had some problems with the sound of its name. Grandfather had tried to straighten it out early on, when he adopted the spelling, and hopefully the sound: Ri-VETT. Quite likely, in Canada, the family had spelled it Rivet, which was pronounced Ri-VETT, or, among the purists, Ri-VEH or Ri-VAY. Green Island was not home to many linguistic purists. Oddly, I later played baseball against young fellows from Cohoes whose names were spelled Rivet or Rivest, but said Ri-VETT. Unfortunately, the strangers, for the most part, tend to pronounce Rivett as Rivit. When Uncle Art married a lady named Arlene Stanley in 1910, she fancied herself as socially a notch above Rivit and, to ensure that her name was said to her liking (that is, Ri-VAY), she improvised a spelling RIVEAGH. She placed it on her mailbox and the postman delivered mail there to Rivett or Riveagh until she died in 1938. When Uncle Art married again, his second wife was content to be Rivett.

❑

Enough of digression. Let us return to Vincent Carratû's story. That first Carratû, he explained, had been rewarded for valor, given a Papal title and lands in Sicily, then a separate country, where he married into a local family. Sicily was an even fiercer environment then than now, and, as a result of one of the uprisings, the original Carratû packed up his family and fled to the mainland and Cava di Tirenni, in the safer jurisdiction of Naples.

A Farflung Family

"I have traced the Carratû family back to the early eighteen-hundreds," Vincent told us, "but there is a lapse of records between that time and the original namesake. It is clear though that in the mid-eighteen-hundreds the family fortunes declined and the younger Carratûs started emigrating in search of fame and fortune. The first exodus was to South Africa and South America. Soon after, others traveled to the United States. My father and his brother were the first, as far as I can tell, to travel to England. It wasn't until after the second World War that another brother came to England after moving first to France and then the Channel Islands." (My wife's grandmother and her family had come to the United States around 1900, among the first Carratûs in this country.)

Vincent Carratû, at age fifty-seven, already had begun reducing his role in the family business, looking toward retirement but not inactivity. That was clear from the way he questioned Carmela about her family ties. He said that he had already prepared a number of family trees showing how all the branches of the family are linked together and was now looking for more clues to more connections. Carmela offered some help: she was related, distantly, to the Flushing Carratûs.

Fascinated by Research

"I've been fascinated by research into the family," Vincent said, "but I find that I don't have the time now to go into the history prior to the early 1800s. When I retire I hope to complete the work." Whatever the outcome of Vincent Carratû's studies, he's sure that future family historians will have much to add. He has two sons, his brother Tony has three and his youngest brother Nicola has two. As he said: "We're making sure that the Carratû name continues." The prospect of future generations of Puccios also is assured; at last count there were no fewer than seventeen male Puccios of the third American generation.

It's going to be a lot easier to keep track of future Rivetts. I have one son and he has one son, and it may be up to that grandson to keep the name going. My brother Douglas, who died in 1995, had three sons, but none seems in a position to extend the family line.

Now seems the proper occasion to revisit the subject of Rivett family birthdays and coincidences. I must disavow any planning that led to the birth of my son Guy Stanley on May 6, 1953, the twenty-second birthday of my baseball idol Willie Mays. Guy really hadn't been expected for another two weeks, but, while I was out of town one weekend, Helen inadvertently hastened his arrival by cleaning our apartment. (Guy shares his birthday exactly with a chap in England who has become quite famous: Tony Blair.) Helen picked the names: Guy as an Anglicized shortening of her father's middle name Gaetano, and Stanley for the third generation in my family.

Not a Good Planner

My son also was not guilty of planning the birthdates of his son and daughter. The son, Joseph Salvatore, arrived on October 3, 1981, the thirtieth anniversary of Bobby Thomson's memorable home run. My grandson's names came from his mother's father Joseph Pasceri, and from (select one), his great grandfather Puccio's first name, or the restaurant where Guy and Maria had their wedding reception. Then came Lauren Nicole, whose birth date should not have been so planned, on April 1, 1988. Her names were selected probably because they sounded nice; no connection with either family. When her brother was informed of her arrival, he responded: "April Fool!" Right idea, wrong occasion.

All this is as much help as I can provide for future genealogists of the Rivett family. If anyone is interested in digging further back than Doctor F.A.W. Rivett, perhaps they could buy that Three Centuries of Rivetts.

Getting a Hearing

Pa always maintained that his hearing was OK. Of course, he thought a lot of people mumbled and he didn't always understand them.

Ma never said anything about her hearing. But she didn't always answer people. Just smiled a knowing smile and nodded a knowing nod.

Pa said that he had a great test for his hearing and that it always passed the test. The way he explained it was: *I could stand way at the other end of the bar and hear someone say to the bartender, Give Stanley another one too. They didn't really speak loud and I could hear them OK. As long as I didn't miss a drink, I guess my hearing is OK.*

Pa was in a line of work that didn't require him to discern subtle sounds: railroading. Locomotives couldn't sneak up on him. Pa's avocation was another matter. That's where he needed a certain degree of aural acuity to maintain his economic equilibrium. I didn't realize until much later (and Pa probably never realized at all) that he didn't have to hear that voice from the other end of the bar. Any bartender worth his title would have made sure that Pa got the message--and the drink.

❑

Ma got by with the knowing smile and the nod most of the time. Occasionally, though, even when she wasn't quite sure what she had heard, she'd say, My, isn't that nice? Like the morning she was sitting on the front stoop--I was there too--and Mr. Stoddard stopped by to chat. Mr. Stoddard was the Episcopal minister; he wore the standard garb: a clerical collar, a black broadcloth shirt, and a pectoral cross that hung at the middle of his ample belly, but he didn't call himself Father. Mr. Stoddard also wore a bushy mustache that often drooped over his upper lip and thus prevented his basso profundo mumble from emerging in recognizable words. Especially to Ma.

When he stopped and said what must have sounded to Ma like "Ummadm wounedsup tithed zmoanam zapee zeer laa," Ma smiled the knowing smile, nodded the customary nod and said: "My isn't that nice?"

Mr. Stoddard, being an unshakable if unhearable man, nodded back and strolled on. But he must have been shocked, at least dismayed, at Ma's response. He was talking about a lady who lived down the street and what he said was: "Mrs. Lowndes died this morning. It's a pity. Dear lady."

Pa occasionally would have some trouble with Ma's lack of hearing, or of attention. He would mumble to her and get no reply. Whereupon he would mutter one of his mildest epithets. "Six months in the pie factory. With a muzzle on. Talking to yourself."

Ma's hearing was good enough anyway that she never missed a number at the numerous bingos she attended after Pa died. Or so she claimed and she might have been right. She played a dozen or twenty cards at a time and won often enough to keep up her interest and her pocketbook.

Always the Acoustics

I always blamed the acoustics when, as a reporter, I couldn't pick up all the words in a lecture or missed a punch line here or there in a play. I knew most auditoriums and lecture halls had their dead sound spots. I figured I just found one every time. I knew I could hear perfectly well, because in the noisy city room, I could hear everything on the police radio (even the routine time checks) and intercept questions from my colleagues above the din of the clattering typewriters and chattering reporters. I suppose that, like Pa in the bar room, I never realized that everyone else was boosting the conversational volume or relaying the word across the room, so that they could be heard above the background noise.

When I went out to cover a talk, I developed a clever approach to beating the acoustics. I'd arrange to meet the speaker beforehand and, pleading that I had been burdened by so many assignments that I couldn't possibly stay for the entire lecture, but of course I'd hate to leave without a good story, I'd ask, humbly of course, if you could just briefly give me the high points. And they did. No one took umbrage at the implication that they'd be padding out a few kernels with an awful lot of cob. They seemed glad to get their message across as they wanted it--an early version of the sound bite.

Then came a time when I was having trouble with the acoustics when there were no acoustics, like conversing with someone right across the desk. Most people I worked with understood what was wrong before I did and they SPOKE UP. Others repeated before I could even say "Huh?" So it took me longer than it should have to realize that my trouble wasn't the acoustics, it was the genes.

❑

Much too late, I went to an ear doctor who confirmed that my hearing was faulty. At first, I used a single hearing aid, on my right ear, one of those obvious over-the-ear models that for a while aggravated my astigmatism by twisting my reading glasses out of focus. That device was, as I mentioned, obvious and most people took its presence as a sign they should speak s l o w l y as well as LOUDLY to me.

Checking on Reality

Even so, that single hearing aid sometimes distorted reality--enjoyably. Like the day when I was having a discussion with one of the Public Service Commissioners and I heard her say "You're erotic!" I never cared much for the lady but I take compliments where I find them. With some pride, I mentioned that conversation to a colleague. He had heard it too. "Oh hell, she didn't say 'erotic'," he told me, "she said 'erratic'." It sounded better the first time.

As time passed, the hearing-aid seller found that one hearing aid wasn't enough for me, or for his finances, whichever came first. He prescribed two, fitted neatly enough into each ear so that they were hardly noticeable, especially when I needed a haircut. Now I'm back to two, slung over my ears, highly visible. People who can see them speak LOUDLY and s l o w l y; others don't and I have to say "Huh?" or "Sorry" to them.

I try to observe the convention that hearing aids should be seen but not talked about. Other people's hearings aids, that is. Sometimes, though, the others bring up the subject. In one of my volunteering efforts, I met a composer-pianist at the airport and was driving her to her hotel when I noticed that she appeared to have a hearing aid, too. Before I could mention it, she did, and we spent much of the ride comparing notes on our experiences. I couldn't match hers: she had to have a hearing-dog to alert her to doorbells and phones when she had her hearing aids off.

Once Upon a Time

Once upon a time . . . .

Oh, this is a true story. It just happened once upon a time. Once upon a time when doctors made house calls, when doctors did not flaunt their wealth, because most doctors weren't wealthy, when doctors would stop to talk to little kids.

So, once upon a time, a doctor drove to the home of a patient and parked his car outside. A nice car. A Cadillac. As close to flaunting fiscal fitness as he'd ever get.

And, once upon a time, a little kid, about nine years old, a son of the patient, stood outside and, when he saw the car, marveled at it. The biggest, nicest car he had seen. A Cadillac! The little kid knew was still admiring the car, standing right up close to it, when the doctor came out.

"It looks as if you kind of like my car," the doctor said. "How would you like a little ride?" A wasted breath. The kid reached for the door handle and let himself in. The doctor drove the kid around a couple of blocks. "You know," the doctor said as the kid was getting out, "you could get a car like this when you grow up. You just have to work hard and save your money."

That was once upon a time.

A Long Wait, But Worth It

When I met my friend Joe Pasceri—a friend and the father of my son's wife--he was standing beside his new car. A new Cadillac. He wore a driving cap at a rakish angle, and he told me the story of *Once upon a time* . . . Joe said he was glad the doctor had told him how to get a Cadillac. "Only one thing wrong," Joe said. "He never told me it would take fifty years." I asked if it would have made a difference. Joe was honest: "Not a bit."

Once upon a time, when I was a kid, doctors made house calls too. But Green Island was different. No doctor's Cadillac; no anybody's Cadillac. Lots of Fords; after all, Henry Ford had built a plant in Green Island. Some Buicks . . . about the biggest and fanciest I remember from my early days.

I became acquainted early--when I was about five--with a Model T Ford, a tin lizzie owned by Mr. Jermain, the plumber who lived up over his shop, two doors down the street. He used to let me watch him wash the car and dry it down with a "shammy". And I watched--and listened to--him start it. He had to pull on a crank to get it going. Sometimes, one yank and a burst of pops and bangs and it was going, More times, it was yank the crank, a pop, just one, and silence. Adjust the spark. Another yank. Another pop and silence. Over and over, till something he said to the car worked. Once in a while, he would yank the crank and it would spin back and hit him on the arm or the hand. That's when I learned that the car had a name. He called it "sonofabitch." He never gave me a ride.

Not Glamorous, But –

It wasn't until I was ten or eleven that I found a car I could love. It was a brownish Hupmobile, a Hupp for short, that belonged to Mr. Bennett, the Methodist minister. It was a couple of years old but looked new. Mr. Bennett--his first name was Fred, but not to us kids--gave us rides in his Hupp. A couple of times, he took us down to Hawkins Stadium and to watch the Albany Senators play. Kids got in free, if an adult was with them. Ministers also got in free. Another time we talked Mr. Bennett into taking us up to Cohoes, to the swimming pool. He asked for directions. So I said "Go up Hudson Avenue and turn over on Arch Street . . ." And he said "Oh, Frannie,"--he was the only person who ever called me Frannie--"I don't think it would be a good idea to turn over with you boys in the car." Well, we got there. Kids could get in free. Ministers too, but Mr. Bennett said he didn't swim.

That summer I became a virtual driver of the Hupp, thanks to imagination not technology. Mr. Bennett parked it in the yard alongside the parsonage behind the church on Hudson Avenue, where I could see it every time I came to call for his son Gardner to come out to play. Every time I hollered for Gardner, someone would come to the door and say He's eating. So, I waited and drove the car. Probably put more miles on that Hupp than Mr. Bennett had.

I never got in the car. I could stand on the running board alongside the driver's seat and put that car through its paces. *Turn the key on, step on the starter, maybe try it again. OK, the engine is running. Push in the clutch, move the gearshift into first, let the clutch out s l o w l y. Ah, that was smooth. A little push on the gas pedal. Back to the clutch, up to second gear. And now, more gas again, the clutch in, up to third, high gear. Watch the speedometer. Fifteen, twenty, thirty. My goodness, that's fast enough. Slow down for a turn.* And on and on, mile after mile. Or, sometimes, I would stand on the running board like a cop in the movies, and tell the driver *Follow that car. The green one. Keep him in sight. Watch out for the trolley. There he is. Speed up so he can't get away.* Before I could catch the other car, Gardner would come out to play. He never drove his father's car like that.

A Look, But No Touch

A year or two later, I met another car that I wanted to drive--virtually. Never got a chance to. It was a lovely Stutz Bearcat speedster, a two-door, a convertible coupe, and bright bright red. The fanciest car I ever saw. There it was, suddenly, parked in front of our house. Well, nearly. Most of it was in front of Bennett's sheet metal shop. Beautiful.

Inviting. But, just as I stepped closer to the shiny metal running board, someone shouted from Bennett's: "Hey kid, get the hell away from the goddam car. You wanna wreck the paint job or something? C'mon, get away." I gave a defiant look, and went away.

I was fickle about cars. I came to admire the Franklin that the Keating sisters owned. They lived on Hudson Avenue, in a big brick house with an extra big side yard and they kept their car in a garage back near the riverbank. Oh, it was a large car, even bigger than a Buick. A boxy thing, soberly black. I never learned how fast it could go, because it never did. The Keatings were careful drivers, and Norine, who drove it to work at the Watervliet High School every day, never went faster than a canter.

When I went to Watervliet High, I had a fleeting affair with a car that was even bigger, and surely faster: a giant black Graham-Paige touring car--a four-door convertible--that Punk Wehmeyer drove to school. Punk, whose real name was John, used to stop to pick up riders, like me. He provided a sometimes thrilling ride down Second Avenue in Watervliet, a new two-lane concrete road atop the filled-in Erie Canal. Occasionally we'd find our way impeded by Miss Keating and her Franklin, rolling serenely, so Punk would toot the horn--an awesome sound--and, roaring at perhaps twenty-five miles an hour, rush past Miss Keating on the broad gravel right hand shoulder of the road.

It was great fun until the day Miss Keating decided enough was too much, and, as assistant principal of the high school, she influenced the principal E.J. Sanders to call a special assembly at which he denounced such wild behavior. "I heard that someone is driving a big barouche recklessly on the way to school. That has got to stop," he thundered. "If I hear about that happening again, you can just keep on going in your sea-going hack and not bother to come to school again." He sounded as if he meant it, so Punk avoided Miss Keating the remaining few weeks of the school year.

Some Cars I Owned

In all these encounters, no one advised me how I might become a proud owner. The first car I bought, in 1938, was a used, very tired, Ford of a certain age. It cost twenty-five dollars and may have been overpriced. It lasted long enough to be worth the investment but not worth repairing. That Ford was succeeded by a Chevrolet four-door sedan that I paid a hundred and twenty dollars for. It was somewhat younger than the Ford, and it met my need to transport an entire baseball team at once. Age and abuse brought the Chevy to a timely end.

A decade passed before I was able to buy another car. With the aid of my bride of a year, I selected a brand-new car, a dream car. It was a tough time to buy a car: the Korean War made prices high. Especially for us. Then we found a car we could raise the credit to buy, priced at fifteen hundred dollars: a British car called a Hillman Minx. We bought a sedan, a solemn black model, that looked quite spiffy. A big selling point was the turn indicator, a lighted arm-like device that popped out of the side where you wanted to turn. It worked well. It was the only part of the car that did. Our dream car turned out to be a nightmare. So, at the end of a year, we turned in it on another new car. Excuse my blushing. Another Hillman Minx, and it was just as good as the first one.

We've had a lot of cars since then. Some lemons, some lemonade. Both too numerous to mention.

Some People
I Worked With

(And One I Didn't)

When Life Imitated Artie

*An expensive anti-abortion campaign, which
has sparked debate over advertisements
advocating points of view on controversial
issues, has begun running on New York Area
television stations . . . .*

*The two-year-old campaign is sponsored by
the Arthur S. De Moss Foundation, which
was created in 1955 by a wealthy evangelical
Christian insurance executive. The trade
publication Adweek has estimated that the
foundation is spending $20 million annually
on the advertising, which had run only on
national cable networks . . . .*

The New York Times, October 14, 1993

The TV spots showed on local cable. Very polished. So
polished that I was not quite sure what they were selling,
until the punch line.

❑

Arthur S. De Moss. I knew him as Artie DeMoss
(familiarly Li'l Abner), a young hustler who took a job as
copyboy at the *Times-Union* to fill in time after school and
to enhance his earnings opportunities. Artie was eighteen
then and he was a senior at The Milne School, which was a
good school for a hustler to go to, because the name made it
seem private and important, when in fact it was the campus
school for the State College for Teachers.

That was about sixty years ago. I was a newish sports
writer for the *Times-Union*. Artie was a remarkable copyboy,
even for that paper. He was the only copyboy who ever brought
a girlfriend to work. Artie hustled his girlfriend Junie, an
otherwise bright classmate of his, into doing his job for the
first few hours each afternoon. Artie had a better use for

that time: booking bets on horse races. He booked bets at work as he did at home, and, because the pay for copyboys provided him little working capital, he passed on to more affluent bookies any bets that seemed to have a chance to win, while holding on to the stiffs that promised a full profit. He didn't need working capital for that, just hustle, since the bigger bookies operated on the honor system roughly. They trusted you to honor your obligations or be treated roughly.

He already had built a thriving business in his home neighborhood, a fact I learned only years later, when we bought the house next door to where he had lived. The older settlers still spoke with awed admiration of Artie and his business associates.

An Unusual Driver

The DeMoss family also was remarkable. Artie's father ran a small jewelry store downtown, but his reputation in the neighborhood was based on his world class inability to drive an automobile. Once he managed to jam his flivver sideways into the driveway between their house and (eventually) ours. Another time, he missed the driveway altogether and drove right through a large wooden porch on the front of our house. The people who owned the house used the settlement to do away with the porch and build instead a small concrete stoop and install a distinctive bow window, the only one on our street. I have a warm spot in my heart for DeMoss *pére.*

❏

Whatever brought Artie to the *Times-Union*, he found his tenure there highly profitable. An often chore of a copyboy was to carry the reporters' and editors' bets to one of the several private off-track betting establishments in the neighborhood. The one preferred in journalistic quarters was a half-block away, around the side of the Capitol Hotel, that provided fuller and faster news of the races. Just as those established bookmakers had done for years, Artie found the news editor Bert Bearup a steady source of income. Bearup felt it a bounden duty to bet on every race at every track in the country (not that there were many of them in those war years) and, making up for the paucity of tracks, to dream up and back various exotic combinations, three-, four-, five-, or even six-horse parlays, roundrobins, and other if-coming adventures. His individual wagers were mostly small--a buck or a deuce, sometimes a fin--but they ensured a high standard of living for anyone booking his bets, who mostly was Artie. While Artie thus entrepreneured, Junie ran copy, sharpened pencils, refilled pastepots and went out to the nearby greasy spoon for coffee and stuff for the staff.

A Labor of Love?

It never was clear how Junie was compensated; perhaps it all was a labor of love. Artie treated her well. He never asked her to work after six o'clock, by which time the racing was over for the day. Artie finished the shift alone, staying on duty till midnight, sometimes later, though those long hours were something of a hardship, if not a danger, for they cut into the hours of sleep Artie needed to maintain his intellectual strength, not so much for school as for bookmaking. Artie often sneaked into the women's rest room, into a cranny furnished with an antiquated wicker chaise longue, for a quick and quiet nap. Women in the city room never felt threatened by a sleeping male. Artie's napping was noticed, however, by one of the copy editors, and one night, working ever so deftly, he decorated Artie's face with burnt cork. Then the editor shouted from the city room, *Hey Artie! Hey! Copy! Artie, get your ass down to Coulson's for the tabloids.* Artie, suddenly alert but not very, dashed to pick up the bulldog editions of the *Daily News* and the *Daily Mirror*, from which the *Times-Union*, saving rather large telegraphic costs, extracted the columns of Ed Sullivan and Walter Winchell. Part way to the newsstand, Artie chanced to look into a store window and saw a reflection of his graffiti-ized face. He dashed back to the office to wash his face, not an easy task, and then went once more to get the tabloids. The back- and forthing caused the final edition to go to press late, but no one ever mentioned why. Don't ask don't tell had an early vogue.

Artie stayed around the paper a while after that, and he also stayed awake. His departure was hardly noticed. He was just another copyboy in a succession of wartime copyboys. No one ever expected to hear from Artie again. Everyone missed Junie more.

❑

Artie went on to open a small local insurance agency after the war. A natural switch for a hustler. For bookie and insurer both sit back secure in the enriching knowledge that eventually form and the actuarial tables will prevail. In the long run, the horses will be slower and life longer than the clients expect.

I lost track of Artie in the early nineteen-fifties, because I left the *Times-Union* for a job with the American Newspaper Guild in 1952. I didn't return until late in 1955.

A Reborn Artie

Several years passed before I learned what had become of Artie. Just before I returned to Albany, Artie was Born Again spiritually. As he told a reporter in 1973, he was (in the mid-1950s) worth a million dollars but his life "lacked direction". Suddenly he was struck by a "lightning bolt . . . right between the eyes" as he drove past an evangelist's venue in the Fort Orange Stables just outside Albany. He stopped abruptly, parked his car, and walked in on the nationally active evangelist Dr. Hyman Appleman, once a lawyer. They read a few verses of Scripture, Artie said. And Artie was reborn as Arthur S. De Moss, in a stable. The symbolism was real though the stable was actually a large enclosed riding academy.

Artie the hustler was no more. In his place was Arthur S., living by the Good Book, not the kind Artie used to make. Somehow revelation also struck Arthur S. that a big insurance business was better than a small one. Within months, he had left the local agency to become an entrepreneur, writing his own book again. He had discovered that the road to millions was a detour around the middleman. Strong advertising and direct mail sales. No runners--that is, agents--to cut in on the deal. And Arthur S., thinking like Artie, played the game of the name to perfection. His new company was National Liberty (Corporation) of Valley Forge, Pennsylvania, solider than a rock as a sales base. And the money poured in.

By September 1973, a writer for *Fortune* had listed Arthur S. among the "new millionaires". High up among them, with a bundle that *Fortune* estimated at a hundred and fifty to a hundred and seventy-five million dollars. But that was a lot less than he had been worth a few months earlier; his peak worth was put at four hundred million. (I would not dare translate that into 2002 dollars.) Arthur S. was the president and chief stockholder of National Liberty. What shrunk his fortune was a U.S. Senate investigation of the direct-mail insurance business, one of those periodic and ultimately futile attempts to interest Congress in establishing Federal regulation of the "industry."

Fortune's rating of Arthur S.'s fortune gave rise to the interview in late 1973 in which Arthur S. told of his spiritual rebirth. (The interviewer for *The Knickerbocker News* was a young reporter named Jim Kunstler, who went on to become a locally-famed novelist. He never created a character like Arthur S., or Artie. Kunstler later became a nationally-known polemicist against the blight of urban and suburban homogeneity.) The interview, which followed the Senate inquiry, was a reprise of the local-boy-makes-good theme.

A Different Life

Arthur S. revealed in the interview that he still remembered Artie after a fashion. He told the reporter that Artie had joined the Army at age fifteen (that would have been 1940, before the war) and served six months before his family blew the whistle on him. Then Artie worked on a ranch and tended bar in Uvalde, Texas (known to everyone as the hometown of John Nance Garner[2]), and, after bouncing through three high schools, entered a Navy training program at Cornell, lasting six months before faulty knees forced him out. A very interesting *curriculum vita,* much of which no one had heard of during Artie's stint at the *Times-Union,* which in turn was a part of Artie's life that Arthur S. never mentioned.

❑

He omitted another incident, an earlier fall--not from grace but from a window--that landed Artie on Page One of the *Times-Union.* It happened in 1928, when Artie was three years old and the family lived in another section of town. There on Page One was a deep two-column picture of Artie, under the caption *I'se Not Hurted, Mommy!* And on Page Three, a spread of pictures including the obligatory line of dashes tracing the fall from window to ground. The entire eleven feet. Perhaps the recent travail of Arthur S. had erased the fall from Artie's memory.

Avoiding a Payoff

At those Senate hearings (I found only a couple of news stories about them), Arthur S. found himself in much the position Artie had found himself in that night he napped in the ladies' room at the *Times-Union.* Now,

---

[2] And old John Nance was vice president during FDR's first term and famously described his job as not worth a bucket of warm piss, which the media translated to spit.

however, his reputation, not just his face, was besmirched. The *Philadelphia Inquirer* reported that it had looked into National Liberty's sensational success and learned that the company had acted as Artie never would have dared to do when faced with too large a payoff to his clients: it welshed. The *Inquirer* reported that National Liberty had rejected twelve thousand or so out of seventy-eight thousand seven hundred fifty-five claims filed by its policyholders. The Senate Anti-Trust Committee revealed still another shenanigan: National Liberty had paid a "consultation fee" of three thousand dollars to a Congressman from Pennsylvania who subsequently entered heaps of lavish praise of the company into the *Congressional Record*, praise that National Liberty then quoted in its advertising. A spokesman for National Liberty explained later: "They made a lot of noise. But the advertising itself was what was most in question. The advertising now goes through the [Pennsylvania] insurance department before we can use it." The voice of Arthur S., the hand of Artie.

That exposure before the Senate was costly to the firm, its gross worth shrunk in half in 1973, and more costly to Arthur S. He told Kunstler that he had lost two hundred million dollars. Those numbers jibe with *Fortune's* earlier estimates. Arthur S's late-found Christian faith never wavered. Of the two hundred million loss, he said, "It's the Lord's money." A lovely philosophy, since both the loss and the earlier gain were only on paper, the value of the stock he owned if he had found a willing buyer for all of it at the market price. Of the future, he told Kunstler, "God has a perfect plan for each life."

❑

God's perfect plan for Arthur S.'s life came to an end on September 1, 1979. Or had the plan for Arthur S. gotten mixed up with the plan for Artie? God only knows. ❑

A Legend in His Own Times-Union

Fire sirens sounded near and clear as I sat in the Plaza Grill, sipping my nightcap, waiting for the next bus home at 12:30 a.m. The sound was tempting, but it was too cold to wander about looking for a fire. Someone came in the back door from Beaver Street, and announced, *Helluva fire. It's the Times-Union.* There'd be another next bus. I finished my drink, pulled on my coat and left. If t*he Times-Union* was on fire, I wanted to see if I still had a place to work.

As I reached a slight bend on Beaver Street, I could see that it was a helluva fire, but not the *Times-Union.* Not yet. It was in the Alfred Equipment Company next door, a three story brick warehouse for hotel and restaurant equipment. Hose lines went up the front steps at the paper. Firemen inside the plant. The second alarm just in. Fire apparatus lined up on Green Street. People, all chased from the paper, lined up across Beaver Street. Printers, copyreaders, stereotypers, the Associated Press staff, everyone except reporters and photographers; they were probably covering the story. One copyreader greeted me, "It's going to be pleasant vacationing next week in Palm Beach." Someone rebuked a colleague, "You were the last one out. Why didn't you drop a match in a wastebasket?"

Firemen on a truck at the corner had raised their aerial ladder and a man on the platform was turning it into place when he slipped on the wet metal surface, grabbed for support and pulled the wrong lever. It brought the ladder down across his body and, as the ladder kept rotating, someone on the ground hollered, "Hey, Jimmy, where the hell are you going?" Wherever it was, Jimmy had gone. His mates stopped the rotation, but couldn't get his body free.

His death made the fire a big story. But there already was a clear sign of that. The publisher and the business manager were standing on the front steps, and they never came to the office after dark. I strolled over to see about *vacationing next week.* Before I could ask, I learned the answer was no. The publisher Fred Archibald spoke first, "Doc, I want you to cover this story. I talked to A.J."--A.J. McDonald, the publisher of *The Knickerbocker News* down the street--"and he offered to let us use his plant. We'll be able to run our presses, but we've got to set the type at the *Knick.*" With unaccustomed modesty I said, "Fred, you've got a lot of reporters around here; want me to round them up?" He knew what he wanted. He said, "No, I know about them. I want you to do it."

So I did. I had no pencil, no notepaper, but I picked up some information at the scene and the rest by telephone from the *Knick,* which is how I learned the dead fireman's name was Emil Durand, close enough to Durante for nicknaming, wrote a story--two-thirds of a column--and a banner headline, and escorted one of our printers who carried the type back to the *T-U,* and oversaw the makeover of Page One. Hours late, the paper hit the street, carrying a big bold line:

Fireman Killed in 2-Alarm Fire

I went home satisfied. A fine job, I thought. Especially for a sports writer on his night off.

But that afternoon, February 5, 1948, I learned why the managing editor George O. Williams had become A Legend in His Own *Times-Union.* He had missed the action, stuck at home in Niverville, some twenty miles away. That gave him time to think how the story ought to be covered: the real story was the paper and its coverage. His banner read:

Mid Fire, Ice and High Water
Times-Union on Street

with the bottom line in second-coming type, festooned with flames atop and icicles beneath. . Dropping off it was a two-line, five-column head. That's important! Stories by five reporters about how they covered the fire or otherwise engaged in heroics. By everyone except me. Virtue, however, had its own reward: four hours overtime pay for a couple of hours work.

I didn't come to work until about 4:30, so I missed the action, but I could visualize George taking charge. I had seen it before. He would stand, leaning over the city desk, edging the city editor aside, waving his glasses as a pointer, clearing his throat time after time to signal attention, marshalling his forces, and, finally, at deadline, hovering over a reporter (or a rewriteman) and muttering *no, no . . . no, no . . . you should be saying*, and dictating a paragraph, all in a voice at least an octave above normal.

In that same edition, Williams gave us still another Legend, though we all were unaware of it at the time. On Page One, sharing space with the booming headlines was a three column photo of the fire taken by a copyboy named Bernard Kolenberg. He soon became a Legend that deserves his own story.

Stories About Stories

The stories about Williams were legion as well as Legend. Old-timers insisted, for example, that in 1930, when two out-of-town small-time badmen had murdered one State Trooper and shot his partner, George had concocted banner headlines about the ensuing manhunt centering down-county, reputedly at the request of the circulation manager to increase street sales. That sort of faking did happen.

Dick Walsh told me about the way George handled the story of the discovery of the body of the kidnapped Lindbergh baby in 1932, the "crime of the century" of that period. Dick was in charge of the late baseball extra and had the paper ready for the press when the Associated Press sent a flash LINDY BABY FOUND DEAD. Dick told me, "That's all I had and I didn't know when I'd get more and I didn't know where I'd put any more if I got it. So I called George and told him the situation. And he said 'Hell, you don't need a story with that headline. Just put that headline in the biggest type that will fit and put an EXTRA ear on the page. It'll sell.' So I did and he was right, the street hustlers sold thousands of papers."

Great stories. Authentic sounding. That's the way the newspaper game used to be played. Truly legendary but perhaps not true, as I learned recently. I looked it up. The 1930 manhunt actually had been centered down-county. (The killers were caught, however, in Oklahoma.) The Lindy Baby story might have been true; the microfilm files did not carry the Baseball (or LINDY BABY FOUND DEAD) edition.

A Wonderful Era

But those are just facts. Williams could have done those things. He was the Managing Editor, the boss of all bosses in the newsroom (and often slightly more than equal to the Publisher). Williams had come to *The Times-Union* as managing editor in 1928, toward the end of the Era of Wonderful Nonsense, when there were no media, only a medium: newspapers. The only competition an afternoon newspaper faced was another afternoon newspaper. As the *Albany Evening News* fancied itself a "family" newspaper, the brash *Times-Union* seemed to compete against itself with the emphasis of its multiple banner lines on Page One changing from edition to edition.

Williams's early days at the *Times-Union* were the days of trained seals (fancy writers who were assigned to cover sensational events, such as the "trial of the century" that occurred at least once every year) and sobsisters (who chased the women's angle thereof), of reporters who didn't (and probably couldn't) write, and rewritemen who didn't merely write, but embellished. The days also of composite photos and faked interviews. The days long before the success

of *USA Anyday* stirred editors to devote a large chunk of
Page One to a feature story.

I became interested only recently in tracing Williams's
days before he came to the *Times-Union*. He had started as
a reporter in 1908, when he was 18 and just out of high
school, at the *Baltimore World*. How long he stayed there is
not clear. He turned up as a reporter in 1917 in Johnstown,
Pennsylvania, beginning a decade in which he seemed to
be a job-hopper: five jobs, a couple of years at a time. The
last stop before Albany was a term as city editor of the
Buffalo Times in 1921-1922. From city editor to reporter is a
move that few would consider upward or even sideways. He
came to Albany, as closely as I could place it, in 1923 as a
reporter for the *Albany Evening News*, which had just been
started by the Gannett Company. That was the same year
William Randolph Hearst acquired the *Times-Union* from
its editor-publisher Martin H. Glynn, a local boy who had
made very good in politics as well as publishing. In the city
directory of 1927, not always a reliable source, the listing for
Williams was "rem[oved] to Baltimore". If he had moved, he
likely went to work on the *Post*, which also had recently been
acquired by Hearst and was edited by William Baskerville,
who it appears had been Williams's early mentor. In any
event, in 1928, George became managing editor at the
Times-Union. Where had he been the year before he came
to Albany?

A Real Source and Alive

Not satisfied with the indirect research, I found
someone who had been there. At a lunchtime gathering
with alumni of the *Times-Union*, there was Henry Matteo,
who, I suddenly realized, had been newspapering in Albany
even before Williams came to the *Times-Union*. I told him
I had written something about Williams but needed more
information. He said he'd like to see it, so I mailed him a
copy. Within days, I received a three page note filling in

some of the gaps. "My earliest recollection of Williams goes back to the late 1920s." Henry told me. "He was on rewrite at the *Albany Evening News*; I was a sports writer on the *Knickerbocker Press*- both staffs worked in the same room." More to the point: "It was from there, if I'm not mistaken, that he joined the *Times-Union* as managing editor." I've never known Henry to be mistaken.

How ever Williams came to be managing editor, the. first thing he did, Matteo recalled, was to induce Marshall Taylor, with whom he had worked in Buffalo, to come to Albany as his city editor. Not long after, George recruited some of the *Evening News* reporters and editors: people like H. (for Humphrey) F. Wood, a marvelous rewriteman; Charley Willoughby and Cliff Carroll, who were desk editors, and others who had already faded from the scene by the time I got to Albany. (By that time, H.F. Wood had died too. As Matteo explained, Wood had trouble sleeping, so he began taking pills to go to sleep, and then pills to stay awake. He failed to come to work for a few days; someone was sent to his apartment and found him dead. Too many pills.)

A Novel Figure

Williams, under a fictional name, got credit, in the William Kennedy novel *Legs,* for legendary foresight in December 1931 when he novelistically ordered a headline written (purely in preparation) about the killing of the gangster Jack Legs Diamond. I looked that up, too, and it could have been true. Except for one thing: in the novel, the headline read **DIAMOND SLAIN BY ENEMIES.** Williams would not have considered that news, but **DIAMOND SLAIN BY FRIENDS** would be worth a banner. Diamond had just been acquitted after a trial in Troy of charges that he had kidnapped and tortured a smalltime Catskill moonshiner named Grover Parks and his helper. That occurred late in the afternoon of December 17, too late for even the Late

Final Extra Peach edition. So Williams began preparing for the follow-up story.

Whether he wrote a preparatory headline doesn't matter. By next day, he needed it. Diamond had been thoroughly shot dead in his bed in a rooming house on Dove Street barely twelve hours after the acquittal. Someone properly had called a *Times-Union* reporter first and the police second, and the reporter Ray O'Connor dictated his notes for the first story over a phone in Legs's room. What with the stories of the acquittal, the victim's last night on the town, the murder, the search for suspects, George Williams was left with little space (and that on Page Three) to report a most remarkable event: Grover Parks showed up, a few hours after the killing, at the funeral home where the body had been taken. He had just happened to be driving by in his truck. (Parks was perhaps the only person in New York State who could NOT have killed Diamond; he was still under escort of State Trooper Francis Hilfrank, who had been assigned to protect him during the trial. Hilfrank was still at his side in the photo. A legendary coincidence: it was Hilfrank who had arrested Diamond in the abduction case.)

A Novel Recollection

Again, in 1933, another part of The Legend, in which fiction barely outshone fact. As I heard the story a decade later, George Williams had sat on a story of the kidnapping of the scion of the all-powerful O'Connell family for three days "to protect the victim," and still was able to run the story first. Action worthy of a Legend. The reporter Bill Kennedy must have heard the same story, for, when he became the novelist William Kennedy, he wrote much the same tale in *Billy Phalen's Greatest Game.* (Williams had had his William Kennedy, a lookalike of the movie star Warren William, who wrote a column under the classically Albany name DeWitt Schuyler.)

What we heard was pretty close to fact, as well as I could determine from the microfilm. Leo W. O'Brien, the *Times-Union*'s political reporter, had learned about the kidnapping within hours after it occurred at 1:15 a.m. on July 7 and promised the O'Connell family that he'd keep it out of the paper until they said it could run. Once O'Brien got around to telling his editor about the deal, Williams also agreed to it, perhaps grudgingly. A day or so later, other reporters got onto the story or at least the idea that there was a story, but O'Brien and Williams and the O'Connells talked them into agreeing not to run it right away. The story finally broke at 7 p.m. on July 10 in the form of an announcement by the Albany Police Chief. And the *Knickerbocker Press* of July 11 was first with the story under a banner headline: **O'CONNELL JR. KIDNAPED IN ALBANY.** A story in that same edition revealed that the press in general had known of the story for forty-eight hours, which meant that Williams and O'Brien had kept it to themselves for a day and a half. Close enough for Legend.

The *Knickerbocker Press* had gained a premature, but unstoried, lead on the kidnapping in its Sunday edition, wherein the abductors had caused the O'Connells to place a classified ad that named, in a simple numerical code, possible go-betweens in their quest for ransom. Once the story broke, it was *The Times-Union* that ran subsequent coded ads and dominated the continuing coverage of the O'Connells' tribulations and the kidnappers' trials. (In a trial, O'Brien calmly admitted that a wonderful interview with a kidnapper was just a figment. Williams and the paper shrugged it off..)

End of Competition

On July 1, 1937, the circulation rivalry of the afternoon papers came to an end. As a result of a complex deal with the Gannett Co., *The Times-Union* became a morning and Sunday paper. Gannett eliminated the *Knickerbocker Press* on mornings and Sundays and changed the name of its afternoon paper to *The Knickerbocker News*. Instead of the hectic pace of four or five editions each day, George had two widely spaced editions with separate audiences. The first edition went to press at 7 p.m. for street sales, principally to sports fans; the final came out about 1 a.m. for home delivery and newsstand display for the commuters heading for work.

The day after the merger came the news that Amelia Earhart had vanished while flying across the Pacific Ocean on a round-the-world flight. A great story! And, thanks to the difference in time, a morning paper story. It was the kind of story that eked out details day by day, slowly enough to prolong an editor's attention span for days, even weeks.

But Williams had an off-day, or perhaps a day off. The story was only a day old, but on Page One of the Sunday paper of July 4, the first Sunday without the opposition of the *Knickerbocker Press*, the two line banner headline was: **3 DIE IN ONEONTA AIR CRASH;/ FLIERS HUNT AMELIA IN VAIN.** Perhaps Williams gave in to the adage "All news is local". Possibly, the circulation department asked for help in developing a market some eighty miles away. George got back on track the next day with a two-line banner on Amelia, and kept the story alive for several days.

When Greenland Was Local

Despite the shift in operations, big bold banner headlines would still dominate Page One. Big stories would still command big display. And little stories still could be made big. George Williams still had an eye for the big local story even if he had to look a long way off for it. One of those was the cracking of a good-sized gambling ring in Plattsburgh, not usually in the local coverage area. George assigned reporter William Lowenberg, Jr., who covered it in workmanlike fashion. And it was printed under the byline **By "Hotspur"**. George's little joke. Lowenberg was no Hotspur but a quiet chap who enjoyed a quiet hobby: casting about the Internet of the time with his short-wave radio in Morse code and voice. In 1947, after an Air Force B-29 crash landed on the Greenland icecap, Lowenberg used his wireless to interview the survivors, one of whom had local ties, and Williams produced the strangest local dateline in *Times-Union* history: BLUIE WEST 6, GREENLAND.

World War II had provided its own big stories and usually demanded at least two Page One banner lines a day. There were some days, however, when local events took over the banners. Mostly these were incidents in various investigations of Albany's political leaders, ordered by Governor Thomas E. Dewey in his typical Mister District Attorney manner, and counter-investigations of Dewey's Republican cohorts by the O'Connell minions. While each was accorded its banner headline, the reports were distinguished by their length, not by any colorful writing. Just the facts.

After the war, Williams went back to the local scene for his big, or big-looking, stories. In the early fall of 1946, when a sixtyish woman named Emma Moccio disappeared the same day her husband had gone to work at a local marble dealer's with a gun in his hand and malice in his heart, for both of which he was arrested, Williams sent some reporters delving into backyards, abandoned icehouses, and brush-covered lots. But no Mrs. Moccio, though people reported for weeks having seen her on the street somewhere in Albany, Soon she ceased being Page One material.

Girl Goes Missing

Just as Mrs. Moccio's news value waned, a new, more interesting Disappearance: a seventeen year old girl named Paula Welden vanished while walking near the campus of Bennington College, where she was a sophomore. It took Williams a few days to find the proper Hearstian treatment. The college authorities had withheld the report for three days; and Hearst had taken over Page One for special stories and editorials inveighing against John L. Lewis and the Miners Union for calling a strike in the coal mines just as winter approached. (History note: coal was the major fuel then, by a wide margin.)

When Williams at last got the opportunity to cover the Welden disappearance, he sent his favorite reporter Richard J. Lewis Jr. to the scene. Lewis, a court shorthand reporter who moonlighted at the *Times-Union,* knew what Williams wanted. And he produced it: one new angle every day. One day, it was the police quizzing two strangers who had happened to be in town the day Miss Welden vanished. Then a daylong excavation of a large gravel pit. And the appearance of two Connecticut State Troopers, brought in by the missing girl's father. Further charges that the Vermont State Detective was incompetent. And, to give Lewis a day off, Williams had his outdoors writer prepare a piece, complete with map, of the perils a missing girl faced in the wilds of Vermont. But all to no avail. Around Christmas time, the searchers declared a recess, and never really resumed. Williams tried to keep the story alive, and Lewis went to Bennington occasionally in quest of a new angle. All he ever had to show for it, though, were a few pleasant days out of the office and on the expense account. Several months later, Williams demonstrated once again the power of the Welden story; he hired a reporter named Pete Stevenson, who had covered the search for *The Bennington Banner* and possibly had some other qualifications.

❑

Science news--of the pop-science kind that William Randolph Hearst liked--also appealed to Williams. One night, at home in Niverville, he heard on the radio that a huge radioactive cloud was heading for the Capital District. He called to leave word for the city editor to obtain a Geiger counter--*first thing, no delay, understand?*--so that the *Times-Union* could test for fallout. I heard about the call and left him a note like this, *George: No need to get that Geiger counter. I just finished counting the Geigers for you. There are seventeen in Albany, twenty-two in Troy, and twelve in*

Schenectady. There may be a few more in the towns, but I thought that was close enough. --Doc. The day staff found a Geiger counter and someone to run it at RPI. George took their word over mine. By the time I came to work, he was laughing about the note.

A Medical Discovery

Soon George made a much more startling scientific discovery, then sought the facts to back it up. A mysterious ailment that resembled polio without the paralysis raged in the Town of Coxsackie, downriver a bit, where mushrooms, nurtured by horse manure from nearby racetracks, were the principal crop; at the same time a serious equine disease called swamp fever was epidemic at those tracks. George made the immediate connection: swamp fever in horses causes polio in humans. So he assigned Lewis. For a few weeks, Lewis told George every day what he had learned, but didn't write a word until they were satisfied that the story would hold up. At last, a blaring two-line banner on Page One proclaimed the connection. It was a wonderful story. Not long afterward, however, the State Health Department issued its report, based on some facts that Lewis hadn't learned: the illness that plagued Coxsackie was not at all like polio, was not related to swamp fever, and was not carried by horse manure--not the real kind, anyway. The Health Department agreed that the disease had a local angle, and called it the Coxsackie virus.

George also gave legendary 1930ish treatment in 1948 to a couple of murders that had local connections. One occurred in Boston where a shop owner was beaten to death in a holdup and a set of keys dropped by the killer led to his identification: an Albany native and World War II veteran named Dunning Powell. Along with the banner headlines, Williams ran larger-than-life pictures of the key keys. As

the hunt continued for Powell and the rare English sports
car he was driving, Williams kept up the Page One play.
Powell eventually was caught after he made a U-turn on a
one-way street in San Francisco and the cops noticed his
fancy car on their wanted list.

Then came a murder most foul right in Albany, in
which the victim was trussed up in a manner that tightened
a noose if he so much as twitched a muscle. He more than
twitched. The *Times-Union* dubbed it "The Japanese Noose
Murder." And, when, with startling speed, the perpetrator
was captured, George Williams splashed his confession
under a banner that said **NOOSE SLAYER'S STORY**. The
tale lived up to the headline's promise.

That is some of the Legend as editor. There must be
other legendary tales that I never had heard about.

A Legend as Manager

Williams was a Legend as manager too, though
sometimes decidedly unmanagement-like. His duties
required him to sit on the management aide in Guild
negotiations. But not to speak. One day, as we strolled back
toward the newsroom from North Pearl Street, he said, "I
hope you fellows get a good raise, because when you get one,
I get one." At the door to Keeler's Men's Bar, he invited a
couple of us in and bought us a drink.

When he became a manager, he brought some people
over from the *News*, but mainly he inherited a cadre: Bert
Bearup, who became news editor; Ray O'Connor, who
starred in the real-life Legs Diamond legend; Joe O'Heaney,
a latter-day police reporter; Paul Howard, reporting from
a news office in Hudson Falls; and Marie Avery Myers, the
society editor (as Nancy VanDyke) and occasional sobsister.
And Matt Sweeney, who had started newspapering in 1896
and had, by his account, covered some high class stories in
his day, before falling back in the thirties to covering odds
and ends in Rensselaer, a suburban backwater.

Remembering Pals

Williams also remembered his friends and associates from the early days in Albany. In 1930, he hired Dick Walsh as a copyreader after Walsh's job as telegrapher for United Press had been eliminated. When Williams was at the *Evening News;* the United Press office was next door. Later in the 1930s, he found a job for John Bowen, who had been his boss as managing editor of the *Albany Evening News* in the twenties. (Bowen, slight, squeaky-voiced and crew-cut, went to work one Monday and found someone at his desk. He began to protest. The man told him, "It's my desk now. I'm Joe Torbett and I am the managing editor.")

After the Gannett-Hearst deal in 1937, George also found jobs for two other of his old colleagues who had lost out in the merger: Ray Mowers and Jo Leonard. Mowers, short, portly, and middle-aged, was a superb writer who found a terrible fascination in the one-armed bandit slot machines that lined the walls of the backroom at Coulson's newsstand at State Street and Broadway. (He killed himself in the early forties by turning on the gas oven in his apartment.) Jo Leonard had been active in the Guild at the *Knick*, but George knew her as a friend and as a good reporter.

The Williams I knew seemed a benevolent sort. But, I learned, in his earlier days, he could be a tyrant. As he was to Henry Matteo, who was then, as now, slight, frail-looking, soft-spoken and a genuinely gentle man: a perfect target for a bully. Henry, for some reason he has forgotten, found himself the target of George's mean streak. "He could be very hard on anyone he harbored a grudge against," Henry told me. "It became so unbearable that one night, as I was working at my desk in the sports department, I collapsed. Jack McCann, who had been talking with me, thought I had breathed my last. I heard him exclaim 'He's gone.'" Henry was unable to hear or see Williams's reaction, but once he had revived, he found that George seemed to mellow toward him.

The Perils of Drink

In Williams's early days when Prohibition was the law if not the rule, George never blinked at the presence of a gin glass alongside the bowl of library paste in front of each copyreader. (Scissors, paste and heavy black pencils were tools of the trade.) He realized that the editors needed the healing fluid when they came to work at 5 a.m. Occasionally--this is on the word of Dick Walsh--someone would, his aim impaired by the night before, dip his paste brush into and quickly, and without a word, out of a neighbor's gin glass, and said neighbor, on sipping his potion, would remark, *A lot smoother today, kind of minty. Where'd it come from?*

The shift to morning publication cleared the gin glasses away as people changed the venue. Williams was just as benign in his neglect of latter-day drinking later in the day. Even when the Dick Walsh each day assembled a pile of emptied (quart) beer containers alongside his chair. George laughed with the rest of us when a young photographer named John Burns devised a drinkometer that measured drink by drink how far the spectacles had slid down the nose of a fellow cameraman, Ken Moore, on payday afternoon. Of course, there were O'Connor, and O'Heaney, and Sweeney, and Bearup, and Don Call, whose Martini drinking outshone his political writing, and Paul Howard, whom Williams had brought in from the sticks, to name but a few.

Williams often indulged in a few nips at Keeler's Men's Bar. George's nips led to naps. When that happened, he seldom had time to close his office door, right at the head of the main stairway, and often dozed, head on desk. The first person to pass the office closed the door, lest a visitor leap to the right conclusion.

Williams must have fired people for their drinking or for the results of their drinking. Dick Walsh told me about a sports writer who was fired when he was caught covering a golf tournament from the Capitol Hotel bar, right across the street. (Even that might not have been Williams's doing;

Henry Matteo is certain that Walsh did the firing.) The only reporter in my time who lost his job to drink was Paul (Pussy) Howard, and that was accidental. Paul's dulcet tones had earned him a job offer from a local radio station. But he sought a going-away present: severance pay. Often, after a few drinks, he confronted Williams with an offer: "George, if you give me my severance pay, I'll quit." George didn't give. But there came a night when Paul said, "Dammit, George, I quit." George said, "I accept your resignation." (There was no severance pay anyway, just dismissal pay, except in a very terminal way: on death or retirement. The only reporter I knew who lived to tell of his severance pay was Joe O'Heaney, who qualified for about a year's pay; he used his nest egg to open a bar.)

A Benevolent Mistake

George's benevolence toward drinking kept me out of the doghouse the day the *Times-Union* failed to carry the news of the first arrest ever made in a basketball point-fixing scandal. A sports story, naturally, or so George considered it. So it was the night sportswriter's fault when it didn't appear. By rights, I should have faced an inquisition. I was saved (!) by Roy Travis, the late-shift news editor, who reached the office before I did. Asked about the story, he told Williams, "Oh, that must have come in while Doc was over at Steve White's having a beer." Williams never asked me about it, which meant I didn't have to explain that I was in the office all the time, while Travis was so busy playing gin rummy that he failed to notice the single, unadorned, paragraph that the Associated Press had moved on the state news wire, which was delivered to his desk, not the sports wire, which was delivered to mine.

His patience with drunks on his staff sometimes wore thin. Especially when the drunkenness was too readily apparent to the publisher, or, even worse, an advertiser. Such as occurred one night when the cartoonist Robert

L. Ripley, believe it or not, brought his Chinese junk *Won Lei* to Albany and provided it as the venue for a party at which the *Times-Union* publisher entertained important advertisers. George sent a reporter, Al Rockefeller, and a photographer to record the scene. Rockefeller was very drunk and arrogant about it, causing a scene that dismayed the publisher and many of the advertisers. Williams told me (I was then an officer in the Guild), "I've got to suspend that guy without pay for two weeks. It's the least I can do." I quickly responded: "I didn't hear you; I don't want to hear you." So George suspended Rockefeller, who made no complaint to the Guild.

❏

Williams was tolerant too of the weekend poker game. The game was a tradition by the time I began work. Office lore had it that the game gained official approval the night of April 19, 1940. That's when the New York Central's Lake Shore Limited ran straight off Dead Man's Curve at Little Falls, some sixty miles west of Albany, and killed thirty-one people, near midnight, and, the story went, staffers who had been playing poker rushed to cover it. Really, Herbie Campbell, the city editor, and F. Leonard Ottman, the chief photographer, drove to the scene and produced exceptional prose and photos. Neither was a poker player, so, most likely, one of the poker players had alerted Campbell and Ottman.

The only time Williams objected to the poker game, it was not even a poker game. He saw the relics of an all-night knock-rummy game, a deck of cards and a few empty beer bottles, near the sports desk, and posted a notice that ruled out, right then, poker-playing and beer-drinking. I posted a counter-note that you can't expect us to play bridge and drink Martinis on our pay. George clarified his position, telling me, not in writing, "just tell those stupid bastards to put away the cards and hide the empty bottles. It looks bad if the publisher happens to come in." Since I was one of the stupid bastards, I made sure we all complied.

In those days before the human resource profession was discovered, George enhanced his Legend by his hiring and (especially) his promoting practices. He was proud of his talent for finding talent among the copykids (to desex the job title). Not all of them worked out, of course, but his pride didn't count those who flopped. All in all, he was entitled to be proud. He found among the copykids a sportswriter-reporter named Martin P. Kelly, an editorial cartoonist with staying power in Hy Rosen, and a fine reporter and editor in Hal Kallenburg. He also discovered photographers: Bernie Kolenberg, later a Legend, and Roberta Smith, the first woman news photographer in Upstate New York, and Gates Barnett.

How Gates Closed the Gate

Some months ago, while shopping, I encountered Gates Barnett and told him I was writing about the good old days. He grinned and told me his favorite story about the Legend. He said, "When I first went into the darkroom, George put me on the nine to five shift with weekends off. I don't know how I got such good hours and I never asked. One day when I came in a few minutes late, George was already there--the first time--and he was mad. There was a bad accident, a couple of trucks and some cars, down near Hudson, I think it was, and he jumped all over me. 'Dammit, you picked a helluva time to be late,' George said. 'We've got to cover that accident. Now get going and when you come back, you're fired.' Of course, I went, but I was worrying all the time about being fired. I managed to get some pretty good pictures and when I got back, George was still mad but he talked to me again. 'I've been thinking,' he said, 'and I'm not going to fire you. You did a decent job. But you're going on two to eleven with Tuesday and Wednesday off, starting tomorrow. See if you can get to work on time.' You know, I never got off that shift. Never, until I quit."

The Legend died in legendary manner. George Williams went out with some of his old pals for dinner the Saturday night after he supervised coverage of Dwight Eisenhower's election as president in 1952. They went to Duncan's, an excellent restaurant in the suburbs, and late in the evening, George excused himself: a stomachache. He didn't return to the table and, several minutes later, one of his pals found him in the men's room: dead on the throne. Without his hand to guide the coverage, the *Times-Union* noted his passing in less than legendary fashion: a modest three-column head on Page One with column after column of quoted tributes from the governor, the mayor, and assorted bigwigs, all of whom offered stilted praise for a man they really didn't know. No mention of Legs Diamond or of Paula Welden or of the great horse-manure caper. Nobody thought to ask the Boston and Albany train crews, or the bartenders at Keeler's or VanHoesen's in Niverville, the people who knew and liked George Williams. I had no opportunity to comment, either, having taken a leave from the paper in September to work for the American Newspaper Guild in New York City.

A quarter-century later, George Williams received his entitled treatment as Legend--in the guise of Emory Jones--in *Billy Phelan's Greatest Game*. Kennedy described George/Emory like this: *[his] hair was white, with vague, yellowish implications that he might have been the fair-haired boy of someone, a mother perhaps, somewhere. . .* And pictured him moving to greet his star reporter: *rumbling across the crooked, freshly-swept floor of the city room. Here he came: pear-shaped, bottom-heavy, sits too much, unhealthy fear of exercise in the man.*

That was George.

A Burning Ambition

Bernie Kolenberg was the kind of kid Norman Rockwell often used as a model: skinny, gawky, unruly hair, a big Adam's apple. The kind of kid who always looked like a kid. And that's how he acted, too. Enthusiastic, impatient, trusting, trustable. Not at all the kind of kid you'd expect to become a Legend. But here it is thirty-five years and more after he died, and people are still writing about him. As a Legend.

Bernie came to the *Times-Union* in 1946, just one in a long line of copyboys (and girls) in the old *Times-Union* building at Beaver and Green Streets. He was eighteen and had not gone far in school; he could have become a career copyboy. He quickly caught on to the routine: fetching copy from the Associated Press desk and the International News Service teletype, or from the city desk (only a couple of steps away) to the copy desk in the corner of the room, and then to the antiquated rope-pull device that carried copy to the composing room, and filling paste jars and sharpening pencils, and, even more important, rushing for coffee and other vital necessities for reporters and editors. He did his work well, but his heart wasn't in it.

He had his heart set on becoming a photographer and soon became one. Not for pay. He bought his own camera. Unheard of. The photographers, for pay, snickered at the idea of a copy boy taking pictures, and, sillier, buying his own camera. But they allowed him to use their darkroom and their paper and chemicals, which weren't theirs but the company's.

Bernie had limited opportunities to use his camera at lunchtime, which usually was eight or nine o'clock. But often walked down Green Street, over Madison Avenue to the Dunn Memorial Bridge, snapping pictures as he went. His subjects mainly were jakey bums, what we now call the homeless alcoholics. Some of us worried that he might get punched or otherwise hurt, or robbed. Bernie went on taking pictures, naively unimpressed by the dangers we saw.

A Midnight Fire

His big break came just after midnight on February 5, 1948, when the building next door caught fire and the staff photographers had long since gone off duty. Bernie was there with his camera which he took everywhere, maybe even to bed. Bernie took pictures from outside. One of them caught flames darting from the top floor, silhouetting firemen on ladders. The managing editor George Williams played it in three columns on Page One the next day along with a story that described Bernie as "a copy boy with high aspirations to be a staff photographer." A burning ambition was more like it.

Not long after, Williams promoted him to staff photographer. But not before the kid had turned in a picture of a strangely shaped large piece of ice he had found outside his door one morning. A mysterious piece of ice. And mysteries appealed to Williams. He used it on Page One, three columns wide. The next day, Bernie sheepishly dispelled the mystery. He reported to Williams: "My brother John told me he put that ice in the doorway to play a joke on me. He said he took a block of ice and kind of rounded it off. I didn't know." So the next morning: another story. George never even criticized Bernie. (A few years ago, someone at the *Times Union* came across the original picture and story in the microfilm file and ran it again, still as a mystery.)

As a staff photographer, Bernie was still a kid at heart. He was a steady customer of novelty shops: a bowtie with a remote-control light at the knot, fake eyeglasses with wipers run by a battery, things like that. He also bought a rubber stamp; first a two-liner STAFF PHOTOGRAPHER/ BERNARD J. KOLENBERG, later, the same information inside a circle.

As a staff photographer, Bernie had expected to find action and danger. Instead, he found routine and boredom: assignments to proclamation signings, dinner speakings, gavel transferings. His boredom showed in his captioning: the names typed on the back of the print, sometimes with a word or two as to where it was taken or the occasion, seldom both, and almost never the date. But there were other assignments where he supplied his own excitement: a steeplejack might find himself looking up at Bernie's camera, or a convention-goer surveying downtown by leaning out his hotel window might be snapped by Bernie leaning further out a nearby window. One night while experimenting with infra-red film--it produced images from heat rather than light--Bernie took pictures at a local movie house. One of them caught a prominent and married State legislator from New York City sitting with his Albany wife, a secretary with whom he had formed an attachment many years earlier. That sort of thing never was mentioned in the public print, or public pictures.

An Easter Holiday

Bernie sometimes used a day off to go afield for pictures. One Easter Sunday, he decided to snap the Easter parade on Fifth Avenue. He went to New York by bicycle, assisted by a tiny one-cylinder motor that pushed its top speed to perhaps thirty miles an hour. It was not a bad day at the start but the weather turned cold and windy and his return trip was harrowing. The first any of us in the city room knew of Bernie's trip was when Williams called from his home in Niverville. Bernie had turned up there, hungry and half-frozen. The Williamses had fed and warmed him and George ordered someone to drive down and take Bernie home.

Bernie's schooling had been limited to his years at Hillside School, a boys' institution in South Troy operated by the Christian Brothers. He remained loyal to Hillside and the Brothers, and to LaSalle Institute, a military oriented high school they ran in Troy. In the 1950s, when a group of Hillside boys were starting a train trip from Albany, Bernie photographed the occasion. He wound up with some cute shots of a couple of kids smuggling their dog aboard to the amusement of the conductor. All staged, of course, but no one objected.

Photo by Truman

In the mid-fifties, Bernie recruited another legend as a one-shot *Times-Union* photographer. Bernie was covering a visit to the city by former President Harry S Truman. He shot (with a camera) the former President a couple of dozen times. He offered the camera to Mr. Truman—who could have been a Norman Rockwell subject, too—and asked him to take a picture. The President obliged. His work ran with a credit line Times Union Photo by Harry S Truman.

Bernie also enlisted a local celebrity—the Mayor of Troy, Ed (Dynamite) Fitzgerald—to liven his picture-taking. Assigned to take immortal images of the opening of a municipal pool, Bernie asked the mayor to dive in. The mayor promptly did so. In his business suit.

For years, we thought the camera was not only Bernie's life but also his love. He never spoke of girls, or even a girl. Then, one night, he returned from an assignment with photos, and a girl he introduced as Mary. A petite, dark-haired, quiet girl. Other nights, other visits from Mary. We learned her name was Mary Hahn. Soon we learned that romance had blossomed. They were engaged and, in due course, married. Office gossip: Bernie will make up for lost time; they're going to have a big family. Bernie must have heard it, for one night he blurted to me, "You guys are talking about Mary and me having lots of kids. Well, we aren't and I wish you'd stop talking like that." In fact, they were unable to have children and wound up adopting a boy they named Kevin.

Courting Trouble

As a staff photographer and family man, Bernie continued to buy his own equipment: special lenses, a car telephone, a foldup bicycle. He also continued to seek, and, at least once, create danger. I didn't get to share assignments with Bernie until I became a reporter again in the fall of 1961.

I missed out on one of Bernie's odder Odysseys early in 1962. I was kept inside to write of the capture of the man who had killed an Albany cop a few days earlier. Another reporter and Bernie were assigned to stake out the crime scene, because an editor thought the cops might bring the perpetrator there. Some people in the neighborhood noticed Bernie's car and, still worried after the recent murder, called the police. A radio car was dispatched. Bernie heard the call on his car radio and moved out fast.

The following summer, a propane tank truck blew apart in Berlin, a town some thirty miles east of Albany, and the resulting firestorm engulfed a large part of the village. A perfect setting for Bernie, but he never showed up. He had better things in mind. He called a friend who had a small plane and they flew over the scene for excellent panoramas.

A year of two later, Bernie and I went together in his Volkswagen convertible to Whitehall, seventy-odd miles away, to produce a Sunday feature about some Albany University students working with local kids on a summer project. Routine. Until we were returning, with the top down, on the Northway, and Bernie noticed two horses ambling southward in the wooded median. He pulled over to the left lane, partly on the shoulder, unlimbered his camera and with both hands off the wheel and foot off the gas, began shooting. He told me, "Hold the wheel and keep it steady." I did. I also protested, "Bernie, you're going to get us killed going this

slow"--about twenty–"with all the cars doing seventy." His
response, "Those poor horses. They might go out on the road
and get hit." They didn't. Once we passed the horses, Bernie
resumed normal speed. He printed the pictures, but they
didn't get used: horses' posteriors were no novelty in the city
room.

Bernie and I also were assigned separately one evening
to cover a train accident near Hudson. A remote place south
of the city, a mile or so from any road. I parked near the
freight yards east of the crash and walked in. Bernie parked
near the station, about as far to the north, and rode in on
his unfolded bike. A passenger train rolling north had run
head-on into a switch engine going south, where it was not
supposed to be. The force of the collision detached a caboose
from the switch engine and sent it rolling backward down
the track into some standing freight cars; the conductor, in
the caboose, was fatally hurt. Otherwise, there was little
damage. Bernie got his photos, I got my story, and the
trainmaster offered us a ride to Albany. Bernie folded his
bike and climbed aboard. I walked back to my car and drove
in. He had his photos printed by the time I reached the office.
But I knew where my car was.

Scooping Rockefeller

One of Bernie's scoops (how he loved the word!) helped
me to get one in 1963. Governor Nelson A. Rockefeller was
about to unveil the detailed plans for a grand new erection
called The South Mall and I was assigned to develop a story
in advance. The Governor's people were, naturally, saying
nothing. But they were assembling a display of photo murals
of the project in the Capitol and had walled off the area with
plastic curtains. But Bernie walked in and was snapping
away, until someone realized he didn't belong there and
asked him to leave. By then, Bernie had snapped everything
I needed for a story. We both scooped the Governor, who was

monumentally upset to read all about it in the *Times-Union* hours before he planned to break the news.

In mid-January 1964, the day after a historic snowstorm, we went separately to cover an unusual murder. A restaurant owner was shot dead by his dishwasher as he sat at his bar. Bernie got pictures of him still seated on the barstool covered by a tablecloth as a shroud. A great shot, as even the desk recognized, It ran four columns on Page One. Just in case anyone couldn't discern the victim's body, a black arrow pointed it out. Bernie came back to the police station where I was waiting for a prosecutor to give out the suspect's name which we didn't know for sure. (I had phoned in all the rest of the story earlier.) But there was no regular phone handy when the perpetrator was identified. Bernie let me use his car telephone, which worked beautifully.

The Only Failure

Bernie failed me only once, and it was on an architectural assignment. George Dudley, by then dean of architecture at RPI, had invited me to attend a lecture by Edward Durell Stone, who had designed the new University at Albany. I brought Bernie along. To him, it was a routine job, akin to a proclamation signing. To me, it was a big story, for Stone had posted drawings of an expanded university, with academic podiums and dormitory towers sprouting from all the land about, including a couple of cemeteries. I tried telepathy to get Bernie to snap them. That failed, so I nudged him and pointed. Dudley saw me and said, "No pictures, they're out of bounds." I gave up. So, uncharacteristically, did Bernie.

In November 1963, after President Kennedy was assassinated, Bernie pleaded in vain for an assignment to cover the funeral in Washington. The *Times-Union* didn't believe in spending money like that. And Walter Hawver, the city editor, planned to have Bernie: cover local reaction to the funeral: routine stuff that Bernie detested. So it was no surprise when, on the day of the funeral, Bernie left Hawver a note that he was taking the day off: vacation. And it was no surprise to Hawver when Bernie hustled into the city room close to deadline with rolls of film from the funeral. In Washington. They showed up in a picture page next morning. Bernie had been taking pictures of John F. Kennedy in and around Albany since his 1960 campaign for the Presidency. In 1964, the *Times-Union* put out an 82-page book of Bernie's best entitled *John F. Kennedy: A Memorial Tribute. Albany to Arlington.*

Covering a Kennedy

In the fall of 1964, Bernie and I covered part of the campaign of another Kennedy: Bobby, running on the coattails of his brother's shroud for U.S. Senator. We went to the Glens Falls airport when Bobby Kennedy was starting his campaign with flying visits to several upstate cities. The candidate was late, then later. Our deadlines came and went. Finally, after midnight, the Kennedy plane landed. Bernie and I joined the touring press in the bus that followed the candidate's open car past the thousands of people who lined the rural roads and city streets. Each time the entourage stopped, the driver would open the door so Bernie could duck out, snap a bunch of pictures, and step back in. The touring press groused. Bernie just smiled. A week later, Kennedy campaigned in Albany and Bernie was there again, right in the thick of the crowd.

The same zeal--some called it *chutzpah*--led Bernie into some peril and out of it. Hawver recalled the time he and Bernie, covering a crime story, wound up in a State Police station while the troopers questioned a suspect in a backroom. As deadline neared, Bernie talked to a trooper guarding the interview room, and then, when the door was momentarily ajar, he shot from the waist. No flash, no focusing. No one noticed. He left quietly and dashed for the city room, just in time for the final edition. Hawver stayed to wrap up the story, which he phoned in. Meanwhile, the rest of the newspack waited. They were still waiting when a *Times-Union* delivery truck rolled up and left a final edition, with the photo Bernie had taken.

Bernie's peril came later, when the perpetrator went on trial and his lawyers asked a judge to rule that the Troopers had connived with Bernie to the prejudice of their client's right to a fair trial. When Bernie was called as a witness, the Judge asked him how he had come to take the pictures. Bernie stood up, opened his jacket and--click-click--shot the Judge. He could have been slammed for contempt of court right then. But the Judge just said, "Just unload the film and give it to me." Bernie did and *his* case was closed. The Judge also ruled that there had been no prejudicial connivance.

Off to Vietnam

By 1965, the war in Vietnam had become Mecca for news photographers, The new Mecca and Bernie's zeal for action, dangerous action, meshed. In the summer of 1965, he took vacation time and, paying his own way, headed to Vietnam. He was armed with his still camera and a hand-held movie camera provided by a local TV station: Channel 10, where Hawver had become news director. In a couple of weeks, he was back with, as usual, excellent still and movie shots that were still news. He also had sold some photos to news services while in Vietnam.

A month or so later, Bernie received an offer he couldn't refuse: a chance to return to Vietnam to cover the war for the Associated Press. The AP's photographer Horst Fass had been working eight months without a break and sorely needed time off. Bernie took a leave of absence, and went off to war.

Late in September, Bernie reached Vietnam. He was still the kid next door, the model for Norman Rockwell, exuberant at being where the action was. "Great to be back again," he proclaimed at press headquarters. He went out on some ground forays, took some excellent shots from a helicopter advance, and, about a week into his stay, was assigned to fly with a couple of Air Force Skyraiders on a strafing mission against a Viet Cong post. Finally. As the planes swooped in for the kill, they brushed against each other and went down. The pilots and Bernie were killed. It was October 2, 1965, Vietnam time. Bernie was thirty-eight years old. He left a wife and an eight-year-old son.

In a eulogy printed a day or so later, reporter Bill Kennedy called Bernie "a folk hero among journalists, a myth maker whose exploits were so exceptional when you retold the stories of Bernie's deeds people thought you were lying."

In a word: a Legend.❏

---

* An OpEd piece in October 1995, marking the 30th anniversary of Kolenberg's death, by Walter Hawver, the *Times-Union* city editor in the early 1960s, refreshed my memory about Bernie's day in court and supplied some details of his Vietnam experiences. Thanks, Walter.

Father John and the Indian

Whenever the phone rang at my office, I tried to answer it myself; I knew I'd have to eventually. And it was fun hearing the caller, usually a reporter, asking for me, sputtering at finding I was on the line.

When the phone rang one morning in April 1987 not long after the bridge on the Thruway near Amsterdam collapsed into a raging flood and killed (eventually) ten people, both caller and called were surprised. It was a long-absent voice that spluttered enough for me to recognize and greet the speaker. Nonetheless, he announced: "This's John Douglas. "The fucking Indian did it. The fucking Indian put a curse on that bridge." His diction had assumed the exaggerated precision by which he meant to convey Great Importance and Unquestionable Truth. "The Indians had an encampment up there just when they were dedicating that bridge. Remember. The fucking Indian put a curse on it. Pointed right at it. Hal Kallenburg had it in his story. Look it up: 1958, October 18th. It's all in there."

❏

Sure, John, I'll check it. It was the least I could offer a guy I had worked with at the *Times-Union* for several years. That was before he heard the call and became the Rev. John Douglas, Episcopal priest. But I said it with fingers crossed, because I knew that John was never so wrong as when he was right in such minute detail: picking the very day something had happened twenty years before.

John had a few more words to say about the Indian and the curse, and demonstrated once more that, though he had changed from the Fourth Estate to the Third, he had not left his old vocabulary behind. When he stopped for breath, I asked where he was calling from. California, courtesy of his local diocese. So we chatted a bit about John's service to

God and the church and humanity. He sounded as if he was keeping a straight face.

❑

But I remembered how John heard the call. It wasn't from God. John was covering the anti-poverty activity of the mid-60s and became acquainted with one of the poverty-fighters, the Rev. Alfred Lee, from whom--if from anyone--John heard the call. Father Lee, who had been an airline pilot before he became a sky pilot, served a once-rich now-poor parish in the South End, and lived in a well-to-do neighborhood on the hill. John asked how he could afford such a fine house on a rector's small salary. Said Father Lee, "The Diocese owns it, no rent." And he told John about other lovely large old houses the Episcopal Diocese owned and was waiting to make available to new clergymen. That was the call John had been waiting to hear and heed. As he told me over beers one night after hours at Jack Shaughnessy's Towne Tavern (the site now of Mammoun's Middle Eastern Restaurant) , several blocks from the paper, "Father Lee was telling me about all those big houses the old fucks had left to the Diocese, just waiting for somebody to move in. I said to myself, as long as they're there, I think I'll get a piece of the action." The Albany Diocese, needing priests in the worst way, put John through a brief course for late-choice clergy and he was duly ordained. He never got a chance to move into one of the houses, however, as his wife decided that he should follow her back to her home state of California where she would become a judge.

Did He Get the Files?

John's cursory information would have been a good story. I checked the local public library and learned that the microfilm file of the *Times-Union* for October 1958 could not be found. Ah, another curse? Then I phoned Joe Picchi, one of the old-time reporters I had worked with. He also knew John well, but he checked anyway and told me, "Geees, he had the time right and all that. Hal had a story, a couple of stories, but no curse, nothing like that." [Later I consulted Edmund Wilson's *Apologies to the Iroquois*. Wilson had a chapter about the encampment, and identified the Indian--Douglas's and Kallenburg's--as Standing Arrow, the leader of a powwow of mostly Mohawk high steel workers, some of whom had worked on the bridge. No curse there, either.]

❑

Douglas had come to the *Times-Union* quietly in the mid-1950s. He made a reputation as an investigative reporter by quoting extensively from affidavits that the State Commissioner of Investigation had filed in court. He was a spare, fairly tall fellow, probably younger than his baldishness looked, given to wearing dark suits that made him resemble a clergyman or an undertaker. He also fostered a reputation as a kook. But a shrewd kook. The stories he worked on often were datelined as if he had visited some far reaches of our coverage area, glamorous places like Lake Katrine, or Fort Plain, or Hoags Corners. He regularly claimed car mileage expenses that passed review by the city editor and the managing editor and the tougher scrutiny of the business office, which diligently checked the number of miles he had claimed. Not one mile too many. The office was so impressed by his accuracy that no one noticed that John was driving all those miles without a car. After about six months, those expense claims provided a down payment on one.

John, Meet Sputnik

The high point of Douglas's career occurred the night the Soviet Union launched its Sputnik. Douglas was idling away the late-night shift when the story came over the news wires. John promptly put in a phone call to Moscow or the Soviet Union's Mission Central and reached someone who would talk to him, someone surnamed, according to John's story, Comeinyankee. Just like the greeting *Come in*

Yankee. John wrote a sidebar--a localized I-was-sort-of-there piece--that ran alongside the main wire story on Page One. Bert Bearup, by now the managing editor, was irked that John had called Moscow without permission, and refused at first to let the company pay for the call. Bearup relented, but John paid, though not in money. He quickly and irrevocably became known as Sputnik. So it shouldn't be a total loss, a later managing editor, no doubt impressed by his nickname, assigned him to cover, in person, a launch or two of U.S. satellites from Cape Kennedy..

❏

The last time I saw John Douglas--and that was several years before he phoned me--was at a testimonial dinner for the Columbia County Democratic chairman, a hail fellow named Larry Novak, which attracted a cast of hundreds. Whoever had brought John to the party some thirty miles from Albany was unable, or perhaps unwilling, to drive him back. So my wife and I offered him a ride. We were repaid with forty minutes or so of vintage John Douglas. He was in Albany, the guest of Bishop Wilbur Hogg, on assignment from his diocese in California to conduct research for a biography of the Bishop Kennedy who had died mysteriously some years earlier in the desert in Palestine. We asked about his parish in California. No parish; he was the chaplain at a school or home for wayward girls. As we dropped John off, we all agreed that we must get together again. Of course, we didn't.

He Bounced Away

I learned of his departure weeks after he had gone, when I stopped in the Towne Tavern. The second generation of Jack Shaughnessys broke the news, "I know you don't care, but that sonofabitch Sputnik left town. And that fucking phony stuck me again. I swore I would never cash a check for him after he stuck the Old Man the first time. But that Roman collar and the cross. And he said he was good for it. Another rubber check." Politeness dictated that I not ask how much. But I had heard that Douglas considered a hundred the least he would ask a friendly barkeep to cash.

❑

A few years ago, I told some of the Father John story to my sister, who is versed (and active) in matters Episcopalian, and asked if she could determine where he was. She found that the national directory of the church listed a Rev. John Douglas in the Diocese of Boston as "adj-staff" --for, we thought, adjunct-staff, a priest on assignment from another Diocese. The only Rev. John Douglas in the entire directory. I have not heard of any further passage through Albany. If John should favor us with a visit, he would learn that young Jack Shaughnessy had sold his business. His son ran another Towne Tavern several blocks up the street. He has since gone out of business. No place left for a fellow with a Roman collar and a cross to cash a rubber check

Homage to John Maguire

John Maguire had come to the *Times-Union* city room while I was working in New York. By the time I returned, he had become the paper's first real medical writer and its master of the light touch. He also worked, to some degree, for the state Health Department, where his duties included writing speeches for the commissioner.

Maguire had come to the paper for his health. Some time earlier, as he operated a small but apparently prosperous public relations agency in Manhattan, he had suffered a serious heart attack Go somewhere less stressful, his doctor advised. So he came to his wife's hometown, to freelance and to volunteer as a writer for the local Heart Association. Bert Bearup, the managing editor, was on the association's board of directors and offered Maguire a job. (He was Bearup's best hire.) John then lived in North Albany, on Center Street, a block long, between Broadway and the railroad tracks, with his wife Helen Gregory and three children.

A Birth, a Death

In June 1954, the *Times-Union* reported in an informal column called *Strictly Personal* the birth of a fourth Maguire child, a son Gregory. Barely a week later, the paper reported the death at age thirty-nine of Helen Gregory Maguire from complications of childbirth. Left with four children and still not in robust health, John had to call on his in-laws to take care of the children and, as son Gregory recalled much later, placed them briefly in an orphanage He regained them when he married Marie McAuliff, a best friend of Helen's. They had three more children.

With the family growing, John and Marie needed a bigger house and found one in the Pine Hills. They had to dispose of the house on Center Street, and another on

North Pearl Street that belonged to Marie's family. That circumstance gave rise to one of John's better anecdotes. He was enjoying a drink and conversation in the City Line Tavern, across from the bus barns, when a neighbor barkeep who had lost his saloon to fire, spoke to him: "John, I heard you got a couple of houses you got to get rid of. It's a tough sell in this market. But you're a nice guy and I like you. John, if you ever need a fire let me know." The real estate market was not that tough.

❑

John also was the bug editor at the *Times-Union*. Not bug as in entomology. Bug as in flake, eccentric, nut, weirdo or wacko. His subjects ranged from Bill Gannon, the peripatetic postman, a flake who traveled more than Owney the post office dog, and Dave Marks, who had gotten rich as a pioneer seller of radio and TV parts, an eccentric (a well-off flake) who also was a world traveler, to Four-Star Hennessy[3], a nut who wore a Mr. Peanut costume as an ad, and Bishop Tomlinson, a wacko who was the Emperor of the World. There were a lot of other bugs in between. John treated all his bugs with the respect an entomologist would show for a newly-found genus of centipede.

A Remarkable Schedule

While working full time at the *Times-Union* and some time at the Health Department, Maguire also found time to string for Time, Inc., with such magazines as *Time, Life, Fortune* and *Sports Illustrated*; and for McGraw-Hill, principally for its magazines *Business Week* and *Engineering News-Record*. As a stringer, he was supposed to file only memos, but he reported in story form, which must have upset his editors because he wrote better than most of the magazines' writers.

---

[3] In recognition of the stage of his syphilis.

John was a usually cheerful man, of average size, with a gray mustache and thinning hair that he kept cropped close "so people won't notice it's thinning." His good cheer often was reflected in his news stories. Each summer, it seemed, he wrote several stories satirizing the coverage of the Saratoga racing season and particularly racing handicappers. He also wrote funny weather stories, which gained him wide praise.

Not everyone accorded him accolades. On a day that his (serious) story about a snowstorm ran in the paper, John entered the doctors' dining room at the Albany Medical Center Hospital for lunch, and was greeted by a very loud, "John, that was a lousy story about the snowstorm." Promptly, another doctor rose to his defense: "John is a very good medical writer." The loudmouth replied, "Yeah, but he don't know shit about snow."

Profiling the Mighty

In 1960-1961, John wrote *John Maguire's Profiles* for the Sunday paper, a task that involved a long interview and a long story. Not all of them sparkled, because the subject sometimes was beyond John's help. He returned from one interview with a wonderful—but unprintable—story. As he told me, "That guy must be afraid he'll die of thirst. At every doorway, going into or out of a room, he had a little table, and on each table he had a bottle of good Scotch and a couple of glasses." A couple of years later, he produced another profile for a good cause. At the behest of the county Health Commissioner, John wrote a paean about a lady who was retiring as the last of the "granny" midwives. The Commissioner had talked the granny into retiring, offering her Maguire's profile and a proclamation by the mayor as incentives. As he said, she had been talking too much about how she took care of the "bad babies".

John's affability did not overcome his natural caution. When, in the mid 1960s he began assembling material for an obituary of the political leader Dan O'Connell, John parked it in his desk in a folder labeled Air Pollution. "In case any of those guys on the *Knick* come nosing around, that might throw them off," John explained to me. His stock of air pollution came in handy on February, 28, 1977, when O'Connell died at age 91. John put together nearly two pages—two newspaper pages—about the lost leader.

One night when John stayed late, I returned from a P-TA meeting at a local school and mentioned that the speaker advocated early sex education. "A good idea," John said. "Teach them to get it early while they're still strong."

❑

Maguire's offhand stories were more apt and thus funnier than some of the set jokes that he loved to tell. I tried to be enthusiastic in all cases. I wanted to be sure he'd show appreciation for my efforts. Some of John's stories involved meetings with stars of the International News Service (and others) in the Pen and Pencil, a Manhattan watering hole that attracted news people. (His attendance there led to my conclusion that he had a successful business.) He also had a wealth of anecdotes about the Dodgers of World War II and earlier whom he had watched many times at Ebbets Field. Though John did not have a Brooklyn accent, he could report perfectly that a Dodger pitcher named Waite Hoyt (1932) had been injured: "Hurt got hoit!"

Bring the Kids to Work

Saturday morning was bring-your-kid-to-the-office time for me and John. He usually had two or three little ones in tow. At noon, he would announce, "Let's go down to the coffee shop and get a hamburger." Someone was sure to remark, "Attaboy, John, everybody in on one hamburger." I think each kid really got one. On such occasions, I told John about all the stuff I was reading to my son. "You shouldn't," he advised. "If you read to kids, they won't bother to learn to read." His kids learned to read, and to write. Oldest son

John G. became a reporter; Gregory a writer of children's books and, recently, adult fantasies based on *Cinderella* and *The Wizard of Oz*, among others.

John always wore a suit and, of course, a necktie, Always the same necktie, a narrow knit thing of black or navy blue, which he knotted only once. From then on, he loosened the knot while at work, loosened it more to remove the tie at night, and simply slipped it back and tightened it next day. To save time, he said.

❑

Having grown up in Brooklyn, Maguire didn't learn to drive, because, well, because it was Brooklyn, and, after he had the heart attack, he told me, didn't want to risk imperiling others by driving. In Albany, he became one of The Bus Boys, joining the non-drivers John Cassidy and David dePorte. He had met both of them in his reporting. Cassidy was the sardonic public relations expert at Albany Medical Center Hospital; dePorte was a partner in a small but classy ad agency. Cassidy defected from The Bus Boys when he learned that it was possible to drive a car to an Off-Track Betting parlor. Cassidy was the most principled PR man I knew: he quit (with no job in sight) to protest a decision by the head of the Albany Medical Center trustees to publish the institution's annual report in the *Times-Union,* against Cassidy's recommendation. Cassidy went to work months later for the state Health Department. David dePorte had painted murals for the WPA in the Great Depression. He came by his surname, courtesy of an immigration clerk who shortened David's father's name from John D. Portugaloff to John D. Port, which the recipient retranslated to John dePorte, which had a much nicer ring.

Bus Boy was an inapt title for Maguire. He walked nearly everywhere. Miles and miles at a Harry Truman pace. Therapy for his heart. Another therapy—doctor's allowance if not doctor's orders—permitted him to smoke cigars (no inhaling) and to drink Scotch (in his moderation). When he felt chest pain—several times I knew of—he walked to the hospital for a checkup.

No Column, No Maguire

So Maguire went on, covering a variety of stories, writing his column, stringing for magazines, and preparing speeches, until, in 1977, a new editor took over the *Times-Union*. The new editor Harry Rosenfeld had new ideas about Maguire. No more column, he ruled. He offered John a good deal to remain a columnless reporter. John balked: no column, no Maguire. He quit. John continued his stringing, free-lanced some articles and resumed public relations. He described his PR strategy to me: write on plain paper, no letterheads; take three or four days to deliver the product, and charge a hundred and fifty dollars per release. Actually, he dashed off a release in ten or fifteen minutes, and held on to it for a while to impress his client that he had put a lot of time and talent into the job.

While still at the *Times-Union*, John experienced difficulty swallowing. The doctor found a large growth in his throat: a malignancy. He underwent major surgery and follow-up therapy to clear the cancer and save his voice. He \seemed in good health again, but a few years later cancer struck him again and could not be conquered. He died on January 19, 1986. He was seventy.

The Morning After

My wife decided that we should take dinner on folding tables while we watched TV. I agreed, though I really didn't want to see TV or have her see TV. I knew what was coming.

Just before the news came on at 6 p.m., Helen put on her own news. She said, "I got a ticket today." I told her, "Oh, that's OK; it's tough to park in Albany." She said, "But this wasn't for parking, for speeding. I was very upset at the cop. I thought the limit was fifty-five and I was only doing forty-seven. The cop told me the limit was thirty." I asked, "Where? I thought you were going to Delmar." She answered, "That's right, I was on Delaware Avenue. That's fifty-five, isn't it?"

Before I could tell her, "No, dear, you were still in Albany, and it's only thirty, and even in Delmar it's only forty-five," the local news came on and abruptly changed the subject.

Our top story!! State official arrested for assault! The words went on, *a warrant charging Francis Rivett with assault on Fred M. Dusenbury, a candidate for Mayor.* The picture: me, flanked by two large-looking Capital Police officers, doing the perp walk. I kept my arms apart, body language for *Look everybody! Look! No handcuffs!*

She looked from the TV and said, "Did you really strike that miserable wretch of humanity?" The short answer was *Yes.* But it was a long story that got longer.

❑

The event that led to my arrest had occurred a week earlier, the day of a Public Service Commission session, the morning after a farewell party for the former director of our Office of Accounting and Finance, Eric Leighton. One should never have to confront a Commission session on the morning after. What made this morning after a particular problem was that the Commission was about to adopt a set of rules to conform to a new law regarding utility customers' rights. Though there really was nothing new in the proposed rules–they merely repeated what the Commission had been doing right along–the session attracted a large crowd of utility lawyers and public interest lobbyists. Among the latter was Fred Morgan Dusenbury, who, despite occasional tinnitus, had heard the voices urging him to run for Mayor. Dusenbury had been a media-styled gadfly for several years, and he was gadflying me that morning about a copy of the new rules. I told him and told him and told him that I couldn't make them public until the Commission acted on them, He told me one of our staff lawyers had said he could have the rules. So go get them from the lawyer. No. He wanted them from me. I went on to another office. As I passed through the crowded lobby outside the boardroom en route back to my office, he beckoned to me and renewed his nifnawing.

The First Collision

His persistence collided with my morning after. As I spoke, I shook a finger at him. He said, "Stop pointing your finger at me." I responded, "I'll point a fist at you." He was just arm's length away, squarely in front of me. He said, "You haven't got the guts to." He moved, threateningly I thought. I preemptively wound up and swung a roundhouse right, dead on. But he had moved sideways and my fist bounced off the top of his head. I added a couple of quick wrist taps. He shouted, "I've been assaulted, call the police." Nobody moved. He reached the phone on the receptionist's desk and called the cops. I went back to my office.

Dusenbury's call brought a number of cops from the Capital Police. He insisted that they book me for assault. They held their counsel. We all went to the police station in the Empire State Plaza. The Commission chairman Paul Gioia sent along a staff lawyer, Howard Read, to protect me. He had never been involved in a criminal case. The cops gave him his first lesson. They showed him the criminal law book and explained that whatever I had done was no more than harassment, a mere violation, not assault, a misdemeanor. While the police interviewed Dusenbury elsewhere, I sat alone. One officer came by and said, "You couldn't have hit him very hard, his hair isn't even mussed." Another: "I can see why you did it." A sergeant came by and asked, "Are you the hitter or the hittee?" I replied, "Hitter" – pause – "alleged." He said, "Of course." The police did nothing; they hadn't seen a thing.

The Conquering Hero

Back at the office, I found myself hailed as a hero. I tried to be modest about it. After all, I had only done what lots of people would have liked to do. Hilda Wenger, a dear lady who had worked with me on my first press release a decade earlier, had come in late that day, and when she heard of the incident, said, "I hope the poor dear didn't have to wait in line."

The Dusenbury incident was big news, except to TV, and I had to answer all the questions about it. The *Times-Union* buried the story at the bottom of Page 33 (or so) where my wife didn't see it. Mayor Erastus Corning 2nd did--he saw everything--and he called to ask about the story. I told him all the details and he said, "Oh, I'm so pleased, so pleased that someone finally gave that little cocksucker what he deserved." I never thought to ask if that was an epithet or a description. Out on the street, people I knew crossed the street to compliment me; people I didn't know waved their greetings. A couple of people even offered to help my defense fund.

Dusenbury was upset when he learned I was given a hero's accolade. He came to the office and told Gioia that he wanted a written apology. I gave him one, a very general apology for whatever he thought I had done wrong. He wanted something specific, such as, "I apologize for hitting you three times." When I stood on generality, he swore out a warrant for me. Which brings me to the perp walk. The Capital police called me to report that they had to serve the warrant, but the judge had left the bench for the day, and if we serve it now you'd have to spend the night in jail. so will you come over in the morning? I did and was formally booked: photos, fingerprints, etc. Then a policeman offered me a chance to leave by a back door to avoid the TV cameras. I said, "No, let's go out front so they can't yowl about a coverup."

The Judge Breaks Up

No TV or press at the police court. And a good thing. They missed a story when the judge, Thomas W. Keegan, read from Dusenbury's complaint: ". . . that you, Mr. Rivett, did hit him three times . . ." He paused, looked up and laughed: "You! Doc! You hit him three times?!" Back to the reading. I kept a straight face. He offered me a week to get a lawyer.

I came back with Jim Banagan, an unknown associate in the well known firm Rutnik & Rutnik. The corridor outside court was filled with complainants and defendants, bail bondsmen and lawyers. One gentleman, most likely a defendant, greeted me enthusiastically, though we had never met before. He introduced me to several of the group as the guy who punched out the guy that's running for mayor. Murmurs of approbation and admiration. As I left court, a TV crew asked for a quick interview. With the camera rolling, a reporter asked, "How do you, as a PR man, handle a situation like this." I gave him what a colleague who saw the news show described as a *you stupid bastard* look and replied, "The same way I handle everything else: fully, frankly, and fearlessly." No more questions.

On December 14, I came to trial, on a charge of harassment, just as the Capitol police had called it. Dusenbury tried to take over the prosecutor's role. After I admitted that I had hit him, he asked, "How many times?"

I responded, "Any number you say." Thereupon, the judge declared the case adjourned in contemplation of dismissal (ACD) on February 14, the usual disposition of such trivial cases. If I kept my nose clean till then, the charge would be dropped and my record cleansed. I did and they were. A Valentine present.

❑

While I behaved, Dusenbury did not. Though he cloaked himself in the peaceable role of a Quaker, his tongue was non-pacific. A few years earlier, when an old couple in Schenectady who not only refused to pay their utility bill but also declined to accept money to pay it froze to death in their unheated unlighted flat, Dusenbury accused the utility officials of murder. On occasion, when I declined to provide him material that had not yet become public information, he threatened publicly to get me fired. Which leads up to his gross misbehavior a few days after the judge declared my lack of guilt. Dusenbury, in the presence of an undercover cop in his neighborhood, declared, "If I want justice, I'll have to get a gun and go after Rivett and Keegan and Muia." (Joe Muia was the prosecutor. My lawyer Jim Banagan escaped the threat probably because Dusenbury didn't know his name.)

So Don't Worry

I heard the story a few days later and it went like this, "It took a while to catch up with Dusenbury and tell him, we breaka you face, and in the meantime, Judge Keegan had a detective in his house, practically in his Christmas tree. They gave Muia some protection too." I asked, "What about me? Nobody even told me." And was told, "Oh, we didn't want you to be worried."

End of the story? Not nearly. Dusenbury sued the State and me for damages. The State won, without ever going to trial, by claiming correctly that my punching was not in line of duty. When my case came to trial in August

1983, I lost heavily because I committed what Al Smith used to call *mopery*. I was terminally dumb. The day Dusenbury's claim—he was seeking eight thousand dollars—went to trial, I was sick, too sick to concentrate on anything. I was burning with fever, my nose was runny, and I hurt all over, even my hair hurt. My lawyer reported that the Judge wanted to get the case settled and Dusenbury wanted two thousand dollars. Too much, Banagan said, and I agreed.

The case went to trial before a jury that would rather have been somewhere else and probably saw me as the embodiment of guilt: the watery eyes, the runny nose, the flushed face. Our side was not doing well until Banagan decided to call one of my colleagues as a witness. Then our case collapsed. The colleague, Bob Garlin, a thirtysomething lawyer who still giggled, had proclaimed loudly that he had seen nothing that October morning. I knew he had been in his office, well down the corridor from the scene of the encounter. But he giggled about it and, when asked by the DA's office, he gave a statement about what he had not seen. As he testified, as my witness yet, I learned about the statement for the first time. *Mea culpa!* It was a thrilling story: that I had dashed eighteen feet across the reception room to pop Dusenbury. There hadn't been two feet of clear space that morning after, but here was my witness—**my** witness—saying I ran eighteen feet. I now had more than my fever, my runny nose and my hurting hair to worry about. The jury was out twenty minutes and I was out six thousand dollars. My lawyer managed to delay the payoff by about a year and cut the loss to five thousand dollars. I also had to pay the lawyer a fee of one thousand dollars. Banagan told me why I had not been billed for the police court work. Mayor Corning had called the office of Rutnik & Rutnik and said he didn't want my police court trial to cost me anything. If there was a bill, he paid it. The Mayor died in May 1983, a few months before the civil trial.

In the 1981 election, Dusenbury received about five hundred votes, largely, I'm sure, because of the name-recognition publicity I provided him. Dusenbury died in October 1996, at a relative's home in Siloam Springs, Arkansas. The death notice in the *Times Union* fit neatly in `fourteen lines, the maximum space for which there was no charge.

Acknowledgements

We now reach the point where the author generally passes around credit–or blame—for the outcome of the product.

Sorry, there is none of either to spread. All of the writing, all of the drafts, all of the editing, and all of the research are mine.

At early stages, I asked Lise Bang-Jensen, Ann O. Treadway and Marggie Skinner to read various drafts and they offered some helpful suggestions. But mainly, it was my wife Shorty—my severest friend and best critic--who provided the most telling critique: "Too long-winded." I cut somewhere between twenty-five and fifty pages.